Time and Tide

Adventures on Alaska's Copper River Delta

DICK SHELLHORN

Dick Shellhorn
13 Dec 14

Publication Consultants
Since 1978

PO Box 221974 Anchorage, Alaska 99522-1974
books@publicationconsultants.com—www.publicationconsultants.com

ISBN 978-1-59433-489-4
eBook ISBN 978-1-59433-490-0
Library of Congress Catalog Card Number: 2014947886

Manufactured in the United States of America.

Disclaimer

This book is what I would categorize as historical fiction. I have used real names and places, and described events that actually happened. How accurately is open to debate.

Very little of history is not fiction to some degree. Based on the number of times my wife corrects my stories these days, the accounts in this book clearly fit in the category of tales. One of my favorite sayings from Alstad's *Savy Sayin's* is "An oldtimer is a man who's had a lot of interesting experiences, some of them true."

I don't have to look in the mirror to realize that somehow I have attained that Exalted Status, which also comes with graying hair, declining eyesight, and more frequent trips to the cabin outhouse. When some people say I am "full of it," they obviously know what they are talking about.

I respect and greatly admire each and every character in this book. How could I write this story without them?

Even the biggest adversary, a USFWS Protection Agent that was just doing his job, earns my regard. Although Officer Crane was the recipient of some rather spicy invective from Mom, Dad in reality got off very lightly. A $25 suspended fine, plus forfeiture of hunting license for 30 days. Since Dad only hunted on weekends, basically his trusty 16 gauge missed action for a maximum of 8 days. Assuming he made it out for every hunt possible, of course.

I still do, and will continue to do so as long as I can. A world of adventure awaits. No two days are the same; there is magic in sunrise and sunset, and all between.

And perhaps a tale or two more.

February 2014

"Nae man can tether time or tide."

Robert Burns, *Tam O'Shanter*

Dedication

This book is dedicated to Dad.
He taught me about duck hunting, and life.

Shoot! The air's full of wigeons!

Acknowledgments

This book is the result of contributions from so many Cordova people with tales of the Delta's history. Hopefully I don't overlook anyone.

First and foremost, Randy and Jackie Bruce. There is hardly a page that wasn't discussed over coffee at their kitchen counter. Ironically, in the home where I was raised as a child. Their kitchen was the living room in our tiny house. Mom chewed out Dad in that very place when he brought my brother Bobby and I home late from our first duck hunt.

Special kudos also to a pair of resident old time duck hunters who have done it all, and know how to tell about it: Jimmy Webber and Bobby Maxwell. I don't know how many times Randy and I would be scratching our heads about names, dates, or events, and he would say: "You better call Jimmy or Bobby." They hunted and fished the whole Delta, and recall with amazing detail, and accuracy, the highlights of those great times.

Another rich source of stories I had never heard was Dan O'Brien. His father, Bill O'Brien, was another early hunter and partner in the first duck shack on Alaganik.

And who can over look Harry Curran, who passed away a year ago. I will never forget sitting in the sunshine at his kitchen table at his hillside home overlooking Orca Inlet as he recounted his life story. The twinkle in his eye matched the sparkles off waves on the bay. I had a tape recorder going, and a 90 minute cassette ran out before we even started building our duck cabin. When I made the mistake of suggesting we could jump ahead to 1959, he interrupted me with: "Now wait a minute. We'll get there." Oh, I loved the Scotsman.

So many others. Sue's parents John & May Ekemo, and her uncles Bill Ekemo and Pete Lovseth. Ken & Bruce Van Brocklin. Merle, Barb, and Ardy Hanson. Danny Glasen. Justin Strom Jr. Fred Newirth. Sig Gildnes. Julius Reynolds. Trudy & Jerry Bendzak. Al Jardinski. Don Scutt. Pete & Robin Blake. Robby Maxwell. Tom Justice. Jack Stevenson. Virgil Carroll. Gary Weinrick. Virginia Nicoloff Lacy. Tom & Bob Simpler. Dick Renner. Jerry Behymer. Kenny & Wayne Smith. Jim Iliff. Ron Horton. Luke Borer. Robert Beedle. Mark King. Sylvia & Mae Lange. Mike Webber. Norman Swanson. Ira Grindle. Mary Behymer. Thorne Popelka. Bob Lenz. Mike McHone. John Goodridge. Jay Beaudin. John Davis. Al Cave.

Bob "Moose" Henrichs. Toni Bocci. Mike Collins. Rene Pettingill Rankin. Beth Pettingill Pirtle. Larry and Kathleen Kritchen, and their daughter Kay Adams. Many are gone. But their tales endure.

USFS personnel, especially Dede Serb, Bob Behrends, Dan Logan, Dana Smyke, and Milo Burcham. The help of the local District Ranger Office, and access to maps, archives, and background was invaluable. The same applies to Kelsey Appleton at the Cordova District Fisherman's United office, which has enough historical material on the fisheries of the Delta and Prince William Sound to qualify as a second local museum.

Cordova Museum Director Cathy Sherman and her assistant Nancy Bird, plus Kristen Carpenter of the Copper River Watershed Project, and *Cordova Times* Editor Jennifer Gibbins for their help with maps, background materials, reviews, and encouragement.

My sister Sharon Ermold. At age nine, she was there when we built our cabin in 1959. Reminded me it rained every day. Each was sunny for me, so that's the way I wrote it.

Last, and most importantly, my family. Wife Sue would roll her eyes when I woke up at 5 a.m. on dark Cordova winter nights, made a pot of coffee, and started typing on the computer. Recognized the look from the greetings in the early days of our marriage, upon returning late Sunday from the cabin, of course stopping first with Randy at the Powder House to recap the weekend. Her archive of photos, plus the Cabin Scrapbook she and Sharon put together, were invaluable resources. Most of the photos in the book came from that album, which also provided an excellent timeline of events at Pete Dahl.

Duck hunter's wives are a special breed, and I knew I had good one after our first overnight trip to the cabin with my parents in 1966. Find details in a Chapter titled Alaganik Redux. I love you, sweetie.

Daughters Heidi and Gretchen, a constant source of pride, inspiration, and joy. "How's the book going, Dad?" Both made it to the cabin at a very early age, as did their children Huck and Ellie. All were so small they couldn't stand to have their height marked and dated on the interior wall by the entry door, which became an annual event in the years that followed.

Then there are my son-in-laws Tom and Scott, who, in keeping with tradition, constantly chip in to provide fresh material for this book. My daughters know how to pick em.

And of course, Mom and Dad. Without them, there wouldn't have been a cabin, or Cabin Logs. In many ways, this is their story.

Family. It all comes down to that.

As you will see.

Contents

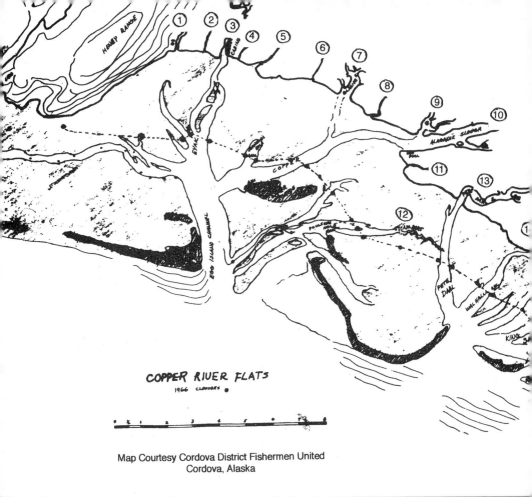

COPPER RIVER FLATS
1966 CLOSURES ●

Map Courtesy Cordova District Fishermen United
Cordova, Alaska

Copper River Flats Map Key

See "Detailed History of Slough and Name Places" on page 384 for more information.

1	Mountain Slough	6	Johnson Slough	12	Steamboat
2	Center Slough	7, 8	Big Glacier and Little Glacier	13	Pete Dahl Slough
3	Eyak River			14	Walhalla Slough
3a	See Map, Page 12	9	Tiedeman Slough	15	Gus Stevens Slough
4	Joe Reeve Slough	10	Alaganik Slough	16	King Salmon Slough
5	Government Slough	11	Whiskey Pete Slough		

17 Castle Island and Castle Island Slough	21 Cottonwood Point	27 Gus Wilson Sloughs
	22 Dago Slough	28 Martin River
18 Storey Island and Storey Slough	23 Russian River	29 Mirror Slough
	24 Little River	30 Softuk
19 Grass Island	25 Shit River	
20 Kokinhenic Island	26 Cudahy	

Area Game Unit Management Map

Courtesy Alaska Department of Fish and Game sub-units for managing a diverse population of deer, moose, goat, bear, and waterfowl in the Copper River Delta Area

12

Introduction

This is the story of a duck cabin on Alaska's Copper River Delta. And much more.

In 1959 we built a duck cabin on Alaska's Copper River Delta. From that very first July day on the banks of Pete Dahl Slough, we began keeping a journal of events there. Over the ensuing 54 years, this chronicle has evolved into 1600 pages containing 3,100 entries by 458 people in seven loose-leaf 8.5X11 binders. In what we now call The Cabin Logs.

While Copper River king and red salmon have gained worldwide fame for their quality and flavor, many may not know of the fabulous duck hunting once available on the 50 mile wide Delta formed by that river as it exits the Chugach Mountains and races to the Gulf of Alaska. Its unique intertidal habitat, full of ponds and braided with waterways, is a natural nesting grounds for waterfowl and also a special stopping place for migratory birds.

While early explorers and prospectors traversed the region, it was salmon that first drew pioneers to the outer shores of the Delta, with fishermen building camps on the edges of the sloughs to operate stake net sites. Then there was the famous Copper River and Northwestern Railway, cutting directly across the upper reaches of the Delta, enroute to the fabulous deposits of ore 200 miles away in a place called Kennicott.

Here is a chronicle of the exploration of the Delta, beginning with Lt. Henry Allen's amazing expedition up the Copper in 1885, as well as a history of fisheries, war, roads, fires, storms, floods, earthquakes, and duck hunting.

Meet characters such as Long Shorty, Curly Hoover, Kernel Korn, Hook Van Brocklin, Scotty Curran, Eyeball Leer, Nord, Les Maxwell; and of course, the Mayor of Pete Dahl, Don Shellhorn.

Learn about duck shacks such as the Pair-a-Dice Inn, Last Resort, Lame Duck Inn, and the Korn Hole; and the rich history hidden in their walls. Delight in the foibles of hunting in the wild weather and water of the Delta.

Revel in the Ode to Family and small town Alaska found in countless quotes from the Shellhorn Duck Cabin Logs, a unique journal of life and adventure covering 637 visits to their cabin near the edge of the Delta.

Full of laughter, joy, and also tragedy; replete with lessons and truths; ribald and poignant; *Time and Tide* is a story of 129 adventuresome years on the Copper River Delta.

This book began as a story of life at Pete Dahl, based on all that written history. Somehow it evolved into much more.

BOOK I
Beginnings

"In the beginning, God created Heaven and Earth,

and the Copper River Delta."

Chapter 1

Crane

CRANE: 1. Grus Canadensis. These are large, long-legged wading birds. Cranes are among the tallest birds in the world.
R. H. Armstrong, *Guide to the Birds of Alaska,* 1980
2. "A shitheel from way back." Anita Shellhorn, Pete Dahl Cabin Log, 1959

"It get's late early out there."

Yogi Berra, describing left field in Yankee Stadium.

Part I

The sun was setting in splendid fashion as two duck hunters headed back to their riverboat. It was September 1959 on the Copper River Delta, and in those days before the uplift from the Great Alaska Earthquake of '64, the region was called "the Flats" for good reason. High tides flooded the entire area, filling shallow ponds with brackish water while preventing the growth of brush and trees, and you could see everywhere for miles, including all the way to the end of the Heney Range where the sun was slowly sinking near Whitshed Point.

Back then the Flats were full of ducks and hunters; and not only could you see forever, you could hear forever. Duck season was in full swing. Gleeful hunters were blasting away west toward Eyak, Government, and Glacier sloughs; north toward the road; and west toward Pete Dahl and Alaganik. The evening shoot was on, with lots of lead and excitement in the air as legal hunting hours were about to end.

It happened to be a bluebird day; clear, calm, and warm. A flock of high flying pintails went zipping by, and the duo fired off a six shot volley, more in jest than

"The region was called the Flats for good reason … you could see everywhere for miles."
View of hunters returning to the Pete Dahl cabins, in the early days following the
Great Alaska Earthquake.

hope, as the birds were clearly out of range. None came down; they trudged on
through the grass and marsh.

As the pair approached the boat, Don Shellhorn, who had stayed by the craft
to make sure it didn't hang up on the bank of the slough in the rapidly falling tide,
stood up, and silhouetted by the sun, somehow became two.

And thus began what was to be one of the most famous tales in the history of
our duck cabin on Pete Dahl slough.

The hunters approaching the suddenly doubled pair of boat watchers were
Harrison Leer and me; the second figure beside my Dad was a Fish and Wildlife
Protection Officer named Crane. Who wasted no time.

Which one of you just shot?

Leer, a baby faced character who thrived on the art of verbal repartee, loved
having a good time, and could frankly care less if he ever shot a duck. Always
quick witted, he immediately and intuitively recognized this was a chance to make
up for some dismal hunting by having a little fun. Born and raised in Cordova, his
father worked on the Copper River and Northwestern Railway. Leer graduated
as Valedictorian of Cordova High's seven member class of 1936 . Even then his
peers recognized his sharp verbal skills, as among his activities was included Editor
of the Northern Lights, the high school newspaper.

Leer was bright; he attended the University of Alaska, and then went on to graduate from Medical School at the University of Oregon. After practicing in Petersburg, Alaska, he went back for more schooling in ophthalmology. He set up shop in Juneau, Alaska; and traveled around Southeastern putting on eye clinics. Cordova was one of his stops. For many years he held eye ball exams in the lower level of our house, which had a long recreation room perfect for his purpose. In reality it was probably just an excuse to come back to his old home town for a rollicking good time down at the duck cabins.

Along with his eye equipment, Leer always brought a pet phrase he had been polishing all winter. One year it was "Oh, turn blue" in honor of the year's previous waterfowling misadventure, in which he and Dad had been caught in the vast mud flats beyond Eyak River while returning on a falling tide from a hunt up the very slough we were now on. They spent a cold, clear night huddled in the bow of a open plywood skiff, and came home with "frost-nipped" feet from the caper - hence the "turn blue" maxim.

It wasn't Dad's first overnighter on the mud flats beyond the slough mouths. Raised in Seward, he had come to Cordova in the mid- 30s to work in a clothing and hardware enterprise, and had spent a similar eve in almost the same area a couple decades earlier with legendary local Bob Korn. The duo had left Korn Hole near the mouth of the Eyak to run across the Flats to Tiedeman Slough enroute to the Haystack, a single huge rock deposited eons ago by receding Sheridan Glacier, and famous for good goose hunting. A falling tide caught them also, and Dad often told the story of shivering all night in the bow of the boat while the amply built Korn lay with his wool jacket unbuttoned, snoring away, until they had enough water to return the next morning.

Hunting being slow at Pete Dahl, some 25 year old memory, plus a few B & B's (Beer and Blast, usually V.O.), convinced the pair that surely there were geese still to be had at the Haystack. So here we were.

Dad's standard load for any hunt was his faithful old Model 12 sixteen gauge, a pipe, stubby Lucky Lager beers, and a few shells.

Enforcement of duck hunting regulations was nonexistent back then, and Leer's first reply to this mysterious lawman's opening gambit almost caused Dad to choke on his brewski.

What did you say, I can't hear you?

Perplexed, and perhaps not aware of his adversary, Crane repeated the same question. Louder.

Leer put his hand up to his ear, cupping it to magnify sound, and repeated his question. Also louder.

This was turning into a shouting match.

Crane, who was quick to agitation, decided to cut to the chase.

Look, it's after shooting hours. Which ONE of you shot?"

Ah, the opening Leer was seeking.

Whatever the hour, back in those days, no respectable duck hunter headed back to the cabin until the birds stopped flying, however late that might be. Many a time we arrived back at the shack using spotlights to find our way; and more than a few would even admit to listening for the sound of ducks splashing in the pond to determine if they had hit anything at "dusk." One memorable hunt even coined the phrase "Moon Shoot."

So as Crane began the opening rounds of his interrogation of what he felt were violators, all about us the sound of duck hunters merrily blazing away continued. The Boys at Glacier, shooting three inch mags just a slough over, were in particular good form.

Leer turned to my dad, acting puzzled.

Can you hear him? There's so much noise, I can't understand a word he's saying.

As this exchange continued, the sun also continued to do its thing, gradually sinking below the horizon. Later, after I began my career as a high school mathematics teacher back at my alma mater Cordova High, I often pondered the relationship between tangent lines and circles. Shooting hours are from half an hour before sunrise to sunset. When has the sun actually set? Not a simple question if the horizon is obscured by clouds or mountains, for example. Orbital mechanics and astronomy also enter in. The hunting regulations have shooting hours listed, but are they correct for the latitude and longitude of the Copper River Delta? Or more specifically, since we were west of our cabin at Pete Dahl, and the Boys at Eyak were even further west of us, wouldn't the true sunset time be progressively if ever so slightly later?

Before Crane could reply, Leer, who clearly was on the CHS or U of O Debate Team, shifted gears, changing verbal tactics to forestall a logical response. The Eyeball Specialist pointed to me.

If you asked which ONE of us shot, it was him.

Hey, what are hunting partners for?

Somewhat surprised, and pondering why Crane had asked which one of us had shot, which was puzzling since six shots had been fired, meaning either he couldn't count, or assumed one of us had the plug out our gun, I was quick enough to point back at Leer.

What! He was the one that shot.

I felt like adding I never miss, just to seal the indignation at my partner's betrayal.

Crane, perhaps realizing this was deteriorating into an Abbott and Costello routine akin to "Who's on first, what's on second …," decided enough was enough.

That's it. You're both under arrest.

At which point Dad stepped in. Using his pipe as a pointer.

Wait a minute. You can't arrest him. He doesn't even have a license.

What! That's another violation.

He's only 15, and doesn't need one!

While showing considerable restraint not to add "You Horse's Ass!

Way to go, Dad.

I glanced sideways at Leer while clutching my brand new Model 12 sixteen gauge tightly, and couldn't resist a slight grin. With Leer momentarily stymied, and unbelievably at a temporary loss for words, Crane realized he had better be speedy with his statement before Leer regrouped.

OK, then the two of you are under arrest.

Call it Guilt by Proxy.

Sparks of Half and Half tobacco were now flying everywhere. Before Dad could pull his furiously smoking pipe out of clenched teeth, Leer jumped back into the fray.

What? You've got to be kidding. Don didn't even fire a shot. He was here watching the boat.

With gun fire continuing to echo all around us and the sun now obviously below the horizon, an added comment, of course:

Is it just me, or what is all this background noise? Sounds like shotguns to me. How can you bust us when everyone else on the Copper River is still shooting?

Crane was adamant.

Let me see your licenses, and then I'll take your guns and ducks.

Which he did.

Both Leer and Dad were stunned, and more amazing, Leer was speechless.

So that was it.

With the tide rapidly falling and twilight upon us, we piled into our fiberglassed plywood 14 foot runabout and bade farewell to our new Antihero. I vaguely recall Mr. Eyeball using another word that starts with "A" to describe him as we pushed the boat off. I cranked up the 18 hp Johnson, Dad and Leer cranked open a Lucky, and we headed back through the Lower Cutoff to the cabin at Pete Dahl, a fifteen minute run, with the sun setting on Dad and Leer's hunting for the year.

Gunless but not beerless, I recall a surprisingly pleasant ride. It WAS a beautiful evening, there was still ample water, the sloughs were flat calm, the colors in the sky were marvelous as stars were just beginning to pop out in the east.

And the pair of criminals in the bow of the boat were laughing and having a good time.

It was a unique adventure.

What a story to tell when we got back to the cabin.

Dad, who was nicknamed Izaak Walton by hunters all over the Delta for his well known casual approach to the sport and probably never shot a bag limit in his life, had to see the irony of the situation. He, who hunted for the joy and fun of it all, and hadn't fired a shot, was arrested for shooting after hours.

Leer was ecstatic. It had to be one of the crowning moments of his life. In twenty short minutes, enough material for years of story telling. I could see his mind churning through possible sayings to describe this one.

It was the best evening shoot ever.

And we didn't have a duck.

Leer had picked up three widgeon when we were walking in earlier, "on the rise," which was code for in the late stages of swimming and the early stages of flight. He might have been an ophthalmologist, but he had a lousy eye for wing shots.

Crane had confiscated the birds for evidence.

Part II

By the time we idled up to the cabin, it was getting pretty dark. All the other hunters were back. Their boats were anchored in the slough, and Coleman lanterns were hissing away in all the shacks, their noisy yellow light in bright windows and open doors, casting long golden rectangles across the tranquil water.

Clinks of glasses, laughter, boots thumping on floors above elevated pilings, scrapping of chairs, the clatter of hunting gear being stowed. The Second Hunt, also known as the Evening Shoot, was on. Ammo for this one came from the day's adventures, unique for each group of hunters, as well as from the amply stocked shelves and cabinets brimming with firewaters of choice. The air was already full of raucous noise rather than birds, as B.S. shooting was in full swing.

Oh boy, I thought.

This is going to be one to remember.

And I wasn't to be disappointed.

Leer and Dad hopped out of the boat and headed up the bank to the cabin. I backed the boat out and dropped anchor amongst the other rigs, all swinging down river on the falling tide, offshore enough to not go dry at low water.

Four cabins lined the banks of the slough, three clustered together, the other 100 yards to the east. Each had its own unique design and character. The small, tidy one furthest west belonged to First National Bank of Cordova President Dick Borer; next was a long metal clad structure built by locals Andy Swartzbacker, Bill Ekemo, and Pete Lovseth. These two shacks had been there for two years. Then there was ours, framed in and very roughly completed in five days just a month earlier. Off to the east stood the Castle on the Rhine, an architect-designed, hurricane proof, pre-cut, finish lumber structure carefully assembled by a professional contracting crew at the same time Dad, Smokey Bernard, Harry Curran and I were puzzling through random stacks of scrounged lumber and metal, no two pieces the same length or width, to create our masterpiece.

The ring leader from the Pete Dahl Hilton, owned by a Conglomerate of Six, was seine boat captain Les Maxwell. A stocky transplant from the coast of Washington state who took his duck hunting pretty seriously, and also was undoubtedly the best wing shot I have ever seen, he could often be seen standing bare chested on his cabin porch or roof, untangling binoculars from his portly, hairy superstructure to scan the horizon for Northern Birds. Like Ahab's Moby Dick, Les had an obsession, his for Old Red Eyes, the fastest flying and best tasting duck around, alias Drake Canvasback. A fine cook and waterfowl connoisseur, Captain Maxwell disdained hunting the skinny early season locals. After every hunt he would wander to our cabin and fondle the breasts of the ducks us dumb nimrods wasted time shooting, not out of some strange perversion, although Les did go through wives as fast as ammo when the shooting was hot (I think he was married four times), but to see if they were "pluckers," fat enough to be worthy of his skills, well feathered out to mean the Migration was on.

"I backed the boat out and dropped anchor... off shore enough to not go dry at low water." Our workskiff anchored in front of the cabin, September 1959.

This was ages before the days of tweeting, texting, e-mail, and Internet, but word of The Bust spread with fiber-optic speed. I had barely made it up the bank before lights bobbing in the dark started converging on our cabin from both sides, agitated neighbors stomping up the stairs to hear the story. Over and over. And with something beside flashlights in their other hand.

What happened? Who was this guy? He did what? You got arrested, and you didn't even shoot?

In the background, whispers. Don Shellhorn has never shot a limit in his life, and they took his shotgun away?

And of course, in the midst of it all, Toastmaster Leer, M. C. of the late evening

23

"The narrow cabin table began to sag under the weight of a mounting supply of liquid reinforcements." Don Shellhorn, Mayor of Pete Dahl, on the right.

Pete Dahl Tonight Show. Come to think of it, he did look a little like Johnny Carson, and emulated his style.

The crowd continued to grow, and the narrow linoleum-covered plywood table Dad had recently built began to sag under the weight of a mounting supply of liquid reinforcements for expressing overall incredulation and mass indignation. Back then everyone smoked. The cabin was now wall to wall with hunters puffing on cigars, cigarettes, and pipes. The front door was open, yet despite pungent clouds billowing out, Coleman lanterns barely cut the fog, with visibility down to a yard and the ceiling at four feet by FAA standards.

As everyone knows, where there's smoke, there's fire.

Something had to be done. Outrageous. The Establishment is attempting to infringe on our Inalienable Right to hunt whenever we want. This is Alaska, the Last Frontier, for Pete Dahl's sake, not the "Lower 48." Suffering for a long time as a Territorial serfs under the carpet-bagging oppression of a distant and ignorant U.S. Federal government with completely irrelevant policies created by corrupt politicians, the Colonists were about to revolt.

Shooting hours? You've got to be kidding. They're going to take away our best hunting. How are we going to make it through the winter without those teal breasts on the table?

Alaskans, and Cordovans in particular, have a proud history of feisty protest to Outside interference. Back in 1911, when the freshly completed Copper River and Northwestern Railway was hauling price loads of high grade ore from the mines at Kennecott to the new port at Cordova over one of the most amazing train tracks ever built, the Feds stepped in to force the line to burn coal imported from stateside, rather than allowing construction of a short spur down the coast to Katella and the cheap high grade fuel that could be found right there.

The mining-based populace was outraged. Inspired much as this Pete Dahl mob by fuel other than coal from the many watering holes that seemed to occupy every third building on the city's freshly built main street boardwalks, they bamboozled the local U.S. Marshall on a wild goose chase and poured down to the dock to greet a steamship arriving from Seattle laden with bags of coal. Before it was all over, much of this cargo was floating in Orca Inlet, inspiring the local daily newspaper to report of the Cordova Coal Party. Folks back in Boston probably saluted by raising their cups of tea when they read about it in the morning papers a few days later.

I sensed a Pete Dahl Protest in the making. And thought, by golly, my high school social studies teacher was right: History does repeat itself.

And let's face it. No one are better students of history than duck hunters. They can tell you who shot what, when, where, and how, 50 years ago. Half or more of duck hunting is sitting around telling stories about past hunts. Didn't this whole thing start because Dad decided to take Leer back to the place where he had shot his first goose more than 25 years ago?

Didn't the British navy used to issue a ration of grog to their sailors before charging into battle?

Crane didn't realize it, but for a crowd always seeking late night entertainment, his actions had cranked open the spigots on the Good Ship Pete Dahl, rationing be damned, and the merry crew was steaming full bore ahead.

It felt like the cabin was going to fall off its piling.

Something had to be done.

Part III

To this day it is not clear who came up with the idea. Likely it was one of the more practiced Moon Shooters, well inspired by moonshine, despite the absence of that orb.

Back then there were no smoke alarms, but suddenly the cabin was emptying with incredible speed.

By motion, second, and unanimous ballot of the Peed All Borough Assembly, Mayor Don Shellhorn semi-presiding, Crane Season had been officially declared open, twenty four - seven. And we're not talking about the sharp billed, long-necked, slow flying migratory pterodactyls. If only other democratic institutions could respond with such alacrity in the face of crisis.

Everyone was racing back to their cabins with highballs in one hand and spotlights in the other. The open riverbank between our cabin and Maxwell's was quickly lined with Revolutionists not nearly as stealthy as Washington's troops on the Delaware, but with equally intense fervor.

And not nearly as concerned about ammo as their forefathers.

Spacing themselves in a formation that would have made LaFayette proud, the Pete Dahl Regiment of the Copper River Revolutionary Army, an elite group of frontier sharpshooters, bent on declaring Independence from the USFWS Fiefdom, was about to fire the shots heard round the Delta.

In unison, as if by hushed command (it was too dark for hand signals), all set down boxes of shells and smoothly loaded their shotguns with a speed that would have astonished Washington and his ragtag musketeers.

No big deal. From years of night shooting, these woodsmen could have done it blindfolded.

Instead of "Ready, aim, fire" someone hollered "Take that, Crane" and rows of flames were suddenly erupting from barrels all along the line.

If you've never fired a shotgun at night, the torch that flashes a foot out of the muzzle is quite spectacular. Equally inspiring was the noise. Twelve, sixteen, and twenty gauges, pump and semi-autos, Winchester, Remington, and Browning; someone even reeled back after a volley from a ten gauge, Pete Dahl's equivalent of the sixteen inch guns on the Battleship Missouri.

The Pete Dahl Regiment of the Copper River Armed Forces had a diversified arsenal, and like military outfits anywhere, was enjoying putting its firepower on full display. Plus the length of several volleys indicated a few of the troops were hunting without plugs in their weapons.

Intermixed with the noise, flashes, and smoke were yells and screams that the heat of battle has forever generated, and shall not be repeated here. It was impressive. I was proud to be there and be part of it.

The demonstration lasted a considerable time, until ammunition - liquid, verbal, and powdered - started running low. The troops realized they better save a few rounds for the Morning Shoot, which wasn't that far away, judging by a faint glimmer in the eastern sky.

I crawled into my bunk as the barrel of my nearby trusty 16 gauge cooled down with strange creaking sounds, wondering what the Boys at Eyak, Glacier, and Alaganik must be thinking, staggering out cabin doors to ask each other : What is going on at Pete Dahl?

Are the Northern Birds trying to sneak by at night? Guess Les ain't gonna let that happen.

It's awful clear. Did the Feds offer a bounty for shooting down Sputnik?

Oh, I bet I know what it is! They're trying to signal town for more beer. Listen to the pattern in the shots. I think it's "S, M, B" in Morse Code. Clever.

I also thought about Crane, Homo Sapien rather than Grus Canadensis. Where is he? Did he camp somewhere down river for the night? Or is he back in town? I wonder if he can hear this, or see the flames in the eastern sky? Speaking of seeing, will he show up tomorrow with a posse of Federal agents armed with massive search and arrest warrants to suppress this uprising?

I snuggled a bit lower in my U.S. Army WWII surplus down sleeping bag atop a U.S. Navy WWII surplus pipe-framed, canvas-spanned bunk, probably from a troop ship that sailed the Pacific, based on the drawing of a naked lady on its bottom side that guests in the next tier down never mentioned for some reason, and said to myself:

"Who cares? This *really* is the best hunt ever."

I can't recall what happened the next day. Neither, I suspect, could most of the denizens of our newly declared Free Nation.

Mom's cabin log entry before we headed upriver on Sunday, September 27, indicated rather low morale, to put it politely.

Part IV

The court hearing was set for Tuesday, 29 September, at 1 p.m. Back then justice was swift and exacting. Cited Saturday, 26 September, late in the day; at the Magistrate's Office three days later. No O.J. Simpson trial dragging on for years in those days.

It was a school day. I finished a quick lunch and headed to the Courthouse, which at that time was on the third floor of the U.S. Post Office Building. Located on Second Street, it was only a block away from the high school, and you could see the bars in the jail rooms at the rear of the building from the Science classroom. Maybe shortly I'd be waving at Dad and Leer while studying biology.

The accused were already there, seated in a small crowded room on high backed chairs in front of a big wooden desk, like students sent to the Principal's office. Easing myself into a side chair, I noticed they were rather subdued. Not contrite, but quiet. Must have already laid out their defense strategy, I thought, certain the brilliant and quick Eyeball Specialist wouldn't let us down.

A side door opened, and Magistrate Todd Moon, followed by Mr. Crane, strolled in. Or should I say, in Her Honor's case, chugged in. Moon was portly, to put it politely. Shaped like her name. Years back, rumor among us pre-teen hellions was that she liked her wine and cordial, salmonberry and blueberry, respectively. Homemade from the heavily laden, and even more heavily guarded, bushes in her front yard. Which just happened to be conveniently adjacent to the head of a 1930s CCC era trail up Mt. Eyak. Which gave us a golden opportunity to cop a few of her finest before scrambling off in the woods with her shrill voice and waving broom encouraging us to pick up the tempo.

Based on Moon's semi-quick entrance and serious demeanor, it looked like this was going to be speedy and by the numbers. Hopefully it wouldn't be vindictive. Dad was already on trial for a crime I supposedly had committed. I wondered if she recognized me, a Salmon Berry Fugitive on the loose. What does double jeopardy mean, I asked myself?

In fact, since The Bust, I had been pondering many of the vagaries of our legal system, analyzing this case into the wee hours, tossing and turning while conjuring up Perry Mason-like last minute courtroom dramatics.

How about the Classic Clock Defense? Time lines are a crucial part of any case. Time pieces back then were notoriously unreliable. While hunting, Dad wore HIS dad's old wind-up pocket watch on a leather cord around his neck after ruining so many wrist watches changing shear pines, pulling decoys, or falling in sloughs. Santa Claus left a new one in his stocking every Christmas.

What made Crane's ticker the Golden Standard for Copper River time? Maybe he forgot to wind it, banged it against his canoe, or submerged it in mud while stealthily sneaking up on us at Tiedeman.

Come on, Dad, Leer, my brain screamed. Ask Crane to pull out his watch and give us the time. Then ask Miss Magistrate to read that dainty little thing barely visible on her chunky wrist. I'll bet they're not the same.

Case dismissed!

Or ask Crane what his first words to us were when we arrived at the boat. Remember? He asked: "Which ONE of you just shot?" How come the TWO of you are being charged? Clearly he thought only one hunter shot, and by his very question couldn't tell who. As long as you don't crack under tough cross-examination, you've got him!

Or bring up USFWS's very own procedures for signaling Universal Time to fleets of aggressive seine boats jostling for that first big 7 a.m. Monday morning salmon set out on Prince William Sound. Fed up (no pun intended) with skipper's claiming their clock said exactly seven when they slapped out their gear prematurely with everyone else quickly following suit, Protection came up with the bright idea of having their Officer on Scene fire off his pistol or rifle at exactly 7 a.m., Government Time. Wasn't this an implicit admission on their part that every one's time would be slightly different? (Incidentally, some bright fisherman on the other side of the bay merrily fired his rifle while yelling "let er go," so that enforcement technique didn't last long).

And what about the sun, with correct time so clearly elusive?

Forget about the latitude/longitude spin, thought I. That's only good for seconds, at best. But was the weather clear? Maybe cloud cover is what made for that incredible sunset. Did it obscure a view of the sun setting completely?

Wait. Oh my god. From Tiedeman slough, you can't see the horizon. Hinchenbrook Island juts up thousands of feet. So even if the sun had completely vanished behind those peaks, perhaps it hadn't officially passed below the hidden line that demarcated sunset. Brilliant.

Moon read the charges. Crane presented his case. Dad and Leer said nothing. How do you plead? Dad: not guilty. Leer: not guilty.

That's it? What ?

Sadly, life and fantasy are not the same.

Her Honor rapped the gavel. Guilty. $25 fine suspended. License forfeited for 30 days. Case closed.

I hadn't said a peep. My law career was over.

And Leer. What a disappointment. Where was that quick wit? Those cool baby blues? That rapier-like dialogue? He had already packed his vision charts, fitting equipment, and cases of eye glasses. The southbound PNA plane to Juneau left at 4 p.m.

I headed back up the hill to Algebra class, guilty but innocent, saved by a birth date, a notch higher in that strange peer ranking system of adolescence, and perplexed by the capriciousness of our legal system.

Coppola's *The Godfather* hadn't come out yet, but it was a classic Italian gangster movie theme: Father took the rap for his son.

Dickie got off! He's free. He can still hunt, anytime he wants.

Dad was my retriever for the rest of our first duck season at Pete Dahl.

Part V

Truth be told, right now it's evening, 5 September 2011, almost 52 years later, and I'm sitting at that same cabin table writing this story.

Even at age 67, I don't miss too many morning shoots. Yesterday was very good. Filled my bag limit in an hour. Even got a triple on a big flight of pintails high balling into the decoys, while being pelted by rain and 30 mph winds. Unusual for me, I'm an average shot at best. We'll talk about the rest of the time some other time.

This was supposed to be our traditional Family Labor Day Weekend at the cabin: wife Sue, daughter Gretchen, son-in-law Tom, and our wonderful little three year old granddaughter Ellie Dahl Carpenter. Daughter Heidi and husband

Scott are in drought plagued Austin, TX. Wish I could send them some of this rain. Guess where our first grandchild got her middle name. She loves it down here, was barely a year old her first trip. Same for our kids. I'm sadly disappointed the gang isn't here. But for once the weatherman was right. It blows so much and so often out this way that we've come to accept and ignore most wind and rain predictions. But when "Cape Suckling to Gore Point, Hurricane Force winds, at 60 mph with gusts to 75," came over the radio, a 40 minute ride through exposed quarter mile wide sloughs in a 17 foot open metal riverboat was out. So no tacos, alder blaze in the fireplace, cards, games, stars, sleeping in bags, taco omelet with Pete Dahl Snappers (our famous Bloody Mary's), naps, and fun.

Maybe next weekend.

I came down two days ago with a boatload of supplies. My 14 footer is pulled up on the bank as far as I can get it so the winds, now at 50 plus, won't blow water over its side and combined with three inches of rain in the last 24 hours cause it to sink. A small automatic bilge pump can only do so much.

The ducks and I get a day off. So it's coffee now, and maybe a little Peachtree Schnapps later, along with a lot of memories as the cabin shakes and the damper on the old oil space heating stove squeaks.

"Grampa, that need double dee," would Ellie my little helper say, already knowing the name for that wonderfully magic spray that eliminates screeches in her swing set below our home in Cordova. I glance out the now dark window above the table and notice faded signs in the roof pitch above it.

Water stained and barely legible posters from the 1959 New Year's Eve Fireman's Ball at old City Gym, now Bidarki Recreation Center. In red letters on tan poster board in Dad's classic self-taught printing style, the left one says, from top to bottom:

1st Class
100 Percent
Wiolator
Confirmed Member
After Hour Club
Peed-Al Slew

while the one on the right states:
"I Bawl"
Special
Wiolator
Associate Member
After Hour club
Peed-Al Slough.

In between, a six inch diameter cardboard model clock, with the hands set at 6:40.

Mom and Dad's costumes at the traditional New Year's blowout were famous city wide. With things slow and nights dark in Cordova's long and often wet winters, there was lots of time to come up with creative get-ups before smuggling forbidden beverages into the second floor City Gym to usher in the New Year. Technically a public facility, consumption of alcohol was forbidden. Which only stimulated the cooped up populace into shrewd ways of sneaking in contraband or spiking the punch. Heck, that was half the fun.

Folks wanted to cut loose, laugh, and have a good time dancing to The Kolenuts, Ramona on the piano, Callahan on the drums.

Just this spring, when my Mom passed away at age 91, Dad preceding her in 1995, more than one local stopped to tell me the thing they remembered most about my parents was Dad in his tux, Mom in her cancan dress, and the pair wowing the crowd with their wonderful dancing on New Year's Eve.

One year, Dad, recalling his wild and crazy days as a debonair bachelor when he first arrived in Cordova, came up with a portable street lamp that looked just like the ones lining Main Street. It had a big yellow globe on top, a perfect image of the real deal. Powered by a battery in the base, it actually lit up, much to the delight of the crowd. Even more ingenious, and also even more popular with everyone, the base also held a secret compartment for storing Liquid Inspiration behind a sliding door in a clever tribute to Prohibition Days. Dad had no problem dressing and playing the part of a merry reveler hanging on the pole for dear life; I hear he even danced with it more than a few times. When the light was on, it wasn't the only thing shining, as patrons from all over the gym came to bask in its 80 proof glow.

Long time Cordovan Jim Webber remembered their dancing and the fake street light too. One Saturday morning while our family was waiting for sourdough pancakes at the CoHo, he interrupted his daily coffee klatch with the boys to tell me about the year he and his brother Bill, both still in high school, sneaked into the Ball wearing masks and costumes.

"We had heard about your Dad's lamp post, and made a beeline for it. He didn't recognize us, but happily slide open the door. That shot of whiskey from his hidden compartment is something I'll never forget."

So is it any surprise that an arrest and loss of hunting privileges served as artistic inspiration rather than demoralizing defeat?

Dad as himself; Mom as Leer, wearing these very signs now on the cabin wall, on the backs of their duck hunting costumes.

Who says crime doesn't pay?

First Prize, Most Creative Costumes, 1959 New Year's Eve fireman's Ball, goes to Don and Anita Shellhorn.

Part VI

What history in reality is not fiction? Hell, I can't remember what I did yesterday, let alone 52 years ago. Life today is a stack of 3X5 cards lest I forget who I am.

For years, I have been telling cabin visitors the story about the signs on the cabin wall. Weeks ago, it dawned on me that there might be actual records in the local justice system of events those days half a century back.

Enter local Magistrate Kay Kritchen Adams. Former math student, outstanding in academics, sports, and everything she did and does. Daughter of Cordova legend Larry Kritchen - hunter, trapper, fisherman, policeman, you name it - and a wonderful story teller before passing away recently. Heard great tales of duck hunting at Pete Dahl in the good old days, usually at the Post Office, his favorite place to meet, greet, and B.S. with half of Cordova. A daughter of Larry's had inbred respect for history, and within three days of a phone call, Kay had found and photocopied 10 pages of court records from that infamous day in 1959.

What a find. It honestly gave me chills. Spent the first day driving around town with the documents showing everyone how proud I was that my Dad was a criminal.

The copies lie before me, and will be inserted in the 1959 Cabin Log as soon as I am done writing. Priceless information, as well as misinformation, unanswered questions, omissions, and possibly a few outright errors. Appeals lawyers would have a field day.

For starters, Leer's name was spelled incorrectly as Lear on all documents related to him, including sentencing. He could have stood up and said give me my gun and ducks, I'm outta here. You got the wrong man.

Or he could have used the Classic Eye Exam Defense. You know, the witness who fingered the suspects is asked to identify them again from ten yards away and can't tell a dog from a duck. Leer is an eye doctor, why didn't he notice his name was spelled wrong, and think: "If this Crane guy can't tell an "a" from and "e," maybe he can't tell a 5 from a 6. Maybe he has such bad eyesight he glanced at his watch and thought it was 6:30 when it really was 5:30, the exact time shooting hours ended that day.

Come on. Reach in your pocket and pull out an eye chart. "Read the bottom row, please."

Case dismissed!

The documents show both Dad and Leer plead "Not Guilty," were duly tried, found guilty by Magistrate Moon, fined and sentenced as described earlier. Whether they got their guns back at that time is unclear. Maybe Dad had to mail Leer's to Juneau 30 days later.

I did feel a surge of pride in their pleas and renewed confidence in their innocence. To this day I feel Dad should have said "double not guilty." 1. Crane was standing by him, so clearly he didn't shoot. 2. If he didn't shoot, how could he have shot after hours?

Also unstated is what happened to the three confiscated birds. Did Magistrate Moon dine on savory roast duck slow-cooked in blueberry cordial while sipping chilled salmonberry wine that evening? Was that Officer Crane in his whipcord USFWS outfit, star flashing in the flickering candlelight, seated across from her?

New information surfaced from another document. The signed complainant was "Leslie I. Crane, Game Management." After all these years, his full name, to go with a Pete Dahl Date That Will Live in Infamy.

Page 3, "Warrant Misdemeanor," is strangely blank and incomplete. September 29, 1959 is handwritten on the top. The form then says: "I executed the same by arrest of the within named defendant_____and now produce_____in court_____.

Signed Leslie I. Crane, U.S. Marshall "

First of all, Crane wasn't a U.S. Marshall. Secondly, who did he arrest, and who did he produce in court, where?

No names, just empty lines.

Retrial!!

The last page is a bombshell. A much more detailed complaint, it states that "Don Shellhorn is accused by Leslie I. Crane, Enforcement Patrolman, Game Management, of the crime of shooting after hours, a misdemeanor; in violation of Section 6.4(a) Migratory Bird regulations." More importantly, it goes on to state that on the 26th of September 1959, "at or near Tiedeman slough," the said Don Shellhorn "were shooting 40 minutes after closing hour." Signed by Crane, after the words "being duly sworn, depose and say that the foregoing complaint is true."

Ditto for Leer.

What? Forget the bad English. Forty minutes after hours?!

As an eye witness participant, I find that hard to believe. Really hard to believe. In fact, as former Cordova High English and Home Ec teacher JoAnn Banta would say, "Bull puckie."

I swear, also Under Oath, that the sun was at some stage of setting. Come on, it was still bright out. How could it be 40 minutes after sunset?

Like a good Cold Case cop, I started searching for whatever other empirical evidence might still be around. Tacked on the inside wall of our duck cabin close to the entrance door is a framed, 8X10 typed list of day by day "Shooting Hours, Cordova, Alaska." Covered with glass, it is in remarkable condition. Before listing the daily times, it states "Times shown are one-half hour before sunrise and actual sunset times. Difference of times of sunrise and sunset in this area are so minor they may be ignored." Above the heading at the top, in Mom's handwriting, "Don Shellhorn Special," and at the bottom right, also handwritten, "Anita."

Intriguing. A subtle hint to her hubby, do not violate again? Or just a way to tease; perhaps clever pay back for all the verbal trash talk while playing two-handed pinochle?

Glancing at the times on the table, it dawned on me why this historic document had been ignored for more than 30 years. On 1 September 1959, shooting started at 4:06 a.m. and ended at 6:46 p.m. Glancing out the window on this hurricane-laced evening through wind and rain, there is still plenty of light to clearly see my riverboat bouncing on a huge wind surge tide almost three feet above normal—at 8:30 p.m. on September 5th!

What the hell is going on?

Ah-ha. Back in 1959, Alaska, with its far spread east-west longitudinal reach from the Southeast Panhandle to the tip of the Aleutian Chain which almost touches Russia, had four time zones. Crazy. Juneau was an hour ahead of us. So five o'clock in Cordova was six o'clock in Juneau.

Wait! Maybe Sheriff Crane had flown in from Ranger Enforcement Headquarters in the Territorial Capitol on 26 September, pinned on his star, loaded his six shooter, mounted his canoe, and giddy-upped down the slough to round up some shotgun-totting Duck Rustlers from the notorious Peed All Gang before Sundown. With his watch still on Juneau time! By the 1959 table, shooting hours on 26 September were 5:05 a.m. to 5:30 p.m. He thought it was 6:30.

We're innocent! I knew it.

Two other pieces of written historical data remain. One is Mom's entry in the Cabin Log, dated 25–27 September 1959. Faithful and meticulous chronologer of Events Pete Dahl, it was her idea to start a log, and all the entries from the beginning of building our cabin on July 25th, 1959 to her last visit that year on 10–12 October are in her handwriting alone.

Part of her entry for that fateful 26 September hunt says: "disastrous hunt on Saturday evening at 5:30 Game Warden picks up boys for shooting after dark!!!"

Five-thirty p.m. is the actual time legal shooting ended on that date. It was still quite light when Leer and I walked a couple hundred yards back to the boat *after* we shot and missed those high fliers, so we had to have torched off our last volley somewhere close to that time.

Where did Crane come up with "40 minutes after hours"?

Finally, there's that old cardboard clock on the wall between the two New Year's Eve signs. Its hands are set on 6:40, which, like a lot of things Pete Dahl, makes no sense. If Crane's claim of 40 minutes after hours was correct, that would make the time of our bust 5:30 plus 40 equals 6:10. Mom's Log Entry stated 5:30, so either way, why is it set on 6:40?

Perhaps Dad and Mom decided to change the cardboard clock to match today's current sunset time on 29 September, so guests could look out the window, glance at the clock, and enjoy the story. Between changes to make Alaska all the same time zone, plus adoption of Daylight Savings Time, today's shooting hours on 29 September end at 7:30 p.m.

So who knows?

This I do know.

We'll never know.

Part VII

A late afternoon sun flickers across silty waters, long shadows from tall cottonwoods lining the banks creating ragged leafy-edged patterns on glassy Alaganik Slough. Cruising upriver in my purring riverboat, elevated on today's big tide, I can see across the Delta almost as in pre-earthquake days. Despite scattered forty foot spruces, as well as thick stands of brush, occasional gaps allow glimpses of the Haystack, now covered with evergreens, standing firmly entrenched above Tiedeman Slough.

Yep, there it is. It helps that fall is in the air; and yellow leaves dropping off the deciduous, "falling," vastly improve visibility while sometimes creating havoc with the boat's jet unit intake.

Ah, if rocks could talk. Early U.S. Army explorers like Abercrombie and Allen must have noticed it while cordelling past in the 1880s; perhaps Copper River Natives used it as a lookout for thousands of years.

A huge erratic that has tales to tell.

And to me it whispers, evoking memories of that glorious, unforgettable, transient eve half a century ago.

I hear Dad telling Leer, in reverence to its monolithic power,

"Let's go the Haystack. There's always birds there."

Part VIII

25–27 September 1959

Real good start - Curly Hoover kind enuff to loan skiff - have loan of 35 motor. Doc Leer with us. Dick and Mike Noonan in our boat, Sharon and Harry, Don and myself in big rig. Motor fails on big skiff so are towed down by Dick in the small skiff and Johnson 18.

*Disastrous hunt on Sat. Eve at 5:30 Game Warden picks up the boys - shooting after dark!!! Lose guns and birds must go to court on Tuesday at 1 P.M. No rhyme or reason for any of this **Mr. Crane** a shit heel from way back. Sunday rather sad - so sorry please.*
Bag - Leer -7
3 took by Shmill
Dick - 4
Don -3

Sad state of affairs —Anita

Perhaps, as Mom concluded, it was a "sad state of affairs."
But it was also one of the best times of my life.

Chapter 2

Alaganik

ALAGANIK: 1. The Native word *Alarneq* (Alaganik) means "switchback in the river." SHERMAN, *Images of American; Cordova*
2. "We always called it the Copper, because it was the first slough east of Whitshed that led to the main Copper upstream." Jim WEBBER, LOCAL FISHERMAN

"Just because you know where something is doesn't mean you're going to find it."

PETE DAHL AXIOM

Part I: Lower Cutoff

The fiberglass 14 foot Boston Whaler carved around the tight horse-shoe bend nicely, its double chime hull cutting the muddy waters as designed. Powered by a 50 horse Johnson outboard whose propeller had been replaced with a jet unit, it was well overloaded but still maintained step.

Momentarily.

One minute the pair in the craft was cruising down the river; the next instant they were, as the phrase goes, "hard aground." Surrounded by a wall of card board boxes, ice chests, tools, and equipment, the forward passenger almost went flying over the bow into about 4 inches of water. Astern, the skipper was splashed from two directions: water spraying from the jet unit running 1000 rpm's over limit from behind, and a geysering Lucky Lager on the steering console in front.

Quickly shutting off the engine, Captain Don Shellhorn thought "Uh oh."

Struggling back to an upright position, First Mate Anita Shellhorn's thinking went more like "Oh s--t"

Unlike flat-bottomed lightweight aluminum riverboats that can be pulled off slippery sand bars with relative ease, the heavier Whaler, with its dual deep "V's" that were great in the often rough waters of Alaganik Slough, was a bugger to budge.

Well-drilled in this routine, the couple reacted with surprising calm. Grabbing four plastic-coated seat cushions, they slid them under hull skegs impaled in the mud. And pulled. Nothing moved. Next option was prying with the wooden oars. Again no success.

Plan B: lighten ballast. Quickly they unloaded several boxes onto the few inches of receding water barely covering the bar.

"Don't worry if they float away, honey, the current will take them right to the cabin," said the Captain, a wily river runner.

Still no movement, despite the leverage of oars. They could see the water receding.

"Let's not panic. I'll climb up over the bank and see how far away we are from the cabin," said Scout Shellhorn.

He waded across what was left of the slough, scurried up a muddy cut bank, stood tall while shading his eyes, and scanned the horizon.

"How's it look, honey?', queried his loyal mate, from below.

"Really good, sweetie. Why, I can see the cabin right over there."

Which it was. A mere 800 yards away, as the crow flies. With Pete Dahl slough, 200 yards wide and 10 feet deep, in between. And 12 hours until the next high tide.

Oops.

Well, thought Mom, as she washed the mud off the cushions and began spreading them on the dry ground above the sandbar, plus digging out a tarp and emergency lunch she had learned to always pack, at least we're not lost.

And so, in the words of Samuel Eliot Morison, "the yacht's white wings were folded for the night."

Eyeball Specialist Dr. Harrison Leer, who specialized in acronyms to describe such common experiences while duck hunting with Dad, would have phrased it more succinctly: they were SIM, i.e. Stuck In Mud.

On a small slough less than a mile upriver from the mouth of Alaganik called the Lower Cutoff. It zig-zagged from Alaganik to Pete Dahl, the next major slough to the east. A short cut that could save about ten minutes running time. If you made it through. The tide drained out of the Cutoff from both ends, rapidly. Shortcuts are well known to often be the longest distance between two points. They had come up about 500 yards short.

Ironically, Dad's good friend Harry Curran had run the deep draft, 60 foot halibut-style salmon tender *Copper King* through this very channel back in 1947, "just to see if I could do it," were his words. Harry said he had a heck of a time getting it around the sharp hairpin turn Dad and Mom had successfully navigated,

"The yacht's white wings were folded for the night." Captain Shellhorn with Boston Whaler SIM in the Lower Cutoff, July 1975.

"by putting the bow of the tender against the bank." Of course, that was back before the earthquake when there was much more water. Harry was a natural boatsman. He said more than once he "could feel the bottom under the keel of the boat."

Evidently Dad couldn't. Sand bars across the Delta were becoming well acquainted with the feel of the bottom of a certain Boston Whaler.

The stranded duo were certainly not the first to impale themselves on the Delta's muddy terrain. If only Lt. Henry Allen's Journal, *An Expedition to the Copper, Tanana, and Koyukuk Rivers in 1885,* had been available. It would have made for enlightening reading during their wait. They could have shared his sense of humor by a small bonfire while swatting away bugs. And unlike Allen and Company, known that in a half day, max, they would be in a warm, cozy cabin.

Unfortunately, what should be every Delta traveler's Bible wasn't available until ten years later, when Alaska Northwest Publishing reprinted it.

9 July 1975

After a slight delay - like one tide to another - we made it, at 1:30 a.m - left the landing at 1:30 p.m. Quickest trip we ever made says the "Captain," not so the "oar" he brought along. More when our eye balls are open. —Anita

Slight goof about 30 minutes late so hit the bank, to wait for the incoming tide. Weather great so no great hardship - had our little radio - provisions - beer. Built a good fire - a few mosquitos. Live and learn. —Don

Perhaps Dad was also considering adding a waterproof written reminder of his favorite Mantra atop the steering console: *Time and Tide Wait for No Man.*

10 July 1975

Up? not too early after last nites episode - Great day - hot - 70 degrees at 11 a.m. Unloaded provisions - hooked up radio etc -

In the afternoon went down to check on the strawberry plants - very dismal Laid in the sun. Had a good steak dinner - as a navigator I am a good steak cooker. —Don

Got sorta organized today, oh what beautiful weather. Seems we should be "doing something" never been so lazy before. On the next page will be found my "great contribution" to poetry, verse or curse as the case may be. Composed while stuck in the Mud! —Anita

Sediments of Anita

> On a lovely day in early July
> Off to Pete Dahl were Don and I
> Thru the Lower Cutoff we did try
> Almost to the Cabin and like to die!
> Up on a sand bar we did sit
> Guess you know who said "Oh Shit."
> Pushed with oars with all our might
> Had to give up to spend the night.
> Dinner of ham, cheese, pickles on a bun
> Cantalope, cookies, bugs all part of the fun.
> Radio coming in loud and clear
> 30-06 handy so there is no fear.
> 8:30 now, tide not high til 1:30
> We'll get there yet nice and dirty.
> To flop on a bunk and get some sleep
> Ya can bet your britches we won't count sheep!

"Pushed with oars with all our might, Had to give up and spend the night ... 8:30 now, tide not high til 1:30, we'll get there yet, nice and dirty." SIM in Lower Cutoff, Mom makes herself comfortable, July 1975.

Part II: Early Exploration

March 1885

The Copper River has always been one of several key access routes to interior Alaska, and Alaganik Slough has served as the main entrance to the Copper. From its origin at Copper Glacier on Mt. Wrangell, the 300 mile long river, tenth largest in the United States, races at 7 miles per hour toward the sea. Named for copper deposits first discovered near its headwaters by Natives, the murky concentrated flow of the Copper passes through the Chugach Mountains and races under the Million Dollar bridge between Miles and Childs glaciers at 52 Mile on the Copper River Highway. Then the flow rate slows, as it spreads out to form numerous tributary rivers, streams, and sloughs that cut through a delta it has created over eons with the sand and silt carried by its waters.

The modern day definition of the Copper River Delta extends all the way from Whitshed Point on the end of the Heney Range in the west, to Katella in the east.

The actual flow of the Copper itself is much narrower, with Alaganik in the west and Cottonwood Point in the east as the boundaries of its grey waters.

Early Russian, British, and Spanish explorers all ventured up the Copper and its many tributaries. While Natives had been going up and down the river for centuries to trade, hunt, fish, and also utilize pure copper for implements, the first white men to make it all the way up the Copper were Russians.

In September 1796 Baranov sent a party lead by Tarkhanov to explore the unknown upper regions of the Copper. Details of this adventure can be found in Lethcoe's *History of Prince William Sound*. Tarkhanov spent a long winter wandering throughout the Delta and nearly dying of starvation, but for the help of local aborigines. With Native guides showing the way, he finally became the first European to visit the upper Copper area, ascending the main river in March and April of 1797. Several later Russian explorers also made it up river, as noted in the Historical Section of Lt. Allen's Journal. Early prospectors and trappers, including John Bremner and Peder Johnson, also followed the Copper to the Interior on undocumented trips.

The Russian explorer Sereberinikoff stopped at a place he called "Alagnak," several miles upriver from the mouth of the main slough, during his 1847 expedition. From there, he and eleven assistants made it far up the Copper to Chittyna by September, but were forced by weather to stop at that point. After surviving a cold winter, in May and early June of 1848 they explored further, reaching Tazlina Lake. What happened after that is unclear. It appears the Russians treated the upper Ahtna Copper River Natives badly, and at some point were massacred, never to return.

After the United States purchase of Alaska from Russia in 1867, politicians back in Washington D.C. decided it might be nice to know what they bought for $7.2 million dollars. Various military surveys were conducted; the first two up the Copper were by Lt. William Abercrombie in 1884 and Lt. Henry Allen in 1885. Abercrombie's large expedition didn't make it very far beyond the Child's and Miles glaciers.

It was a small, light weight expedition by Allen and two enlisted companions the following year that made an amazing and epic journey, well documented in his report *An Expedition to the Copper, Tanana and Koyukuk Rivers in 1885.*

Alaska Northwest Publishing Company first printed this report as part of its series *The Northern History Library* in a 1985 ALASKA JOURNAL. That version is no longer in print, but Duane Schuldt through Publications Consultant republished the report in 2009.

Simply put, the documents describe an astounding adventure, and make for fascinating reading. Allen had a dry sense of humor which served him especially well during the wet dreary first months of his expedition.

As with practically all early explorations of the Copper, Allen, Sgt. Cady Robertson, and Pvt. Fred W. Pickett first entered the river's muddy water at Alaganik Slough. The name for this waterway has Native origins, reflecting it's importance and common use for travel by the various groups to a small Native settlement called Alaganik several miles up river.

As mentioned in this Chapter's introduction, the Native word *Alarneq* (Alaganik) means "switchback in the river." From the small settlement of Alaganik the slough did just that, taking a 90 degree turn to the south, and then switching back to the east and upward to the main Copper River. In a sense, this tiny settlement, which numbered 117 in the 1880 census, was the gateway to the Interior, although bearing zero resemblance to St. Louis during the push across the Great Plains.

Sketches in Allen's Journal, particularly one titled "Start from Alaganik," display still recognizable sloughs and forested terrain near the confluence of the McKinley River and Alaganik at Mile 22 of today's Copper River Highway. Four canoes filled with Natives and the Allen party are illustrated, about to veer off the switchback and head up toward the main Copper at 27 Mile. In 2013, lifelong Cordova fisherman Jim Webber recalled the slough there was" almost as wide as it was deep," describing its 50 foot width and 60 foot depth in the 1950s.

The term slough refers to a body of water that is intertidal, and the Copper River Delta is a maize of such waterways. The mouth of Alaganik Slough, where the Delta ends in steep muskeg-based grass and brush covered cutbanks six to ten feet high, is roughly one-half mile wide. Oceanward from that is what locals call "the Flats," a broad, muddy or sandy non-vegetated region braided with small gutters to large channels that is covered by murky tidal water much of the time. The depth of the water fluctuates dramatically with tides that vary from fifteen feet high to minus three feet low, with two high and two low tides daily. A series of sandy barrier island reefs formed by wind, surf, and tides run the length of Delta, and protect the "Inside," or Flats, from the heavy surf of the Pacific Ocean. Modern commercial fisherman routinely pass through shallow water and breakers between these barrier islands to gill net for the famous Copper River Salmon on the edges of the Pacific Ocean.

High tides flood up Alaganik and all the sloughs of the Delta. Alaganik Slough quickly narrows down considerably. Twelve miles upriver where it reaches the upper edges of the flat Delta terrain and the timber line at what was once the site of the settlement of Alaganik, it is only a few hundred feet wide. Prior to the earthquake of 1964, tides flooded all the way up to that point, assisting travelers wise to its ways. The sloughs were clogged with ice, usually from freeze-up in November until late March and early April. From the settlement of Alaganik the slough continued on to connect with the western edge of the main Copper River at Mile 27 near what early 1900 builders of the Copper River and Northwestern

Railway called Flag Point. It was a natural sheltered access route to the main river and points beyond.

Alaganik itself was far enough away from the near edge of the main Copper River at 27 Mile to be protected from the almost constant winds that roar down the river bed and scour the Delta, especially in the winter. The location had well forested, elevated land just above the slough, and a rich salmon run of sockeye salmon headed to McKinley Lake. A logical, ideal place for a small "village."

Adding incentive to the Alaganik Slough route was the location of a major settlement at Port Etches on Hinchenbrook Island, about 50 miles from the mouth of the Copper. Originally a native village called Nuchek, the Russians established a trading post there in the 1790s called Fort St. Constantine. The United Stated inherited it as part of "Seward's Folly." Large sailing vessels routinely stopped to drop off men, supplies, and equipment as the base for ventures all over Prince William Sound. When Allen landed there to begin his expedition, it was a trading station being operated by Alaska Commercial Company.

From Nuchek the explorers, guided by natives who knew the routes well, traversed the sheltered waters along the inside edge of Hinchenbrook until they reached the Cutoff, a shallow passage between Hinchenbrook and Hawkins Islands. Next they canoed across to Pt. Whitshed, still in the lee of the southeasterly weather that anyone who has spent time on the Flats or Delta knows can create havoc. Around the corner to the east lies the edge of the Delta and the Flats, which typically were crossed for seventeen miles on an incoming tide to the first slough that leads upward to the western edge of the main Copper, Alaganik.

The same slough we have used for 54 years to gain access to our duck cabin at Pete Dahl had been used for the previous 164 years by European explorers to go up the Copper, and by natives for countless centuries before that.

A River of History. And a River of hazards. In 1779 the Spanish explorer Arteaga called it "Rio do los Perdidos." River of the Lost. Yet not once did Lt. Allen mention his party being off course. How could they be? They were exploring and mapping a new unmarked area one-fifth the size of the United States.

Allen, a lanky 25 year old West Point graduate from Kentucky, described their adventure in fine detail. And proved to have true grit.

Quotes from Lt. Allen's Journal, Part II, Narrative of the Copper River

"On the morning of March 20 we left Nuchek for the mouth of the Copper river in two boats obtained from the natives…"

"By the time we turned the southwest point of Hinchinbrook Island the breakers were washing our stores in the boat…"

"We continued our struggle. At 5 o'clock, having passed Johnstone's Point, we went into camp on the north side of the island…"

"The old native selected this as a safe harbor, prophesying at the same time the near approach of a storm. The "old man's" prophecy was fulfilled, for barely had we hauled up the boats and made them fast than it began to sleet and rain, nor did we see the sun from that evening until we had passed the limit of great precipitation, north of the Copper River Glaciers."

"The following day we left camp at 4 a.m., and passed through the narrow and shallow channel between Hawkins Island and the most northerly point of Hinchenbrook Island."

"The storm forced us to direct our canoe to Point Whitshed…We went into a small cove on the west side of Point Whitshed, to interview an old native and his wife (Eyaks) who we found by chance engaged in stringing clams.'

"From them we learned that there was no other "harbor" for our boat short of the mouth of the Copper River, unless we ran up into the Eyak, several miles north of our direct course.

"They spoke much of the mud flats, which we afterwards became acquainted with through sad experience."

"To reach the principal channel of Copper River… necessitated a start from Point Whitshed at 3 in the morning, at about the time of flood tide. The wind was dead ahead, and darkness was supreme. Our boats were constantly shipping water, yet for several hours we struggled against all difficulties, keeping close to the rugged and rocky shore, without a beach. The more the tide fell the oftener we grounded on the mud. We had hoped to reach the channel of Copper River (Author's Note, ie. Alaganik Slough) before this state of affairs could arrive. Finally, as a means of economy, we tried to make headway by going out from the shore, but the tide was receding too fast and left us on the mud about 800 yards from shore. A few provisions were then carried by us to the rocky shore over the soft, sticky mud, and were cooked with driftwood found lodged among the rocks."

They were in the vicinity of Government Rock, not yet to the outflow of Mountain Slough and the marshy edge of the Delta. Allen, along with Peder Johnson, walked four and a half hours through mud, ice, snow, and water, to reach a small settlement on the east bank of the Eyak River a mile below Eyak Lake, where he recruited two more Natives to help with the expedition. They returned to find their boats still high and dry.

"After wading out to our stores, we found the afternoon tide not high enough to float the boats, so were compelled to pass the night ashore, and leave at 3 a.m. the following day, when, after struggling against the head wind for two or three hours without success, the intense darkness making matters worse, we turned back to the camp on the west side of Point Whitshed rather than again be stranded on the mud flats."

The next day they tried again, departing on the flood morning tide.

"We again started for the mouth of the Copper River, which we fortunately reached before the tide could drop us on the mud. Had we been half an hour later the same fate as that of the preceding day awaited us. We could only know we were in the channel of the river by the "wind-row" of ice piled on its west bank. A divergence of a few yards either to the right or left was sufficient to run the boats aground. As we ascended this western channel it became wider and the current stronger. The floating ice compelled us to entirely stop rowing. We tried "cordelling," which was unsatisfactory on account of ice and numerous deep inlets along the banks."

"About 7 p.m., after having rowed continuously for thirteen hours, we were stopped by an ice blockade. We had made our mid-day meal on hard bread in the boats. Had we been inclined to cook, the absence of timber of any description would have prevented it."

"Our immediate objective was Alaganik, further up, and our supplies were not so scanty... After reaching the blockade the stores were unloaded and piled on the muddy bank, with nothing to protect them from the mud and rain except the three tent-poles and the tent fly. We had been exposed to the storm for four days; our clothes were completely saturated; some of us, too, had been in the water up to our necks, and here we were entirely without firewood."

"Under the guidance of the "Old Man" and the Eyaks we started afoot for Sakhalis over this flat, barren of everything except swamp grass and a wonderful mixture of ice, snow, mud, and water, made worse by the continuous rain and sleet of the past four hours. Darkness was on us, and our little party of nine divided into three to try and find this village. After two hours' wandering it was found in a small "patch" of undergrowth, and consisted of two so-called houses, very small and equally crowded. These were each about 12 by 13 feet, and in the one where I slept were twenty-nine natives, ten dogs, and the household effects. The "Old Man" and one native strayed and were compelled to weather the storm without fire or shelter."

Sakhalis was a small camp several miles below Alaganik. Eventually, after several portages over ice, the supplies and party reached Alaganik on March 27.

"Since the evening of departure from Nuchek, March 20, we had been continually exposed to sleet and rain, driven by strong southeast wind, which rendered the limbs numb and action at times almost impossible. On one occasion each of the party tried to light a match, but all failed on account of numbness and moisture. These days were severe ones, but an excellent discipline for the even more trying work that was soon to follow."

From there, after a brief rest, on March 29, Allen and his two men, along with Peder Johnson, a veteran of the region, and seven natives, began their ascent of the Copper, using both sleds and canoes. Everything was covered with snow. They had a considerable load of supplies, and made six miles, sinking in the wet snow. On March 30th, after struggling through the miserable conditions for one day, they realized it would be impossible to travel with so much gear. Lightening the load began the next morning.

"We abanDoned about one-half our ammunition, cooking outfit, food, clothing, &c. A few hours later we abanDoned our tent and more clothing and food, and then had with us about 150 pounds of flour, 100 pounds of beans, 40 pounds of rice, two sides of bacon, 15 pounds of tea, some Liebig's extract of beef, deviled ham, and chocolate."

"On the morning of April 1 we left camp with the storm more severe than ever, the precipitation having changed to snow."

On they went. By April 2 they had passed the Miles and Childs Glaciers, and reached the point where the Abercrombie Expedition of the year before had stopped.

"On the night of April 2 we went into camp on an enormous pile of immense rocks, heaped up in the center of the riverbed. On the east side of these was a very small and narrow channel; on the west the width does not exceed 50 yards; and this is Copper River. Its depth must be great, though the ice forbade our march over it and consequently any attempt to determine it. I have called this remarkable gorge "Abercrombie's Canyon."

It was another miserable night.

"No place in it could be found which would permit us to lie at full length, so our night was passed on our haunches, in a severe storm of snow and rain… The

result was a night of watching and longing for day, with clothes as thoroughly saturated as though we had slept in the river."

Finally, they made it above the canyon.

"The 4th of April was the first day that we caught a glimpse of the sun from the time of our departure from Nuchek, March 20, and the first day or night that was free from a precipitation in some form."

A remarkable, and prophetic, experience. Pounded by southeast winds. Betrayed by tides. Lightening the load. Stuck in the mud. Overnighting on the exposed flats. Cordelling up Alaganik. Endless days of rain. Drenched from head to toe. Even battling ice clogged sloughs. Been there, done that. History does repeat itself.

But at least not lost. Exploration does have its advantages. How can you be lost if you don't know where you're going?

Part III: First Trip Down Alaganik

September 1954

The alarm rattled. Bobby and I rolled over in cozy down-filled Army surplus sleeping bags. Candy, our little brown and white cocker spaniel, was curled up between us. It was still dark, and outside I could hear current quietly rippling against a stump in Alaganik Slough. Glancing up, I noticed water had condensed on the inside of the canvas covering above us. A drop hit me in the face. It was nippy.

Dad sat up in his sleeping bag, stiff from a restless night on the hard wooden bed of the truck. Stretched, turned on a flashlight, and crawled out. We all slept with most of our clothes on. The Green Hornet, as we called it, was a 1930s era Ford truck with wood stave sides that looked like something straight out of Steinbeck's *The Grapes of Wrath*. Dad specialized in Creative Engineering, and had bent sturdy metal rods that reached across the tops of the side walls to create a covered wagon powered by cylinders rather than horses. It was our family trademark. At every opportunity, the Shellhorn kids - Donita, Bobby, myself, and Sharon, in chronological order, plus often half the neighborhood - rode in the back on forays out the road for picnics, berry picking, and outdoor fun. Often we would roll back the most forward stretch of canvas and stand holding on to the wooden panel just behind the truck cab, trying to avoid the dust that billowed up while peering over the top like Rommel in North Africa, minus the goggles. Mom and Dad could glance through a little back window in the cab to check on us.

It was almost as dusty up forward. The former Cordova Commercial delivery truck, painted with green XO-type paint to cover up rust and dents, had lost its air tightness somewhere around the thousand mile mark on the city's potholed dirt roads. During the transport's early days, there were only two turnpikes in Cordova: Three Mile Bay Road, and Power Creek Road, seven miles in length. Both were so narrow, curved and rugged they required no speed limit signs. Miss a turn on the first and end up in Orca Inlet; the fresh waters of nearby Eyak Lake beckoned from the second.

As WWII came to a close, railroad tracks from the abandoned Copper River & Northwestern Railroad were torn up, and construction on the "Copper River Highway" began. Cordovans had visions of extending the road over the famous train path all the way to Chitina, and then connecting to "the lower 48" via the Alcan Highway, which the military had hastily built at the onset of the war. The local "highway" was basically just gravel dumped over the railroad grade, and by 1954, had more than doubled Cordova's drivable mileage.

Dad dropped down from the back of the truck, and lifted Candy out, so the two of them could answer Nature's Call. He then reached back in the truck to grab a wooden Blazo box. Slid it out, dumped the contents on the ground, and turned it over to use as a table. Handy items, those boxes, in which rectangular metal cans of gasoline or kerosene were crated and shipped from Seattle to Standard Oil and other local businesses.

We could hear him pumping on a gasoline lantern; then a hiss and the Coleman's bright light. "OK, troops, up and at 'em " were the first words of the day, as he started an old canister-type single burner gas cooking stove inherited from his Dad and the glory days of hunting and camping on the Kenai Peninsula. "Hot chocolate on the way" came next.

Funny the stuff you remember. This was my first duck hunt, and what I recall most was the scorched-milk flavor of steaming cocoa on that early morning beside the Alaganik.

Cooking was never Dad's strong suit.

Outside it was starting to brighten. Pre-dawn. A glimmer to the east. Could see where you were going without a flashlight. A nice day was on the rise. Fall and excitement in the air. A small twelve foot cedar craft lay along side the road near the murmuring slough. Had been a lifeboat of longer length on the local U.S. Coast Guard buoy tender until a mishap crushed the stern and banged up the sides. The military termed it a total loss and took it to the dump. Dad, one of Cordova's Top Scroungers, was quick on the scene. Hauled it home, cut off the damaged end, patched the sides, slapped on a transom, paid a month's salary for a little 10 horse Johnson from the rack on the hardware side of the Commercial, of which he was now a partner, and we were in the water-fowl business.

The craft was light and had a tradition of seaworthiness despite its tippiness. What was left of it barely stuck over the end of the truck bed. The three of us had turned it over and lifted it into the back of the truck after Dad came home from work at the store. All of us, plus wildly excited Candy, rode up front for the late evening drive out the road. Mom had admonished Dad to be careful, which we knew as Code signifying the Boys Were In For An Adventure.

Boat #2 in our succession of family vessels was a considerable improvement over Model #1. Dad had made that one by laying plywood on the floor and building sides. Long Shorty, a local fishermen who stood 6 foot 8 inches and fancied himself to be a boat builder when his legs weren't sticking out at weird angles from a bar stool at the Club, was the design engineer. Right.

Cordova's denizens spent many hours leaning on bars dreaming up nicknames for the fellow tipplers. Long Shorty was so tall he had to bend down to enter the pubs lining Main Street, and soon became in the habit of walking that way full time. Many other monikers weren't so obvious, Digger Davidson clearly being an exception. He was the local undertaker.

Anyhow, Dad must have mentioned to his bartender friend Kenny Van Brocklin that he was looking for a boatbuilder. With a free drink for incentive, everyone at the Club Bar raised their hand. Kind of hard to miss Long Shorty, who obviously knew how to bend things into shape.

Together they created the Ultimate Flat Bottom. Fourteen feet long, not an inch of flare or rise. Plywood with a rib here and there. Powered by a 12 horse Johnson, it flew, as long as there wasn't a ripple. And slid from bank to bank like an otter. Talk about anticipating the next corner. By the time it arrived at the Boxcar, the vertical sides were covered with grey mud from bouncing off banks, and the boatsmen were black and blue. After so many crashes, it's no wonder the next craft was a lifeboat, or at least part of one.

We chowed down on sweet rolls while Dad slapped together some salami sandwiches, his lunchtime specialty. Whew. At least it wasn't the other favorite, sardines. Usually with a layer of mustard. Mmmm-good, we would say. Toss in a bag of candy bars, soda pop for us, beer for the Captain, and we were set. Dehydration was never an issue when hunting with Dad.

Alaganik Slough, here we come.

Bobby was twelve, and two years my senior. He had already been "road" hunting with Dad, and bagged his first goose the year before above 8 Mile in a place appropriately called The Goose Pasture.

Me? I didn't have a clue. Before the day, and night, were over, I would.

We were parked on a small gravel turnout just opposite the spot where the Pipeline Lake Trail begins. This was back before the earthquake, so the tide came all the way up to that point. There was plenty of water in the slough.

The plan, as I later learned, was to go down to the mouth of Alaganik, hunt through the low tide, and then come back up on the incoming tide. Twelve hours of glory on the Delta. It was also the first time I learned that Dad never could really understand a Tide Book, ever. I think he just glanced at the numbers, looked at his watch, and uttered one of his favorite phrases, "Ah, the hell with it."

Have sometimes wondered if that's why I went on to become a mathematics teacher, most of my career at Cordova High. Tide books are great illustrations of negative numbers, commonly known as minus tides, of which I was soon to become familiar.

We dragged the boat down the bank through the bushes. Dad went back to grab the outboard as we ferried a box loaded with lunch, pop, and beer, plus shotguns, decoys, and hunting gear to the boat. Then added gas tank, tool kit, spot light, oars, life jackets, seat cushions, etc. Candy was racing all over, barking with glee. Oh boy. She wouldn't be quite so chipper twelve hours later.

"Me? I didn't have a clue. Before the day, and night, were over, I would." Bobby and I in our earlier years, already toughening up for future adventures.

The little outboard fired off after a coupe cranks, and away we went. "Cruising down the river...," which later became our family boating song. Wow. It was awesome. My first real look at the waters of historic Alaganik and the lower reaches of the Flats. Grass changing from green to yellow, a nice clean "V" trailing the boat as the Johnson purred along, a cheerful little rooster tail just astern, Dad at the motor tiller, startled ducks jumping out of the water and off the banks, and that deliciously crisp autumn air in our faces.

We ran, without any problem, for about 30 minutes, all the way to within a mile of the slough entrance. On the east side just above a tributary that branched off toward Pete Dahl were a string of ponds that Dad had hunted before. The birds would come off the mud flats, zip along the slough, and then cruise into the ponds to feed.

We stopped there, pulled the boat up over the gradual muddy bank, carefully tied and anchored it off, grabbed our gear, and trudged over a small cutbank to the edge of the marsh. The sun was barely up, golden grass waved in a slight breeze, and nearby ponds sparkled.

We walked 100 yards to the edge of the first long pond, jumping several ducks in the process. Dad was a stickler about gun safety, especially with us youngsters, so none of us had loaded shotguns. Bobby was carrying a single shot .410; I had inherited his older bolt action .410, also single shot. Dad had a trusty Winchester Model 12 sixteen gauge pump, his Dad's shotgun from ptarmigan hunting days in Seward. The 12 came from 1912, the year Winchester introduced what was to be one of the most popular pump shotguns ever.

The pond was roughly 100 yards wide, and about 300 yards long. Bobby, the veteran, was allowed to head to the upper end to set up a little blind and put out half a dozen rubber inflatable "Deeks"; within Dad's sight but out of shotgun range. The two of us dropped our gear, and started cutting low brush to make our own blind. We had folding duck stools to sit on, and after getting set up tossed out the remaining six decoys. Candy had taken off with Bobby; maybe she recognized I was a rookie, and knew she would have better luck retrieving for my brother.

I would like to say the hunting was great, but actually it wasn't. The weather was just too nice. The birds were flying high. A single would decoy in occasionally. I found out in a hurry that a .410 isn't much more deadly than the Daisy BB gun I had been shooting for several years. At least not in my hands. Dad was the model of patience, coaching me with the idea of swinging the gun, not pointing; and remembering to lead the bird. Back then shotgun shells were made of waxed cardboard, and even on a dry day such as this, they tended to require effort to be chambered. And more effort to extract, as once wet, they swelled in a hurry, becoming jammed in the barrel. Dad always carried a 3 piece gun rod for such contingencies.

We could see Bobby bag a couple birds, Candy splashing out to retrieve. I blasted a few times, to no avail. Dad tossed a beer bottle out into the pond so I could practice shooting at a stationary target and get some idea of the pattern size.

By midday, the birds had quit flying entirely. We walked back to check on the boat, and eat our lunch there. It was so nice we all took a siesta in the grass on the riverbank.

Tired from lack of sleep the prior night, plus all the fresh air, we all snoozed later than expected. Not a problem, said Dad; the birds always move right at dusk. Back to the pond we went, with the sun slowly setting in colorful fashion behind us toward Whitshed Point. We, actually they, picked up a few more birds. Then it was time to pull the decoys, pack up the gear, trudge back to the boat, and head back. No sun visible by this time, but the sky was still yellow, red, and purple to the west.

Strangely, the boat seemed to be quite a bit further from the water. No problem. It was light and slid easily across the mud. We piled in, Dad fired off the outboard, and up river we went. Slower. Gee, the current was ebbing out, at a pretty good clip. Maybe it had been doing the same when we came down river, and that's why we had zipped along so nicely.

Also ebbing, as in fading, was daylight. It was starting to become dark. The lower part of Alaganik is wide and deep; then it tapers down at a place about halfway back to our launch site, at a junction known as Snag Point. Where we of course hit our first stump, and sheared our first pin.

For those unfamiliar with shear pins, they are basically just a small metal rod about one inch log, of relatively soft metal, that fit through a hole in the lower unit drive shaft and also a slot of the propeller to keep it from spinning freely on the shaft. They are designed to break off, or shear, when the propeller, while spinning at high speed, hits an underwater object. This prevents major damage to the shaft, motor, and prop.

"Just what have you done with these kids, Don Shellhorn?" Early family photo, faithful dog Candy, plus Grandmother Meda Shellhorn, Dick, sister Donita, Mom, & Bobby, in front of our little house in Cordova. Mom was already becoming adept at interrogating Dad after duck hunts.

Dad carried them by the pocket full, as well as the cotter pins that locked the prop in place. For good reason. He could change them in record time, having had considerable practice.

No sweat. Pull over to the bank, take off the prop, replace the pin, reassemble, and off we go. Two shear pins later, and the further up slough we traveled, the shallower the water, the more the snags, and the darker the evening. And also the lower the temperature. Clear weather means nippy nights.

The last half mile was by boot power only. Dad and Bobby dragged the boat, stumbling in several pot holes. My boots were too short for the task; Candy and I curled up in the bow trying to stay warm.

It was pitch black by the time we made it back to the truck. Dad and Bobby were wet and exhausted, I was shivering, and Candy wasn't zipping around any more. After loading everything back in the rig, Bobby and I stared at headlights shining on the dirt road for about 5 minutes, and then fell asleep with Candy at our feet and the car heater pumping out BTU's.

We woke up with a jerk as the truck pulled to a stop in front of our tiny house on the corner of Second Street and A Avenue. Considerably later than the promised hour. Well, we reasoned, what duck hunter worth his feathers gets home on time anyhow?

Mom was at the door, with the classic question indicating someone was in the Dog House, and it wasn't Candy.

"Where have you been, Don Shellhorn?"

Nothing is more indicative of a successful hunt than a wife chewing out an unshaven and often hungover husband upon late return. Bobby and I had witnessed this phenomena many times.

"Why, hi, Sweetie."

"Just what in the world have you done with these kids, Don Shellhorn?"

Mom continued to chew on Dad. We knew a question ending in "Don Shellhorn" put him in Hurricane Category Trouble. The phrase ending with just "Don" meant mild weather. If it ended in "Honey," life was good.

We didn't dare smile or giggle. Stood and watched silently and patiently, nodding seriously. But inside there was great joy, for we knew we had just joined a Special Fraternity known as Duck Hunters, initiated by the Grand Mallard. Dad.

We unloaded our gear, piled out of wet clothing, and headed up the narrow stairway to our tiny bedroom.

Candy, traveling mate for much of the voyage, hopped on my bed, as Bobby and I called it a night. We slept well and happily.

Little did I know it would be the only duck hunt my brother and I would ever make together.

Chapter 3

Eyak

EYAK: 1. Native name derives from the village and lake above it. The word *eyak* (igya'aq) refers to the "throat" of a lake.
CATHY SHERMAN, *Images of America: Cordova*
2. "Up river, down river," regarding choices of direction when navigating the Eyak. RANDY BRUCE

"For the most part who they were and how many and when is unknowable, unregistered in that scattered, paper-and parchment, half-reliable remembrance that we call history."

JOHN GRAVES, *Goodbye to a River*

Part I: In The Beginning

As long as there have been ducks, there probably been duck hunters. Can't you envision early prehistoric man salivating at the sight of a fat juicy mallard?

Natives of the Copper River Delta undoubtedly felt the same craving. Especially in the early spring, when migratory birds returned, but salmon runs were yet to arrive.

It is interesting to note that Lt. Henry Allen made no mention of ducks, geese, or swan in his 1885 Journal. Perhaps they hadn't appeared when he traversed the Delta in late March. Typically, migrating birds show up in mid-April through early May. But there was also no mention of sea ducks, which winter in the salt water areas; nor mallards, which are quite common year-round on intertidal areas near Cordova.

Allen's Journal describes the meager food stores Natives had left by late spring, surely another incentive to hunt. But evidently not for birds. Soon, however, their eggs would be on the menu. Local Natives still make annual expeditions out to nearby sandy barrier islands to gather them in May and June. Egg Island, five miles below the mouth of Eyak River, is an aptly named favorite spot for sea gull eggs. Easily accessible by the same craft used to ferry Allen across the flats, and only a few miles away from the place where Allen and his Native guides spent miserable nights before making it to the mouth of Alaganik, it was a natural subsistence site.

Natives may have also stumbled on to much larger Dusky goose eggs scattered on nests throughout the Delta. Prior to the earthquake, there was little cover, and their nests were often quite obvious. It is also possible Natives discovered that geese went through a flightless molt stage in late July and early August. Modern game biologists use this time to herd Duskies into shoreside pens, and gather data while banding them.

However, bird hunting as we know it didn't begin until explorers, trappers, prospectors, cannery personnel, fishermen, and then railroad builders arrived on the scene, all toting rifles, and shotguns. Salmon, copper, and ducks are all intertwined.

Part II: The First Canneries

It is startling to realize that canneries and fishermen began appearing on or near the Delta in 1889, only four years after Allen's Expedition. Central Alaska Co. built a cannery at Wingham Island in the spring of that year. The cannery made a fairly successful pack that first season, but the location was not ideal, and it was moved to western Alaska the following spring. The Peninsula Trading & Fishing Co. built a cannery on Wingham Island, also in '89. Two years later it was moved to the Coquenhena Slough of the Copper River Delta.

Now spelled Kokenhenic, this slough carves its way for twelve miles directly below 27 Mile of today's Copper River Highway. Wind and water erosion have almost completed erased Kokenhenic Island. I visited Kokenhenic in 1958 while on a gillnetting trip with commercial fisherman Leonard Lange and his stepsons Jim and Woody Allain. It was a mile around the sandy cottonwood-covered islet at that time. The cannery operated in 1891, was closed for two years, and then was re-opened by the Pacific Steam Whaling Co. It ran until 1897. The cannery had difficulties gathering fresh water, which all came from a rain catchment system. The company established a cannery near the present site of Cordova in 1889, and moved its equipment to Orca, three miles north of Cordova, in 1895.

Also in 1889, Pacific Packing Company built the Odiak cannery on a slough in the heart of Cordova. It operated two years, was closed during the 1892 season, joined the Alaska Packers Association in 1893, and was operated through the 1905 season before being sold to the Copper River and Northwestern Railway Co., which was preparing to build a railroad from Cordova to copper deposits at Kennicott, 196 miles up the Copper River. Cordova's present day modern hospital is located on this very spot.

Plus an interesting sidelight. After the railroad was built, another cannery was established far up the Copper River. In 1915, Copper River Packing Co. built a cannery on the Copper River at Mile 55 of the railroad line and put up a successful pack that year. The cannery had an arrangement with the CR&NW to haul fish from the fishing stations to their operation and then bring the finished product to Cordova for shipment by steamer. Archival photos from 1915 through 1919 show fishermen dipnetting from the river banks at 55 Mile, and a saltery right along side the railroad tracks. The name was changed to the Abercrombie Packing in 1918. It was abandoned in 1920.

Part III: Eyak Canneries

Soon came two canneries that had a huge impact on duck hunting in the Eyak area, which was the home turf for most early waterfowl efforts.

In 1916, Clark-Graham Co. built a cannery on Eyak River a few miles from Cordova. The plant was sold to the Eyak River Packing Co. in 1919 and sold again to the Pioneer Sea Foods Co. in 1924. It was destroyed by fire in November, 1935.

An article in the November 30, 1935 *Cordova Times* described the loss. The plant was owned by James E. Parks of Seattle at the time. About 100 small seine boats and power skiffs, many of them owned by individuals, were burned up. The cannery building was about 200 feet long and two stories high. All under one roof, it was divided into boat storage, gear storage, coal storage, office, commissary, cannery, canned fish storage room, and a general utility storage room with a can loft upstairs. The fire started from an exhaust backfire when a watchman tried to start a gasoline engine. A watchman at the Crystal Falls cannery, about a mile to the west, noticed it about 3:55 in the afternoon. Calm winds prevented the fire from spreading to several nearby dwellings, as well as the oil house and bunkhouse.

The cannery was never rebuilt. The small homes and cabins along the river bank which housed cannery workers and staff were abandoned.

In 1923, Northern Light Packing Co. built a cannery near the mouth of Mountain Slough and operated it until 1932. The cannery was located by a large waterfall that cascaded from the Heney Range, two miles east of lower Eyak River. In 1934 the plant was taken over and operated by W. Utness. In 1939 it began operating as the Crystal Falls Fish Company, and continued processing until 1964, when the uplift caused by the Good Friday earthquake made access and operations there impossible.

What made these last two canneries so significant in duck hunting efforts was the numerous summer cabins built on piling adjacent to the main facilities. These small dwellings housed the many workers involved in fish processing. They were literally surrounded by ponds and sloughs full of ducks and geese, and were used in the fall as a base for hunting. In particular, the ones near the burned out hulk of the Eyak Cannery soon became hunting headquarters for several local waterfowlers.

Part IV: Early Fisheries

Where there are canneries, there are fishermen. The evolution of the Copper River fisheries is what established the first cabins that later became duck shacks.

An article by Jim Payne titled "Local Fishing Methods and Gear Progressed" that appeared in the 30 April 1981 *Cordova Times* described how the early fisheries operated. Highlights are summarized here, as where the fishermen went, their shotguns followed.

Much of the early salmon packs came from Eyak Lake, using stake nets. Gradually the fishery expanded down Eyak River and out to the edges of the Delta. By 1900, fishing in the Eyak was so intense that boats hauling fish up the river had difficulty getting past nets strung across it and sometimes just ran right over them.

In the early days after the fishery expanded across the Delta, some fishermen lived in cannery bunkhouses along the sloughs, with stake nets directly off the nearby cut banks. Others built small tent frames which evolved into cabins at their favorite sloughs. Many of the cabins were designed to house two fishermen. The mouth of Eyak, in particular, was a popular spot. A 1936 USFS Survey shows eleven cabin sites along the east bank close to the steep edge of the river. In the early 1900s these fishing cabins were located on the opposite side where the water was deeper. However, river flow eroded the banks, so the cabins were eventually moved across the slough to avoid this problem.

Fishing rights to the best sets on sloughs and gutters came on a first come, first serve basis, with camps being set up early in the spring. Some fisherman traveled across land by sled before the spring breakup to stake out the premier locations. Shallow draft stern wheel tenders came by to pick up fish seven days a week, and drop off supplies. Fishing was done by row boat, using set nets on poles.

Sockeye salmon stake-net near Center Slough at low tide, 1922. Note the salmon hanging in the net. The slough was named because of its location midway between Eyak and Mountain Slough.
REFERENCE: APPENDIX, HISTORY OF NAME OF SLOUGHS OF COPPER RIVER DELTA.
PHOTO BY NORMAN SWANSON, COURTESY CORDOVA DISTRICT FISHERMAN UNITED.

Eventually a system evolved in which fish were delivered and consolidated at "tally scows" that were anchored near the mouths of the sloughs. Gradually Columbia River double enders appeared, and conservation regulations moved the efforts off the cutbanks. Fishing was done by open skiff, with bigger boats anchored at the mouths of the sloughs as floating headquarters. It wasn't until 1923 that fishing in the breakers and beyond started, with Utness a pioneer in experimenting with power boats and drifting those areas.

Many of the sloughs were named after fishermen who camped out at particular fishing spots year after year. Tendermen knew exactly where Pete Dahl, Joe Reeve, Pete Olsen, August Tiedeman, Gus Stevens, Gus Wilson, the Johnsons, and Cudahy fished. A whole gang of Scandinavian fishermen "homesteaded" at a big slough to the east of Pete Dahl, so it was naturally named Valhalla, which morphed into Walhalla. Boxes of supplies in town were labelled with fishermen's names for delivery to the appropriate slough by the tenders, a tradition that continued through the 1970s until fishermen using fast, high powered bowpickers began running to town between openers which often lasted only 12 to 24 hours.

Part V: Early Duck Hunting

Of course, every camp and slough mouth was surrounded by nesting ducks and geese, quacking and honking away, with shallow ponds directly behind loaded with waterfowl. Undoubtedly a few plump spring birds ended up cooking slowly in camp dutch ovens.

In those early years, tenders often hauled something besides fish back to town during the fall silver salmon season. Fishermen scattered across the Delta and staying out for weeks at a time would send in boxes of ducks. Jim Webber talked about his dad sending in hundreds of birds, which were shared throughout the community.

Waterfowl also served as subsistence fare. Mae Hanson Lange told the story of her family living in Katella from 1920 through 1936, and relying on fish and ducks, plus an occasional bear or mountain goat, for meat. "I remember one time we were just about out of food and low on ammunition. Mom sent my brother out with one shotgun shell to get some ducks. He came back with fifteen. I hated plucking ducks, but was pretty happy to do it that time."

Back in that Era there was usually only one U.S. Fish and Wildlife enforcement agent for the whole area. There wasn't much constraint on hunting effort. Early southbound migrators such as yellow leg geese, which usually pass through before the season opens, were especially popular. Legendary Otto Koppen patrolled the area for 25 years in the double ender Wingham, beginning in the late 1920s. He was inducted into the Cordova Elks in 1935, and was famous as one of the town's best duck cooks and connoisseurs all the way up to his passing in 1979. Koppen had a practical, flexible attitude toward enforcement in the early Wild West Duck Days.

"His policy was to resolve the issue out in the field. He never brought anyone in on some "iffy" case. When he brought them in, they were guilty," said Hollis Henrichs in Koppen's *Cordova Times* obituary. And he probably shared more than one choice, slow cooked, tasty yellow leg goose with generous fishermen.

Part VI: Eyak Hunting

Because of the fisheries and easy access, most of the early recreational duck hunting was concentrated on the western end of the Delta. At that time there was no road. It was iron rails from Cordova to Kennecott. However, everyone knew how to run a boat across Eyak Lake and down Eyak River. Hence most of the early duck shacks were concentrated in the Eyak area.

Lifelong Cordovan Jim Webber described a flotilla of boats laying behind the protective Spit built at the town end of Eyak Lake. "Prior to the road beyond Mile 13, and during the early fishing days, the lagoon behind the spit at the end of the lake was packed with boats. All the duck hunters tied up their skiffs in that sheltered area. Plus there were at least three floating docks and two floating covered boat houses. That's where everyone started when they were going to head down river."

Webber mentioned Harry Hawes, nicknamed Long Shorty because he stood about six foot six inches tall but always walked bent over about a half foot shorter, helped the navigation process near the outflow of Eyak Lake into the river. "There were all kinds of stumps and submerged logs there, so Long Shorty put up poles just above the Eyak River bridge to mark the channels so boats and skiffs going up and down the river could avoid them."

Webber also remembered boat landings just below the bridge. "Utness, who owned and operated Crystal Falls, had one there. This is where he would haul his fish pack up in a little power scow and unload supplies to haul back down. Several skiffs also tied up there. Later the Forest Service built a landing just below it."

Although fishing created the first source of major duck hunting activities, a second wave of hunters arrived with the construction of the Copper River and Northwestern Railway. Starting in Cordova, it cut a swath right across the upper reaches of the Copper River Delta. Construction began in 1907 and was completed in 1911. In particular, the stretch of tracks from Mile 5 to Mile 27 went across countless rivers, sloughs, ponds, and meadows that were prime waterfowl country. The few track speeders available were used by lucky individuals to ride the rails and access this area.

A Naval radio station near Ibeck Creek at 7 Mile that was established in the early 1900s also spurned bird hunting in that region. Old black and white photos show duck hunters, including Curly Hoover, standing on the tracks with shotguns and geese beside a Ford speeder, at that very spot. Many avid duck hunters had railroad roots. Nicolet, Lydick, and F.A. Hansen were all to establish duck cabins on or near Eyak River; they or their parents worked for the railroad.

In his book about Cordova from 1929 to 1941 titled *The Cordova That I Knew*, Al Swalling wrote "When September 1st would roll around, it seemed every able-bodied male, including young lads old enough to carry a shotgun, and even many women, would head for the Eyak and Copper River flats to hunt ducks and geese. It wasn't only the birds for the larder that counted, but the freedom from the daily grind, as well as the special camaraderie that the outing produced. If early winter held off, the season could be as long as two months. Aa special event during the hunting season was the annual duck dinner hosted by the Elks Lodge."

Swalling went on to help build the WWII railroad tunnel at Whittier, and eventually own one of the biggest and most successful construction companies in Alaska, based in Anchorage. He clearly cherished his young days in Cordova, had an astute sense of observation, and a keen memory. He could write. And must have had some very good times duck hunting.

Decision thousands of miles away in Washington, D.C. also affected the Delta and hunting.

In 1907, President Theodore Roosevelt established the Chugach National Forest, which includes the Copper River Delta. Its creation seemed to have almost no impact on early activity. Railroad construction went full bore. Fishermen and canneries had already built camps, cabins, and bunkhouses on the mouths of the sloughs, and continued to do so. Many were undoubtedly used for duck hunting, particularly during the silver salmon season, which typically starts in mid-August and lasts through late September. The Crystal Falls and Eyak River canneries were built, with several houses and cabins adjacent. All on what had become public land. Under what guidelines and restrictions is not clear. So it is not surprising that individuals started tossing together duck shacks in nearby areas. It was the Wild West Days of Duck Hunting. Lots of birds; lots of slough and fire water; lots of hunters; and as Swalling intimated, lots of "special camaraderie," often of the Spirited Brand.

Part VII: Big Arc Cabins

Duck cabins and duck hunting stories. Can't have one without the other. Today there are 22 cabins left standing on the Delta. Many others have vanished in the unforgiving forces on nature: amplified winds roaring down the Copper, water in every conceivable state, weather of unlimited category from all points of the compass, vegetation exploding after the earthquake uplift, erosion and flooding from constantly changing glacial rivers, and beavers building hundreds of dams to alter sloughs and ponds forever.

Ah, if cabins could talk. What tales they could tell. Hunters of those gleeful early days, and their stories, are also gone; chronicles lost.

Some basic data is preserved. The cabins are on lands managed by the United Stated Forest Service (USFS), and require Special Use Permits. Local USFS archives reveal basic information about the cabins and their holders. Such as who built them, where and when, and the succession of owners.

However, even that information can be misleading. Time lags often existed between the date a cabin was built and the date the first USFS Special Use Permit was issued. Understandably so. Back then the Forest Service Office in Cordova consisted of a District Ranger, an Assistant District Ranger, and a Secretary. Two trucks, no boats. A huge area. They had their hands full. Much of the emphasis was on timber sales. No wonder paper work was sometimes tardy or non-existent.

Additionally, many of the original cabins were tiny, temporary structures, built on untreated pole pilings. They were fish shacks that completely vanished. Several of the sites along Eyak which at one time held fisherman's quarters stood empty for years through the 50s and 60s until a mini-building boom took place in the early 70s.

Since early duck hunting effort centered around Eyak and then spread to the east, it seems logical to start its history on this famous river. Not surprisingly, ten of today's cabins are located side by side at the mouth of Eyak on a large bend called Big Arc. All sit on what were originally fishing cabin sites. A USGS Survey completed for the Forest Service of the Big Arc group by Harold Smith in late September of 1936 shows all ten lots, varying in size from 1.05 acres to 0.5 acres. Smith's survey indicates it was done with Standard F.S. compass and 200 foot link steel tape. One has to wonder if a shotgun was also included but not mentioned. Birds whizzing by, along with cabins of rowdy hunters, had to be a major distraction.

Many of these early cabins had clever nameplates adorning their entrances. Others were simply named after their owners, origins, or design.

Pair A Dice Inn
Perhaps no cabin on Eyak was more famous than Frank Hoover's place. Hoover, who was as bald as a cue ball, was naturally nicknamed "Curly" by local pundits. He arrived in Cordova in 1932 to dig razor clams. He and Carl Edmonds started a taxi business, which by 1936 evolved into a trucking and freight business called Hoover's Movers. Hoover was an avid bird hunter, as an early black and white photo of a group of hunters, including two nattily dressed ladies, standing beside a Ford track speeder at 7 Mile on the railroad tracks, all holding shotguns and birds, indicates. Curly's shining pate was easy to recognize in the photo that dated before 1938.

Curly hunted out of one of the abandoned Eyak Cannery cabins before acquiring a downriver Eyak cabin in the early 40s from William Smith, who had owned the site since the early 30s. The first USFS Permit issued for that site is in Frank Hoover's name, and dated August 14, 1944.

Curly was quite a ball player, a catcher who played two years of summer ball in the professional Northwest Baseball League before coming to Cordova. But his real passions were ducks and dice. Hence the sign outside his cabin door read "Pair A Dice Inn." When visitors showed up at his place, it was a good idea to have a pocket full of cash. And hope you left with a shirt on your back.

Hoover eventually retired and headed south. In 1969 he sold the cabin to Johnny French, proprietor of the Cordova Outboard Shop. They probably came to know each other through duck hunting, as repairing outboards damaged while chasing birds was a big part of French's business. And likely from rolling the ivories too.

Merle Hanson, retired teacher who came to Cordova in 1969 and ended up owning a cabin at Eyak, recalled: "Johnny French bought the cabin from Curly

Duck hunting, railroad style, at Mile 7 on the CR&NWR in the 1930s. Curly Hoover is third from the left.

Hoover when he decided to leave. But the dice tradition continued. Every time we dropped over for a visit, Johnny would start shaking the dice in a cup and say "Let's roll a few." And you didn't leave until he had some of your money. It got so I would just walk in, put ten bucks on the table, and say "You won! Now can I have a drink?"

Randy Bruce, another Eyak cabin holder, worked several years at French's outboard shop. "Those guys loved to roll the dice. Johnny installed a special fold-down board on the wall for just that purpose, with a 1X8 back to bang the dice against."

No wonder some fall days, while sitting in our blinds at Pete Dahl, it was well past sunrise before we heard shotgun blasts to the west. But also no doubt why we heard late night whooping and hollering when the wind was stiff from that direction. French was bad of hearing. Lost it while in the Marines in WWIII, during the battle for Iwo Jima. Never talked about it, but once confessed to Dad "It was bad." Had good reason to celebrate life at a duck cabin on a river.

Al Jardinski, Outboard Mechanic Extraordinaire at the Cordova Outboard Shop for more than 50 years, bought the cabin from French in 1980. One of the first things he did was put up three flag poles, for the Polish, American, and Alaska flags. He passed away in 2011, and with him knowledge of thousands of repairs intrinsic to outboard lower units damaged going to and from duck cabins. When I showed up at the shop's back doors, he would glance up from a workbench buried under parts, hands covered in grease, and say "Shellhorn! What is it this time?"

Parks Double Decker
All the duck cabins on the Delta were structurally unique, usually starting very small and then added on at whim. Eyak featured the only two story duck shack on the Delta. It first belonged to Parks Canning Co, which had overseen the

construction of all the original cabins along the river. This unusual building was taken off a pile driver barge that was towed right up to the bank of the river. Norman Swanson, who worked on cannery tenders in the early 1900s, indicated it was set in place in 1919, and was one of the first buildings on the east bank of the Eyak. As mentioned earlier, the shacks on the west side were relocated across the river because of erosion. This new location also provided safer anchorage in the lee of the bank out of the predominate gales from the southeast.

The bottom level of the double-decker was a covered open-bay work area, with the upstairs living area accessed by an outside stairway. Justin Strom eventually became superintendent of Parks Cannery and hence landlord of all the cabins along the Big Arc.

Kenny Van Brocklin remembers the double decker in the 1940s. "It was a fisherman's camp at that time. Gillnetters would tie their boats right up against the bank and pull their nets off to mend them in the bottom level out of the rain. They all lived on the top floor."

Sig Gildnes recalled the lower floor being used as a fuel storage area, with 55 gallon drums of gas and oil lined up on planks out of the weather. He also recounted that Parks built all the original cabins, so it was their fishermen that used them. When Sig stayed in a small cabin next door during the early 60s, longtime fisherman Louie Nelson and his wife spent the summer on the top floor of the double decker.

Gildnes remembered it well, because during the weekend fishing closures, Mrs. Nelson would invite him up for hot cakes. "They had to be perfectly round, and were great," said Sig. "Also bacon on the side, and lots of coffee. Louie loved Kent filtered cigarettes, and would sit back and smoke while I ate. Not a man for a lot of words."

Justin Strom Jr., who spent many nights there as a youngster, remembered all the racket from the nearby Pair A Dice Inn. A trip down Eyak wasn't complete without a visit to Curly's place. They had a great and unusual view of the action from their second story perch.

The first official USFS Special Use Permit for the Double Decker was not issued to Parks Canning Co. until January 1963. Evidently, up to that time the cannery had some other agreement with the Agency. In 1970, the permit was transferred to Morpac, the company that took over Parks.

Fred Newirth, whose father-in-law John Hewitt supervised the fish operations at Morpac, eventually started using the cabin. "It was in rough shape. Very little use or maintenance for many years. Kids were camping in it, with lots of vandalism. Even started wood fires in the oil burning stove. So I told Bob Morgan, the Superintendent of Morpac, that I would fix it up and take care of it for a half share in the cabin. Which I did, including a new roof. Eventually Bob wanted to sell out, so I bought his half and became sole owner. I remember Julia Nordman was the bookkeeper and office manager at Morpac at the time, and drove a tough bargain. In fact, Bob was going to accept my initial offer, but Julia convinced him to double to price. Which was still a pretty good deal."

After all the repairs and improvements, Newirth faced additional challenges in the late 80s when the bank of the river eroded right up to the edge of his cabin. Julius Reynolds, who had recently retired as Area Game Management Biologist from the Cordova office of AF&G, was busy working on his nearby cabin. Newirth hired he and Mike Jackson, another ADF&G retiree, to save the cabin. By moving it. Engineering straight out of Annie Proulx's *The Shipping News*.

"What a job," said Reynolds. "We had to jack it up, put 3X12's down, and then ease it back on two inch pipe rollers about a foot long. Used a come-along tied to an anchor to pull it an inch at a time. It was a slow process. The planks would sink and the cabin would slip off the rollers. Took us five days, and a lot of crawling around in the mud, to move it back about 20 feet. We also destroyed at least two come-alongs."

Newirth eventually sold the cabin to Pat Fagan, who is now the current owner.

Last Resort

Pete Gildnes was a Norwegian who started fishing the flats in the 1920s. Pete's son Sig was born in Norway, and started coming north from the western Washington area to fish with him in 1949. It was all hand pulling of the 150 fathom length gill nets back then. They lived on a 33 foot cabin boat, and fished mainly to the east in the Grass Island area, out of an open skiff, which was the style at that time. During closed periods, they would run to the mouth of Eyak, anchor the bigger boat, and then head upriver to town in the open skiff.

Sig remembered almost all the lots along the mouth of Eyak had cabins on them, originally built by Parks Canning Co., under some sort of agreement with the USFS. At that time, Pogey Paulson, Parks Canning Superintendent, was in charge of the cabins. In 1960, Sig approached him about buying the cabin next door to the Parks Double Decker. It was in rough shape. In shrewd Norwegian style, Sig described its condition, and then asked: "How much would you want for it?"

Pogey replied $50.

Sig asked why so much?

Pogey replied because that's the Forest Service lease fee.

Sold. Not bad, even for a tarpaper shack with a leaky metal roof that was leaning slightly on wobbly old posts. Sig and Pete started camping out there during fishing closures. Pete was so worried the cabin would fall over in a storm that he cut several small alders and stuck them under the cabin to help support it.

Randy Bruce, a friend of Sig's who eventually bought the cabin, actually counted the number of what he called "pecker poles" after one particularly rocky night. There were 48.

Sig recalled the cabin had a small coal burning stove in it. Which I could verify, since a young fellow named Dick Gardner from Iowa and I stayed in the cabin during a 1962 ADFG salmon tagging project.

We used a 16 foot open skiff and 50 fathom set net, fishing during closed periods only. Would pick the reds and kings as quickly as they hit the gear, handle them gently, insert a pair of disk tags attached to a long wire just in front of the dorsal fin, weigh and measure the fish plus identify sex, and release them immediately, noting the time and place for each disk number. The project was not popular with fishermen, as the disks tangled in their gill net web during commercial openers. The goal was to gather data about migration patterns and estimate fish populations.

Our goal was to stay warm and dry. Pretty easy to verify Pete's concerns about the stability of the cabin; and ventilation was not a problem, given the sunlight shining through cracks in the walls and holes in the roof on nice days. We came very adept at quickly building a coal fire in the old metal stove. Bags of coal were still available at the Service Transfer in Cordova at that time. We often ran over to the Crystal Falls Cannery for groceries, as their small store was just ten minutes away on high tide. Between fish slime and coal dust, it was quite an operation.

The following year, Pete complained about waking up to a cold cabin in the morning, so eventually they converted the stove to oil. Bob Summers, a famous Copper River tender captain, brought the materials and a 55 gallon drum of fuel right up to the bank in the big red-hued power scow Teal, and also dropped off fuel and supplies at the adjacent Parks Double Decker.

Sig came up with the name Last Resort for the shack, from a TV program he watched during winters down south in Washington. He painted the moniker on the door. In reality, maybe it was because he never thought it would last through another storm or winter.

The first USFS Special Use Permit for the site was issued to Gildnes in October 1964.

Sig, a Norwegian, befriended Randy Bruce, a Swede, while they were enrolled at Skagit Valley Community College in Mt. Vernon. The term "enrolled" was used loosely, because of the impression that neither of them attended classes very often. It was a way to kill time in the winter until heading North To Alaska in the spring.

Sig began skippering tenders for the local Alaska Packers Cannery, and both Randy and I at one time worked on deck for him. He was not a hard-nosed Captain.

Back then the crew was paid hourly wages, plus time and a half during the week. It was double overtime for extra hours on weekends and holidays. Sig payed close attention to the calendar. Norbert Hamm, the Accountant in APA Superintendent Merle Wickett's office, went ballistic when Captain Sig submitted a time sheet which had us working 25 hours in a day. On a holiday. Sig's justification: "Come on, it was the 4th of July. They deserved a bonus."

Sig eventually moved on to the tugboat business, and Randy bought the cabin from him in 1977.

He, wife Jackie, and their boys Dave and John spent the first summer sprucing things up, and endured a chilly but happy fall in their own duck shack. Strapped with buying a house and a duck cabin the same year, Randy began scrounging creosote piling and decking materials to build a new cabin the next summer. Carpenter friend Bud Banta came down, eyeballed the old place, and ventured "It might stand for one more year - if it doesn't blow too hard."

Randy and Jackie patched holes in the roof and cracks in the walls, and kept a nice new oil heater going full bore most of the fall. The following summer Randy and I built the foundation for a 16X28 cabin directly behind the old one. Staying in the original shack for the project brought back a flood of memories, even though it didn't rain. Took a couple days to get the piling all set in place and braced, as well as run beams and lay decking. Since the beams were nice 4X6's running the length of the cabin only eight feet apart, and we had a big pile of full dimension 2X12's sixteen feet long, we decided to forgo floor joist and just run them laid flat as decking.

Which worked out great, until late in the day, when we came up one plank short. It had been one of those sunny days when everything was clicking, including the pop tops on beer cans. We had merrily been nailing down planks and looking forward to dancing in celebration on the completed deck. Only to be so near, yet so far.

We were both in t-shirts and jeans. Off to the west, against the base of the Heney Range, a few miles away, only a 15 minute boat ride, sat the abandoned Crystal Falls Cannery. We knew scrounging that last 16 foot 2X12 would be a cinch. The collapsing buildings were already in the shadows of Heney Range, as the sun fell behind its peaks. But this wouldn't take long.

"Let's finish 'er up!" was the rallying cry. Wonder what Custer hollered to his troops.

No problem. We tossed on cotton long sleeve shirts, threw in our jackets, jumped in Randy's 16 foot light aluminum Quachita with a six pack of beer, a couple hammers and pry bars, and a 3/4 tank of gas as our supplies. Went roaring up Eyak to take the narrow, winding cutoff to Crystal Falls. Which turned out to be a bit shallow, i.e. full of sandbars. No problem, current with us, we went racing through, kicking up mud and sand in a couple spots. Randy was an outboard mechanic, I had nothing to worry about. We did have a tool kit.

Made it to the old Cannery, found our plank, loaded it in the boat. All in about half an hour. Debated about going back up the shallow slough, or instead going down stream, out to the middle of the flats, taking a left, and running back up Eyak. Would be much easier in terms of water, since the tide was still in, albeit ebbing. However finding the mouth of Eyak can be a challenge, as the entire cutbank looks the same from out on the water.

We had both worked on tenders throughout the area, and felt pretty confident. Somewhere Dad, Leer, Bob Korn, and countless others who had spent the night on the Flats grounded by falling tides were laughing.

With the 16 foot 2X12 jutting over the bow, we took off down river. No problem, hit what is called the Home Channel and cut left. By then, it was dusk. Ran awhile, and then headed up what we thought was Eyak. Into a dead end. Looped back, ran further to the east, and repeated the process. Now it was darker than dusk. Tried it one more time, probably all the way over to the east near Glacier Slough. No cabins in sight.

Randy picked up the gas can, and jiggled it. "The next one better be the right one."

At some point the 2X12 went overboard. Lighten the load. Anything to extend our mileage. We headed west, and by now it was a maize of mud and water. Welcome to the World of Lt. Allen.

Dumb, Dumb, Dumb. In the words of G.O. Young, from his book *Alaskan Yukon Trophies Won and Lost*, "We were very much provoked by our carelessness."

I had on a cotton Army fatigue jacket from my Signal Corp days in the late 60s; Randy a dark blue float coat. No radio, no light, no luck. He shut off the engine, and we hunkered down for a long wait until the next incoming tide. Luckily it was a short summer's eve; and also, no one was waiting or expecting us back at the cabin. Rescue attempts can multiply screwups exponentially. We would be OK and just fresh as daisies at dawn's early light.

Kicking ourselves for such stupidity kept us warm though out the night.

I'm not sure when Randy put in the final plank to complete the deck. Maybe it was during duck season that fall, while I was over at Pete Dahl chasing ducks with Dad. I hope he scratched a special memo on it for posterity.

It wasn't until the next summer that carpenter/fishermen friends Bud Banta and Eric Johnson came down as what Randy called "Prime Contractors" and hammered the cabin together, with help from Randy and other neighbors. They stayed in the old cabin during construction. I suspect their "Building Fee" was the same steaks, plus B & B's, or perhaps Bud beloved martini's, that had been the going rate for the foundation work.

Randy and I did feel considerable pride when Bud remarked that it was quite a deck, almost perfectly square and very sturdy, although the last plank on the end didn't seem to match the others.

When the new cabin was complete, it took about ten minutes to knock the old one down, salvage whatever material was reusable, and burn up the rest.

Randy tacked up a new Last Resort sign, and the Bruce family had a cabin which to this day has been their greatest pride and joy.

Pete's Point Resort

Julius Reynolds bought the other Gildnes cabin from Pete in October of 1983. It was the southernmost, consisted of a cabin and a warehouse, and occupied two lots. Harold McDonald held the first USFS Permit for the lots, issued on December 5, 1962. Pete obtained the property in October of 1966, and gradually added more and more cabin to the original tiny structure. Pete's son Sig remembered McDonald and his wife Henrietta, who came up from Oregon every summer to fish out of the cabin. A 1976 photo shows how it had morphed from a tiny, rickety shack into Pete's Point Resort by that time.

Reynolds did considerable remodeling and repairs over the years, and renamed it Decoy. The warehouse, built in Pete's Norwegian Style, collapsed in 2012 under the huge snow fall of that winter. Julius rebuilt a small storage shed closer to his cabin in 2013. He and Randy remain the two most active duck hunters at Eyak, and each evening I call via VHF radio from Pete Dahl to get the Daily Duck Report and Forecast. Often parts of it would be edited before public broadcast. Julius and I are both Oregon State grads, and our beloved Beavers gave us much to commiserate about during the fall football season.

The Hide

Five other cabins complete the Eyak Group. In 1982 Merle Hanson, who hunted for years at the Korn Hole, purchased the cabin owned by Norman Borseth. Borseth was a Parks fisherman, and is listed as the owner on the first USFS Permit issued for the site on July 15, 1942.

The original cabin was about 15X10, a tiny shack, not much bigger than the cabin on small boats back then. Norman, with his wife, kids, and a dog, lived there during gillnetting season. Must have been quite cozy.

Norman later shared the cabin with a fishing partner named Dick Long. The original cabin grew in size to 19X10, with a 14X16 addition, plus an 8X25 deck. The pair were still using the place as a base for fish operations when Randy Bruce

Pete Gildnes shack on Big Arc, Eyak River, in the early 60s. Note the poles leaning against the front of the cabin and the outhouse for support, the tilted chimney stack, and the beginnings of a foundation for an addition on the right of the cabin. Not quite a "Resort" yet.
Photo Courtesy USFS

was building his new cabin in the late 70s, and would drop over to inspect the operation. Both Randy and I would shake our heads while nailing roof rafters and hearing comments like "Ooooh, I like watching you fellows drive nails." Hmmmm.

Borseth's brother John ran the Parks Cannery on Eyak River, and was in town the afternoon and evening it was destroyed by fire back in 1935. Remains of the destroyed buildings were likely a major component in Norman's cabin, as well as several others downriver.

Merle, wife Barb, and kids Kelly and Ardy had trudged across the growing marsh and brush to a nearby cabin called the Korn Hole for several years before the Borseth cabin became available. Merle spent many summers helping Bob Korn keep his cabin up and running. Like the Bruces, they were thrilled to finally have a place of their own. They came up with the nickname The Hide, because it was a great place to get away from town.

Both Merle and Randy had hunted often at our cabin at Pete Dahl before obtaining Eyak sites. Their sons all shot their first ducks at Pete Dahl. I always remember young John Bruce sitting beside me in a blind, and dozing off. Woke him up when a flock of teal came in; he had to stand on the bench to see over the brush and fire away. Brought back memories of my first duck, which also wasn't very airborne.

Glasen's

Danny Glasen now has the northern-most cabin of the Eyak group. Sig Gildess recalled the site was empty until Ralph Pirtle built a small cabin there in the early 60s. It gradually fell into disrepair, and Pirtle sold it to lifelong Cordovan Walt Mantilla in the late 70s.

Mantilla was head of the local State Department of Highways Maintenance operation, had countless years of experience on the Delta, and decided it would be best to build from scratch. He tore down the old shack and built a 18X26 cabin, and later added a 10X12 storage shed.

Dar Glasen's son Danny bought the place in 1992, and his son Danny Dar is now the current owner.

Three Lady Cabin

The next cabin south from Glasen's was famous as the only all-female shack on the Eyak. The site was owned by Mary Ann Addington, with the first USFS Permit issued in October of 1971. When the cabin was built, Bud Banta was lead carpenter for the project, with Addington, Julia Nordman, and Pat Goodrich as his crew.

Randy Bruce remembers it was a regular "Who's Who of Cordova" when the cabin was completed and a Grand Opening was held on Sunday, August 19, 1973. Teenagers Ron Goodrich and Jeff Pettingill ferried passengers to and from the cabin in a riverboat.

"The bank was lined with river boats as people came down to celebrate," said Bruce. "Frank Burns, who ran the Alaska Steamship office all the way back in the railroad days, was there, along with his wife. So was local banker Dick Borer, and countless other locals high rollers. It was quite a party."

Among the guests were Don and Anita Shellhorn. It was noted in their Pete Dahl Cabin Log that they, too, enjoyed the gathering, and stayed for an hour visiting with the crowd. The lady guests had purchased a Flamo double mantle propane light as a cabin-warming gift, which the new owners greatly appreciated.

The cabin became quite a card parlor. Trudy Bodey Bendzak, a recently arrived teacher, became friends with Addington, who also taught at Mt. Eccles Elementary. She remembered the ladies played using a deck featuring Chippendale models.

"It was their favorite. Had nicknames for each one, including some male teachers on staff," chuckled Bendzak, who confessed one time she had to head out of the cabin for some fresh air.

"Mary Ann came out and consoled me. You know, Trudy, you don't have to keep up with us older gals."

"There wasn't a lot of hunting done out of that cabin, but I sure remember boatloads of ladies coming down to play cards," observed Merle Hanson.

"And having a lot of fun, too," he added, mentioning that one time the same gang headed over to Louie Hasbrouck's cabin on Little Glacier for an overnight outing. Fred Pettingill was running the crew down from 9 Mile in his airboat, and somehow flipped the craft on its side trying to cross a gutter.

Fred's wife Betty didn't do much shuffling of pasteboards for awhile, as she broke her arm in the crash.

And Three More Cabins

For years, three sites formerly used by fisherman lay abandoned on the banks of Big Arc. That changed in the late 70s and early 80s.

"It was a stretch of time when there was a group of active parents with young kids who really enjoyed getting out, and took advantage of vacant lots to build new cabins," said Bruce. "Things were hopping on the old river at that time, and it was a great crowd of fun lovers."

Jim Kassen, a surveyor and friend of Walt Mantilla's, built a 16X24 cabin on the site between Hanson and Jardinski. The first USFS Permit was issued to Mantilla in October 1977, and then transferred to Kassen a year later. Peter and Robin Blake bought the place in 1981, and their sons Scott and Brandon became avid duck hunters as well as outstanding basketball players for Cordova High.

Just south of Jardinski, Tom Cooper built a 20X24 cabin in the early 80s, on a lot that was one of three fishing sites held by longtime Parks gillnetter George Adams. Cooper sold it to Jim and Peggy Rankin in 1989. Current owner John Wiese bought it from Rankin in the late 90s, when Rankin sold his Cordova clothing and sporting goods store and headed south.

Right next door to the Wiese cabin, local carpenter Roger Koegling built an 18X20 cabin for Bob Halvorsen and Harry Nicolet in the early 80s. That cabin was held by Rankin for one year, before being sold to current owners Jon and Teri Stavig.

Part VII: Little Arc Cabins

A pair of narrow sloughs above the Big Arc cabins angle eastward back toward the Copper River Highway. The first, half mile upstream, is named Little Arc; the second, a half mile further upriver, is dubbed Stump Slough. Their identical appearance created marvelous opportunity for navigational blunder and increased business at the Cordova Outboard shop.

The headwater of Little Arc is glacial flow from Scott Glacier passing under the 9 Mile Bridge. Its grey runoff pours through a small gutter 500 yards below the road, depth fluctuating wildly depending on temperature and rainfall.

Stump Slough meanders into a maize of shallow ponds and beaver dams. And, of course, its moniker is well justified. Perhaps it should have been named Shear Pin Alley.

Patrons eagerly headed for the Boxcar would routinely make a Left Turn too soon. When Dad began conning his early succession of floating derelicts, it was his favorite blunder. Patrons lounging on the Boxcar deck would hear an outboard headed their way, followed by the high-pitched screech of a prop spinning in the air.

"Hmm. Shellhorn must be coming down," was the standard comment.

In short order, they would hear the engine fire up. Dad became very proficient at changing shear pins and replacing propellors with missing blades. And stopping by Cordova Outboard on Monday for replacements.

Little Arc was home to two cabins. One was the most unique on the Delta. And that's saying something.

Boxcar

Ah, the Boxcar. Literally that. The Copper River and Northwestern Railway shut down in 1938 when high grade copper ore at the Kennecott mines ran out. Low prices were also a factor. If it had operated for a few more years, the 196 mile line would probably still be going, for when World War II rolled around, the demand for metals skyrocketed.

Have always dreamt about riding those rails. What a trip through terrain and time that would be. Dad, who came to Cordova in 1934, told stories about clickety-clacking off to play baseball. He was third baseman on the Town Team, and they would chug up to challenge the Railroad Nine every year. Traveling at a modest 20 miles per hour or so, with several stops along the way, the ride would take at least nine hours. Gained the impression from his stories that the locomotive wasn't the only thing chugging. Like baseball teams all over American, killing travel time in that era involved some serious effort at poker and avoiding dehydration enroute to the next doubleheader.

The ball games were played at either McCarthy or Chitina, wide open towns near the processing mills at Kennecott, for good reason. The mine was a tightly run, dry camp. One evening by our cabin fireplace Dad confessed to "losing his shirt" on one of the train rides back. Must have been a rather major debit, seeing as he was manager of the clothing department at the Cordova Commercial. Perhaps that's why a mini-couch at our duck cabin was made out of seat backs and seat cushions hijacked from abandoned railroad passenger cars. Recouping the losses, so to speak.

But I digress

The Boxcar. Located a mile up Little Arc Slough, the last major left before reaching the mouth of Eyak River, it was a full length, bonafide railroad boxcar. Originally built in 1898 as a crew car, featuring bunks and a pot belly stove. It was sidetracked in 1938 along with two others when the railroad shut down that year. F.A. Hanson, who was the Railroad Superintendent, had ready access to much of the abandoned rail stock near the roundhouse and railroad yards located around the site of today's Cordova Community Hospital. As a young boy, I can remember playing in the huge circular concrete pit that was at the center of the operation there, where the loco-motives were maintained from below, rotated, and shunted in and out of a semi-circular warehouse behind it. The building was called the Roundhouse, for obvious reasons. For awhile we kids hoped the pit might someday become a swimming pool. Instead it became a costly cleanup problem for the Kennecott Corporation due to the oil and pollution beneath it. No EPA during the railroad and WWII days.

F.A., an avid duck hunter, realized the crew car would make a great duck shack. He partnered with Bill Leibe, a local grocer, and lined up some help that must have been engineers left over from the construction of the amazing and famous railroad itself. Loaded it on a barge. Walt Mantilla used his 20 foot power boat to tow it across Eyak Lake, down Eyak River, and up Little Arc. A big tide flooded water right up to the edges of the river bank . Used rollers and pulleys to slid it off. Plopped it on the marsh, leveled it with wood pads, and had them selves a duck cabin.

Here I thought moving outhouses at Pete Dahl was big time engineering.

By 1944 Hanson had left, and Leibe sold the cabin to the Van Brocklin broth-ers, Bob, Don, and Kenny. In 1946 the new owners jacked the cabin up and installed pilings-under it. Harry Curran, who was later instrumental in helping us build our cabin at Pete Dahl, helped with the project.

"Before that it was basically sitting on the ground, and the big tides would flood the inside," said Kenny Van Brocklin. "We actually had to drill holes in the floor to drain out the water."

Nice

By the time Randy and I were ready to begin our apprenticeship as duck hunters, Kenny and the Boys did most of their hunting out of this railroad days relic. It was to be our basic training grounds, the site of our initiation into the many rites and mysteries involved in pursuit of the Sacred Duck.

Kenny was nicknamed Hook, not because of the shape of his nose, but due to his famous basketball left-handed shot employed with random success when he suited up in purple for the Cordova Elks basketball team. City League roundball was a popular winter-time passion back then. The B.P.O.E. squad always did their pre-game at the local lodge a couple blocks away from the City Gym. This had varying degrees of impact on Kenny's accuracy and their won-lost record.

By the 50s, Kenny had moved on from the hardware section of the Commercial to become a co-owner of the Club Bar and Liquor Store, right next door to his former place of employment. In fact, every third business on Main Street was a pub, with barbershops strategically located, so a patron could have a cold one and get clipped in efficient fashion. Kenny's shift in employment was a logistical boon to efficiency in preparation for trips to the retired railroad car.

As with all duck hunts, getting to the Boxcar was half the fun. No coal powered engines or glistening steel tracks involved, but a whole lot of tooting going on. I'm not sure of earlier modes of transportation, but by the time Randy and I started hanging on for dear life enroute, Hook had a 22 foot wooden cabin skiff powered by an outboard of locomotive proportions. A monster Johnson 50 horse, the biggest motor of its time. Every one of the steeds was needed to attain step. Shoe was the name of this craft.

Sailing author William Snaith noted that "The choice of a boat's name is the semantic key to a man's dreams, a revealing decision."

Evidently Kenny just hoped to arrive at the Boxcar still standing on his feet. Or perhaps the name simply honored the craft's distinctive profile. Regardless, Hook and the Shoe "were made partners in the presence of the antagonist," Snaith's description of the on-going battle between Man and Ship versus the Sea; or in this case, the Eyak River.

Hang on, you laddies.

The yacht had outside steering, a pair of large windows up forward, and a windshield atop the cabin to keep hats and beer cans from flying overboard. First class passengers rode inside; riffraff stood exposed astern. As soon as the boat reached cruising speed, the transom drain plug was removed, as the rate of water flowing out this portal closely coincided with hull leakage.

Despite all its deficiencies, the Shoe could pack considerable tonnage, particularly of Liquid Inspiration, although "lighten the load" was an oft heard phrase used to justify downing a few cold ones enroute. Always seemed a mere shifting of ballast to me, although it did lift spirits.

The Boxcar was really Club Bar #2. Finding a place to anchor on the slender nearby slough could be challenge, so wild was its popularity. It was not uncommon to see vessels left hard aground on steep banks as shoreside captains' humor rose and the tide fell.

A very unique cabin it was. Stairs and a small deck led to an entrance facing the slough. At one time conductors had shouted All Aboard out the door. Which was often a challenge for newly arrived passengers-to-be.

Eventually an entrance railing was added after patrons kept falling off the deck and spraining arms or legs trying to avoid spilling their highballs. A storage shed was attached on the non-slough side amidship, with another door, small deck, and steps leading to the nearby outhouse. However, dual approaches to the Facility proved to be confusing, especially late at night. Baffled geese probably thought they were being called when hunters stood outside on both porches hollering for their woe-be-gone partners who had become lost stumbling to the privy a mere twenty feet away.

The cabin interior was long and narrow, "boxcarian." A kitchenette with propane cook stove, sink, and cabinets right inside the main door; a counter-bar combo plus small table nearby; next an oil space heater; and then racks of bunks far in the rear. Randy and I learned in a hurry we better head back to the safety of the sleeping area, for the action was fast and furious elsewhere.

What a Show. Saturday evening. Dad standing by the table, a Transoceanic short-wave radio blaring Glen Miller music. Banging an overhead cabinet door back and forth. Finally Kenny hollered, Shellhorn, what the hell are you doing? If you're looking for the V.O., its over here. Dad's had obviously already located the first half of a B and B, and proudly replied, Hook, I'm playing the drums, can't you tell?

"Eventually an entrance railing was added after patrons kept falling off the deck and spraining arms or legs ..." The Boxcar, 1950s.

Right.

Randy and I watched and learned.

Despite the size of Kenny's Supply Ship and his ready access to Firewater, it was quite common for the troops to run short. Especially if it was a three day Labor Day weekend.

Labor, Indeed. Randy loves to remind me of one such trip.

We had headed down river a day before the season opener to clean up the cabin and get organized. "Gotta get organized" was a perennial catch phrase. Kenny and Dad's grocery list included 2 cases of beer, a bottle of V.O, and a box or so of groceries. Organizing a duck cabin and building blinds is dehydrating work. Supplies dwindled rapidly.

To the Dynamic Duo's credit, we made it up and out for the morning shoot, and did well. Now we were back at the Boxcar having breakfast, and the crew realized the B & B stock was almost gone. Running out ammo was no big deal, the ducks deserve a break every now and then. Running out of Oly, Rainier, Black Label, Lucky Lager, or Higher Octane thirst quenchers was a crisis demanding immediate action.

Kenny headed for the boat. He could be to town and back in an hour if he really pushed it. As he pulled the anchor and started turning the boat around to head down stream, Dad raced out to the porch, cupped his hands, and hollered plaintively: Hook, Hook, don't forget the V.O.

You could almost hear it echoing off the Heney Range two miles to the west. Kenny waved over the roar of the engine as he turned sharply around the first bend. Randy and I headed to the bunks for a nap.

Ninety minutes later, we awoke to the sound of an outboard returning. Hook back from his resupply mission, to a Hero's Welcome. Unloaded several cases of beer, ice, a meager box of groceries, and went to anchor the boat. We hauled the supplies into the cabin and unpacked a loaf of bread, slab of bologna, and steaks.

Dad was restocking the liquid provisions. No V.O.

Kenny came into the cabin.

Distraught Dad: Didn't you hear me yelling at you?

Kenny: Sure, that's why I waved. Thanks for reminding me not to turn up Stump Slough.

Dad: Stump Slough? I hollered don't forget the V.O., you Horse's Ass!

Kenny: Oh my God, I can't believe I forgot that. Somebody at the bar asked me a question, and I got distracted. I don't think I have enough gas for another round trip.

The demoralized troops decided to make do. It was time for dinner, preceded by cocktails.

Damn, I sure could use a B and B, said Dad.

Kenny: Me too. Oops, that reminds me. I better check the boat before it gets dark.

Hook went out to the Shoe, lifted the lid to a hidden compartment, and quietly removed a bottle of Seagram's finest, carefully sticking it in his coat pocket.

Dad was frying up steaks when he came back in the cabin. Heard clinking as Kenny set the jug on the counter. Turned, and saw a smiling Van Brocklin. Look what I found in the boat - You Horse's Ass!

In classic Charlie Chaplin style, Dad let go of the frying pan, raced to Kenny, hugged him, and gave him a smooch on the cheek. Oh Hook, I love you!

The first USFS Permit for the Boxcar was issued to Don Van Brocklin on 2 August 1950. It was transferred to Ken Van Brocklin only 5 months later, on

18 February 1951. The Permit remained in his name for sixty one years, until officially taken over by Clay Koplin and Connor Halloran in August of 2012.

Little Arc Slough has silted in badly, and it now takes an airboat to reach the Boxcar. I visited it on cross country skis two winters ago. Age and elements are taking their toll.

Snow had drifted almost to the eves. I dug a small snow pit by the front door, and could peer through its glass pane inside. Sat in the wind's lee, drank a thermos of hot tea. Sun reflected off white plains toward Heney Range, as a flood of memories warmed my face.

Maxwell Cabin #1

Half a mile above the Boxcar sat another cabin. This small shack was originally built by avid duck hunter Carl Edmonds. Curly Hoover was his partner. Buel Maxwell was also in on the cabin somehow. Edmonds eventually gave his half to Buel's son Les, who arrived in Cordova in 1946. Les later bought the other half from Hoover. There is no record of a USFS Special Use Permit.

A small black and white photo of the cabin in its earlier days shows Buel and Bob Gill standing on the deck with a black lab. Numerous ducks and geese hang from the front wall. The door to the tarpaper-covered shack was shorter than both hunters, and the chimney which extended twice the height of the cabin had to hold a record for the tallest on the flats. The foundation appeared to be interlaced layers of 6X6.

Buel Maxwell and Bob Gill, with black lab, at Maxwell cabin #1, late 1940s. Judging by the number of birds hanging on the wall, hunting was very good.
PHOTO COURTESY BOBBY MAXWELL.

Les's brother Bobby recalled hunting out of the cabin in his first two years in Cordova, beginning in 1949.

"It was a cool little cabin, but in pretty rough shape by then," recalled Maxwell. "Dad was a helluva shot, and there was some good duck hunting right near the cabin. Also lots of honkers in a place we called the Goose Pasture above the cabin."

The Maxwell Gang was always on alert when heading out to hunt.

"I remember seeing a big spread of ducks on a pond right above the Boxcar while we were running up the slough. We stopped, snuck up, and blasted away. They were Don Van Brocklin's decoys. "

The cabin was still standing in 1952, and visible from the Boxcar. By the mid-50s nothing but stub pilings remained.

Part VIII: Bygone Others

So there you have it. The cabins on Big and Little Arc of the Eyak. A fascinating mix of old and new. But is that all the Eyak area cabins? Not really. Up river, buried in mud, hidden in brush, and lost in time, are scarce remnants of others. Plus a few that are still standing, but in rough shape. Scenes of past glories and raucous good times.

A bleached four foot long 1X6 sign with the words "The Duck Inn" professionally lettered in black paint circa the 1920s decorates a wall of my Odiak Slough warehouse. In smaller print, underneath: ""Storehouse Kid - Prop.," and also "Chickens Allowed."

Where did that come from? My sister Sharon found it stashed under our Pete Dahl duck cabin, which was built in 1959. Dad must have "requisitioned" it somewhere. Shar has a knack for decorating with collectables, so took it to town and mounted it on the exterior wall of her porch. Ended up in my possession when she built a new home. Artifacts travel interesting paths.

Sis didn't "have a clue" about what cabin at one time proudly displayed the sign. Given the penchant for clever name plates in the early days, it likely came from a shack in the Eyak area. Maybe from one of the upriver sites.

At least four duck cabins were located on a pair of sloughs a mile down the Eyak, where it emerges from the forested edge of Heney Range and enters broad open marsh. One slough swings to the west, and is the cutoff to Mountain Slough and the old Crystal Falls cannery. The other, named Lydick Slough, is just a few hundred yards further downstream. It branches to the east and back toward the road. Both are now almost entirely filled in with sand and silt.

Back in the cannery heydays, both Eyak River and Mountain Slough were key transportation waterways. Large boats, including the *Northern Lights*, a deep draft schooner-style 60 footer, hauled supplies and canned fish from the lower reaches of Mountain slough to nearby ocean channels and also tendered fish back to the cannery. By the 80s, only remains of the abandoned, deteriorating vessel lay on the bank near Crystal Falls Cannery site. Randy Bruce salvaged its bow name plate and propellor before they vanished in mud and vegetation. Both are now displayed as mementos at his Big Arc cabin.

A small power scow named Beaver was used by used by Utness to run fish and supplies up Mountain Slough to his landing and warehouse on the banks of Eyak

A successful hunt from an abandoned Parks Cannery cabin on the upper Eyak in the 1940s. Notice the old dock piling in the background. From left to right: Charlie Simpler (local fisherman) Andy Anderson (Cordova District Forest Ranger), Dr. Coffin, (local physician) Rolland Nipps (School Superintendent), and Ralph Renner.
PHOTO COURTESY TOM SIMPLER.

River just below the Mile 5 bridge. Local fisherman and boat builder Glen Lankard eventually used the bow of the Beaver when constructing a tender named the *Wilignee*. As the main Eyak continues to fill in and is now only only a few feet deep in many places, it is hard to imagine all that past traffic and activity.

Jim Webber remembered one of the duck cabins on the upper Eyak these craft routinely passed.

"Dr. Council had a cabin called the Lame Duck Inn on the upriver side of the Mountain Slough cutoff. You could reach it by hiking down the Eyak trail, and then following a boardwalk that crossed over several smaller gutters. In fact, you could walk all the way to the Crystal Falls cannery, using the boardwalks, plus some larger bridge timbers they had strung across some of the bigger gutters. Dr. Council was quite a rounder. One time back in the 30s my Dad (Jim Sr.) did some market hunting. He was coming back up Eyak, it was late, dark, and cold. He saw lights over at the Lame Duck Inn, and decided to stop and warm up. Council and the boys were having quite a party. Dad had more than 100 ducks, and Council asked him if he wanted some more. They planned to stay and hunt more and had way too many birds already. So Dad took them too. Had a deal worked out with someone on Alaska Steam. Boxed em up and sent them to Valdez on the steamship where they were sold there."

Webber recalled The Lame Duck Inn later belonged to a fellow named Bridgeman. He also remembered three cabins on the eastern bank of Lydick Slough just above its mouth. The first belonged to Harry Nicolet; the second to the Lydicks; and the third, "by my time," to a fellow who worked for Army ACS (Alaska Communications System) in Cordova named Blackett. Name plates for cabins were a big thing back then, and Webber recollected the last cabin being named The Rogue's Rest.

Dan O'Brien remembered finding remains of the cabins still there in the late 60s when he and Mark King were in high school and trapping that area. He also mentioned a cabin labelled The Red Rooster in a stand of timber on the downriver side of the Crystal Falls Cutoff slough, about 100 yards down from the Eyak.

Lame Duck Inn, Red Rooster, Rogue's Rest, Duck Inn.

Hot damn, the good old days.

A half mile down river from Lydick Slough sat the abandoned cabins and houses of former workers at the destroyed Parks Cannery. Several of these were adopted for duck hunting. Karl Barth, who came to Cordova as a hospital lab technician and later owned a hardware and sporting goods store, hunted out of one.

"Karl was great," recalled Jim Webber. "He would encourage us to use his cabin at any time. Sold lots of shotgun shells that way, too." Obviously a shrewd business man.

Ralph Renner, another longtime Cordovan who arrived in the late 30s and managed the Cordova Utilities, chased ducks out of another one, as did Dick Davis.

A few of the cabins were still standing in the early 60s. Sylvia Lange remembers her family spending the summer in one, while she and her father Fred Lange ran downriver to gillnet out of open skiffs just beyond the markers at the mouth of Eyak. It was nicknamed The Swallow's Nest because so many birds had occupied the cabin eves and attic. She felt a twang of envy toward the Honkola's, who occupied a bigger two story cabin next door, used for the same purpose.

Most of the Parks Cannery cabins eventually fell into disuse and were abandoned, to gradually vanish with time. By 2012, only one small cabin remained, windows and door gone, paint peeling, a tilting reminder of days gone by. A few piling and rusting boilers still line the banks of the old cannery site.

A similar fate befell the cabins at Crystal Falls, as the access slough became almost entirely silted in.

Eleven is the number of cabins still standing on the Eyak and its tributaries.

Chapter 4

To The East

EAST: 1. The direction toward the point of the horizon where the sun rises at the equinoxes, on the right-hand side of a person facing north. WIKEPEDIA
2. Early Delta duck hunters' inaccessible Promised Land. LOCAL FOLKLORE

"Maybe all the good times could have happened somewhere else; its people, not walls, who give a place a heartbeat."

MICHELLE BOOTS, "FIRE DESTROYS HISTORIC COPPER CENTER LODGE," *Anchorage Daily News*, 20 MAY 2013

Part I: Joe Reeve Slough

Korn Hole

A number of duck shacks popped up east of Eyak during the earlier days of duck hunting. Still visible from the Big Arc cabins are gradually decaying remains of perhaps the most historical and famous cabin of the Delta, the Korn Hole.

Bob Korn's place on the edge of the Delta cutbank at the mouth of Joe Reeve Slough is half a mile from Eyak. It has the earliest USFS Permit on record, dated February 11, 1937. Like most of the other duck shacks, it was undoubtedly there much earlier. The slough was named after Reeve, a set netter who utilized the site from 1919 to 1922. Reeve wintered at a cabin on Eyak Lake, and traveled the Eyak River by rowboat and later a skiff powered by a 5.7 Alto outboard. The cabin was eventually acquired by Korn. Randy Bruce mentioned finding a paper invoice on the floor of the abandoned Crystal Falls Cannery

"The Korn Hole ... was perhaps the most historical and famous cabin on the Delta." Bob Korn stands on the upper left, with quite a crew of hunters, in the 1940s.
Photo courtesy Kathleen Kritchen.

store that was a bill to Bob Korn for some dish towels and other supplies. It was dated 1934.

Korn was a big heavy set man who came to Cordova in 1920. A lifetime bachelor, his cheerful, generous nature was legendary. A community swimming pool was named after him for all his donations to school and youth activities. While the clam industry was going full bore, he made huge vats of razor clam chowder for the entire community on the 4th of July.

Korn loved the outdoors and a good time. In 1938, my parents spent their honeymoon at his cabin on a little island on Eyak Lake four miles out Power Creek Road. The name says it all: Passion Island. Yes indeedy, those were the good old days.

Before the1964 earthquake, access to the Korn Hole was easy. Exit the mouth of Eyak River on high tide, take a left, and arrive in a jiffy. Which a lot of folks did. An undated black and white photo from Swalling's booklet shows seven hunters sitting on the front porch of the early Korn Hole. Three gals and four guys. Bobbie Dooley, George Dooley, Bill Date, Ms. Brown, Minnie Dooley, Bob Korn, and Al Swalling. Sometime in the twelve year span between 1929 and 1941. Looking at the cabin behind them, it must have made for some interesting sleeping arrangements.

Bob Korn was nicknamed Kernel Korn. For years, as a youngster, I thought it was Colonel Korn, and he was some sort of military hero. Not true. As discovered in a roundabout way sixty years later.

Merle Hanson hailed from Choteau, Montana, and came to Cordova in 1967 to teach science at CHS. Housing was tight, so Cordova School Superintendent Barney Anderson found him an apartment on the third floor of the Alaskan Bar and Hotel. Owned and operated by Bob Korn. Who took him under his wing, so to speak. Merle admitted many a night it was so noisy upstairs that he said the hell with it and joined the locals for insight into Cordova lore and the byzantine family trees of his pupils.

Hanson's high school English teacher was none other than A.B. Guthrie Jr., who won a Pulitzer Prize for his novel *The Way West*, and wrote several other classics about American expansion and exploration. Perhaps Merle recognized in Korn a character befitting of Guthrie's literary art. Hanson recalled empty vodka bottles in the back seat of Guthrie's car when he pulled up for petrol at the Choteau gas station, Merle manning the pumps. A week of Montana rapscallions would be enough to drive any Pulitzer to drink.

Hansen arrived in the twilight days of Korn Hole Glory, but there were still adventures to be had. In the spring, Bob invited Merle to help open up the cabin and do repair and maintenance work. Korn, of full bodied proportions, had an equally heavy work skiff, which was stored in a warehouse alongside the Powder House. Step One was to get it loaded on a small rail tram and lowered into Eyak Lake. Which was quite a splash. From there, downriver they went, following the path of earlier Delta pioneers. The Way East, to Korn's infamous bungalow on the banks of Joe Reeve Slough.

By then, access to the cabin by tidal water flooding to the edge of the cutbank was impossible due to earthquake uplift, so Korn had purchased a small four wheel drive contraption called a Desert Rat to haul supplies back and forth. The route was crisscrossed with deep gutters, so little bridges had to be built across them. Merle and Bob were on track, sort of, when Korn stopped to inspect a crossing, stepped in a gutter, and vanished. Merle helped fish him out. Bob stripped down naked, wrung out ever stitch of clothes, put them back on, and said "Let's go, what are we waiting for?"

"Everything was wool," said Hanson. "Plus he had a nice layer of built-in insulation."

Made it to the cabin in short order. While tidying up things in a back storage shed, Merle stumbled across several bags of dry kernel corn. Asked Bob what they were for. Well, it seems the Korn Hole Gang had read about geese being attracted to cornfields down south. So for as far back as Korn could remember, they had several bags of corn shipped in every year, and scattered it all around their blinds in open meadows behind the cabin, as well as on the mud flats in front. It was a great plan. Why chase geese when they will come to you? Hence Kernel Korn, the Hunter, rather than Colonel Korn, the Military Leader. Korn would never tell Merle whether it worked or not.

"Bob confided in me they also tried making goose pits by digging and sinking barrels, like they saw in hunting books," said Hanson. " Mumbled something about water tables, and said that didn't last long."

Jim Webber confirmed the Korn Corn Plan. "One time they ran out of booze, and called town on the CB to ask for a resupply, including ice. Paul Mulcahy and I ran down with a load in our airboats. You could run all over the flats then. When we crossed the mud in front of the cabin, we noticed it was turning yellow. What the heck? Turned out if was dry kernel corn spread in a big area, gradually tapering down to a narrow path leading to a goose blind. But we didn't see any geese hanging off the cabin."

Merle mentioned that Korn had intentionally built his outhouse right near the edge of the back pond close the cabin, with the door facing the water. Always had a few decoys floating nearby.

"One of the Delta's first multipurpose rooms," said Hanson. "Bob always took his shotgun and a newspaper with him when he headed to the outhouse, and more than once came back with a few ducks."

Korn had a gaggle of Anchorage friends in the bar business who would come down every fall for a rollicking good time. One was Paddy Kissane, who became quite a regular. Evidently Goose Fever spread all the way back to the Big City. Fred Pettingill, Louie Hasbrouck, and a couple other Cordova characters were at Kissane's downtown Mermack Lounge for Paddy's birthday, and presented him with a goose call. Which they encouraged him to try out right there in the pub. Patrons laughed while Kissane blasted out a few honks, and said "Wow, this sounds great" at about the same time as four live domestic geese the Cordovans had hidden in the back room came marching into the bar.

Kissane was a proud Irishman. A three foot tall Leprechaun statue stood in the middle of the back bar for patrons to admire. One day he went to the storage room for supplies. When he returned it was gone. Paddy was really upset. Later that fall he came to Cordova to hunt at the Korn Hole. After a lively welcoming party that went well into the wee hours, he headed to his bunk. When he crawled in, there it was in his sleeping bag. The Boys roared in laughter.

Several years ago, Merle was at the cabin with Korn and Kissane, and Bob was fretting about Paddy not feeling well. That night the Irishman sat on the deck watching a pretty sunset, and said this would be a great place to die. Which he did that night.

After Korn's death, the cabin ended up in the hands of Terry Kissane, Paddy's son. By 2012 it had changed hands two more times. Like several other older shacks, the Icon of Delta Duck Hunting has fallen into disuse and disrepair because of poor access and accelerated growth of brush and timber. It will soon be gone.

Part II: Government Slough

Sherman's

Next to the east from the Korn Hole, a mile from the mouth of Eyak, lies Government Slough. Its waters originate from Scott Glacier, whose terminus is ten miles north of the Copper River Highway. The runoff passes under a pair of bridges at 9 Mile, and from there travel roughly five miles more before reaching the edge of the Delta. At one time a large highly visible tripod was built at the mouth of the slough, and was used by the U.S. Coast and Geodetic Survey as a reference point for mapping the Delta; hence the name "Government."

Because of its proximity to Eyak entrance, it was also fairly easy to reach this slough, running offshore close to the cutbanks on big pre-earthquake tides. In fact, the Korn Hole was midway refueling stop on this journey, and the Government Gang often stopped for a quick warmup nip with Bob and the Boys before continuing their cruise.

The Sherman cabin sits 3/4 of a mile up the far side of Government Slough. The first USFS Permit was issued to Corliss, Date, Lydick, and Sherman in 1950, but the cabin had been there for several years prior to that.

Another fascinating cast of characters. Bill Sherman came north from Tacoma, Washington. Operated Bill's Cab Company for awhile, then partnered with Bill Gragan in Bill's Bar. Later sold his interest to Bill Hall.

"Didn't even have to change the name," chuckled Ken Van Brocklin. Sherman later partnered with Van Brocklin in the Club Bar and Liquor Store.

The other partners were a perfect fit for duck shacks. Walt Corliss ran the local Standard Oil fuel distributorship. Standard Oil owned all the units in Alaska at that time.

Bill Date operated a local lumber yard. The Lydicks were a railroad family, and veteran duck hunters that also had a cabin on the upper Eyak River.

So lets see: Sherman for the beer and booze; Date for the cabin building materials and construction; Corliss for boat gas and cabin stove oil; and Lydick for the river and duck hunting expertise. A Corporate structure that must have left the Guggenheim Conglomerate which financed the CRNW railroad in awe.

Eventually Tom Gilmore joined the cabin syndicate, with he and Sherman listed as sole Permit holders later in the 50s. Gilmore and his wife Molly ran Pop's Liquor Store. Perfect. Dual sources for the most important ammo in Delta duck hunting. And we're not talking about shotgun shells.

According to Van Brocklin, "Tom loved to hunt ducks. And roll dice. I remember every year when the USFS Permit payment came due, Tom would come into the Club Bar with the bill, and he and Sherm would shake dice to see who paid it."

Van Brocklin's Boxcar and Sherman's Shack were a mile and a half apart, as the crow flies. Most of the hunting from the Boxcar was done by walking past a series of ponds toward Government Slough, a swift, wide glacier stream at that point. One fall Kenny and Dad enlisted Randy and I to drag a yellow Navy-surplus life raft all the way to the slough, with a case of beer inside, of course. Then we rowed across the slough. The adults opted to drift down stream enjoying cold beer while Randy and I walked, jump shooting ponds on the way. We rendezvoused near Sherman's cabin and replaced the beer with ducks. We were of course elected to pull the raft back up river. At least they didn't insist on riding.

One of Kenny's all-time favorite hunts occurred across Government. It was late fall, most of the ponds were frozen, and the slough had dried up so much you could wade across the shallow water. Dad and Kenny decided to hunt a long narrow pond half mile above Sherman's. Upon arrival, they heard the quacking of a lone duck. Turned out to be a bird that had been "winged" by hunters and was frozen in the ice. They broke it out, and the duck responded by merrily quacking away. They decided to call it Oscar, made a big hole in the ice, and let it swim around.

Which attracted considerable numbers of birds migrating south.

"It was cold," said Van Brocklin. "We always took a bottle of Christian's Brothers Brandy on days like that. Your dad was on one side of the pond, I was on the other. He would holler he needed some brandy, and I would send it skimming across the ice. Could hear that trademark laugh of his over the sound of the glass bottle sliding on ice as it went across the pond. Next thing you knew it was zipping back my way. It was a hunt I will never forget."

Part III: Glacier Slough

Maxwell Cabin #2
Farther to the east, on this side of Alaganik, stood two other early cabins that were also accessed from Eyak. The Korn Hole and Sherman shacks were just a quick trip around the bend from the mouth of the Eyak. The Glacier cabins were six

miles away, and required traveling across open water that had confounded natives, explorers such as Lt. Allen, and commercial fisherman, way before sporty duck hunters, often fortified with water of a different proof, sampled its wares.

"Before the road was extended far enough to access Alaganik (aka "The Copper") from above, we did all our hunting right close to Glacier," said Webber. "The Copper was a nasty place back then. Big tides and bad weather, all exposed. Very wide, wind would scream down, tough in an open skiff."

The Maxwells were avid duck hunters and prolific cabin builders. Seems like every major hunting area on the Delta - Eyak, Glacier, Alaganik, Pete Dahl, and even Walhalla - was at one time or another the site of Maxwell Hunting Enterprises.

Bobby Maxwell recalled two cabins at their Glacier site, originally owned by the Clemens brothers. This duo operated a floating cannery at Eshamy every summer, towing it from its winter anchorage in Odiak Slough with a small WWII Navy surplus sub-chaser across Prince William Sound. It was always startling to see this grey port-holed ship come cruising up the slough, its superstructure at road level on big tides, maneuvering a barge laden with a red two story cannery in the hundred yard wide waterway.

The uplift from the 64 earthquake left the barge and cannery high and dry. Its Eshamy days were over. Eventually locals Bob and Rose Arvidson purchased it, and began remodeling and adding on. Bob had a PhD in psychology from a Canadian university, but discovered he would rather outwit salmon than people, thus returning to his roots as a commercial gillnetter. He spent the offseason building entertaining structures around the original cannery, including a replica of the mast of a British sailing ship, a registered lighthouse, and a cement sculpture of the Greek god Sisyphus, pushing his huge eternal rock. Bob's theory of psychology was that everyone had their own rock to push; and he certainly did his share, adding hundreds of yards of rock and gravel around the structures.

And of course all the while maintaining the barge was a floating structure, and thus not subject to city property tax.

Dates of the original Clemens cabins at Glacier are sketchy. It was well before the road was extended beyond Mile 13. Buel and Les bought the pair of cabins from Al Rathsenberger. The larger one was about 9 feet wide and 22 feet long. Tom Justice, who eventually owned the cabin, recalled the roof was lightly supported by 2X4's on two foot centers, but the wind always seemed to keep it clear of snow. The other cabin was smaller, about 10 foot by 12 foot, and was used for a storage shed.

More interesting was Justice's description of old heavy steel water heaters used as ice breakers.

"There were 20 of them surrounding the cabin. All were about 3 feet round, partially buried, and stood vertically 5 feet out of the ground. Their purpose was to prevent ice from nearby ponds from taking out the cabin on big spring tides."

The first USFS Permit for the cabin was issued to Robert Max in January 1961. Bobby recalled hunting with Les out of the cabin in the 50s.

"We would run in an open skiff from Glacier to the cutoff on the far side of Alaganik that eventually leads to Pete Dahl. There was lots of water back then, so we just ran right along the cutbank to get there. We hunted right up the first turn in the cutoff, in a series of ponds on the right. It was great hunting; we would come home with hundreds of ducks."

Which was not surprising. Les was an outstanding wing shot.

"Would drive me crazy," said Jimmy Webber. "We'd sit in the blind, and when a flock of birds came in he would tell me to shoot whenever I was ready. I'd stand up and miss half the time. Then Les would get a double on his first shot, every time."

Les was also quite the character, and not coincidentally, story teller.

One of his favorite Glacier cabin tales was about a foursome of Anchorage hunters who arrived at Mile 13 on one of Cordova Air's DC-3's for a weekend hunt. At that time in the late 50s both Les and the Swartzbacker-Ekemo-Lovseth group at Pete Dahl were bringing down "friends" who paid them well for what was essentially guided hunting.

"They stumbled down the plane's tiny stairs in hip boots, carrying shotguns and hand bags stuffed with booze," said Les. "Bandoliers of ammo across their chests, big hunting knives on their belts, hunting hats askew, had obviously taken the afternoon shoot at the airport bar."

"Anyhow, turned out to be a fun loving bunch. Probably had never shot a duck in their lives. We headed down river in an open skiff to Glacier, got everyone settled in, had a couple cocktails, and then I started grilling steaks for dinner on the porch."

"One of the guys, with a squeaky voice, came out with a jelly glass full of whiskey and asked: Hey man, you got a pair of binoculars?"

"I said sure, they're hanging inside the cabin. Help yourself."

"He came back out, scanned out toward the ocean, and then asked me: Hey man, which way to Anchorage? I pointed off toward the mountain range at the west end of the Delta."

"He stood leaning on the railing, peering intently in that direction while taking an occasional sip of Seagrams. Finally I couldn't stand it any longer. Asked him what he was looking for."

"Hey man, I just wanted to see if my wife was chipping on me."

A joke that Les could truly appreciate.

For when Randy and I were asking Bobby about Les's numerous wives, the younger Maxwell scratched his chin, taped his finger on the kitchen counter, and said: "Jesus Christ, let's see. First there was May Gill, Bob Gill's sister. Then there was Virginia Nicholoff. Then Diann, the good looking blonde Scandinavian. And then Shirley, Clede Wilson's ex-wife. I think that's it. Four."

A short pause, sip of coffee, sly grin, and then: "Plus a whole lot of chippying…"

Les passed away in 2012, but his legacy lives on.

Eventually, the larger old cabin was in such bad shape it had to be replaced. The smaller one was gone. In the 70s, Bobby's son-in-law Tom Justice, plus Randy Bruce, Tom Branshaw, and Bobby hauled material for a new cabin to the site on Maxwell's 44 foot seiner, the *Carol Ann*.

"I remember pulling right up to the cutbank to unload everything," said Randy Bruce. "I also remember navigating back around Whitshed using radar because of a snowstorm."

A modern 16X20 cabin with a 6X16 porch was built, and the nearby old cabin was torched. Bobby eventually transferred the Permit to Tom and Leslie Justice. They spent years cutting alder, willow, and cottonwood that was sprouting up everywhere, just so they could see through the cutbank brush line to the Flats beyond. Eventually they sold the cabin to Gene Wooden, and moved to privately owned land at Boswell Bay.

Nicolet Cabin

Harry Nicolet was born and raised in Cordova. His father came to Cordova in 1911, and worked for the railroad. He later became Steward of the Cordova Elks Lodge after the railroad shut down, and then owned his own Main Street pub, Nick's Bar. Harry graduated from Cordova High School in 1947, and like many young men of that era, was into commercial fishing and duck hunting.

He and Walt Mantilla, who graduated from CHS in 1937, built the original cabin in the late 40s, using an open skiff to haul the materials there. Old trees three to four inches in diameter were used for pilings. On big tides the skiff could be tied right up against them.

Harry also had a small wooden 14 foot v-hulled skiff powered by a 15 hp outboard that he would use for hunting the entrance area of Alaganik when the weather was good. A 1952 black and white photo shows a Fedora-hatted Harry sitting on the covered bow of the craft, one hand stroking the chin of his retriever, a full string of ducks draped around his neck, trusty Model 12 shotgun in the other hand, with a treeless Glacier cutbank in the background and the Heney Range tapering to the horizon.

Harry Nicolet hunting in style at the mouth of Alaganik, 1952.
PHOTO COURTESY ROBIN NICOLET BLAKE.

The first USFS Permit for the cabin was issued to Harry Nicolet in April 1955, with a lease fee of $10.

Virgil Carroll eventually bought out Mantilla's share in the 70s. The cabin was in rough shape; in Virgil's words, "on its knees." In the early 80s, Carroll and Company tore it down and built a new 15X22 cabin on treated piling at the original site, hauling the materials in on Virgil's seine boat, the *Miss Carroll*.

The old cabin wasn't the only structure in disrepair. Virgil, who is a big fellow, told the story of an outhouse adventure that lead to more construction.

"I was sitting there, and it actually collapsed around me. The walls were gone, I fell through, and all that was left was the frame. Plus me, with my knees up to my chin."

Venture after ducks at your own risk.

Chapter 5

Boom

BOOM: 1. To progress, grow, or flourish vigorously. WEBSTER'S
2. The deep, resonant sound of a shotgun's blast; which is not to
be confused with another type of Blast. PETE DAHL DEFINITION

"If you build it, they will come."

MOVIE *Field of Dreams*

Part I: Flyway Highway

Up to this time, all the Delta duck shacks were accessed via the Eyak River. That
was about to change. The 1950s saw a revival of cabin construction. In the words
of Dick Renner, "It was a regular building boom out there. Cabins were popping
up everywhere."

Why? Well, even ducks were not immune from the impact of national and
worldwide events.

The price of copper plummeted at the same time high grade ore ran out at
Kennicott, resulting in the shut down of the mines and the Copper River and
Northwestern Railway in 1938.

A local landing strip, built in 1934 alongside Eyak Lake using FDR Public
Administration Funds, was not long enough to handle increasingly larger
planes. In 1938 the recently created Civil Aeronautics Authority provided
additional federal monies to extend the runway to 3000 feet. It also noted
only four runways in Alaska adequate for most modern aircraft. Cordova was
not included.

By 1940, with war raging in Europe, Congress considered Alaska's defense,
authorizing creation of the Alaska Defense Command in May of that year. Soon

Lend Lease airfields were being built throughout Interior Alaska and Canada, with select additional locations for coastal defense and an alternate route.

Cordova was one of those sites. CAA work had begun on an airfield at Mile 13 on a low priority basis in the fall of 1940. That all changed with the attack on Pearl Harbor. Enter Morrison-Knudson Construction, one of the biggest public works contractors in the country. They immediately took over the project, hiring several former CRNWR employees to re-activate the railroad so construction could progress at top priority.

In 1942, two companies of the U.S. Army 42nd Engineer Regiment arrived in Cordova to combine with MK in completing the project, while establishing a large camp north of the airfield. By early 1944, the two runways were completed, and MK moved on, leaving behind heavy equipment which the Army used to construct interconnecting taxiways. As the war moved west, Cordova troops were shifted elsewhere, and by June of 1944 the garrison was down to less than 100 men.

Soon after that, with Japan clearly no longer a threat to Alaska, the facilities at Mile 13 were turned back to the CAA. Not long after that Army quonset huts began showing up in Cordova as homes, along with a multitude of other abandoned WWII booty.

In 1945, work began on construction of a gravel road over the railroad grade to Mile 13, and then to points beyond. By the early 1950s, the road had reached as far as Alaganik and the McKinley River at Mile 22. This opened up vehicular access to Alaganik Slough, which runs right along side the road from Mile 21 to the McKinley River Bridge.

Prime duck hunting on the hitherto mostly inaccessible Delta areas east of Alaganik was suddenly just a car and boat ride away. The Glacier and Tiedeman areas were also now readily available. No more need to travel all the way down Eyak River, cross the exposed flats, hang on to your hat, and hope a southeaster didn't show up.

A Highway to the Flyway. Yippee ki yay! The Boom was On.

Perhaps some older drake widgeons, tan bald pates flashing in the sun, basking in the tranquil shallow waters of Walhalla pond, suspected something was up. The rumble of guns off to the west seemed to be approaching, and there was the disconcerting sound of outboards roaring in nearby sloughs.

A few may have even remembered disturbing events back in 1951, when a trio of hunters showed up and camped near their here-to-fore private reserve. It was the Maxwell brothers, with a Camp Cook, of all things.

"Les was pretty competitive about duck hunting," said his brother Bobby. "We hunted quite a bit out of Glacier just on the other side of Alaganik, using an open skiff. Anyone hunting east of us would get him pissed off. Plus we always saw lots of birds headed past us toward Pete Dahl and Walhalla. So we took 2X4's, a wall tent, Coleman stove, plus a 55 gallon drum stove we borrowed from Pogey Paulson at the cannery, and headed to the far side of Walhalla slough in an open skiff. Set up camp in an alder patch right along side the cutbank. Great hunting. Birds everywhere. Ray Guerrero was along with us. He was a great cook. One day Ray shot several mergansers by mistake. Les told him to throw them away. Instead Ray soaked the breasts in salt water, and then made Duck Adobo. Les wanted nothing to do with it, but it was some of the best duck I ever ate."

Soon, many others would also discover some of the best duck hunting they ever had.

Part II: Snag Point and Alaganik

O'Brien, Lantz, Nicholoff Cabin

One of the first cabins built after the road reached Alaganik Slough belonged to Bill O'Brien, Freddie Lantz, and Pete Nicholoff. Buel Maxwell was also in on the combine, but was bought out very soon after its construction.

"He and the other guys didn't get along," said Bill's son Dan O'Brien.

What a fascinating trio of owners.

Bill O'Brien came to Cordova in 1936 with Standard Oil doing exploration work along the Gulf Coast in the Cape Yakataga and Katella areas. He spent the winter of 1937 at Cape Yakataga with Ira and Helen Grindle, and came to know Mudhole Smith that way, as Smitty flew supplies to them on a regular basis. O'Brien helped pay for the provisions by trapping and also by a 50 cent Federal bounty on eagles. Later he became owner of the Service Transfer Company, and combined with Smith and Dick Borer to start the local 1st Bank of Cordova.

Pete Nicholoff was a Prince William Sound legend who was born in Bulgaria in 1892 and gradually made his way to Cordova area by 1916. He was most famous for his 65 foot wooden mail/tug boat Siren, which he bought in 1942 at an auction in Valdez. Nicholoff hauled fuel and freight on barges towed by the Siren for years, and entire books have been written about his many amazing exploits. Hauling construction materials down five miles of protected slough from the landing at McKinley River bridge to their cabin site a mile below Snag Point must have seemed like child's play to him.

Freddie Lantz was manager of the hardware department of the Cordova Commercial Company, as well as a co-owner with my father Don Shellhorn, and Edith Date. He was a character who loved to pull pranks on customers and Edith.

At that time, the Commercial sold Johnson outboards, and had a long wooden rack of them on display right on the main floor. A fisherman was complaining about how hard the often cantankerous Workhorses were to start. Freddie walked out from behind the counter, hooked up a gas tank, and fired one off on the first crank. Prop out of water, you can imagine the roar.

Edith, the store accountant, worked in an open balcony office that overlooked the hardware section. She tended to the excitable side, so naturally the Nuts and Bolts Underlings, including Kenny Van Brocklin and Harry Curran, made sure agitation was part of their stock and trade.

She just about hit the ceiling. Freddie merrily hollered up over the racket, "Don't mind us, Edith. Just showing Slim how easy these new ones start." Harry and Kenny were laughing so hard they headed to the basement, lest they be fired.

Never a dull moment at the old Commercial.

The original 16X24 O'Brien-Lantz-Nickoloff cabin was built in 1954. The first big load of material, including pre-cut roof rafters, was hauled down in a Columbia River double ender belonging to Shorty Jessup. That size boat, 30 feet long, with deep draft and cabin up forward, routinely traveled up "big" Alaganik Slough all the time. The first load also included 3/4 inch "cement" plywood, which came off forms used in building a modern bridge over Eyak River at Mile 5 to replace the narrow wooden railroad span. There was enough of this sheathing material to cover the entire cabin as well as the floor.

Remaining construction supplies were hauled down by skiff from a narrow gutter at 20.3 Mile, halfway across what was called the "Goose Meadows." Pre-earthquake tides flooded this entire open marsh, and skiffs were often anchored on the up-road side of a 60 foot piling bridge across the gutter, so they would not float off during bad weather. On big tides only the top three feet of the gravel road were not immersed, and it was impossible to get the open boats under the bridge.

Jim Webber recalled a slough packed with boats in the fall. "There would be a line of skiffs right below the bridge, bow lines tied to the guardrail, with a stern anchor out, during duck season.

The gutter connected with main Alaganik Slough a mere 500 yards below the road. From there it was clear sailing down to the Flats, passing the present modern-day Alaganik Landing enroute.

Today, that original launch site is a small brush-choked clearwater stream clogged with beaver dams, almost impossible to navigate even by canoe. The bridge has been replaced with a culvert, and a large gravel turnout is the only remnant of a once bustling duck port.

Jessup was a fitting character to team up with O'Brien, Lantz, and Nicholoff. For years he had worked for Otto Koppen, USFW Enforcement; and later for the

"Lantz was a character who loved to pull pranks on the customers and Edith ... the Nuts and Bolts underlings made sure agitation was part of their stock and trade." The Cordova Commercial Hardware Gang, April 1954. L to R: Freddie Lantz, Harry Curran, & Kenny Van Brocklin.

Protection Division of the Alaska Department of Fish and Game. Shorty was of course barely 5 feet tall, and always wore a pair of pistols on his hips. He was still working for ADFG when I tagged salmon in 1962, and must have become even shorter in the ensuring years, as I recall the revolver barrels almost dragged on the ground. Turns out he was in on the operation for good reason.

According to Dan O'Brien, the cabin location was selected not for ducks, but for fish. Back then a big run of king salmon migrated up Alaganik to reach the main Copper at 27 Mile. Salmon went right past the cabin site, all the way up Alaganik to a slough that branched off near the McKinley river bridge, and then continued on up to the main Copper.

Jim Webber described a waterway 40 feet deep and 50 feet wide that veered off just below the Mckinley River bridge, and was used by salmon heading upriver. It was the same route that was used by Natives and early explorers to access the main Copper, and can still be seen on old USGS maps of the area.

The Alaganik Three had two 50 fathom shackles of king gear hanging in their cabin. Shorty would putt up in his double ender and help Lantz set it out at night. Freddie would then run the fish upriver and take the haul to town, where Pete would smoke them in a shed behind his home. Quite a set up. And they weren't alone.

Webber verified the hot king salmon fishing, especially just up-river at Snag Point.

"Larry Kritchen and I sounded out a big hole there when depth finders first came out. It was 80 feet deep. Fisherman would sneak up and make sets right off the point. At one time there was even a pole on the bank you could tied your gear off."

Kind of hard for Shorty to pull out his six-shooters and make an arrest while pulling in kings at the same time.

Virgil Carroll mentioned Harry Nicolet telling him about gillnetting at that very spot. Tales of fishermen ramming boats to get the best set on 7 a.m. openers are common; wonder if they bumped into each other in the dark at Snag Point.

Dining and poker were also high on the list of priorities for the Alaganik Gang. Dick Renner, a junior in high school at the time, was among a group of hunters that pulled up to the 20 Mile landing after a weekend chasing ducks. His favorite dog, a golden retriever named Rusty, hopped out of the boat. Freddie, Bill, and Pete were loading gear in their rig to head down river. Rusty was running around, and started sniffing at their supplies.

Freddie said to Dick, "Why, that dog looks like he's interested in hunting with us."

Dick replied, "He'd hunt every day if he could. But I'm all out of dog food."

Freddie: "No worries. If we can take him along, Rusty will have a T-bone along with the rest of us tonight."

Probably more than one, based on the size of the ice chest.

"I'm sure Rusty ate very well on the entire trip," said Renner. "Turned his nose up at dog food for a few days when they dropped him off in town."

Once, on an early Sunday afternoon tide, Dad and I stopped at their cabin on the way home from Pete Dahl. We knocked on the door, nobody came to open it, but some one hollered "come on in." Bill, Freddie, and Pete, all with sizable bellies, were sprawled out on this big couch, so stuffed they couldn't move.

Freddie pointed to this huge mountain of french toast and ham on the table, and asked "Have you guys had breakfast yet?"

Dan O'Brien was a young and impressionable lad during those early cabin days. Dick Borer was President of the 1st Bank of Cordova, Bill O'Brien was the Vice President, and Fred Pettingill was the Secretary. Bank Bylaws said they had to have a Board meeting every month. They would stop on the way to Borer's cabin at Glacier for a meeting of "the board," and spend the whole night playing poker. Pat Flinn and Bill Zahradnicek would often be along.

"I remember a quart of booze and glass at each station on the table," said Bill's son. "Often they never even made it to Borer's place."

Duck hunting? What's that?

Part III: Big & Little Glacier

First Bank of Cordova Cabin

Things were happening further down Alaganik, if the Bank Board made it that far. West two miles beyond the mouth of Alaganik were a pair of interconnected sloughs called Little and Big Glacier. They could be accessed by going out on the Flats and then cutting back to the entrance of main Glacier slough. Prior to the earthquake, the two branches could also be reached by taking a right turn up Tiedeman Slough, which entered Alaganik just before it opens out on to the Flats. Not far up Tiedeman, a smaller slough branched to the left, zig zagging for a mile until it hit the upper part of Glacier Slough and access to the cabins below.

Depending on weather, hunters either ran their open skiffs on the "outside," or through the Tiedeman cutoff, which was longer but more sheltered. Prior to the road reaching 20 Mile, the only access to the three older cabins already in the Glacier/Government slough areas was by going down Eyak and across the flats. The two new and safer options, plus the development of airboats which could run down directly in almost no water from 9 Mile, opened the area up for more hunters.

Early records of the First Bank cabin are sketchy. It was built in the mid-50s. Dick Borer was the owner. Airboats were just coming into play on the Delta at that time. All were small and powered by airplane engines at that time.

Jim Webber described construction of the 14X24 cabin. "Dick hauled all the material down in a twelve foot airboat with 16 inch sides, if you can believe that. Started at the 9B landing. Later he got a little bigger one. Mary Joe Evans came to Cordova as a Kelly Girl and went to work for Borer in his insurance business. He and Mary Jo would run both airboats to haul more stuff down. She became a heck of an airboat operator. Even back then they had to jump out of Johnson slough and cross the pond to get there."

The first USFS Permit for the cabin was issued in 1967 under the name 1st National Bank of Cordova.

Tom Justice recalled a 1st Bank of Cordova plaque nailed to the side of the cabin. In the late 50s and throughout the 60s Dave Rogers and Glen Criner also used it. Criner would land his Super Cub on wheels, and tie it down right in front of the cabin. In 1982 the Permit was transferred to Thomas Tierny, and then passed on to Gary Baugh in 1992. The current Permit holder is Jack Stevenson Jr., and the site is now accessible primarily by airboat from 9 Mile.

This cabin is also the site of one of the better kept, and literally most explosive, duck hunting secrets on the Delta. After the earthquake and uplift, ponds drained and vanished. And so did the ducks. Particularly near Borer's cabin.

Jim Webber described the planned solution. "Somewhere Dick had read an article about using dynamite to create duck ponds down south in the plains States. It described the process, which was basically dig a narrow deep hole, fill it with dynamite, and set it off. The sides of the crater would sluff as it filled with water, creating a nice pond."

"Dick decided to do it behind his cabin at Glacier. Hauled loads of dynamite down, but then discovered it was impossible to dig a deep hole down there without it rapidly filling up water. So the dynamite was left stacked under a tarp at the planned pond location. At some point someone came down and set it off. Not sure how. It didn't make any pond. But it shifted Borer's cabin on its pilings. Almost knocked it off. He was really mad. Of course everyone else laughed about it."

When Jim Webber doesn't know who did what on the Delta, *that* is a well kept secret.

Which I somehow stumbled on.

It took a sworn oath of confidentiality, and promises from a former Signal Corp sergeant with the Army's top security clearances, to pry this one loose. Perhaps the fact that we were fellow Oregon State Beavers helped. As well as vague references to Statutes of Limitation.

The first hand account came from Passenger Y, who was riding in the back seat of Pilot X's Super Cub when it landed several hundred yards away from the stack of old dynamite. No quotes or names, of course.

X thought it would be a great prank to pull on Borer. We landed at what we thought was a safe distance away. X got out his rifle, and said something like watch this. Nothing happened on the first shot, disappointing. The explosion after the second round knocked us to the ground. We stood up to see smoke rising in the sky, and mud started landing on us and the plane. We wiped the plane off as quickly as we could and got out of there. Back then there was still so little brush you could actually see the tail of an Alaska Airlines jet that had just landed, as it taxied on the Mile 13 runway. We were sure the FAA was going to see the explosion and report it. We flew all the way to a nearby island, landed beside a clear stream, and washed all the mud off the plane before we flew back to town.

The new pond? What pond? Barely made a dent in the muskeg.

Flinn - Hasbrouck Cabin

Pat Flinn and Louie Hasbrouck built a cabin at Glacier about the same time as Borer. The first USFS Permit in their name was dated 6 February 1956. Flinn ran a clothing and sporting good store; Hasbrouck fished and operated tenders. Who built the cabin and how the material made it there is uncertain.

In the early 60s Flinn, who was Dad's competitor in the local clothing trade, invited he and I to come and spend the night. Wow. I was still in high school at the time, and remember late in the evening Flinn and Dad having a contest to see who could jump up and climb over a cable that stretched across the ceiling about 8 feet high. It extended through the walls, and then angled down to secure the cabin to buried "dead men." These were usually creosote pilings buried horizontally under ground, and were intended to prevent cabins from blowing over in the wind, or being knocked off their pilings by floating ice.

Am proud to say Dad won the Cable Climbing Contest. Unfortunately, in the long run, the "dead men" lost a different battle.

Jimmy Webber again. "The original cabin was kind of a boxcar shape. During the big tide surges caused by the 1964 earthquake, it floated off its piling and up toward the road several hundred yards. It ended up right in the middle of a pond. Abandoned. After Louie built a new cabin near the original site, Pat told Billy McCullough, Paul Mulcahy, and I we could have the old one if we wanted. It was still sitting about 300 yards away in the pond. We had plans to jack it up and re-locate it."

"One night, while staying at Louie's place, Pat got drunk, borrowed a little punt, and rowed out to see it. Got sentimental, dumped two 5 gallon jugs of stove oil on the floor, and lit it on fire. The whole thing burned down."

Louie's new cabin was 20X30. It was built in 1967 by North Star Builders, the same company that built many Main Street buildings in Cordova following the big downtown fire in 1963. Louie used his 42 foot seiner, *the Sea Hunter*, to haul in the material, which was given to him by Les Peterson, Superintendent of North Star. Louie had worked construction for Peterson when not fishing or tendering.

At that time the slough in front of the cabin was 8 feet deep, with 80% of Sheridan River running by, so he pulled the large seiner right up to the cabin site. Webber and McCullough also ferried in supplies by airboat.

Later, Gary Weinrick, who had a big second generation airboat powered by an automotive engine, helped Hasbrouck with the cabin and spent considerable time there. In 1984 Louie gave the cabin to Weinrick, who owned it for 27 years.

After the many wild nights at Glacier, Louie would have chuckled to learn that every summer for many years Gary airboated a group of ladies down for quilting, Book Club, and other more civilized activities. Although it is rumored that the Ladies All-Night Card Sessions were worthy of the cabin's previous history.

Gary and his wife Carol recently retired and moved south to Arizona. He gifted the cabin to highly regarded local pilot Mike Collins, who put the Permit in the name of his young son Noah.

Mudhole Smith Cabin

Located off Glacier on the biggest lake on this side of the Copper is a cabin originally belonging to Mudhole Smith, famous early local bush pilot. Merle Smith came to Cordova via Kansas in 1937 to fly for Cordova Air Service. Glacier Pilot Bob Reeve game him the nickname Mudhole after he hit a hole on takeoff near McCarthy and his plane nosed over into the muddy runway, its spinning prop loading the engine and coating the plane and Smith with mud. Merle went on to own Cordova Air, which eventually merged with Alaska Airlines. The airport at Mile 13 is named in his honor.

In 1953, Merle and his oldest son Ken had such a good time hunting at the nearby Sherman-Gilmore-Lydick cabin he decided they needed a place of their own.

"Dad got the bug to have his own cabin after that hunt," said Ken. "Happened to get in at the end of the build anywhere era."

Smitty hired John Foode, a fisherman who also worked at Cordova Air, to build the original 16X20 cabin. On big tides, Foode hauled several loads of material to the site in his work skiff, and lived in a small "dog house" cabin on the boat while building the shack.

The nearby lake was fairly deep. Amphibious Widgeons, plus Cessna 180s and Super Cubs on floats, routinely landed and idled up to a dock near the cabin. Smitty would fly hunters down, including Kenny and his friends Dick Renner and Dennis Lape.

Kenny's favorite duck hunting story was about a memorable night at the cabin with his Dad. "We were down to hunt for a couple days. In the middle of the night the cabin started rattling. Dad thought it was a bear getting after ducks hanging outside, so he stuck his shotgun out the door and shot three times. The rattling stopped. The next morning we heard on the radio there had been a big earthquake. So after that we always called it The Night Dad Shot an Earthquake."

By 1959 Kenny was also flying small planes for Cordova Air. Smitty hired locals Jimmy Iliff and Ole Peterson to build an addition and improve the dock on the cabin. Kenny and his Dad flew them in, and ferried supplies to the project. Iliff somehow developed blood poisoning from a creosote splinter, and realized he needed to get to town for medical attention.

"Smitty wasn't called Mudhole without reason," said Iliff. "Some of us were a bit nervous flying with him. When he showed up with a load of material, I mentioned the problem. He looked at it and told me we better takeoff for town."

Iliff looked at the plane; looked at Smitty, who had on his trademark grin and knew of Iliff's trepidation about flying; looked back at the plane again; and said, "Do I have any choice?"

After the earthquake of '64, the lake gradually silted in and the cabin fell into disuse.

"The water changed and began running under the cabin," said Gary Weinrick. "It took out some of the pilings, and was leaning sideways."

Ron Horton obtained the shack in 2003. He did considerable work on the original part of the cabin. "The back addition was in rough shape from frost heaves. The pond in front of the cabin was good for early goose duck hunting on the sand that has filled it in, but that's about it."

Horton plans to put the original cabin on skids and slide it across winter ice to the highway, which is only 3 miles away. Figures a four wheel drive truck with chains will do the trick. From there it will be relocated to property near Mile 13. The tilting addition and outhouse will be demolished.

A duck shack migrating off the Delta. The first in history, reversing the path of earlier cabins floated in to hunting sites, such as the Boxcar, the Parks Double Decker, and another noted cabin, next on the list.

Part IV: Cutoff

Dar Glasen Cabin

Midway between Alaganik and Pete Dahl, on a maize of interconnecting sloughs, sits Dar Glasen's cabin. Dar was another Cordova fixture. He wore the same wide brim, olive-drab sou'wester hat, rain or shine. Never saw him in a baseball cap, duck hat, or any other type of headgear.

Glasen was an avid bird hunter, and purchased Edmond's share of Curley Hoover's famous Pair-Of-Dice in 1948. Later he bought Curley's Hoover's Movers operation. Dar drove a red Ford pickup out the road at a maximum speed of 10 miles per hour, looking for moose or checking out favorite cutthroat hot spots. He was a top local sports fisherman, and when moose transplanted from the Kenai in the early 50s generated a herd large enough to harvest, the most patient road hunter around.

"He would ask me to go out moose hunting with him," said son Danny. "We would park and sit for hours, and I mean hours, in one spot, waiting for one to come out. Drove me crazy."

Despite the slow speed, every ten years or so the truck would wear out from all the potholes in the gravel surface. Not a problem. Once a decade Ford Motors came out with a custom-built red Dar Glasen Special, ready to ship to Cordova.

Dar was a big fan of movies, especially Western's. Would take his wife Katy to the tiny old North Star Theatre, sit a few row's back from the screen, and then send her to get popcorn. Service in the little concessions stand wasn't speedy, but all the other movie goers soon came to expect Dar's gruff "Down here, woman" as Katy stumbled through narrow aisles trying to find their seats in the dark.

Like at least two other Delta duck shacks, the original Glasen cabin came pre-built. Sort of. This one was two small shacks off razor clam scows that used to be anchored at Whitshed. At one time Cordova was known as "The Razor Clam Capital of the World," and Dar dug clams commercially, as did many of his hunting partners. Dar talked his neighbor and local cannery superintendent Merle Wicket, who also enjoyed duck hunting, into donating the shacks for the Cause.

In the summer of 1956, Dar, along with his oldest son David, plus David's buddy Dick Renner, went down from 20 Mile, and set in all the creosote pilings for the cabin foundation. Dar had been in on the abandoned Parks Cannery cabin on the Eyak where Ralph and his son Dick hunted. The strapping young high school lads made an ideal work force.

Getting the clam shacks there proved to be quite an adventure, and involved two other commercial fisherman and hunting partners, Rudy Becker and Charlie Simpler.

Charlie's oldest son, Tom Simpler, described the operation. "At the cannery in town, Rudy, David Glasen, and I loaded the two shacks on to the stern of the C.B, Rudy's little seiner. The C.B. was only thirty feet long and not very wide. The shacks overlapped off the deck. We ran all the way across the Flats. It was a beautiful night. We came up the entrance to Pete Dahl, but didn't want to risk going dry with the cabins on the deck, so we had to wait until daylight to go up the slough and the cut over to the cabin site."

"Dad and Dar came down Alaganik in a skiff to meet us. We pulled right up to the bank with the C.B., but had a heck of a time winching the cabins off the deck, and getting them back to back on the pilings."

At that time this was the easternmost cabin on the Delta.

"We went right by the little slough that branches off to where the four Pete Dahl cabins were eventually located. Back then there was no brush, and on a big tide you were level with the top of the river banks. There were no cabins there at that time," said Simpler. "I'm sure we would have remembered seeing them if there had been."

The first USFS Permit for the Glasen cabin is dated 19 April 1957, in Durwood Glasen's name.

By 1986, the original cabin was in rough shape. The Glasen's salvaged part of it for a storage and generator shed. Friends from Anchorage that worked construction came down and build a new 20X24 cabin, with a porch and deck.

Prior to the explosion of brush and trees following the earthquake uplift, the late night lights of the Glasen cabin could be seen shining brightly from Pete Dahl. Dar and the Boys always like "a hot one" after the evening shoot. On a clear night with a soft northerly breeze, you could vaguely hear voices and laughter that went with them.

Part V: Cabin Construction Halts

Sooner or later, the USFS was bound to notice a distinct upswing in duck cabin construction on the Delta. Maybe it was the line of skiffs tied off the bridge at 20 Mile, or the steady stream of trucks heading out the road laden with scavenged building materials and returning empty. Several District Rangers were enthusiastic bird hunters. Perhaps they were startled to see cabins standing on newly accessible Chugach National Forest land when they headed down Alaganik for a weekend shoot.

Remember that Alaska was a Territory until Statehood in 1959. Cordovans weren't alone in viewing landlords back in Washington D.C. with considerable disdain. Hunters and fishermen had been building cabins all over the Delta and Prince William Sound since the late 1800s. Fifty years later, second and third generation sourdoughs were just following traditional practices. Hell, Alaskans proudly touted their land as the Last Frontier. For locals, the Delta was their Wild West.

Not to the Forest Service. It called a halt to construction of further cabins in the mid-1950s. Dar Glasen's cabin was the last one built on the Delta at a new location without USFS approval.

Almost.

For every hole, there is a loophole. Right?

Remember the Walhalla tent frame operation by Les Maxwell, Bobby Maxwell, and Ray Guerrero in 1951?

Ah Ha.

Some clever duck hunters discovered that the construction of tent platforms was still allowed. After all, the Delta was a swampy area, shelter was necessary for any long- term hunts, and camping nice and dry out of the muck and water sure would be nice.

Oh my, how one thing leads to another.

A mile above the mouth of Pete Dahl slough, a smaller tributary branches off to the east. This narrow waterway is sheltered from the rough waters that stormy southeasters generate in the 500 yard wide main Pete Dahl slough. This small slough winds its way east to a string of shallow ponds just this side of

Walhalla that were known for some of the best duck hunting on the Delta, especially for widgeon.

The area was a natural flyway for Northern birds heading south, due to the geography of the edge of the Delta, just a mile below this waterway. From the mouth of Alaganik eastward, the Delta cutbank angles outward. In late September and early October, big flocks of migrating Northern ducks and geese would come skimming along the Delta's edge to the mouth of Alaganik, and then blaze across Whiskey Pete and Pete Dahl Sloughs, pouring into shallow ponds in the Walhalla area.

Now it was possible to leave the road at 20 Mile and run all the way to this area in an open skiff without having to go across "outside" waters.

If Pirate Duck Hunters had been given a map marked with an "X" for Buried Bird Treasure, this was it.

Remember when the Dar Glasen cabin-building crew went floating upriver past this tributary on the C.B. in 1956, and noticed its banks were empty? That was about to change.

Part VI: Pete Dahl

Tent Platforms

Two groups of veteran duck hunters decided the tributary off Pete Dahl would be the perfect location for tent platforms. Andy Swartzbacker, Pete Lovseth, and Bill Ekemo partnered to build one; Dick Borer of the First Bank of Cordova the other.

Bill Ekemo was the younger brother of John Ekemo. The latter became my father-in-law when I married his oldest daughter Sue Ekemo in 1966. John and I shared many hunting stories, as well as moose and duck hunting moments. His particular Norwegian Pride in outfoxing The Government shined when recounting the Saga of the Tent Frame Cabins. Andy Swartzbacker worked in the hardware side of the Commercial; Pete Lovseth was born and raised in Cordova, married to John and Bill's sister Lil, and hence was Uncle Pete to Sue. Got all that?

Basically, both groups constructed platforms that in any other situation would be labeled foundations. The base of the 12X16 Borer platform was built using creosote pilings, with a plywood deck sitting on 2X6 floor joist. The Swartzbacker-Lovseth-Ekemo Conglomerate (Hereafter abbreviated SLE) opted for a 16X24 platform, built on a mixture of untreated 6X6 posts and creosote piling, also with plywood floor on 2X6 joists.

From there, it was standard 2X4 framing for the walls and roof, with shiplap purlins on two foot centers running across the 2X4 roof rafters. This was not your typical tent frame construction. However, both "frames" were then covered with heavyweight Navy surplus treated canvas tarpaulins that were so big they covered the entire roofs and longer walls in one single piece.

Hmmm. Looks like a tent to me.

Where Borer found the canvas is a mystery. He also had a number of pipe-framed stretched-canvas bunks labeled U.S. Navy that likely came from the deep recesses of WWII transports. So many, in fact, that he later gave Dad six to use for bunks in our cabin. They came with chains that were used to suspend the racks in tiers of 5 or 6 on what had to be just delightful cruises across the Atlantic or Pacific in the bowels of rolling troop ships. More than one rocky evening, after typical late night duck shack shenanigans, hunters probably felt like they were swaying in rough seas too.

The exact time line of evolution from tent frames to cabins is as murky as the water in Pete Dahl slough, but somewhere soon after, roofing metal mysteriously appeared over the canvas, windows and doors filled openings, and Wa La, there stood two duck cabins, side by side. The SLE shack, replete with oil space heater and cook stove, was built by its three partners; the Borer cabin by a hired crew.

That fall the Pete Dahl hunters had great success and a rollicking good time. Word of which spread faster than the pattern of #4 shot from of a Model 12 with an improved choke cylinder.

Cooks planning the Annual Cordova Elks Duck Feed, a traditional fall event dating back to the 1920s, marveled at the piles of resplendent widgeons, mallards, and pintails arriving in town, and had to hire extra pluckers at higher wages to keep up.

"Where are all these birds coming from?," they asked.

Followed by "Crap, we're screwed. The Forest Service won't let us build any more cabins out there."

Small town secrets don't last very long, especially at the Lodge Bar during an Elks Duck Feed. Liquid Lubricant Loosens the Tightest Lips.

"Two tent frames had morphed into cabins, after the deadline for cabin construction. At Pete Dahl. That's where all these plump Northerns are coming from."

Patrons were drawing plans for their own tent frames on bar napkins while waiting for their next highball. There were so many designs and scribbled maps revealing possible new hot spot locations the bartender had run to the back storeroom for more paper towels.

They did it, so can we.

Oh boy. There could be an explosion of tent platforms on the horizon, unless…

Under community pressure from envious shotgun-totting locals, the Forest Service decided to give hunters one last "shot" at a cabin lease site on the Delta, while prohibiting any further "tent platform" construction. Five small lots adjacent to the now already existing tent frame cabins at Pete Dahl were surveyed in June of 1958. A lottery was held, with names drawn for Forest Service Special Use permits on those sites. Lot #1 was already occupied by Borer, Lot #2 by SLE.

Lot #4 was reserved for the Alaska Fish and Game, as a base for enforcement and research operations. Interestingly, they already had built a small A-frame style shack 20 yards west of Borer, but evidently wanted to relocate due to the severe bank erosion at that spot.

Who drew the rights to Lots #5 and #6 is a mystery. Cabins were never built there. Lot #7 went to a familiar Delta name: Les Maxwell, whose Delta Cabin Building Clan was involved in a shack above the Boxcar, a cabin at Glacier, the early stages of the Lantz-O'Brien-Nicholoff cabin on Alaganik, and Lord knows where else.

Oh. I skipped Lot #3.

It was drawn by Don Shellhorn.

Chapter 6

Pete Dahl

PETE DAHL: 1. A major slough three miles east of Alaganik, named after early local fisherman Pete Dahl. First reported by Lt. Commander J.F Moser, U.S. Navy, in 1898.
Alaska Dictionary of Name Places
2. Correct pronunciation is "Pee-Doll" or "Peed-All," not two distinct words "Pete" and "Dahl." Pete Dahl Archives

"We've only just begun, to live…"

The Carpenters, song of that title.

Part I: Lost

June 1959

The fog was so thick the opposite slough bank wasn't visible. Dad reached down, smoke from his pipe adding to the grey haze, and shook the gas tank. "Hmm. Hope we're almost there."

Not only was there fog, it was becoming eerily dark. Dad had a spotlight out, moving its beam from side to side, a yellow ball of light reflecting off flat water to vaguely illuminate brush, logs, and the adjacent mucky river side.

An 18 horse Johnson was idling along at low rpm's, the Misty, our little 14 foot runabout, making a quiet gurgling "V" in the muddy gentle flow. Its name seemed to match the situation. Couldn't see far enough to go any faster, plus in gas conserving mode.

Wonder if Dad is going to start blowing the fog horn, thought I. Passed a stump sticking up in the water. Another good reason to be going slow.

Strangely, the muskeg to our port morphed into gravel. What The Hell passed through my fifteen year old mind, as Dad verbalized the same thing.

In the words of Maurice Herzog, "We were well and truly lost."

Or were we?

Our vessel crunched to a stop, Dad stepped out, walked ten feet up the incline, and was almost speechless to find a long, narrow, maroon-colored 1950 Ford van with the words Cordova Commercial Company lettered along the back side panel. A step up from the Green Hornet it was, and we called it the Maroon Monster.

"We're back," came his cheerful holler through the haze.

Mom and Sharon piled out of the boat as I tossed the anchor on the beach. Indeed, paraphrasing the famous MacArthur, "We had returned." Not to the Philippines.

To the very 20 Mile boat landing we had left two hours earlier.

The Misty, our 14 foot runabout reclaimed from the dump, being towed by the Maroon Monster, aka the Cordova Commercial freight van, 1958.

Our first trip to Pete Dahl was quite memorable. We didn't get there.

On board were steaks and sundry provisions to spend the night at Swartzbacker's cabin. Everything else we might need was already there, Andy had assured us. The afternoon had started with excitement and anticipation. A first visit to the USFS site where we would build our own duck cabin.

Guiding us was an early USGS map, circa the 1940s, with a route to Pete Dahl drawn by oldtimer Alex Colner, who had sketched it for Dad while buying a pair of Kingfisher hip boots at the Commercial. Several troublesome issues : #1: the map scale was so big, the pencil route he had drawn covered entire sloughs, and many of the tributaries weren't even displayed; #2: the map wasn't extremely accurate; it showed cabins that weren't there, and didn't show ponds and sloughs that were there; and #3: Alex's eyesight and memory weren't exactly 100%. But he was a fascinating character, and probably could have steered us there blindfolded, if we had brought him along.

Swartzbacker had assured us we didn't even need a map, it was so simple. His directions went something like this: RRLLLRRLRL.

Right. Literally, and figuratively.

R = right turn; L = left turn.

We discovered concerns regarding this directive. #1: This code was for "big" sloughs only. How wide does a slough have to be in order to qualify as "big"? As we were later to learn, there are at least 25 distinct sloughs that branch left or right from the launch site at 20 Mile to the cabin sites at Pete Dahl. Many look "big" at high tide, especially when zipping along for the first time. #2: Fog and darkness. Not allies of navigation in any situation. If you can't see the opposite bank, especially near the mouth of Alaganik, which is almost half mile wide, how do you know if you passed a "turn" slough or not? #3: One wrong or missed turn, and The Code is shot. Duh. Why didn't we think of that?

Today, after running the river for 54 years, I could tell you exactly what Andy's Code meant. Yet it is always entertaining, when taking friends to the cabin who have been there before, to ask them, at a fork in the sloughs, "Left, or right?" Most bat about .500. Often less on the way back. Hmm.

In *The English Major*, Jim Harrison wrote "As the sky lightened it occurred to me the sun was rising to the east behind me. When you're on the road it's hard to keep your directions straight."

Which is also true when you're on the water.

Anyhow, we had a marvelous boat ride. And in hindsight, deduced what happened. We made it to the lower end of Alaganik, where we had hunted before. And took the correct left turn up the Pete Dahl Cutoff slough. From there a long slough later nicknamed the Racetrack runs parallel to Alaganik almost all the way back to where we started.

For years, fishermen had called this parallel waterway the "Little Copper," as one of its upper forks split left to Snag Point and Alaganik slough, with the other meandering all the way to the main Copper below 27 mile.

The Racetrack has several forks and branches soon after entering it from below. Three of them are options for accessing Pete Dahl. The upper two are only 300 yards apart, and converge a half mile later after several 180 degree zig-zag bends. We likely took a turn at the wrong time, circled round and round, and raced up and down the Racetrack until low on fuel.

Verifying this theory is the fact that we never reached Glasen's cabin, established in 1956, and located halfway between the Racetrack and the upper entrance to Pete Dahl slough. Dar's place looms over the river bank, and would be impossible to pass without noticing.

So there we were. Back at the landing. Yes, indeedy. Casting our vote for Spanish explorer Arteaga's 1779 name for the Copper. "Rio do Los Perdidos."

Dad had this uncanny ability to turn a foul-up into fun. Steven Ambrose wrote of Lewis and Clark's *Undaunted Courage* in their pioneering first mission across America's wild frontier. Dad possessed undaunted optimism, a perennial enthusiasm; he relished a challenge, perceived adversity as an ally, and had a knack for creating it. Maybe this came from being raised in an outdoor and adventure loving family in the Kenai Peninsula during the early 1900s. When the Shellhorn clan arrived in Seward in 1915, he was three years old. He surely gained much first hand experience in dealing with misfortunes inherent in their many hunting, fishing, camping, and homesteading ventures in that wide open Alaska countryside before moving to Cordova in 1934.

"Hope is the power of being cheerful in circumstances we know to be desperate" was one of G.K. Chesterton's many famous quotes.

Our situation was not desperate, but certainly disheartening. Dad's response, as we hauled everything back to the truck: "The hell with it. We're not going back to town. Let's head out to the McKinley shelter cabin, cook our steaks, and spend the night."

Which we did. No utensils, no sleeping bags, no Coleman lantern; a spotlight and Chesterton's cheerfulness. Parked on the very spot where four years earlier our family had been dealt a devastating blow. Only years later did this dawn on me. I wonder now what thoughts went through Dad and Mom's minds as we unloaded the van. They, too, possessed undaunted courage.

We found candle stubs in the cabin, and built a rip-roaring fire in its old wood burning stove. Scrapped rust off its flat top with the cabin axe, polished the surface slightly with a rock, and slapped steaks on red hot metal. I carved flat "spoons" out of kindling for eating beans which we heated in the can; Mom had potato salad and chips, plus paper plates, salt and pepper. I remember opening the stove to toss in more firewood, and noticing the blackened beef was quite rare.

But the best ever. We slept in our clothes on bare wooden bunks, and dreamed of a cabin at Pete Dahl.

Part II: Cabin Construction

Day 1 — 25 July 1959

Birds were chirping, geese were honking, ducks were quacking, and early morning sun was sparkling off dew-soaked marsh grass when the Revenge pulled up to the bank of a sixty yard wide tributary one mile above the mouth of Pete Dahl slough.

Delta Dawn. The first of oh so many. Our first glimpse of the site where we would build our cabin. After wandering through well-mapped wilderness, we had arrived at the Promised Land.

It had been a long day and night. The Revenge had been put through her paces. Harry Curran's small 30 foot craft was a converted Navy shore launch originally piloted by hand-rudder astern. He had added a small cabin and topside wheel to the heavy but extremely seaworthy cyprus-hulled vessel. Deck-loaded with material scrounged for the past year by the Shellhorns, she had pulled away from the Parks Cannery dock in Cordova early in the afternoon a day prior.

Mudhole Smith's oldest son Kenny remembered standing on the pier watching the boat being loaded, and couldn't believe how much was onboard in both the small hold and topside. Anita Shellhorn, nine year old daughter Sharon, as well as Smokey Bernard and his ten year old son Dennis, waved from the crowded bridge as Curran headed down the bay.

Smokey was a good friend of Harry's, a jack-of-all-trades. His uncle was Cap Bernard, legendary Arctic explorer in the early 1900s, famous for expeditions on the *M/V Teddy Bear*. Cap eventually settled in Mud Bay on Hawkins Island right across from Cordova. Young Smokey came from Prince Edward Island, worked at Mud Bay, and attended high school in Cordova before going back to join the Canadian Navy during WWII.

Harry's Dad worked in the railroad locomotive shop in Cordova. The Currans were friends with the Mud Bay Bernards; Harry and Smokey met as young teenagers. Soon after the war Smokey returned to Cordova with his wife and three boys. They settled in a house just up the street from us. Sharon and the Bernard boys became playmates, and we immensely enjoyed their cheerful character and Canadian accents.

Orca Inlet was flat calm, the tide was flooding. Harry set a straight line course from the harbor to Big Point, the heavily laden Revenge chugging along at six knots, carving the glassy waters. Trailing behind was the Misty, our red and silver fiberglassed -plywood runabout. Its 18 horses would be put to the test in a crucial phase of the operation.

Meanwhile, Dad and I headed out to the Eyak River landing, just off the road at 5 Mile, to busily loading lumber, plywood, pilings, roofing metal, and other material on to a small power barge owned by Kenny Watson, a local machinist and fisherman. Harry and Smokey would run up the Eyak River in the Misty to rendezvous with us after they had rounded Whitshed, crossed the Home Channel Flats, and anchored at the mouth of the Eyak. Then, aided by current, we would tow the barge downriver, fire off its deep draft engine, and head across more mud flats in tandem fashion from Eyak to Pete Dahl, twelve miles distant to the east as the crow flies, but almost twice that via the channels we would have to navigate.

Someone had been too big a fan of MacArthur and his famous multi-prong amphibious assaults. One of El Supremo's famous quotes was "You are remembered for the rules you break."

Right. Just ask Custer. The plan quickly went awry. Hitting high tide was as crucial to our success as it was for the Inchon landing in Korea. We fell behind schedule.

Phase One went fine. Don't they always? Harry and Smokey's trip to the mouth of Eyak was eventless. They anchored the Revenge, and came cruising up the river on time. Nice evening, clear, warm, even though we were already in the shade of the Heney Range by the time we tied the Misty to the barge. Began towing it down river. And immediately started grounding on sand bars.

"We had a helluva time getting that barge to the mouth," recalled Curran. "With all the weight on board, it kept hanging up, so we would have to stop and wrangle it around."

In October of 2011, over a cup of coffee, Harry was helping me reconstruct details of the trip. It was a sunny afternoon, and from his hillside Cordova home we were looking out the kitchen window toward the very same bay the Revenge and Crew had crossed to begin the adventure. "Don't you remember?," he added, his voice rising with Scottish indignation at my failure, as a then 15 year old, to recall events of 52 years ago, "It was a bugger."

By the time we made back to the mouth of Eyak and tied the barge alongside the Revenge, dusk was in its final stages. Thank goodness days are long and nights are short in Alaska July. Despite the falling tide, we made it across the Flats and through Steamboat Channel to the mouth of Pete Dahl. There we had to drop anchor and wait for tide and light to navigate upriver to the cabin site.

Where we all slept, or if we did so, I do not recall. But chugging up Pete Dahl slough, turning past a small island at the mouth of its first eastward tributary, coming around the bend, with the sun in our eyes, to see where we would build our duck cabin, was unforgettable. Even today I can still feel that crisp early morning air, laden with the rich scents of the Delta; hear water rippling past the boat and barge; and recall the speechless excitement when Harry idled back the engine, and we seven stood on the crowded Revenge deck taking it all in.

Captain Curran pushed the barge up to the edge of the bank. We jumped off and secured it directly in front of 4X4 U.S. Forest Service survey posts marking our one-tenth acre site.

Three cabins stood to the west of our plat. Furtherest away was a small A frame structure belonging to the the Alaska Department of Fish and Game. Next was Dick Borer's 12X16 tarpaper-covered cabin; and then a bigger metal-sheathed cabin belonging to the Ekemo-Swartzbacker-Lovseth combine. This cabin was conveniently right next door to our site. Andy had generously offered us the use of it as a place to stay while building our cabin. The adjacent shacks were recently completed, evolving from tent platforms in a mere year. Indeed. The cabin we were staying in was the reason we were able to build our cabin.

We helped haul all the food and provisions in. Mom, Sharon, and Dennis set up camp, the youngsters then crawling back into sleeping bags while Mom brewed coffee.

The tide was falling, and we scurried about unloading the Revenge first, so Harry could anchor it in the deeper water amid-slough before it went aground. Smokey was the lead carpenter, and at his suggestion, all the roof rafters and wall studs had been precut in town to speed up the on-site construction process. We sorted material into somewhat organized piles while off-loading.

Meanwhile, Mom fixed us breakfast; and before you knew it we were in Construction Mode.

For a young teenager whose biggest prior carpentry experience had been building forts out of scrap material in neighborhood trees or woods, this was the adventure of a lifetime. I also discovered that tasks were assigned in direct proportion to skill level. Which made sense. Let the Learning Curve begin.

First, obviously, came the foundation. A foot of water or more flooded the Delta on big tides, so all cabins were built on pilings. Creosote supports were the best, as they would not deteriorate. We had twenty such short stub ends, all scrounged from dock projects, varying from five to six foot in length.

Working with creosote is delightful. The compound is a liquid, black, tar-like substance, so toxic its use is no longer permitted due to environmental concerns. Logs were soaked in ponds of creosote to create pilings used for docks, bridges, and other underwater construction. To this day, around Cordova there are still telephone poles, house foundations, and many waterfront dock structures made of the durable material. Smokey already knew, and the rest of us quickly discovered, the hazards of cutting creosote with a chain saw. It's tough on the chain, but even worse on the face and arms, as flying creosote chips give off pungent fumes which irritate and burn the skin. Soon we all looked like masked bandits, with bandanas of various colors wrapped around our faces.

First decision concerned positioning the cabin. It was pretty much a no brainer. Prevailing storm weather comes from the southeast, and the slough in front of the cabin runs east to west. So the cabin would be located with the entrance facing southwest, toward the slough, leaving the back wall at an angle to the wind. The front would be 15 feet from the bank, providing 20 feet of clearance behind the cabin to a large pond that stretched the length of all the sites. Our place would be situated parallel to the three adjacent cabins. A large window in front would provide an excellent view of boat and bird traffic, as well as the setting sun.

Now it was time to lay out the foundation for our 16X24 structure, and start setting the pilings. No problem. Locate the corners, check the diagonals, pound in stakes. Align placement for two rows of four pilings to support the outer walls, and then another row down the middle. Everything on eight foot centers. Nice. Start digging. Which of course was my job. Hey, I loved it. Didn't have to go that far down in the mud and silt, just about two feet. Once through the top layer of grassy vegetation, it was soft and easy to work. The idea was to get below the frost line. A mud sill-plate was nailed to the bottom of each piling to give it more bearing surface and prevent settling; this usually was a piece of 2X12 treated with creosote. We would soon discover the cabin shifted up and down slightly every winter anyhow. Doors would be jammed and out of square when we came back in the spring, but eventually settle back into place.

I was going like a gopher. Dad, Harry, and Smokey were plopping the piling in, bracing them upright, and backfilling. Mom brought over sandwiches and chips for lunch. We took a break. The men cooled off with a beer, it was a pop for me. Sharon and Dennis were playing in the back pond, catching little fish, and running around in waving seas of grass highlighted with purple iris and violet shooting stars.

We sat on stacks of lumber, and took in the scene. I was too young to really appreciate how marvelous it was. Dad puffing on his pipe; Smokey and Harry joking; Mom chattering, asking questions; kids playing in the blue breeze; special moments of a lifetime. Is there anything more fun than building a duck cabin? In a totally new place? On the Delta with family and friends?

Then it was back to work. We were cruising. Soon all the piling were in. A forest of crooked creosote. All temporarily in place. Now the tricky part. Square em up, vertical. Square em up, horizontal. Nail on sway braces so they wouldn't tilt under load. And then level off the tops for beams.

Oops. No surveyor's level. How are we going to get them all "even"? Ah, Wilderness Engineering. Smokey wandered off, while Dad and Harry stood pondering. The clever Canadian returned carrying three trimmed alders and a beer bottle. Lucky Lager, of course. The rest of us were scratching our heads, and not because of no-see-um's. Without a word, he grabbed some line, tied the three alders into a tripod, and set the bottle in the center.

"Grab that straight stick and head down to the far piling," laughed Smokey. "We've got ourselves a Duck Cabin Level."

It worked. Just the ticket for Pete Dahl construction. We nailed 2X6's across the edges of each row of pilings, and used them as guides to cut off the tops by chainsaw.

By now it was getting late, and we were all becoming rummy. It had been an incredible day. We admired our first Pete Dahl sunset as we ate dinner. The elders had a nightcap, and then we all climbed into bunks that lined one wall of Andy's cabin for that satisfied, complete sleep one only dreams about in later years.

Day 2 — 26 July 1959

We awoke early the next morning stiff but eager. Sun peeking through clouds off to the east. Pot of coffee for the men, hot chocolate for me, a sweet roll for all. Shar, Dennis, and Mom not visible in their sleeping bags. The sound of soft quiet snores. A duck cabin, our duck cabin, rising from stacks of material thirty feet out the door. Everything wet with early morning dew. Already a light westerly, sure fair weather wind, with a promise to increase later in the day and drive away the mosquitos. Rays of sun casting long horizontal shadows and geese honking. That special time before a project resumes, to pause, breath deeply of fresh air, and visualize what is to come.

Not much Hi Ho, Hi Ho, It's Off to Work We Go necessary. Walked down the steps of Andy's cabin, and there we were. Twelve orderly sway-braced pilings stood before us. Wow. We did a lot in one day. Day Two of Adult Forthood about to begin. Can it get any better than this?

Even a rudimentary carpenter such as I knew that having things square and level was important. Everyone was surprised by the quality and quantity of work produced.

Harry, always with quick the the quip, commented: "Wow, Smokey, we need to patent that Beer Bottle Level."

Dad was stoking up his pipe, packed to the brim with his trademark Half and Half tobacco, guaranteed to chase off half the bugs. All of us tied on flimsy white cotton carpenter's aprons, standard workman's apparel of the day. Would hold little more than a hammer, pencil, tape measure, and a few dozen 16 penny nails.

Most of the lumber was rough cut 2X4 and 2X6 spruce and hemlock scrounged from Vina Young's old dairy building on Lake Avenue, which had collapsed years before in a wind storm. No two pieces were of the same width or thickness, and usually they tapered like icicles from one end to the other. The better ones had already been precut for studs and rafters. A pile of the more dimensionally challenged were stacked aside waiting to be used for blocking and bracing.

Sitting in a separate pile, however, were the Crown Jewels of a year's scrounging by Shellhorn Salvage Co., Don Shellhorn, President. Five sixteen foot long quality 6X6 beams. Where we purloined these I am not sure. Probably on what was popularly known around Cordova during that era as a Midnight Requisition, an euphemism for gathering material of questionable ownership under the cover of darkness. The key to this style of acquisition was to make sure the material quickly became hidden by ensuing construction. Or was utilized in a remote location. Such as Pete Dahl.

This common local pastime probably had it origins in the closure of the Copper River and Northwestern Railway in 1938. When it shut down, the company just walked away, leaving buildings and material everywhere. In remote regions such as McCarthy and Kennecott, everything quickly became fair game. The practice took a bit longer to catch hold in Cordova, and then gained exponential momentum when it became evident that much was truly abandoned and was just going to fall down or rot anyhow.

The same thing happened immediately after WWII, when the Army pulled out of their air base at Mile 13, leaving quonset huts and buildings scattered on a maize of roads in wooded areas north of the runway. As soon as the road to Mile 13 was completed, a favorite weekend activity for many Cordovans was to head out to the old airbase to see what they could load on their trucks and haul to town.

So there was no guilt involved in scrounging, day or night. In fact, it was a proud Cordova Tradition, and the best advocates were highly respected and admired for their ingenuity. Dad would build a couch at our cabin from CRNWR passenger car seats; the cabin entry door we use to this day came from a Mile 13 quonset hut; one of the most comfortable and sought after bunks in the cabin is an old hospital bed that still cranks up and down. Mom and Dad salvaged that metal monster from the Cordova dump and somehow hauled to the cabin in a 13 foot Boston Whaler. The list goes on and on.

Today it is nobly called recycling. Turns out Cordovans were just way ahead of the times. This rich tradition continues, especially when barges go adrift in the Gulf of Alaska and lose their cargo, or crash with vans intact on the shores of Montague Island. For several years in the 50s friends would invite company over to dinner and crack an institutional food size can of peas, string beans, or corn for the side dish. Veggies salvaged from containers on a military barge bound for Elmendorf Air Force base in Anchorage that ended up on Montague. Just recently, seiners could be seen pulling into the harbor deck-loaded with dimensional lumber gathered from the outside beaches after a storm swept everything off a barge in the Gulf.

So who knew, or cared, where those 6X6's came from? They were at Pete Dahl, in our pile of lumber, and therefore ours, about to become the beams of our cabin. Another local Axiom: Possession is Nine-tenths of the Law.

Dad, Smokey, and Harry started setting them in place, while I began sorting through a pile of 2X6 that were also commercial grade to find which would work for floor joist. Since the cabin was 16 feet across, they only had to be eight feet or a bit longer, to reach from the center beam to the outer walls. Rough cut wouldn't work for joist, or we would have one heck of a lopsided floor. I quickly discovered one of the quirks of lumber dimensions; 2X6's are actually five and a half inches across. Or supposed to be. So it took some time measuring and sorting.

By the time the guys had all the beams laid and drift-pinned into the piling, I had stacks of 2X6 ready to go. Smokey and Dad marked the joist layout on the beams, and we merrily banged away. Speeding cuts of the dimensional lumber was a gas-powered generator that growled like an angry bear. Dad called it a light plant, but the darn thing weighed a ton. Perhaps its name came from his early days in Seward, when an occasional lucky homesteader had such a machine to spurt wattage into electric bulbs and other equipment. Second hand, like everything else, this one took considerable hand cranking and generated significant verbal amperage before it would provide voltage of the sought after sort. An equally ancient skill saw would cause the old machine to lug down on tougher cuts. Hidden nails were discovered, with smoke and sparks emitting from the narrow and rapidly dulling blade's path. The show was reminiscent of 4th of July sparklers, and almost as entertaining. Despite deficiencies, it sure beat the alternative.

Setting the floor joist went fast, but nailing blocking between to prevent canting was tedious and hard on the thumbs. Somewhere we had squeezed in time for a quick breakfast after the sleepy heads arose. It was lunch time before we finished the floor joists. Still, good progress.

While enjoying another outdoor repast prepared by the Camp Cooks, we heard the sound of a boat from the west, and to our surprise cruising up Pete Dahl came a seine boat captained by Les Maxwell, towing a large work skiff. Both were laden with materials, as well as a crew of construction workers.

We were about to have serious cabin building competition. The Maxwell's were the Copper River Duck Shack Kings, as well as renowned local duck hunters. Hardly a slough on the Delta didn't have a Maxwell cabin on it at some time. Les and his father Buehl were famous for their pursuit of waterfowl. Recall Les had experienced hot hunting from a tent camp at Walhalla in the early 50s. So he had put in for a cabin site at nearby Pete Dahl, and drawn the easternmost lot. The plot was 100 yards away, with the slough bending out of view beyond it. We hollered greeting as they putted by and pulled up to the cut bank in front of their construction site.

Les walked to say hello and check our progress as their gang quickly set to work. This was going to be interesting. Talk about contrast. Maxwell and a Consortium of Investors had combined resources to build their cabin. It included an architect, Bobby Hamilton, who had designed the local bowling alley and later several buildings after the fire that wiped out much of Cordova's main street in 1963; Pogey Paulson, superintendent of Parks Cannery; Harold Nordman, local accountant; John DeLeo, former Cordovan and a commercial airline pilot; and John Sellen, a contractor from Seattle who was married to DeLeo's sister.

Every piece of building material for their cabin was top notch stuff. It included 8X8 posts that ran from underground vertically to the roof, which was designed to be hurricane proof. Why, they even had blueprints!. Undoubtedly the first duck shack on the Delta designed by a bonafide architect. Everything was pre-cut, with a plan for assembly. The roof was to be slightly rounded to shed rain; the rafters were shaped with a curved taper for such purpose. Much of the material came from the Park's Cannery supply yard. The sheets of siding metal were pristine, not a nail hole in sight. While the Boxcar and the Double Decker at Eyak had been floated intact to their sites, this had to be the first almost completely precut structure on the Delta.

It was going to be an easy assembly job for the pros, who would camp out on the seiner. The skiff would be used for runs down to the mouth of Pete Dahl to pick up additional materials dropped off at the Parks tally scow by Pogey's cannery tenders, including boxes of fresh food and liquid reinforcements.

We watched their operation for a few minutes, and then said what the hell, we're building a real duck cabin. There was pride of hard earned ownership in every piece of material, and we jumped back to work. They unloaded sheets of 4X8 3/4 inch plywood as we looked at a jig saw puzzle.

For next came the decking. We, too, had a stack of 3/4 inch plywood, mostly exterior grade, scavenged from concrete forms. Anytime a foundation was poured in town, or a bridge built out the road, Dad and I were on site, gathering up pieces of plywood coated with cement and filled with circular holes that were used for metal keepers to hold the forms in place.. We became adept at spotting potential highway sources through brush without binoculars, and always traveled with the tools of our trade in back of the truck: sledges, pry bars, hacksaws, chisels, nail pullers, hammers, hand saws, peevee, mattock, shovels, come-along, and more. We carefully monitored every construction project. Dad would pump the Boys for hot tips on Saturday nights at the Elks or Club Bar. MIght have even won salvage rights while playing poker in the back room of either establishment.

Not a single piece of our plywood was a complete 4X8 foot sheet. Harry, who never missed an opportunity to get Dad's goat, held up a small piece, gazed through a tight pattern of holes, and commented: "Well, at least you won't have to worry about ventilation. But bugs, shrews, and weasels might be a problem.."

Dad's rejoinder stopped the Scotsman. "Not to worry. It"ll be covered with battleship linoleum."

Banter is an essential ingredient of any construction project. This declaration was met with silence. Highly unusual. Had Dad actually outwitted the Scotsman? Harry possessed a considerable nautical background, including running boats for the U.S. Army while the tunnel was being built in Whittier, Alaska during WWII. But he didn't know what Dad was talking about.

"You know, Airy," said he proudly. "That stuff a quarter inch thick we pulled off the floor of the furniture section of the Commercial. Between cussing, you said it would sink a battleship."

Touche'

Despite the plywood's random shape, we had it pieced together and nailed down in an hour. Then we were in the phase of construction I came to love: framing the walls. It goes so fast, and is immensely rewarding to see walls suddenly pop up. With studs already precut to length, it was only the odd ball widows that took much thought. One window for each wall, no two the same size. Plus decisions about the height and location of each. The biggest, a square single pane picture window, obviously on the wall facing the slough and the south; a long skinny window to go over the sink, facing the east and weather; a medium size square window on the wall facing the north; and a smaller rectangular one facing west, in the direction of the outhouse, so we could keep track of patrons who might become lost in the dark.

All the windows were framed in wood, but certainly not pre-hung by today's standards. Installing them was going to take time and clever craftsmanship. For now, the key was to make sure the framed openings for them were large enough, square, and well built. Duck cabins on soft slough banks do considerable up and down settling, which could easily break windows not solidly supported.

But walls were flying together. Lay an entire one out on the deck; nail it together, and lift it up in place. Go man go. We didn't quit until late that day, after all the cabin walls were up and tied together. Incredible. The boys stood back and drank a Lucky Lager, admiring their work. Some one suggested this called for a B&B. Imagine that. Dad scurried to Andy's and returned with a bottle of the missing ingredient. The first of many a toast on the banks of Pete Dahl slough. Les came to inspect the project. Complimented us and of course had a shot too.

Mom and her young helpers had another fine dinner ready. We fell asleep with that marvelous exhaustion that comes from a day well done.

Day 3 — 27 July 1959

The fair weather continued to hold; Day #3, early to begin, skeletal vertical shadows of framed walls streaking across the grass as we stepped out from our camp. A chill in the air, despite the calendar; a chill of excitement down my back, at what I was seeing and doing. Pride and wonder; who could envision the years and generations of joy to come, from a pile of scrap lumber, alongside a muddy tidal slough.

We set to covering the framed walls with rough cut 1X6's. Not concerned about gaps between horizontal runs; it would have been impossible to make them all fit with the random dimensions of the material. Beside, the walls were going to be covered with tarpaper and then heavy roofing metal, from you guessed it, Vina's old barn.

The old electric generator was roaring, and the skill saw blade screeching, as we cut the ends to square up on studs. In an hour, we were halfway up the walls. Smokey took a look at the diminishing pile of 1X6, and decided we better shift to roof construction, making sure we had plenty of longer boards to cover it.

Common rafters. Ridge boards. Plumb cuts. Birdsmouths. Collar ties. Gable studs. Overhangs. Facia. A whole new vocabulary. It took all four of us to raise and nail the initial pieces in place, but then the pre-cut rafters went zipping up. Smokey's layout worked great. By lunchtime all the rafters were up, and work had begun on framing the gable ends.

Of course the pros to the east had already caught up. Their pre-fab dimensional lumber and standard size plywood certainly helped speed their progress. In fact, they were already almost completely closed in; soon to install pre-hung windows, hang new corrugated metal for siding, and then cover the slightly pitched roof with tarpaper.

Following a quick lunch break, back to the roof. Harry and I began covering it with 1X6, while Smokey and Dad worked on the gable ends and facia. Harry cut 1X6 to lengths I shouted down over the roar of the light plant. He would shoot them up, and I would nail them in place while advancing up the modest 2 to 1 pitch. Dad & Smokey finished their framing, and joined in. In no time, the roof was covered. Tarpaper next, and then more of that heavy gauge roofing metal. We had sorted out sheets that did not have too many holes or tears for the roof. Fortunately there was no need for purlins, as the entire roof was already rough cut 1X6, giving it a full inch depth. So we just nailed lead-headed roofing nails into every hole in the metal. Bending and wrapping sheets around the facia on the front and back ends took time, but paid dividends. Despite the constant battering from Copper River winds roaring down toward the back wall, the untreated end facia lasted more than 40 years.

By late afternoon, the roof was complete. Except for the ridge cap. Smokey and Dad shifted to installing the windows, one side at a time. First they had to finish running rough cut 1X6's up the wall and around the window opening. The stack was rapidly shrinking.

Harry and I were assigned to the ridge cap project. He cut the roofing metal into 18 inch wide strips which were then bent down the middle to roughly match the pitch on either side of the roof peak, creating a poor man's ridge cap. Naturally, I was selected to nail these pieces into place. Sections of metal with no holes had been selected, as we did not want to have potential leaks in the very top of the ridge line. So that meant nail holes had to be created on the outer edges of each section to fasten the metal down. No cordless drills back then. The tool of choice to punch the holes was a 16 penny nail, hammer powered.

Yipee. Back then roofing metal was the real deal. So thick and tough we later discovered shotgun BB's bounced off it when misguided hunters hit the outhouse by mistake while trying to ground sluice ducks on the back bond.

Nailing in the valleys of corrugated metal is a no-no, since this is where water accumulates and runs off the roof. The ridge cap overlapped the upper edge of metal sheets that ran almost to the roof top. Hence I was driving the 16 penny punch nail through two layers of metal that were not securely fastened down, with a tendency to flex and bounce, while trying to hold it in place by sitting with one leg on either side of the ridge line. Just delightful.

The nature of four letter invective has deteriorated considerably over the years, but I was cranking out a few choice specials from the 60s. And of course smashed the crap out of the thumb of my left hand, which was being used to hold the penetrating nail in place.

Let out a howl, followed by a string of timeless beauties. Stood up, and punished the offending hammer by throwing it as far in to the slough as I could.

G.O. Young's *Alaska Yukon Trophies Won and Lost* is a "must read" for fans of hunting tales. Times and standards were different back in the early 1900s, but evidently guides dealing with horses in their epic traverse across glaciers and rivers had well-polished terminology for every situation. In one particularly challenging area, the pack animals kept rolling down a steep river bank.

"Never before had I heard such profanity as on that day, and it increased as our troubles piled up. I have never heard men inject as many oaths into a single sentence as they did that night and the days that followed," wrote G.O.

Another favorite of mine: "At times it became so discouraging that the men halted and stood cursing for several minutes, even though a horse was down. Bones was so outclassed in swearing that he almost stopped for a while, but would occasionally remark, "Well this is just one continuous round of pleasure; if it ain't one d____ thing it's another."

My, if they only knew what the future held. My metal adversaries were earning a new generation of disparagement.

Dad and Smokey came running out to see what was going on, just as the tumbling implement splashed twenty feet from our anchored boat. Both seemed a bit stunned by the clouds of blue language steaming skyward from the rooftop. When the classic movie *The Christmas Story* came out in 1983, I immediately associated with nine year old Ralphie, who inadvertently cut loose with an F-Bomb after spilling lugs nuts in the snow while helping his Dad change a flat tire.

What's that saying about "a good carpenter never blames his tools"?

I climbed down off the roof. The guys examined the rapidly expanding appendage. Stuck it in a bucket of pond water, cooled off on multiple fronts, and went back to work.

"Not much else we can do right now," said Smokey. "But we'll fix you up tonight."

Oh boy. Something to look forward to.

We finished the ridge cap project. Smokey and Dad had the weather-side windows installed. Harry and I shifted back to nailing up 2X6 on the walls, with the Window Experts following us. It was well after seven before we called it quits. All the sides were covered, and the windows in place.

Definitely a B and B performance. Had I known the medicinal values of the more powerful of the two, I would have probably asked to join in. My finger was throbbing, a deep blue-purple-black discoloration under the bulging thumb nail.

While Mom was preparing dinner, Dr. Bernard went to work. Sought out his Medicine Kit, aka as a tool box, and fished out a small hand-cranked drill. I iced the thumb as he fit in a small bit. Kind of like watching a nurse adjust the needle for a shot, or a dentist testing the tooth drill. The surgical team had another BXB, and decided I was ready. They sure were.

Dad held my thumb down on a board; Harry held a spotlight; and Chief Surgeon Bernard went to work. Sharon and Dennis peered down from a top bunk in fascination.

Dr. B placed the drill bit dead center on my thumb nail, and started cranking.

What the hell, I was thinking between clenched teeth. Don't worry, it'll be over in a minute, said the Good Doctor.

How many times have you heard that, along with "this won't hurt."

It was and it did. Until a geyser of blood squirted upward several inches.

"Thar she blows," chimed Captain Ahab Curran.

The Peanut Gallery cheered.

Amazing. And instant relief. The Surgicial Team celebrated their success with BXB #3, Mom hurried to get dinner on the table before they all passed out, and I couldn't believe how much better my thumb felt. Took a couple aspirin and slept well that night. But surely not as well as the Pete Dahl Medical Team, who killed their aches and pains with another prescription of Ivan Doig's " Dr. Al K. Hall."

Day 4 — 28 July 1959

We arose to Day #4 bleary eyed with clouds in the east. A light breeze from that direction, harbinger of deteriorating weather. All moving slower, but motivated by the possibility of rain. Nothing like finishing exterior walls under water dripping off the roof. We all pitched in to quickly cover the east and west sides with tarpaper and then metal, as the gabled roof sloped in those directions. Then Smokey and I went to work covering the back and front of the cabin, while Dad and Harry tackled installing a space heating stove.

Don't know where Dad found that old Heatilator; they were the predominate source of warmth for many early Cordova homes. This was a beauty, and 54 years later is still one of the main attractions in our cabin when we first arrive, or return from any hunt. Open the carburetor, allow a small layer of gravity-fed stove oil to flow in the pot, light it by hand, wait ten minutes, and the cabin plus people standing by it are toasty.

Harry the Hardware Man was in his element, stringing copper tubing under the cabin, flaring the ends to fit the carburetor and oil barrel, running stove pipe through the ceiling, and installing the chimney. When not helping Harry, Dad was busy building a stand for a 55 gallon oil barrel on cantilevered 6X6 beam ends that extended beyond the back wall. Smokey was doing triple duty, working at all three tasks. Soon Harry had the oil line hooked up to the stove and everything in place. He and Dad lifted the drum on its elevated stand, connected the fuel line, and poured in 5 gallons of oil.

It wasn't noon, three sides of the cabin were covered with metal, and the heating crew had fired off the stove. Nice work. Mom, Sharon, and Dennis came over, climbed up temporary stairs, and checked things out. This is starting to look pretty cozy, was the consensus.

A light drizzle began falling. We took a break for lunch, prepared by Mom, proudly portered over by her Young Staff. Served inside, on upturned Blazo boxes, in our Own Cabin. Warm, dry. Tools and building supplies scattered everywhere. Mixed tang of stove oil, creosote, fresh cut lumber, and pipe tobacco in the air. Tinkle of rain drops on the metal roof. Awesome.

For the first of countless times, we peered out the front window. Light winds were shifting to the southwest, and with them would come gradually clearing skies. Which was a good thing. We still had much to do. Harry and Smokey were to depart on next morning's tide, towing the barge back to town before a run of smaller tides made it difficult to exit Pete Dahl.

At that young age, I was't thinking about the next project in line, but was confident there would be more to do. A half-century later that is still true. The Crew listed finishing the exterior metal; front steps; water barrel; propane cook stove; bracing.

And. Oh Yes, said someone brightly. We need an outhouse for this joint.

So far, a small privy behind Borer's had been our only option. Would be rather impolite to continue enriching some one else's back yard. Dad paced off eight steps from the back corner of our estate toward Swartzbacker's, checked out the view, and said, This looks like a great place. What do you think?

Lovely.

Outhouse technology at Pete Dahl was, and still is, rather basic. Dig a hole, drop in a topless 55 gallon drum, frame up a shelter, and you're almost in business.

The Crew looked at me. What da ya think, are you up to it?

It crossed my mind that perhaps this had been a late evening topic after I had crashed following my Thumbnail Root Canal, and the Drill Team was doing Post Op over BXB #4. But hey, my First Independent Construction Project. A Crapper. Woo - woo! We all have to start somewhere. X marked the Spot.

Proudly, I set to digging, and quickly discovered something called water tables. Silt isn't firm to much depth on the Delta. This was especially true back in the pre-earthquake days, when high tides topped slough banks.

It was hip boot time in a hurry. A 55 gallon drum is 36 inches tall. The excavation had to be deep enough to leave just a small lip above the ground. I had to dig down much further than had been necessary for the cabin piling. It quickly became a race between man and water, with mud sluffing into the constantly expanding hole. When the excavation was deep enough, it dawned on me the top was still on the oil barrel. Had to remove it by using a cold chisel and small sledge hammer, a time consuming process. The hole filled with water as I banged away. Bailed it out and dropped the barrel in. It gradually rose upward as water seeped back in. Oops. Need to punch holes in the bottom so that won't happen.

A sweaty, muddy, and cranky civil engineer was I by the time the barrel was buried to the brim, held in place by backfilled sod and mud, and filling with water again. Senior members of the cabin construction crew would drop by and offer encouraging remarks every now and then. Looks good. You're doing a great job. Keep up the good work. And the ultimate compliment: Can't wait to try it.

Next were four piling, all roughly four feet long, which had to be imbedded three feet down in muck surrounding the barrel. That I had just shoveled back in place. I began making mental notes of all the things I was doing wrong for future reference. Duck hunters are notoriously full of B.S. Something told me I would be doing this again.

Finally the pilings were in place. And somewhat vertical. Measured the diagonals to insure they were "square," as I had learned from watching Smokey and Dad with the cabin foundation. Time to install 2X6 braces, flush with the tops of the level pilings, to hold the foundation in place.

From there it was like building a mini-cabin. Made a small floor out of 2X4 and plywood. Smokey dropped over and quietly reminded me not to run a joist in the middle of the deck, where you know what would fall; and to cover only the forward half of the floor. The back half would be open, a wall to wall seat with a carefully centered hole eventually covering it.

Meanwhile, the guys were cruising. Smokey finished covering the front wall with metal, as well as installing the entry steps. Dad and Harry had the water barrel up, with a rain gutter on the roof edge to catch the runoff and fill the wooden stave drum. They had also carted a small second-hand four burner propane stove, complete with oven and broiler, into the cabin. Dad stacked five wooden Blazo boxes, longer side horizontal, on top of each other in the corner of the cabin. These would be our kitchen cabinets, as they still are today. The stove was tucked in right alongside them. Harry monkeyed around getting the propane lines hooked up to a tank directly outside, while Dad began building a frame for an old porcelain sink adjacent to the stove.

Wow. It was getting late, but this had been one helluva day. Unbelievable, in hindsight. Oil, water, and propane hooked up. Cabin exterior complete. Outhouse halfway done.

The Construction Crew at Maxwell & Co. Estates gave us a salute and wave as their boat pulled away, a brand new Castle to the East complete. Despite our head-start, not much doubt about who was going to win The Cabin Building Contest. We had work to do, but felt pretty darn good. B&B proud, to be sure.

Dinner, another look at what we had done, galvanized grey metal walls reflecting sun streaking through long horizontal clouds toward Hinchenbrook. A quiet, satisfied evening. Harry and Smokey, all of us, going to bed early, with departure of the Revenge and barge at daybreak.

Day 5 — 29 July 1959
Another early start. Mom, Sharon, and Dennis were still in their sleeping bags when the Revenge pulled away. Harry and Smokey had a quick cup of coffee and then piled on the 30 footer to head back to town, barge in tow. The Cyprus Express had performed admirably. We would run upriver to the road in the Misty later that day. Captain Curran took his navigational responsibilities seriously, but could not resist waving a cheerful salute.

Smokey did the same, looking at the cabin for what would be his last time. Sadly, he was one of the 111 who perished in the Alaska Airlines 727 jet crash outside Juneau in September 1971.

Dad and I finished banging the outhouse together, using whatever material was left, mainly 2X4, mismatched pieces of plywood, and the worst of the remaining roofing metal. Dad engineered the interior bench and seat while I finished the roof metal. A little math involved in locating the hole for the seat, but close enough. Installed a door made of 1X6's we had salvaged off an old storage shed, with a classic wooden sliding handle. Turns out the finishing touch, a toilet seat, had somehow missed the barge, and would have to wait for another day. Oh well. A few more deposits at the First Bank of Cordova.

Dad turned his efforts to interior work, specifically, more prep work for hooking up the sink; shelves in the entry; angle bracing on the walls; a temporary small couch made out of seats from an old Copper River and Northwestern Railway passenger car. Wow, were those "cushions" hard. People obviously had much better posture and more patience back in those days. Can't imagine sitting on such rigid, upright seats for the seven hour train ride to the mines at Kennecott.

Most importantly, we installed a door in the recessed front entry, which was set back four feet from the front edge of the cabin. This design would keep the door out of the weather, and also provide shelf space for keeping items cool. The door itself was steeped in history, coming from one of the abandoned Army quonset huts behind Mile 13. The cabin was now officially closed in.

As reward for my great job with the outhouse excavation, I was tabbed for another dirt project, this time digging holes for "dead men." Back then all the cabins were cabled down, so high tides, strong winds, and most importantly, ice moving out on big spring tides, would not shift the cabins or knock them off their pilings. The pond directly behind our cabin was a prime candidate for creating such problems. Heavy cable ran from huge eye bolts midway through the top of the east and west walls. My assignment was to dig a hole as deep as possible, in which we would completely bury piling, laid horizontally, and attached to the other end of the cable. Then large turnbuckles would be used to create tension on the tie-downs. This was SOP for most cabins on the Delta in the pre-earthquake days.

We squeezed in a quick lunch somewhere, scurrying to get as much done as possible on our last day. The southwesterly of the prior day continued, and it was fair, if not totally sunny weather. We had been very lucky to avoid the long rainy stretches common to the Delta, and this had been a key factor in our rapid progress.

Finally Dad glanced at his watch, realized high tide was only a few hours away, and said we needed to start wrapping things up, putting tools away, and getting organized for the trip upriver. Lo and behold, marching out of the next door cabin, came Mom, Sharon, and Dennis, proudly carrying supper over. Fried chicken, potato salad, beans, and a chocolate cake with one candle in the center.

We set up a folding card table in the middle of our spacious new cabin, sat on Blazo boxes, and had what would be the first of so many wonderful times in our Place by Pete Dahl Slough. Lit the candle to celebrate our first official dinner in a cabin that would have so many shining moments in our lives. Bare walls but full hearts, something a fifteen year old doesn't always recognize at the time.

We "lit the candle to celebrate our first official dinner in a cabin that would have so many shining moments in our lives." Our cabin at Pete Dahl, built in five days, by Dad, Smokey Bernard, Harry Curran, and I, July, 1959.

Then it was time to load the runabout and head upriver. Hard to believe it was our first cruise up Pete Dahl, but we found the cutoff towards Glasen's cabin easily. With the 18 horse purring, we zig zagged through sloughs until reaching the Race Track, immediately recognized from our repeated circumnavigations in the futile attempt to reach Pete Dahl a month earlier. The old Cordova Commercial van, plus a small trailer for the boat, were waiting for us when we pulled up to the small turnout and landing at 20 Mile. It had been dropped off by the ever cheerful and helpful Freddie Lantz.

Before departing the cabin, Dad did something that would become a 54 year

"The finishing touch, a toilet seat, had somehow missed the barge, and would have to wait for another day." I hold the ladder while Dad inspects my First Independent Construction Project, the cabin outhouse, July 1959.

tradition. Maybe it was just an impulsive gesture in recognition of how much we had done; perhaps it was unexplainable insight into how much the cabin would come to mean in our lives. I had hand-cranked the outboard, and was about to manually shift it into forward. We were all looking at a cabin that hadn't been there five days earlier. Ours.

Dad stood up, faced the cabin, bowed from the waist, and chanted "Allah, Allah," followed by a toast, this time with his beloved Lucky Lager. Where he came up with this expression remains a mystery; perhaps somewhere in his studies at Seward High. Dad would surprise us with poetry recitation or phrases in Latin when duly inspired. Maybe an extra year of schoolwork paid off. Late one cabin evening it was disclosed that he liked second grade so well, he took it twice.

To this day, we always pay similar tribute to the cabin, and quite often have a toast, before turning the bow west and heading upriver, grey waters and great times receding behind.

First Pete Dahl Cabin Log Entries
"The Beginning" taken from neighbors Log.

25–29 July 1959

"Barged in" with material for <u>our</u> Duck Cabin.

Thanks a million. —Anita

Like your cabin. —Sharon Shellhorn

Too busy working on our cabin to comment. Smashed my finger. —Dick Shellhorn

Swell of you to let us headquarter here. —Don Shellhorn

I sure got cold in the top bunk, only one blanket. —"Smokey" Bernard

Part III: The First Fall

We didn't make it back down again until Labor Day Weekend. Every trip was a combination build and hunt expedition. In those days all the cabins were full of hunters, and each weekend was highlighted by continued improvements on the cabin, as well as visits by cheerful neighbors.

Mom faithfully documented every trip that first year except the last, when Dad came down with Kenny Van Brocklin and Les Maxwell to close the cabin in late October. All the log entries were in her handwriting until October 31. Soon others would contribute. Entries became a tradition which continues to this day, creating a priceless history of people, place, and times.

By the end of 2013, 54 years of cabin history were recorded in seven three ring binders, covering 637 trips to the cabin, and totaling 1602 pages. More than three thousand entries, signed by 458 different family members, guests, and visitors, many now in Duck Hunter's Heaven.

Labor Day Weekend

5–7 September 1959

Took off from town Sat. afternoon for a long weekend at Pete Dahl Cabin. Beautiful weather every day. Frost every morning. Curtains hung and general cleaning done by Sharon and Anita. Outhouse seat on, sink in, walk to outhouse completed, and oil stove fixed. A grand weekend away from town and with ariel ? installed enjoyed marvelous radio. —Anita

Visitors: Dan Traub Busy Neighbors Les Maxwell, Dick Borer, Virginia Maxwell, Mike Noonan, Julia Nordman, Andy Swartzbacker, Mark Borer

Ducks: Dick 3 lost - 4 brought
Don 1 lost - 11"
Sharon 1 duck first shot!

COMMENT: *Gee I hope he didn't hurt.*

12–13 September 1959

Hunt out for evening - arrived too late. Had snacks at 9 P.M. and retired. 4 A.M. the waking hour. No ducks but a beautiful sunny day. 3 bunks put in also table "angled" in. Swartzbacker and Ekemo down with two friends. Callers were Flinn and Pogey Paulson - Pogey slightly cold in a sweat shirt. Used our new sleeping bags for the first time - real cozy. —Anita

No. ducks Dick - 000
Don - 000
Sharon - 000
Anita - 000

Then that memorable weekend in late September.

25–27 September 1959

Real good start - Curly Hoover kind enuff to loan skiff - have loan of 35 motor. Doc Leer with us. Dick & Mike Noonan in our boat, Sharon and Harry, Don and myself in big rig. Motor fails on big skiff so are towed down by Dick in the small skiff and Johnson 18.

Disastorous hunt on Sat. Eve at 5:30 Game Warden picks up the boys - shooting after dark!!! Lose guns, and birds must go to court on Friday at 1 P.M. No ryhme or reason for any of this Mr. Crane a shit heel from way back. Sunday rather sad - so sorry please. —Anita

Bag - Leer - 8 - 3 took by Shmill
Dick - 4
Don - 3

Sad state of affairs -

As is mentioned in Mom's entry, after the first two September trips in the over-laden Misty, we began augmenting our fleet with a boat Curly Hoover had loaned us.

That in itself was quite a story. The craft was a 22 foot plank Tiedeman work skiff that was the primary gillnetter of its era. This one was an earlier model, and had sat for years in Curly's yard near his house across from the Masonic Temple. Neighborhood kids had a grand time playing in it, pretending the tall surrounding grass was rough seas. The make-believe voyage was clearly perilous, for blades of turf jutting through open seams in the bottom indicated the ship was taking on water.

Recall Curly owned Hoover's Movers. Dad eagerly accepted the proffered craft with no prior inspection. It took about two minutes in late August for the derelict to show up on a Hoover's flatbed truck and be dumped unceremoniously in front of our house on Second Street. This was the ultimate in scrounging. Hmm.

The reason the skiff didn't make a run to Pete Dahl until mid-September was simple: it took us that long to make it seaworthy. Dad loved, and taught me a lifelong passion, for what he called Projects. This was a dandy, delivered right to our doorsteps. He couldn't wait to turn off the lights at the Cordova Commercial, hurry home, climb into work duds, fire off his pipe, and start puffing and puttering.

At first sight of our latest undertaking, he muttered something about "The Wreck of the Hesperus." A family phrase that came with him from Seward. Evidently his father must have been both Master Recycler and Longfellow fan.

Wood shrinks when dry and expands when wet. Gaps between the bottom planks were at least a quarter inch wide. Daylight shone through the fissured hull. This was not unique to our vessel. For centuries, shipwrights have been caulking seams on wooden boats. I was about to learn the trade.

From the hardware side of the Commercial came a caulking iron, rolls of caulking cotton, and tar-like caulking compound, with basic instructions printed on the gallon can: Trowel compound into gaps, roll out cotton, hammer firmly in place with caulking tool, seal with more compound, and feather smoothly.

No wonder the fleet was switching to plywood Banta skiffs.

Passing fishermen stopped to offer advice. More than one suggested a different boat. We persevered. The caulking project took several evenings, as well as multiple trips to the Commercial for additional cotton and compound. Freddie Lantz was on the phone ordering more from Seattle.

Finally, bottom seams caulked, we flagged down several passers-by and turned the boat over. Dad began rebuilding the transom and repairing cracked ribs. I placed the end of our garden hose in the boat, turned in on full blast, and ruefully watched the water vanish.

Cordova is famous for its rainfall. Good thing. We may drain the city water supply before the planks swell enough to hold water, thought I.

At least clouds of dust weren't billowing up as cars drove by. Watering dirt roads on sunny days was a Cordova tradition back then. The boat was doing it for us. We left the hose running twenty-four seven. Finally awoke one morning to dry streets and six inches of water in the boat. Hoorah.

Neighbors: What are those crazy Shellhorns doing, cheering for clouds of dust?

Meanwhile, I had continued caulking the planks that ran lengthwise along the sides. Water merrily squirted out those seams until they too became watertight.

Back then fishermen built clever bailers with a flat metal bottom, wooden sides, and a convenient wooden handle, to scoop water out of their skiffs. They were designed to fit between pairs of exposed bottom ribs. Dad made sure we had two.

It was early September before the boat was deemed launchable and perhaps floatable. It then dawned on us that the waterlogged craft had become so heavy an 18 horse outboard wouldn't provide adequate propulsion. We needed that Johnson for our smaller runabout anyhow. Hence Curly's loan of a 35 horse Gale motor. Which of course turned out to be another Project, as the log entry above indicated.

I wonder how long it took to tow the behemoth to the cabin. And if we were able to get the 35 horse outboard running, or towed it back. Neither were mentioned in the log entry. Other events of that weekend had clearly superceded this minor deficiency.

3–4 October 1959

Came down on Saturday around noon. Beautiful day. Dick hunted and got 1 duck. Dan Traub and Bob Mulcahy came over for a hot drink and were our guests for dinner - short ribs were good. Minnie and Al Swalling and Dick Borer stopped over. Smitty flew in and Mrs. Renfro flew back with him. Others around that afternoon Dr. and Mrs. Asa Martin, Mike Swalling and Chris also the Renfros and their boy Mike. Game warden checked their ducks. Saturday evening Pete Lovseth, John Kelsey and Bill Ekemo came over. Don won the game on pinochle we played. —Anita

SUNDAY: *Don and Dick out at five, Don "guiding." Listened to World Series game from L.A. —Anita*

Dad was guiding for good reason. Thanks to Protection Agent Crane and City Magistrate Moon, he didn't have a gun or hunting license. However it meant he did have extra space in the game pouch of his hunting vest for more alternative ammo, aka Lucky Lager. He also turned out to be a decent retriever.

Saturday, 10–12 October 1959

Dick, Kent & Fred Pettingill, Don and myself came down early Saturday morning. Boys hunted Kent got a very big goose. We worked around the cabin. Have a nice coat rack and the bracing is finished. Water froze in the nite as did the pond out back. Ekemo entertained Dick Downing, a geek in a brite red jacket, Banta, Davis of the team. Pat & Dick Borer called. Dan Traub & Bob down also. On Sunday Maxwells, Nordmans, Maxwellls' Jr. and John DeLeo arrived. It snowed a little. Dick Borer broke his 50 horse motor. Fred and Dick will take it in tonite. Also Mike will go in. —Anita

Total game
Kent 1 - 16# honker !!! 6 ducks
Dick 9 ducks
Fred 11 ducks - 1 brought back alive

Dad's 30 day suspension ended on October 26. Am sure Kenny Van Brocklin and the Boys reminded him when he showed up at the Club after work. Probably had to buy a round. Also time to oil up the trusty 16 gauge and head back down river for one more blast, at the birds and in the glass.

Saturday, 31 October, 1959

Ken - Les - Don - left town morning of 30th. Another notable trip - motor haywire had to go back to town for another motor - one good feature - Les got a honker first thing had just got into boat at landing. —Don

"It was early September before the boat was deemed launchable and perhaps floatable." Dad navigating "The Wreck of the Hesperus" down Pete Dahl, September 1959.

Maxwell shot 9 birds in one pond while Issac (Shellhorn) was watching boat too bad he was the last one off. Real good hunting trip my first at my good friend Shellhorn's new cabin, I feel real welcome since I have a part in one of the cabin windows! Total bag to date 1 goose 20 ducks mostly shot by Maxwell I did get six. We are now going to listen to Wash & UCLA and then up the river to home - sure glad (Issac) Shellhorn has his license back so we can get plenty of game. Thanks —Ken VB

Thus concluded our first year at Pete Dahl. Four amazing months. Never did we dream that our next summer would begin with major cabin repairs.

Chapter 7

Wind, Fire, and Earth

WIND: 1. Air in natural motion, as that moving horizontally at any velocity. WEBSTER'S
2. NW Fair, SE Fowl. PETE DAHL ADAGE

FIRE: 1. Burning mass of material. WEBSTER'S
2. Ready, Fire, Aim. PETE DAHL GUIDE TO WING SHOOTING

EARTH: 1. The present abode of mankind, as distinct from Heaven or Hell. WEBSTER'S
2. "Heaven's to Betsy," and "Hell's Bell's," common expressions of Grandmother Meda Shellhorn to describe future abodes. PETE DAHL ARCHIVES

"We can never know about the days to come…"

CARLY SIMON, "ANTICIPATION"

Part I: Foul Winds

"Blow ye winds aye over, blow ye winds aye a…"

OLD SAILING SONG

Early in the spring of 1960 small plane pilots crossing the Delta began reporting damage to cabins in the Pete Dahl area. In fact, one was missing. How could that happen?

No one was there to witness the events, but evidently a thick layer of ice from the pond directly behind the cabins had been lifted by big tides during a strong southeaster. The floating slab must have been blown against the backs of the four cabins located near the southwest edge of the pond. Our cabin and outhouse served as icebreakers, and bore the brunt of the damage. Likely these two structures saved both Borer's and Swartzbacker's cabins from the fate of the ADF & G "A" frame, which was carried all the way across Pete Dahl slough and unceremoniously deposited on its side on the western bank of the Lower Cutoff, almost a mile away.

17 May 1960

Mulcahy & Shellhorn across flats - ice really raised H_____ piling shot outhouse listing - porch gone - Happy Hunting - Mostly working. —Don Shellhorn

Looks like work for the next few weekends, ???????? —Bob Mulcahy

Our cabin wasn't even ten months old, and here we were rebuilding. No wonder Dad sounded discouraged. On June 19th, we came back down in a "new" second-hand 22 foot work skiff, this one a flat-bottomed plywood Banta model, powered by two 18 horse Johnson outboards - one from the Misty, the other brand new. This boat was much lighter, didn't leak, could haul big loads, and cruised along nicely. A big improvement over sCurly's plank "freebie."

We had painted this skiff grey with red trim, and installed styrofoam sheets between ribs under the floor boards, which made it self-bailing. Could leave it anchored at the 20 Mile landing with the drain plug out, rain or shine, and not worry about returning to a swamped boat. Two motors meant always having a backup if one faltered, which happened with alarming regularity. Plus the dual props seems to generate much more than a combined 36 horses in power. When not overloaded, we could keep up with Dick Borer's 50 hp rig. Navigating was a challenge. I had to stand between the two outboards, operating each tiller-throttle with one hand. The forty minute ride to Pete Dahl was particularly enjoyable on wet, blustery days, always facing into wind and weather, it seemed.

June 19th was Father's Day, so it was a family trip. Dad was in high spirits. Who cares, we're all here, headed to Pete Dahl, albeit to a leaning cabin with the porch and back row of piling gone, and a tilted outhouse to boot.

It was a trip of many firsts.

19 June 1960

Fine Father's Day trip, real good steak, everything lovely - work detail tomorrow.
—Don

Tilted outhouse and toothpic piling under cabin rather sad sight. —Anita

First time Copper down at are cabin. —Sharon

I got froze on the way to the cabin. —Joann (Peace)

First time for me at Shellhorn's nice cabin - almost as nice as Boxcar. Enjoyed
Chief Chef Shellhorns steak's - looking forward to more trips here. —Randy

Brought Copper Dahl to Pete Dahl successfully with a no-hitter (sandbars). First
time boat, Randy, Copper, & Joann here. Cabin in pretty rugged shape. Brand
new 18 started on 4th crank. Plan to come back down tomorrow and get with it.
—Dick

Copper was a purebred young golden retriever we had obtained locally as a
pup during the winter. More on him later.

The next day we ran back up river, dropped everyone off in town, picked up
my young friend Allen Swartzbacker, and headed back down with a load of material to begin repairs, arriving at 11:30 that evening. Up at 6 a.m. the following
morning, we replaced the back section of missing piling. This involved jacking
the cabin up to get the creosote supports back in place. A crewman from the tally
scow anchored at the mouth of Pete Dahl brought us up a load of materials that
had been sent out by tender; we looked for more cabin pieces by boat with no
luck. So we ran all the way up the river to 27 Mile for a load of timbers, getting
back late in the evening.

Another 6 a.m. alarm the following morning. Installed and repaired crooked
piling under the cabin. Had to cut the handles off shovels so we could work in
the 30 inch clearance beneath the cabin floor. One of them still lays under the
cabin. Les Maxwell, Harold Pernula, and Louis Hasbrouck showed up around
noon with Les's outhouse, which they picked up half a mile down the slough.

On June 23rd, we finished the piling work, and installed cross braces under
the cabin. Also straightened up the outhouse using a come-along. Dick Renner
and Paddy Fitzpatrick came up river and had lunch with us. Then it was time to
head home. The cabin was back in shape.

20-23 June 1960

I lost 2 bucks on the Johanson - Patterson fight. Patterson knocked the Swede for a loop. —Dick

See Dick and Allen coming back, green grass waving in the wind, sun bright, quite a sight. We are having king salmon tonight, Louis gave us. Better get the pan on. —Don

Made a bomb run and was right on target. —Allen

It wasn't easy but lots of fun. —Don

What followed was the busiest summer and fall in the cabin's 54 year history. We made a total of 18 different trips to Pete Dahl before impending winter shut things down.

The famous "battleship" linoleum was finally laid in late July. Harold, Julia, and young daughter Ann Nordman were along for that trip. The Nordman's were quite a couple. Nord, as he was called, stood six feet tall and weighed around 300 pounds. Most of it amidships. He was a bright fellow, CPA in fact. Ran an accounting and insurance firm. His tongue was as sharp as his pencil, and his ability to mold four letter invective was even better than his talent for making sure every one of his clients received a tax refund at the end of the year.

Wife Julia was almost manly in appearance; slender, short cropped hair, never wore a dress or skirt, liked to hunt ducks and give Nord hell. Her family ran canneries in Alaska; and there was little double about who captained the ship in the Nordman household.

Nord seemed to thrive in his role, and spent most of his time in a small office on Second Street, bottle of "loud mouth" in a bottom drawer. Closing hours usually meant a trip to nearby adjacent pubs, before roaring two blocks up a steep hill in his Jeep Grand Cherokee to their main floor home in a three story apartment building. Often wonder if Julia looked out the window to see Nord, just down the hill, in action. Maybe that's why he moved his office to the back, and hired a receptionist in front. Wearing ear plugs was probably an unwritten part of the her job description, to counter the blue-colored verbiage issuing from the boss's office.

Nord thrived on the art of conversational repartee. One Saturday afternoon on the way home from skiing on the nearby Mt. Eyak area, I stopped by his office to pick up my tax return. It had been a warm, sunny late March day, I was in my ski boots and gear, sweaty from a great day on the slopes. I peeked in the door to his office, and Nord was busy chatting it up with one of Cordova's more attractive young wives. Gathering data for her fisherman husband's tax return, I assumed. Her back was to me, so I just gave Nord a little wave indicating I would wait outside until he was done. Most of Nord's customers weren't this good looking. It might take awhile.

I stepped back, assuming I was out of view, and tried not to eavesdrop on the conversation. Nord liked a warm office. Make his clients sweat a bit. I was already doing that after skiing all day, and it was becoming toasty, to say the least. My long john underwear started driving me crazy, so I reached down and tried to rearrange them a bit. Unbeknownst to me, Nord was watching the whole show.

From his office comes this utterance: "Jesus Christ! Are you just going to stand there scratching your ass all day, or are you going to tell me what the hell you want?"

Mrs. X's pretty black hair flipped in lovely fashion as she turned around, Nord smiling in glee. Talk about getting caught red-handed. Forget the IRS. I mumbled something about coming back later, and ran into the glass door trying to escape.

The Nordman family joined us on every Xmas Tree Hunt. The poor spruce didn't stand a chance. Nord always showed up with this screwball Walter Matthau style hat and a bottle of V.O. Sometimes with a hand saw. Rarely went more than ten yards from the vehicle to get his "bird."

One year the weather was particularly foul, so the women opted to stay home and make chili for us brave hunters. So it was Dad, Nord, and I, all in our little blue Nash Rambler station wagon, off to brave the elements. The Hunt must go on. Wasn't quite apparent where they planned to put two Xmas trees, but there was a large coil of rope in the back, so whatever. Maybe we'd tow 'em in.

Anyhow, the weather was really crappy. A wet whiteout. Trees were covered with so much snow you couldn't tell a good one from a bad one. Nord wasn't about to get out of the car. The bottle of V.O. was vanishing between the Deadeye Duo in the back seat, scanning for the Perfect Tree through fogged up windows. Finally, after a couple hours, Nord realized it was getting dark, pointed out the window in authoritative fashion, and said " Hell, that's a good one right there, let's get it."

Which we, that is, Dad and I, did. As we were dragging the spruce back to the road, a police vehicle pulled up with lights flashing. They weren't Xmas bulbs. Dad asked what the problem was, and the officer replied: "Do you know it's illegal to chop down Christmas trees inside the City Limits?"

The visibility was so bad and the windows so steamed up, we were on the town side of the Powder House.

Oh, boy. First Dad loses his shotgun for hunting ducks after hours; now he and Nord are going to lose their saws for shooting trees inside the City Limits.

The Accountant somehow held his tongue in check. Dad, now an expert at dealing with Authorities after the Crane Fiasco, sweet-talked the officer, imploring the Spirit of Christmas. We drove home with an scrawny tree and a story that spread around town faster than Santa's sleigh.

When patrons were about to leave the Club, barkeep Kenny Van Brocklin would entice them for another round with: "Did you hear the one about Nord and Shellhorn getting busted for illegal Christmas tree hunting?"

Oh. The "battleship" linoleum? Fifty three years, and countless abuse later, it still adorns our cabin floor.

23 July 1960

Don and Dick, with on-the-side help, laid linoleum today. Nord was in his usual form - full of booze - big talk - no action. Go home after midnight on big tide. —Julia

Did lay linoleum. Hootch gone, beer running out. Dismal. —Don

No more loudmouth - sh_t. —Nord

My older sister Donita, a medic in the Air Force at the time, came home on leave and finally made it to Pete Dahl. Welcome back. Was given a paint brush and put to work.

13 August 1960

First trip down - crab good, beer better, aiming for the Sky Tomorrow with an Air Force Blue ceiling. —Donita

Mixed paint for ceiling. A/2nd Donita and Dick got blue (a little on the floor too). Repaired Rose Room (outhouse), got wet fixing external walk. —Don

Doc Leer showed up in mid-September to run his Eye Clinic in the basement of our house, and hunt ducks on the weekend. The road was washed out just beyond Sheridan River bridge. That wasn't about to stop us.

Friday, 17 September 1960

Another notable expidition - (Dick - Harry - Anita - Don). Eyeball Leer (getting his last buck) so he could pay us off, for services rendered, rent, booze, etc, held up start until 5 p.m. Road still washed out - Dick and I forded wash-out. Had punt to lighter - Hank Strom and crew helped pack gear, Mantilla and Mart

*Rude damming water so real low, crossed easily. Used F & W truck to landing.
One motor acting up so little slow coming down - arrived at cabin about 9:30
p.m. Crab feed and then in sack. —Don*

Three relatively uneventful weekend hunts followed. It was becoming late in
the season, and most of the birds had moved through. On the weekend of October
23, the weather was too nice and hunting was poor. Dad, Randy, and I took advantage of big tides to close the cabin.

During the following week, the weather turned southeast, which meant rising
temperatures, wind and rain. The three of us succumbed to Green Head Fever,
and headed back down to the cabin. Yikes. It was one day shy of the latest we ever
stayed in the fall.

30 October 1960

*This is it! - Randy - Dick - Don. Final closing of cabin. Ran out of stove oil,
blowing and cold!! Too much for even the birds - few left but on way south
- Collins buzzed us with his plane - Goodby cabin 'til next year. —Don*

"Closing the cabin" became an automatic process for us, but may puzzle those
not familiar with winters on the Copper River Delta. Cold winds from the Interior
funnel through narrow mountain passes and roar down the Copper River throughout the winter. Pete Dahl Slough is on the western edge of this weather pattern.
The water level of the river drops dramatically, so most of the sloughs dry up. All
the ponds freeze, as does the water remaining in the sloughs. Tides lift and float
the slough ice, creating layers of skim which makes travel by outboard powered
boats impossible. The cabins are inaccessible by river boat from late October until
breakup in April or May.

More than once we have stayed too late. Waking up to snow on the ground,
with ice sheets grinding against the banks and anchored boats, is not a pleasant
experience. Of course there are those late season flights of tugboat-size, four-curl
greenhead mallards as enticement. They and bands of trumpeter swans are the
last to leave, and more than once we have had to break decoys out of ice in the
ponds as part of our Exit Act.

Before departing, the cabin must be protected from six months of brutal
weather. Windows are covered with shutters; water drained from the barrel; rain
gutters taken down. The metal oil barrel is filled to the brim to prevent water
condensation; propane tanks stored inside; chimney stacks covered; all food and
beverage that could freeze returned to town; batteries disconnected; antennas

taken down; equipment such as chain saws, weed and brush cutters, lawn mowers, and generators winterized and stored inside; the more recent solar panel dismounted and stored out of the weather; kayak and punt covered under the cabin; the list goes on and on. A day's work, minimum.

Surprisingly, snow load is not a concern. The Copper Winds take care of that. Ptarmigan hunters on snow machines have found the brush line a mile below the cabin to be a popular winter hang-out for flocks of the white-plumed birds, and have repeatedly mentioned their amazement at the lack of snow upwind of the cabin and on the roof. It just blows away. Of course the lee of the cabin is a different story. There it piles up sixteen feet to the peak of the roof, with wind creating a huge drift that extends all the way across the slough. The packed snow becomes so hard it would be almost impossible to dig in to the cabin entrance, which is totally buried.

The cabins are truly closed during those long winter days and nights.

When the front window shutters had been open, our cabin had a busy year. The list of those that spent nights included Don, Anita, Donita, Dick, & Sharon Shellhorn, Bob Mulcahy, Randy Bruce, Joann Peace, Allen Swartzbacker, Pam Van Brocklin, Debbie Nicolet, Harold, Julia, and Ann Nordman, Jerry Behymer, Jessie Corliss, Bob Daniels, Ken "Hook" Van Brocklin, and Harold Mitchell.

Among the visitors that dropped by to shoot the breeze, share dinner, and sample the hospitality were Les Maxwell, Louie Hasbrouck, Harold Pernula, Dick Renner, Paddy Fitzpatrick, Bob Paulson, Sig Lee, Bill Otey, H.Z. Hanson, Pat Flinn, Andy, Trudy, Linda, and Andy Jr. Swartzbacker, John DeLeo, Dave Savoy, and Dan Traub.

Plus likely several others that forgot to enter the log, or were incapable of doing so.

Part II: Fair Winds

"The summer wind, came blowing in, from across the sea..."

FRANK SINATRA, "THE SUMMER WIND"

The winds blew our way in '61 and '62. Life was a westerly. Ten cabin trips in 1961 alone. Visitors, projects, family, fun, and hunting. Even shot a few birds.

20 May 1961

First time this year to go to cabin... cabin in fine shape... kids in sack... fine radio and a good place to dance. —Don

Lovely day. Walk reinstalled, so time for loafing. ... Will run down to tender on the tide. Thought we saw smoke and a fire at mouth of Pete Dahl so will check... (later noted false alarm) —Anita

Boy is it hot! —Sharon

What a day, and why go to Palm Springs? All we need is a few Palm trees. —Dick

On July 16 Grandmother Meda Shellhorn made her first, and only trip, to the cabin. It was she who fired a rifle to signal help when Dad's father William Shellhorn passed away in 1944 at their homestead cabin on the Kenai River across from Cooper's Landing, directly below the modern-day site of the Kenai Princess Lodge. For some reason I remember one of her favorite sayings when things went awry was "Hell's Bells!" I suspect she had practiced the phrase many times during those incredible years on the Kenai Peninsula. She didn't have to invoke it during this visit.

16–61 July

Arrived at the cabin 9:00 PM. Don-Anita-Dick-Sharon - (Gram) My first trip to the Pete Dahl cabin. Dick Skipper. —Meda

Fine trip - fixed radio antenna - went to scow - leaving at 4 P.M. —Don

Nice weekend - fried chicken and all. —Anita

In late July Mom's sister Evelyn and her husband Al drove all the way to Valdez from Anacortes, Washington, and then took the ferry to Cordova. It was their first visit to Alaska. They quickly discovered it rained in The Friendly City.

23 July 1961

Arrived at the cabin 8:30 PM on Sat July 22 - after 5 days in Cordova's rain belt... After hearty meal in the warmed up cabin - we all dropped into the bunks - and to sleep. By 9 AM Sunday we were up... sun came out - ah - what a treat. We sunned ourselves and took a cruise to the Tally Scow with Dick at the helm, on return with one motor clonked out... We have enjoyed our visit and the relaxing days, even if it was raining. —Evelyn and Al

Mom's older sister Evelyn was a big, attractive, gracious farm gal. Their parents were of German heritage, and owned a dairy farm near Lowell, Washington. The two sisters and four brothers knew all about hard work, and could milk a cow.

Al was about a foot shorter than Evelyn. An interesting couple. He labored his entire life in a plywood mill in Anacortes. Suspect when the horn blew ending the workday, the veneer makers discussed knot holes at a nearby pub before going home.

Somehow Mom and Dad decided Sharon and I ought to ride back to Washington with Evelyn and Al. The visitors thought this was a great idea, so off we went. It was a memorable trip.

The car they drove up the Alcan was a huge Plymouth four-door sedan. Had tail fins that looked like they belonged on a fighter jet, and drank gas just about as fast. Back then the highway was about 50 - 50 gravel and pavement. It was a long and often dusty cruise. Aunt and Uncle took turns driving. Strangely, usually about three in the afternoon, Al at the helm, we would glide to a stop and he would say: "Yup. Think it's time to check the spare."

He would hop out of the car, circle to the stern, open the back trunk, and be gone for about five minutes. Evelyn would slide over to navigate. Al would come back rosy cheeked and re-energized. Hmmm. "Well, the spare looks OK" would be his comment as he slid into the passenger seat.

One late afternoon, right on schedule, Al had checked the spare, and we were cruising along. Evelyn, who had been driving for quite awhile, asked her other half to look at the road map. Whoa. It was quite a ways to the next stop and motel. She needed a break. Al said no problem, he would be quite happy to drive.

Indeed.

We came around a bend, and there stood a flagman. Road work. New asphalt being laid. Gave us succinct directions about driving on the left hand side over gravel subsurface for the next several miles. Away we went. Evelyn dozed off, Shar and I were nodding in the back seat. The seas had become amazingly calm. Next thing you know a horn was honking, lights were flashing, and we all jerked awake as Al took several hundred yards to rein in the behemoth.

An irate construction worker knocked on the window. Al rolled it down. What in the hell are you doing? Heading back to Washington. You're in the right lane! Don't you drive in the right lane in Canada? Not when it's ****************** new asphalt, you *********!

Oh my. Sharon and I glanced out the back window. Dale Fowler, high school math teacher, had taught us that parallel lines never meet. Somewhere on the horizon, Plymouth tires indentations in the still warm asphalt distinctly converged. Al had proved Euclid wrong. Oops. I forgot. Al had made an entry in the Cabin log too.

23 July 1961—Algot Andersen

Early September hunting was slow. But things livened up late that month. First Barton Stanton and Bill Knaack, old friends of Dad's from Seward, came down. Stanton was Dad's boyhood buddy and ptarmigan hunting partner, Knaack was an long time guide from the Kenai who had hunted sheep with Dad and his father. Eyeball Specialist Leer managed to miss the plane out of Ketchikan on the 29th, but showed up on the 30th. It was quite a crew.

30 September 1961

Having a wonderful time (one duck so far) but give us time there's still stuff left to drink. —B.H. Stanton

"H.A." 2nd Class Leeeeer here - Dick and I picked him up at airport. As usual all fouled up - no clothes - Blonde in Ketchikan took him. —Don

Would have wonderful time, except SHELLHORN WAS HERE!

Leer, HA 1st Class Waited 30 years for this trip and sure have enjoyed it. Dick is real cook and top skipper. Hope to try it again. —Bill Knaack

And then, one of the classic all-time entries in the Cabin Log. Leer showed why he was former Editor of Cordova High's newspaper, *The Northern Light.*

1 October 1961

Got up at 3:30 a.m. for the morning hunt. On to Walhalla. The weather was clear. I got my usual limit in ten minutes so sat around and watched the rest of the boys wear themselves out. Shellhorn was his usual unpleasant self, behaving like a Horse's Ass, missing birds, shouting obscenities at the skies, brandishing his gun, giving that loud braying jackass laugh, etc, etc, and finally brought in three birds which I think he found someplace. Don Cook stayed at the cabin and got one. Bill Knaack got three and Barton Stanton five. Dick played retriever. Back at about 10 a.m. for breakfast prepared by Master Chef Dick Shellhorn. It appears that we are way over-stocked on food supplies. When I offered to buy the food and booze I had something sensible in mind like macaroni, beans, cereals and possibly a nice piece of salt pork and a couple bottles of inexpensive wine. So I find we have steak, ham, cold cuts and V.O.! I also suspect that Shellhorn has a couple extra cases stashed away under the cabin which were charged to my account. —Leer

A few more hunts, and then it was close-up time.

22 October 1961

Lock er up for the year. —Nord

I had a real good time all year; thanks. —Jerry Behymer

This is it (Too Bad Joe) —Don & Dick

Fall of 1962 was the start of a ten year stretch in which I rarely saw the cabin. I graduated from high school that spring. Between college at University of Alaska and Oregon State, student teaching, marriage to my high school sweetheart Sue Ekemo in December 1966, a year teaching in Hawaii, two years in the Army Signal Corp, including a 13 month tour in Korea, a year's graduate school at the University of Alaska, a year teaching in Kodiak, and summers spent working on tenders, seining, and doing construction work, there wasn't much free time. Sue and I returned to Cordova for good in the fall of 1972 when a high school mathematics teaching job opened up.

Other than arriving late in August to prepare for the upcoming duck season, there were no trips to the cabin during the summer of '62. On June 2, I dropped by briefly with a fellow from Iowa named Dick Gardner while tagging salmon for ADFG.

2 June 1962

Biologist Shellhorn. I put in the stairs, checked the water barrel. Everything AOK. —Dick

On August 28th Sue and Johnny Ekemo came with me to run our work skiff all the way from town around Whitshed to the cabin. Just a sophomore in high school then, it was quite a trip for Sue. Two hours in an open boat, but nice weather. At that time we didn't have a trailer for the big boat, and stored it in town until we found time to launch it at Park's Cannery near the Cordova boat harbor.

28 August 1962

Dickie brought me and Johnnie down. It's a real neat cabin. I'm glad we came, I got stuck in the mud. Dick's cooking wonderful (?) —Sue Ekemo

Helped (?) Dick open up the cabin for the season hunts. Built some blinds on Pete Dahl point and above the cabin. I lost a game of rummy and had to wash dishes after the delicious meal. —Johnny Ekemo

Late evening fog rolled in, which wasn't unusual after a warm sunny day followed by cooling temperatures at dusk. Had a heck of a time finding our way upriver. Couldn't see the opposite bank of the slough, it was so thick. Dad and Louie Hasbrouck were waiting to pick us up at 22 Mile in the old maroon Cordova Commercial van.

They had sat quite awhile. In fact, ran out of beer and almost headed back to town when it started getting dark, thinking we had decided to wait until the next day due to weather. Luckily they heard the outboards in the fog, and were there when we arrived.

Anchored the boat, tossed the engines in the long back cargo area, and crawled in around them. Louie and Dad were up front in the two bucket seats, puffing on cigar and pipe respectively, as we rattled back to town.

It was Sue's welcome to Pete Dahl Adventures, Inc.

We did make it down for the traditional Opening Day Hunt on September 1st.

31 August 1962

Art Knight, Sharon, Pam, Dick & myself left town early in the afternoon. Had to transfer equipment at 14 Mile Bridge under construction, to Louie Hasbrouck truck. (Maroon Monster still pretty good). Anita slaving away for me (nice gal) at the store. Bright sunny day, took us about forty minutes down. Cabin in fine shape, everything set for tomorrows - first shoot! "Scotty" Curran stopped in with the "Shad" (note: the Shad was a small ADF&G power scow type vessel). First visit to cabin since barge trip with cabin material. —Don

1 September 1962 (Opening Day)

Lots of birds - Art got a goose - Dick and I our limit on ducks. Went to Boxcar to check on construction operation. Nord and Baille there - Ken and Randy in town for material. —Don

3 September 1962

Will skin some ducks for dinner prior to our trip to Anchorage on Wednesday to drive Dick to college. —Anita

Pam and I were cooks and we didn't cook one whole meal!? —Sharon

Sharon and I was cooks, but didn't cook much. Had duck one night. Had fun. —Pammy V.B.

One of most successful hunts we've had, especially the first morning. Thought a couple times might have to stick my gun barrel in the pond to cool it off. Dad did some beautiful shooting- would have really shaken Leer up if he had been here. Wish could hunt some more later on - really going to miss these expeditions. Have lots of successful hunting trips, and enjoy the World Series. —Dick

The next trip to the cabin wasn't until a month later.

Saturday, October 6th, 1962

First time down since Navigator Dick left - no problems. Art Knight, Harry & Dean Curran, Chuck Wright, Jerry Behymer, and myself. Arrived around 7 p.m last night…

Wish you were here Dick. Had to whip the boys to get anything Done! —Don

Had a real good time. Wish Dick was here to get up in the morning instead of me. —Jerry

12 October 1962—Columbus Day

Anita and Cap't Shellhorn down to cabin at noon . Since no hunting partner went up back of cabin - got one duck. Had a fair shot at some snows but missed. Such a beautiful night orange moon out bright and full (Love This Country). Miss you Dick. —Don

The next day, Dad ran up river to pick up Chuck and Peggy Wright, plus Pam and Sharon. Hunting was slow, the weather turned foul, so it was dinner and poker. Don and Hattie Van Brocklin came over from Maxwell's cabin for a card session.

Saturday, 13 October

Swell dinner moose steaks (thanks Dick), fresh crab (thanks Wrights). After dinner had a little poker game with the Wrights and Don and Hattie. —Don

Sunday, 14 October 1962

Marvelous weather and gorgeous view of mountains coming to the "After Hours Club." All the requirements such as good food, fine service (candle-light), wine list the very best. Slept like dead dogs after a lesson in poker playing… Don and Chuck both got in their "morning shoot" from the bunks. —Peg

The following weekend was late October and cold. A very young lad from two cabins over dropped by to warm up and make a memorable entry.

20 October 1962

I had a peanut butter cup. I hope to get two ducks. —Mark Borer

21 October 1962

Now getting ready to go home; it is blowing and half rain and snow. —Anita

Dad was so busy closing the cabin he forgot to write in the log. Dick Borer came over from his cabin for a shot of V.O. before heading up river.

21 October 1962

Goodbye cabins - for another year. May next season be better. —Dick Borer

It wasn't.

Part III: Fire

"I've seen fire and I've seen rain,
I've seen sunny days that I thought would never end…"

James Taylor, "Fire and Rain"

Dad had a saying for almost every situation. One was "Take 'er on a slow bell."

Sirens began howling and bells ringing early in the morning of May 2, 1963. What happened that day was anything but slow, and brought his and many other Cordovan lives to an abrupt stop and detour.

Dad moved from Seward to Cordova in the early 30s to work for Blum - O'Neil Company, a clothing and hardware enterprise on Main Street. Alaska business icon Cap Lathrop purchased it in 1934, and formed the Cordova Commercial Company two years later. In 1944, Dad, Fred Lantz, Edith Paul, and Tom Verig purchased the company. It was the biggest business in town.

When the Army came in to set up camp and construct the airport at Mile 13 during WWII, it was "the Cordova Commercial Company that continued to amaze the regiment by getting them out of one hole after another with the diversity and quantity of their stock," stated a research paper by the Cordova Historical Society titled *Building The Mile 13 Airport and Cordova's Military Base 1941-1944.* The article mentioned 6 inch stove pipe elbows as an example. The Army had lots of six inch stove pipe for Coleman stoves that were used to heat their tents, but no elbows. The Commercial came to the rescue by providing a couple hundred.

In the 50s, I often helped Dad haul freight to the store. We slid boxes down a ramp that opened up on C Avenue, and then stored the stock in a massive basement. Hardware in dark row after row of shelves extended back in history to early railroad days. Miner's helmets at the far end of one aisle fascinated me the most. By 1963, Dad, Edith, and Freddie were the remaining partners in a thriving enterprise selling clothing, hardware, and furniture, as well as housing multiple apartments and offices on the upper floors.

Within an hour, it was all gone.

"FIRE DESTROYS BUSINESS AREA OF CORDOVA," read the headlines of the May 9 *Cordova Times*, published by mimeograph as the Times Building and its presses were among the many structures destroyed in the blaze.

"At 4:10 a.m., Thursday, May 2, 1963 the Cordova Volunteer was called out for a fire that had already spread full breadth of the Club Cafe and back of the Club Bar...Within minutes after starting, flames had spread north and south.."

Old two and three story wooden frame structures, built in railroad days, crammed side by side, lined the entire Main Street block between C and B Avenues. Before it was over, they were all a pile of smoldering rubble.

The flames marching north quickly engulfed the Cordova Commercial, right next door to the Club.

For Dad, the devastating fire was filled with sad irony. The blaze began in the rear of the Club, owned by Dad's closest friend Kenny Van Brocklin, plus his brother Don and third partner Bill Sherman. There were issues with insurance, handled by Harold Nordman, another close family acquaintance. Eventually settlements were paid, but the building was not insured to replacement value. Dad wanted to rebuild; partners Edith and Freddie were older, and decided to retire. Dad approached Andy Swartzbacker about reconstruction. He worked in the Commercial's hardware section, but said no.

At age 51, Dad was back to Square One. Ouch. It was a tough time. He and Mom decided to go it on their own, forming Shellhorn's Clothing, which opened soon in a small space adjacent to the National Bank of Alaska, across the street from the block destroyed by fire.

Another plot twist developed when reconstruction began on the fire sites. Flinns' Clothing, operated by Pat Flinn, had been the Commercial's longtime local clothing competitor. Swartzbacker teamed up with Flinn to build a new Cordova Commercial and Flinn's Clothing on the very sight of Dad's former business.

Meanwhile, Pete and Lil Lovseth rebuilt on the corner where Rosswog's and Flinn's buildings had operated prior to the fire. They leased half the building to Mom and Dad, who relocated Shellhorn's Clothing there, directly across B Avenue from the Alaskan Bar. On the very site of Flinn's Clothing prior to the fire!

No wonder at closing time Dad headed across the street to the Alaskan Bar for a cold one with Bob Korn.

All this history flashed through my mind when noticing Mom's name was not once entered in the Cabin Logs during 1963. Why?

Someone had to mind the store when Dad headed to Pete Dahl. It was his faithful partner and wife.

Dad opened the cabin on July 27th. It was the only time his brother Willard and his two sons visited the cabin.

27 July 1963

Fast trip (1st of year) down about half hour - Willard, Carl, Bill, & me. Saw few flapping honkers. —Don

A Rose Among Three Thorns. —F.W. Shellhorn

I had a blast. —Carl Shellhorn

Some time after that Rae Baxter who supervised the salmon tagging operation when I worked for ADF&G the previous year, dropped by and wrote in the log. No date was given. He used rain barrel water to make a pot of coffee. Seagulls liked to perch on the cabin roof during the summer.

Summer 1963

Stop over from Martin River Salmon surveys - lots of red salmon and brown bears. This water makes the damnest tasting coffee. Reminds me of a chicken coop. —Rae Baxter

Dad, Jim and John Wilson, and I made the opening day hunt. Then on September 3rd we picked up Steve Leirer, a college friend I met at U of A from Seward. It was quite a safari.

3 September 1963

Have seen more ducks here on the flats on this first day than I have seen in a season in Seward. Used one box of shells to get warmed-up. Bagged three. Will have to do better tomorrow. —Steve Leirer

4 September 1963

Steve and Dick to town - Karl Barth gave them 20 ga - instead of 16's - Grrr! —Don

5 September 1963

The great Seward hunter spent the afternoon sleeping in the blind - conserving ammo he says.

Totals to date:
Steve - 15 (1 goose)
Dick - 17
Pop - 3 geese
4 ducks —Dick

The Captain (Dick) slept a while too. He is ahead of me in the bag, but I have more shells for tomorrow. My one goose is worth 5 ducks. —Steve

6 September 1963

Waiting for tide to start in … My shooting is good at times and then bad. I guess it just takes practice. Have had a pile of fun. —Steve

Then we were off to college at U of A. Dad made a couple trips down with Father Wilcox plus Art Knight and his son. On the 20–21 September hunt, crane were moving through, and hunting was good.

20 September 1963

Lots of ducks. All got the limit. Several flocks of crane - finally got one in your favorite spot (Dick). Should have got more - got Crane Fever. —Don

Only problem is to keep them from flying down your barrel. —Fr. Wilcox

The next day was a good one for Art and his son.

21 September 1963

Got two crane - Wow! —Art

Dad told me to load my gun, I and Dad went out. I fired at a duck, it started to take off then hit the water. It was my first duck. I got it in back of Shellhorns. —George

On October 1st Dad came down with Jack Lydick. It was his first trip to the Flats in ten years. Bob Korn, Paddy Kissane, plus Virgil (?) and Alex (?) came over from the Korn Hole to spend a couple nights. The weather was nice, hunting was slow, but a good time was had by this crew of true Oldtimers.

2 October 1963

New York Americans 2, Los Angeles Dodgers 5. Koufax World Record with 15 strikeouts. —Bob Korn

This is the Life - would like to make this Cabin my home for 2 mos each year. —Jack

A beaut of a full orange moon shining - what a scene! Ponds calm shimmering moon lite mountains and all. Nothing can compare. Wish you were here Doll. —Don

Dad returned on October 27th with Nord and Al Jardinski to close the cabin.

27 October 1963

Nord, Al, & myself down to cabin in morning - ice in slough - winter coming. Still a few birds - I got a snow goose and a honker - all big - first time since we had cabin. —Don

28 October 1963

This is it (sad). Ponds freezing snow on ground - good a bye cabin til next year! —Don

The end of an unsuccessful year. —Al Jardinski

Good bye again. —Nord

A season that started with fire ended with ice. Who could have guessed what would happen the next year.

Part IV: Earth

"I feel the earth move, under my feet,
I feel the sky tumbling down …

CAROLE KING, "I FEEL THE EARTH MOVE"

"EARTHQUAKE," screamed the two inch headlines of the 2 April 1964 *Cordova Times*. Detailed stories by Lone Jenson: "Destruction by Tidal Wave in Chenega, Valdez, Seward, Kodiak, and Anchorage; Many Dead," with sub-headlines: "Tidal Waves Hit, One Death in Cordova, Realizing Extent of Havoc, Hardest Hit was the Village of Chenega."

On 27 March 1964, the most violent earthquake recorded on the North American Continent occurred. Had a magnitude of 9.2 on the Richter Scale, at the time making it the second largest earthquake in recorded history.

In her weekly Waterfront Scuttlebutt column of the same paper, Janson led with: "Where are our tides? Will they ever return to normal levels, or has the entire land mass raised between 3 and 6 feet, as some have speculated? All we know is it goes out much farther than normal, and never returns as high as it should. This creates problems."

No kidding. The early prognosticators were amazingly close. The average uplift of the 50 mile wide Copper River Delta was over six feet. But it was a tilted plane, with Eyak rising 6 feet and Cottonwood point 9 feet. Pete Dahl is roughly halfway between those two locations, so an estimate of its uplift would be 7.5 feet.

Yikes! Before the earthquake, a fourteen foot tide would flood over the slough banks and up around the piling under our cabin to a height of a foot. Now the same tide would reach its peak six feet below the level of the bank. Waterways were filled with sandbars, stumps, logs, and snags we didn't even know existed. New high tide was old low tide. New low tide, don't even think about it. Where has all the water gone, short time passing?

Also now visible at low water were huge evergreen tree stumps from some past era. Geologists theorize Delta uplift and subsidence occurs on a 400 to 600 year cycle. One USFS spokesman suggested we were lucky to witness such dramatic change.

Don't know about that. Am sure Cordova Outboard Shop felt fortunate. Props and profanity filled the air as duck hunters tried to make it to their shacks in wooden skiffs ill-suited for suddenly shallow intertidal waters. Mechanics worked overtime to keep up with a late season surge of damaged Johnson's and Evinrudes. Lower units were in particular demand.

For us, the immediate question was how to get to Pete Dahl. The narrow access slough at 20 Mile was a trickle, nearly bone dry, even at high tide. Ditto for Alaganik Slough alongside the road at McKinley River, now bank to bank with stump and log hazards.

Running down Eyak River was sketchy. It had become, in the words of river runners, "pretty skinny." Eyak Lake itself was impacted by the uplift. Not long after the earthquake, a metal weir was installed just above the Eyak River Bridge at 5 Mile to restore its depth. The lake is a major spawning and rearing area for red salmon. The loss of this habitat would have had significant impact on the fisheries.

So what to do? There appeared to be only two choices. One was going all the way from town around Whitshed and across the Flats on high tide, a two hour run in good weather, clearly not a reasonable option on a regular basis.

The other was at 27 Mile, on the westernmost edge of the main Copper. Steel truss railroad bridges still spanned the river at this spot, and during closures fishermen ran their gillnetters all the way up from Grass Island and Kokinhenic to tie up on the bank just above the first bridge, so there had to be significant water.

Plus we had some familiarity with the route. Remember the 1960 expedition from our cabin to 27 Mile looking for timbers to repair the piling damaged by ice?

And other advantages. The run downriver under the big bridge to the top of Pete Dahl was a one mile straight shot. It did not lead into a mine field of obstacles now surfaced in upper Alaganik. Access meant driving 7 miles further out the road to the launch site, but saved ten minutes running time, the course being more direct and shorter.

However, this route was dependent on good runoff coming down the Copper, as tides did not reach that far up the river. This would be a major problem in the fall when the river dried up. As Dad and his late season hunting partners would discover.

Our first trip to the cabin following the earthquake was in July.

13 July 1964

Launched skiff at 27 Mile Sunday. Came down today. Good trip. No problems. Dick, Ronny Ekemo, and myself. Lost part of our walk. Otherwise everything OK. —Don

Nice day for the first trip to the cabin after too long a time. The channel from 27 seems OK; we managed to find a few sand bars. It will be bad for night running due to lots of snags and the broad, flat width of the channel, especially on the upper part. —Dick

So our earthquake damage was minimal. Likely because the Pete Dahl cabins are located on a tributary a mile from the mouth of the main slough, with an island at the entrance of this branch splitting earthquake water flooding in.

Other more exposed cabins were not so fortunate.

"The 64 earthquake pushed ice in and up Alaganik on a big tide surge that came as a result," said Dan O'Brien, regarding their cabin on that slough. "The ice stacked up to the top of the roof of our cabin. It was a straight shot for its push up the slough. The ice was 30 inches thick. The surge lifted the ice up over the bank, and pushed it in against the cabin like a deck of cards. It moved the cabin back about three feet, the pressure slanting all the pilings backwards."

"Originally, the piling were four feet vertical height," continued O'Brien. "The ice pressure slanted them all over so the cabin was only about 30 inches above the ground. Louie Hasbrouck took Dad and Freddie Lantz down to inspect the damage. With many more pressing challenges to repair in town, it wasn't until the following year that they got back down to level the cabin at the lower elevation, since there was no need to be four feet up anymore. The big tides would not come over the banks at all."

"Freddie had a red and white speed skiff tied alongside the cabin, and it was gone after the earthquake. In 1975 while moose hunting up Tiedeman near the Haystack, we found it stuck up in the trees there," added O'Brien.

And of course, there was the Flinn cabin at Glacier mentioned in an earlierChapter. It ended up in the middle of a pond three hundred yards from its original location, because of that same surge.

Due to location or good luck, all the other Delta cabins sustained little or no damage.

On thing for sure. After 1964, cable tie-downs and deadmen to prevent cabins from floating off on ice driven by big tides were no longer necessary.

Not only did the earthquake uplift change the route to get to the cabin, it immediately altered hunting style too. Access to the famous Walhalla pond a mile and a half to the east had always been by boat, as several deep gutters made walking there impossible.

The upriver sloughs that cut over to Walhalla were now empty. Impassable by boat, except on extreme high tides. However, the good news, we discovered, was that it was now possible to hike directly to Walhalla from the cabin, on uplifted drier ground covered with short marsh grass. All the gutters that had been barriers could be waded in hip boots.

1 September 1964

The pioneering expedition this year featured Gary Taylor, Nick Kaiser, Johnny Ekemo, Dean Curran, and myself. Quite a motley crew… We tried running to Walhalla on a +11 high tide with little success from the Upper Cutoff on, so will try walking tomorrow. —Dick

2 September 1964

It was another one of those clear fall days, and hunting wasn't too hot. We walked to Walhalla taking the raft along for deep guts, but found it unnecessary, even on a 10 ft tide. This evening Johnny E. and I took a long walk below, and found sloughs except main ones crossable on a 12 foot tide. —Dick

Two days later a trio of college friends from the University of Alaska at Fairbanks showed up. Wow.

5 September 1964

The Killers from Seward arrived yesterday, and came off the plane all ready this time. Watsjold had a duck hat about 2 sizes too big on; Beaver had an armful of weapons, and Leirer fell off the ramp because he couldn't take his eyes off the stewardess. On the way down, after picking up Iggy and supplies, we ran into some moose, and Igg managed to get a bull from a treetoop late last night. So we spent the night here, and ran up at 4 a.m. to get it out. Had it in the butcher shop by noon, and back down for the evening shoot. —Dick

6 September 1964

Got up early and everyone was anxious to get out and sleep in the blind. Nice beautiful weather and I got a nice suntan. I saw a duck and was so surprised I didn't know what to do. To put it short we had a flop. —Dave Watsjold

Luck was not real good. Heading back to go deer hunting with Bob today, and later down to Martin River for more duck hunting. Still have lots of ammo left. —Steve Leirer

Stopping to shoot a moose interrupted our duck hunting trip to the cabin in September 1964. Standing left to right, beside our big 22 foot Banta work skiff, Dick Shellhorn, Beaver Nelson, Bob (Igg) Simpler, & Dave Watsjold.

Beaver Nelson opted to stay and chase ducks. I picked up Nord and Dad at 9 a.m. when I ran Steve, Dave, and Bob "Iggy" Simpler back up to 27 Mile.

7 September 1964

Beaver picked up 4 ducks this afternoon when Dad ran him up for the noon shoot. We went to pick him up at 3:30, and found his blind, but no Beaver. About 7 pm we started shouting for him, and heard a vocal response from Walhalla which turned out to be fishermen. These guys from Seward, I wonder. Beav walked back to the cabin, and was here when we got back in the black of the night. Maybe its a good thing Dave and Steve left this morning or we'd probably still be out hunting for these Seward H.A.'s. Nord's in prime shape, tip top form, hasn't fired his volley off the porch yet tho. —Dick

Nice and sunny but there's a few birds around. It beats Seward duck hunting any rate. Went out this morning and got a few, had to walk for half of them. Guess we're going to Martin River tomorrow, supposedly there's geese and cranes there. The dastardly duo Leirer and Watsjold should have a deer by now. That's all. —Beaver

Fine cabin shoot - nice sunny day. To H / W / I. —Don

I left for college shortly after the Seward Gang departed. By September 26 the Copper River had begun to dry up, as it does every year when cold weather freezes things in the Interior. The trip down from 27 Mile was a stark reminder of how the earthquake had changed the name of the game.

26 September 1964

Tough trip down. Water low. Don Everly, Don Van Brocklin, Len Hayes and myself. Got to cabin late afternoon. No birds. Going to fly back and run the boat back outside. To run up would beat up the motors. —Don

So let's get this straight. They left the self-bailing work skiff in the slough. Called Cordova Air on the radio, and flew to town. Would have to charter a plane to get back and retrieve the boat. Which would have to be navigated all the way around Whitshed for its return to Cordova. The 27 Mile Route was not working out too well. And the price of ducks was going up.

Most flying to the cabin was done by either chartered Cessna 185's or DeHavilland Beavers on floats. The pond directly behind the cabins was too small for takeoff, so the planes had to land on the much larger lake directly above it. This meant a walk of several hundred yards around the near pond, through soggy marsh, and included jumping across a narrow deep gutter between the ponds. Packing supplies was a chore, so sometimes a rowboat was used to ferry passengers and freight across the closer pond.

The float planes departed from the town end of Eyak Lake. The flight took fifteen to twenty minutes. It was considerably more expensive, and weather was always a factor. Plus air travel wasn't near as entertaining.

Heck, getting lost, hitting sandbars, pounding against whitecaps, becoming drenched or frozen, and knowing a warm dry cabin was somewhere on the horizon, why, that was half the fun.

9 October 1964

Flew down in afternoon. Tom Dooley, W.B. Chase, Bill Stookey, Bob Hunter. Stars out bright tonight. Hope birds flying tomorrow. Shoot the Airs full of Widgeon. Will fly back on the 11th. —Don

11 October 1964

Don, This has been my greatest and my first, you should be a pro, a wonderful host. —Bill Stookey

Guide Don Shellhorn, with W.B. Chase, Bill Stookey, and Tom Dooley. Chase holds a crane, while Dad holds an iconic Lucky Lager in his right hand, October 1964.

My first bird shoot in Alaska and to take the rare Sandhill Crane is an experience I'll long remember. —Bob Hunter

My first hunt on the flats since 1939. Certainly enjoyed it and your hospitality. Be back again next year for sure. —Tom Dooley

*I have fished in Alaska (1937 -The Newhalen River) but this is my first hunt in the new State. Many swans, some geese and ducks. Things are a **little** upset on the flats due to the earthquake. A wonderful time, a wonderful host. I hope I may come back. —W.R. Chase*

Dad flew back down one more time, on October 17th, and was stuck for five days due to bad weather with hunters Jack Linton, Harry Blair, and J. Roth. Who were these guys?

He was so busy closing the cabin he forgot to sign the log.

Part V: 1965

"The times, they are a changin..."

BOB DYLAN, SONG OF THAT TITLE.

The duck cabin logs now span 54 years. 1965 was the year with the least entries.

I was busy the entire summer working on a tender during gillnetting season on the flats, and then crewing on a seiner out on Prince William Sound. Stepped off the seiner, took a shower, packed my bags, and headed to Oregon State, with fall quarter beginning before duck season. Never made it to the cabin or duck hunting that year.

The 27 Mile route to the cabin had proved a challenge, as Dad's late season mis-adventures of the previous year verified. He just didn't feel like tackling it solo. Plus running a clothing store with Mom during the busy summer left little free time.

13 September 1965

Came down with Dick Borer in his airboat. Few birds cabin OK. Out of flamo. Head back tomorrow. —Don

8 October 1965

Down to cabin - Nord - Dennis & Camp Cook Don - via Cordova Air - lots of birds. —Don

9 October 1965

Up early. Went up slough with Al & Chuck. Lots of geese, couldn't hit my hat. But did get 2 honkers and 7 ducks. Nord and Dennis holding down cabin. Listened to World Series. Dodgers over Twins 4 to 0. So. Cal clobbered Washington 34-0. —Don

10 October 1965

Sacked in. Raining and blowing like H- no hunt! Dodgers beat Twins 6 to 2. No chance for plane to pick us up. —Don

11 October 1965

Got up early walked up back of cabin loads of geese - couldn't hit tho - only one mallard. Nord and Dennis stayed at cabin. Sun shining, little wind. —Don

That's it. Dismal, as Leer would say. No mention of closing the cabin. The plane must have shown up when the weather broke, and they had to scramble to get things together.

However, there was some good news, literally on the horizon. North, more specifically. Work had begun on a gravel USFS road that would create a landing on Alaganik Slough three miles below the Copper River Highway. Fred Pettingill and his Eyak Construction gang had started at 19 Mile and were winding their way to the upper portion of Alaganik that was still reached by incoming tides. A cement-slab launch ramp would be installed there, with considerable parking for vehicles and boat trailers.

The River of History was about to come to life again.

Chapter 8

Alaganik Redux

REDUX: 1. brought back, resurgence, returning. WEBSTER'S
2. "It's deja vu all over again." YOGI BERRA, *The Yogi Book*

"Cruising down the river on a Sunday afternoon,
With one you love the sun above waiting for the moon..."

CONNIE FRANCIS, "CRUISING DOWN THE RIVER"

Part I: 1966

19 June 1966

1966 started with a splash. Literally. For on its way to the new launch ramp at the end of just-completed Alaganik Landing road was the latest rendition of Shellhorn river boats. Fresh off the rack at Johnny French's Cordova Outboard Shop, a 14 foot aluminum Quachita, with nary a dent, scratch, patch, or hole anywhere.

Passerby's shook their heads in disbelief. That can't be Don Shellhorn heading to his duck cabin. His succession of crafts was well known to locals. The first was a totally flat plywood box with bow designed by Long Shorty; next a sawed-off second hand cedar Coast Guard lifeboat; then an abandoned ADFG plywood speed skiff rescued from the burn pile that had to be fiberglassed to cover several holes in its bottom; next an ancient plank work skiff leviathan with cracks in the bottom so wide grass grew between them before it was resurrected from Curly Hoover's yard; and finally a respectable used 22 foot Banta plywood work skiff.

And now this? To tackle Alaganik Slough? Shellhorn's had too many B & Bs.

The flat-bottomed green craft slide into the slough with a spray of beer against its bow and splash of water over the stern. Portentous. After a two year hiatus, we were back on our river of choice. Fastened a trusty 18 horse Johnson on the short transom, cranked it up, and roared down Alaganik. Cruising down the river. Back in the saddle again. Home, Home, on the Range. Pete Dahl, here we come. No more 27 Mile.

19 June 1966

First trip to the flats after a year's absence. The new aluminum rig seems quite well adapted to this area - light, easy to handle, and draws little water... No sweat getting here, even 2 hours before high tide. —Dick

Cold, cloudy, windy day. First time in two years to be down at the cabin.
—Johnny Ekemo

Nice Father's Day junket. All in order. Hope to get down again this summer. Anyhow will return when the season opens. —Don

So there you have it. The maiden voyage was a success. Early on the tide, and in less than perfect weather. The Quachita was so light two of us could pick it up; one 18 horse made it fly, drawing a foot or less of water. Plus if we did run aground, it was easy to drag off. Craft #6 was a winner. And we still had the Misty, our 13 foot patched-up ex-ADFG runabout, as a second boat, powered by the other 18 horse.

It was a New Era in river running. The work skiff drew too much water, and was a bugger to pull off sand bars. It had been the perfect boat for sloughs filled to the brim with grey briny, but they were no more. Now sand seemed to be in big supply. Craft #5 was obsolete, and had been sold to finance its sleek little replacement.

Better yet, less than three months later Boat #6 would provide us with the one of the most unforgettable cabin adventures of our lives. It began on the tenth of September.

Once again our little Nash Rambler pulled up to Alaganik Landing towing our new craft. It was a lovely fall morning, sun already warming things up. The tide was pouring in. Dad and Mom climbed out of the front, Sue Ekemo and I piled out of the back.

My brown-eyed beauty was excited. This was her first visit to the cabin since 1962, when she had accompanied her brother Johnny and I as we ran the work skiff all the way from town to the cabin, and then up to the landing at 20 Mile.

Four years later, here we were, heading down river. Based on that first trip, my sweetheart had some inkling of what to expect, or fear. But this was a whole new expedition.

"It was a New Era in river running. ... The Quachita was so light two of us could pick it up ... Craft #6 was a winner." Captain Shellhorn navigating the cutoff at full throttle, August 1966.

For one thing, we were recently engaged. I had spent the summer seining with high-line skipper Olaf Gildnes, while Sue worked at her parent's grocery store, K & E Foodland. We would head back to Oregon State shortly, where I would do my student teaching while Sue continued to work on her degree. Our wedding would be in late December while we were home for Christmas.

Secondly, this would be her first overnighter at the cabin, and with her future in-laws. We planned on staying a couple days, getting maintenance work done on the cabin as well as a little duck hunting. Sue already knew my folks well, but this would be our first time all together at Pete Dahl. Likely she had to be a bit nervous too.

Additionally, it was her first trip in our new riverboat, from the new launch site. This craft was considerably smaller and closer to the water than the work skiff. In fact, a little metal plate fastened to the transom said "Weight Limit: Three adults or 600 pounds."

Right. It didn't take a math major to count noses, multiply by one, and see there were four of us. Plus considerable freight.

Never a trip to the cabin was made without a full load, and this safari was no exception. It took Dad years to figure out that "getting on the step" with a load intended for a 22 foot work skiff wasn't possible in a shallow 14 foot river boat. By the time we crammed all the gear on board, there was barely room for captain and crew. Par for the course. Sue smiled at me timidly when water almost came over the gunnel as Dad jumped in after pushing us off the landing. I nodded confidently. Cast off the Titanic.

The muddy water was flat calm; thank goodness. We had perhaps 3 inches of freeboard. I cranked up the motor, backed out from the ramp, and off we go. Or do we? I tried to shift into forward. What? It wouldn't lock into gear. Put it back in reverse, backed around a bit, tried it again. Nope. What the hell?

We pulled back to the landing, monkeyed around, couldn't get it to shift. Figured out what parts we needed, but then faced the demoralizing thought of unloading everything, heading back to town, missing the tide, and having to wait another day.

Dad, who would probably swim to Pete Dahl with the bow line in his teeth rather than scratch a mission, came up with Plan B.

The Hell with It. A favorite Shellhorn phrase. Let's back down to the cabin, call the air service on the radio, and have them drop the parts off down there.

Say what?

Getting to the cabin going 20 plus miles per hour at top speed in forward is a 40 minute boat ride. It's 4.2 miles as the crow flies from the landing to the cabin, but almost three times as far via slough. How many knots are we going to make going in reverse?

Dad: It's a beautiful day. Plus we can walk part of the way to speed things up.

Really?

Sure, you can drop Sue, your Mom, and I off right below O'Brien's cabin. It's just a big long 15 minute "U" shaped run down Alaganik and back up the Racetrack anyhow. By the time you back down the slough and then up the loop, we'll be waiting on the bank. It's only 500 yards across by land, a twenty minute walk. Plus the tide is flooding in, which will speed you up.

I glanced at Sue. She smiled bravely and said that sounds like fun. Game for anything. Right then and there I knew I had the right gal. In her mind maybe she was thinking this is a test his parents give every potential bride.

So "Cruising down the river, on a sunny afternoon…" we went. In reverse. Steering by hand. Dad popped a Lucky Lager to lighten the load. I dropped them off on the bank by O'Brien's cabin, about two miles below the landing, and waved farewell.

Bucking the incoming tide until I turned off Alaganik just a mile from its entrance to the open flats. Making about 4 knots, standing and holding the motor down so the long lower unit wouldn't pop out of the water and cavitate. And I thought seine boats were slow.

Sure enough, by the time I had reversed my way back up the Racetrack, Dad, Mom, and Sue were there sitting on the bank.

Well, I thought, that only took an hour. I hope we don't run out of gas.

They piled back in, and off we went, the tide still flooding to give us a couple extra miles per hour "speed." From there the sloughs zig-zag through a narrow maize before connecting with the upper reaches of Pete Dahl. We putted along, chatting and enjoying the sights, Sue smiling and cheerful, my hand and arm going numb horsing the motor around sharp corners.

Finally we reached upper Pete Dahl slough. Back then before the brush went crazy you could see the cabin about a mile away. We let up a cheer, and realized we had caught a break. By now, the tide was starting to ebb, so the current was going with us as we headed down river to our duck shack.

Eager to speed our arrival, Dad had me drop the three Merry Hikers off just below the Lower Cutoff to Walhalla. From there it was another twenty minute walk to the cabin. When I putted up to the shack, they were already on the bank waving a greeting. Dad looked awful thirsty. The first item out of the boat was the ice chest full of Lucky Lager.

I glanced at my watch and realized we had arrived about two hours after we left the landing. Quite frankly, I was surprised. Lt. Henry Allen and the Boys would have been jealous. Going backwards sure beat the heck out of walking and pulling the boat, a.k.a cordelling.

Fired off the VHF radio, and called the Cordova Outboard Shop in town. Explained the motor situation to Al Jardinski, resident outboard guru that could fix anything. By now the Shellhorns were Preferred Customers, always bringing in broken Johnsons and shattered props. Johnny French had a little box on the counter titled "Shoehorn's Shear Pins" to save wasted time going back in the parts section to find them, since we showed up every Monday looking for a fistful. Plus a big stack of variously pitched props handy by the cash register. If the shop had a Frequent Flier Plan or Gold Member Card, we would have been Inaugural Members. I'm surprised Dad, a shrewd business man, didn't ask for a 10% discount based on volume.

Al said he would figure out what we needed, and contact Parkair to fly it down. No problem.

By now it was midday. We unloaded all the gear, had lunch, decided it was painting weather, and went to work. The sides of the cabin are covered with galvanized roofing metal, and the paint was peeling in several places, so the first order of business was scrapping away the flakes and wire brushing the bare spots. We all got after it, and before long were breaking out paint brushes and good old oil-based Forest Green XO Rust. This stuff has the consistency of glue and is a real challenge applying, but holds up very well in the brutal winter winds roaring down the Copper.

By dinner time, the crew of four had completed the job. Sue was a trooper. I can still see that long brown hair with blue plaid handkerchief tied over it, those funky black rimmed glasses that were in style back then, sun on her back, merrily slaving away.

The folks were equally impressed. This gal is cabin material.

10 September 1966

On this day of our Lord Miss Susan Ekemo has become half owner of the share of Walter Richard Shellhorn in the cabin known to all men as the "After Hours Club" at Pete Dahl Slough.

After arising at an ungodly hour, helping load her share and more into the boat, smilingly took the jolt and words that go along with shear pins, wrecked motor, continued cruising down the sloughs backwards, and finally walking to said cabin, tackled the paint job with a smile and sense of humor, proving herself a swell gal, the undersigned do hereby take her in. —Anita Shellhorn

By Proxy, Sharon Shellhorn, Donita Cole, Don Shellhorn, Pres., Dick Shellhorn

Had a nice dinner, played some cards, and called it a night. By next morning, the weather was deteriorating. Dad and I were up at 3:30 am, and walked to Walhalla for the morning shoot in light rain with a building southeast wind. Luckily the paint had set up enough before it started raining. Picked up a few birds, headed back to the cabin for breakfast with the gals. Waited for the plane to bring down the parts, but by now it was blowing hard. We weren't going anywhere.

Dad and I went across the slough for a brief evening shoot.

11 September 1966

Weather foul - hunters soaked, but now warm and cozy. No plane, no parts, hermits we are. —Anita

Very few birds flying, weather too foul. —Don

If it's too foul for fowl, it ain't very nice. In fact, by then the wind was up to 40, and it was raining very hard. And nothing, including parts planes, was flying.

Dinner, cards, and then Hit the Kip, a Shellhorn Idiom of unknown origin for crawling in the bunks. By midnight, those same bunks were shaking. Mariners can deduce wind speed by its affect on wave tops; at Pete Dahl, the same can be derived by how much the cabin shakes. The back wall faces directly southeast, the Delta's predominant bad weather direction. The bunks line the back wall. When they start rattling, the wind is up to 50.

It was a restless night. The cabin had certainly withstood winds probably twice as hard as that at some time in its brief seven year history, but toss in the downpour of rain rattling against the windows and pounding the metal siding a 2X4 away from your pillow, and even the hardiest go sleepless.

12 September 1966

Blew hard all nite. Didn't get up until around 9 a.m. Still marooned. Waiting for rescue expedition. No Hunt. —Don

Sue was still smiling. Maybe a tad more weakly. Wished I could have snuggled in the bunk with her. More on that later.

By afternoon, the wind started dropping. Still raining very hard however. Out of the weather and low ceiling from Cordova's direction, the sound of a plane. We run out on the deck, and lo and behold, it's Tom Parker in his Super Cub, on wheels.

The plane buzzes the cabin, banks, turns, loops around, and angles into the head wind to land on the bank of the slough across from the cabin.

Three Cheers for Parkair!

Tom hops out, pulls something from the back of the plane, drops it on the ground, and hollers to us across 200 yards through the wind. Couldn't understand a word he said. The wings of the plane are bouncing around. He jumps back in, cranks up the engine, and is airborne in 100 feet. Love that 30 mph headwind. Super Cubs are the plane of choice for countless Alaska bush pilots, and we just saw a demonstration of why.

Dad and I pile in the boat, row across the slough. And there sits a brand new Johnson 20 horse. Tagged: "Cordova Outboard, Special Delivery to Pete Dahl." What? Wow. We'll take it. Jardinski, intimately aware of Shellhorn Mechanical Prowess, decided on the most elegant and simple solution to our crisis.

Awesome. We row back across, take the old motor off, and hook up the new one. Plug in the gas tank, crank it up in two pulls. It just purrs. As we are giving each other high fives, it dies. What? Oh, no problem. Needs fuel. Pump the bulb, crank it up, it purrs a bit, and dies again. Check the tank, yep, lots of gas. Try it again, same result. So we try pumping the fuel bulb while it is running. Guess what, As Long as You Pump, I Will Run. The tank from our 50s era old 18 horse was not compatible with this new mid-60s model.

Well, what would you rather do? Back up to the landing at 4 mph in reverse for two hours, or pump for 40 minutes going forward at 20 mph? And guess who earned the honor of squeezing the bulb to get us back up river? One more vote for my wife to be!

12 September 1966

Parker down about 4 pm with motor (no tank). Shellhorn (Dick) rigged up direct feed. All OK we hope. Good Bye. —Don

It was a bumpy ride back, especially in the lower Alaganik, which is almost half a mile wide and faces directly into the southeast. An incoming tide against a 25 mph wind creates a lot of chop, and even hugging the cut banks will not get you out of it.

Finally, around 7 pm, we arrived back at the landing. Congratulated each other on surviving another trip to the duck cabin. Sue is thinking: Whew. And while I am now 200 per cent in love with my young Norwegian/Mississippi Lass, she is probably considering research into the Shellhorn Genealogy.

Ah, if she only knew.

As Yogi says, "It ain't over til it's over."

We loaded the boat on the trailer and piled into the Rambler. Headed up the just-completed winding 3 mile Alaganik Landing road, took a left on the gravel "Copper River Highway," and headed to town, 17 miles away. Noticed right away the water on both sides of the road was extremely high, almost cresting the berm. Made it within half mile of the Sheridan River bridge. Dad slowed down, and said something about waves on the horizon.

What, that has to be a mirage!

Nope, the road was washed out. A raging torrent of muddy water of unknown depth spawned by two days of torrential rain on the Sheridan and Sherman glaciers had flooded over the gravel road in several spots. The nearest washout was over 100 yards wide, and we could see more further up the road toward town.

Unbelievable. No one in sight beyond the last overflow. Starting to get dark. No cell phones back then, and not enough gas to go back down to the cabin. Hmmmm. I wonder where we'll be sleeping tonight?

Sue looked at me in the back seat and rolled her brown eyes. Can you blame her?

Well, says the Oldtimer, we camped at the McKinley cabin when we got lost trying to get to the cabin site for the first time back in 1959. It's nice and cozy. Let's see if they're booked up for the night.

Yipee, More Adventure.

We drove back a mile or so, and then unhooked the boat and trailer. No concern about flooding on this high spot, so no point in towing it back and forth on the road. Plus no one else one this side of the highway that could bother it.

About two miles up the road from the Alaganik Landing cutoff, there was a nice cabin just south of the highway that belonged to Chuck Raymond. He and his wife Bird Raymond spent most of their summers there, and often stayed until the snow and lack of road maintenance drove them out. At one time the cabin site belonged to Walt and Jessie Corliss, close friends of our family for many years. Triple A accommodations compared to the spartan McKinley cabin.

No lights on, no cars parked in front. The cabin appeared empty. In Alaska, folks always help each other out in a pinch. Given our circumstances, we were sure they wouldn't mind if we camped there out of the weather for the night. The door was unlocked, but we knocked on it anyhow. No answer of course.

By now it was almost dark. Carrying flashlights, we walked in to what looked like a scene out of a "B" grade horror movie. Carcass of a partially eaten goose on the table, plates half full of food, dirty utensils, empty wine glasses, and things generally askew. It quickly dawned on us that someone had come roaring down the road, warning about the impending washout. They had tossed on their hats, grabbed their '65 Cabernet, and ran. Wow.

We found a couple candles, cleaned things up as best we could, and eyeballed the sleeping situation. The Pete Dahl Gang was pretty well shot.

Two almost double wide bunks that also served as couches

"Dad slowed (the Rambler) down, and said something about waves on the horizon. What, that has to be a mirage!" Sue Ekemo and Mom find humor it the road washout at 16 Mile, September 1966.

lined one wall, with a couple sleeping bags and a few blankets on top. Awesome. Mom and Dad could sleep on one; I could cuddle up with my sweetheart on the other. With clothes on, off course. After all, I was 22, she was 20, and we were engaged. We weren't married yet, but this was the mid-60s. Beatles. 5th Dimension. Protests. Make love, not war. Or so us naive college kids thought.

Mom and Dad plopped on one bunk, I blew out the candles and climbed on the other with Sue.

Mom: What are you doing?

Me: Mom, come on. It's going to get cold tonight.

Mom: No you don't. Get out of that bunk.

So much for The Dawning of The Age of Aquarius.

I looked around. The only remaining option was the floor. Jesus H. Christ. This is going to be one long night. Sue looked at me and shook her head. At least I was allowed a goodnight kiss.

I wrapped up in an old black wool blanket and curled up on the floor directly below my sweetie's bunk. Great. Felt like a dog that had misbehaved. Wished I had its fur.

By two a.m. I had managed two minutes of sleep and was freezing my ass off. The floor was getting colder and harder by the minute. I could hear the folks snoring away, and decided to make my move.

Quietly, or so I thought, I stood up and leaned over next to Sue, who gave me a "shiss" signal with her finger over her lips, along with a cute smile. There might have even been some moonlight for us young lovers. But honestly, warmth and snuggle were all that was on my mind.

As I reached one leg over the bunk edge, some stirring from the next rack over, and then in a gruff voice, from Mother Goose: GET BACK DOWN ON THE FLOOR!

Unbelievable. In 1937, Mom came to Cordova from a dairy farm in Washington to work as a nanny for her older brother John Young and his wife. John had migrated to Cordova from Eureka, California, and had a large boat that he fished quite successfully for herring and salmon. He almost wouldn't let his little sister date this wild young bachelor called Don Shellhorn, who had quite a reputation about the town. High standards had been set in their courtship. One score and 19 years later, they were evidently still in effect.

There was going to be no playing around on Mamma Bear's watch.

Back to to the hardwood I went.

I swear I could hear Sue giggling in her cozy little bunk.

It didn't take an alarm to wake me up. I roused the troop early the next morning, stiff as a board but in tip top form after ten minutes sleep in six hours of below freezing temperatures. There was frost on the windows of the cabin and the station wagon.

Dad: Wow, it must have gotten pretty chilly last night.

No kidding.

Sue was allowed to give me a warmup hug, and down to the Rambler we headed. Hey, it had a heater. I didn't care how far we got toward town.

As we approached the washout area, activity was visible on the road. Something big and yellow. Getting closer, we realized it was a huge D-8 caterpillar that had plowed through the water to work on our side. The operator was none other than Walt Mantilla, head of the State road maintenance gang at Mile 13. Lifelong Cordovan, avid duck hunter. He stopped his monster, scratched his head, and asked Dad what the heck we were doing over here. Laughed louder and louder as the whole story unfolded.

"As we approached, activity was visible ... something big and yellow ... it was a huge D-8 caterpillar that had plowed through the water to work on our side." Walt Mantilla ferries my bride-to-be Sue Ekemo across washouts at 16 Mile, September 1966.

Then offered us a ride back across the washouts. Said he wouldn't recommend trying it with either the riverboat or station wagon quite yet. Also decided he would take us across one at a time, as there really wasn't too much room for passengers on his vehicle. Mentioned it might be a bit bumpy, so hang on tight. I volunteered to go first. It was quite a ride. The D-8 is one big heavy machine, but it was disconcerting to see glacial water roaring at full speed literally covering the treads as you plowed through it.

Recently I was sorting through old slides up in the attic, and it was a wonderful surprise to discover one of them showed Sue, hanging on for dear life to a big metal post that supported the roll over-cage of a massive yellow Caterpillar.

That same long brown hair flying in wind and spray, blue plaid handkerchief keeping it out of her eyes, short black quilt jacket, smiling from ear to ear, with a grinning Walt Mantilla in white hard hat alongside her in the driver's seat operating levers and brakes to transfer her across the Sheridan washout.

By the time Walt had ferried us all across, an older couple named Bob and Chili Lipf happened down the road to see the washout. They received an added bonus by witnessing a Caterpillar Rescue. Greeted us like heroes. Dad explained our situation, they offered us a ride in their tiny sedan. We all crammed in. About a mile before town, there is a famous local pub called the Powder House. As we rounded the bend, the Oldtimer turned to Bob and said: I don't know about you, but I need a drink.

Sounds like a good idea to me, replied our driver. We screeched to a halt, untangled ourselves, and headed inside. The two older couples sat together at one end of a table, laughing and sharing stories. Sue and I snuggled up at the other end. I had a beer, she wasn't old enough to drink.

Looked at me with twinkling eyes, smiled, gave me a peck on the cheek, and quietly asked, Are all trips to the cabin like this?

We were married three months later.

No more sleeping on the floor.

24 September 1966

Sequel to above trip: All OK back to the landing <u>but</u> road washed out on main road - so spent night at Raymond's cabin. Next day Walt Mantilla ferried us across on a cat - car returned on 22nd. —Don

Dad made four more weekend hunts, and closed the cabin on October 18th. It was Alaska Day, and you can be sure the flag Benny Benson designed was flying high.

18 October 1966

Up at 5 a.m. Up slough. Loads of swans - snow geese - some honkers. Both of us (Father Glen Wilcox & I) missed good shots at snows. Very few ducks flying. Going to close cabin, altho no hard freeze yet. —Don

Part II: 1967

12 August 1967

First trip down to the cabin in a year... Head for Hawaii and first teaching job before the season opens this year. May have to charter a 707 back for September 1st. —Dick

17 August 1967

Sue and I down for a three day combined work - vacation party. Painted all of cabin in two shades of green. —Dick

Our first trip down as "man and wife" - how about that! —Sue

Dad found a replacement hunting partner in my longtime buddy Randy Bruce. He worked at the Outboard Shop, which proved valuable. However, neither had paid much attention to the sloughs.

4 September 1967

Goofed on sloughs to Walhalla but finally made it... Randy 2 ducks, I got one goose. —Don

Dad's other intrepid partner Nord wasn't a big help with navigation or mechanics. Plus the sloughs continued to silt in.

7 October 1967

Started up slough to pick up Don V.B and gang. No water up at end. No problem tho. Nord helped pull the craft off and managed to fall on his ass. —Don

8 October 1967

Up at the crack of dawn - that is Pat and Mike - sun bright - no birds. Dennis sneaked on a bird in the back pond, shot around the bird but it got away. Next time blam! —Don

Great time down at cabin, weather has been beautiful. Not many birds though. —Sharon

Had a great time but didn't see many ducks. Thanks Mr. Shellhorn. —Pat Van Brocklin

Real nice time. Too bad couldn't stay longer. —Mike Van Brocklin

Randy and Dad closed the cabin on 15 October, or so they thought.

15 October 1967

So long to Pete Dahl for this season. —Randy

Closing cabin. Going to Walhalla, then up river. Hope to return again before season ends. —Don

They ran into Harold Pernula, Les Maxwell, and Harry Nicolet at the landing. Undoubtedly had a couple B & Bs from the freshly stocked new arrivals. Birds were pouring by. Randy had to get back to work. Dad sent him to town as a messenger to the other half of Shellhorn's Inc. His "hope to return again before season ends" was fulfilled.

Hunting was slow, but the peanuts were good, and the weather was great. On the cabin deck, L to R: Harold & Dennis Nordman, Mike, Pat, and Don Van Brocklin, and Sharon Shellhorn, September 1967.

15 October 1967

Oh no you Don't!! (close the cabin) Shellhorn - Pernula - Maxwell - Nicolet. 2 boats. Balmy weather -overcast - Snows in -ducks in -honkers in. Lots of geese. —Harry Nicolet

Bag - Don - 4 ducks 2 Honkers 1 Snow Harry -7 ducks 6 honkers 3 Snows Harold Pernula - 2 ducks 6 Honkers 3 Snows Les Maxwell - 19 ducks 3 Honkers 0 Snows 18 October 1967

Birds gone this a.m. ponds freezing. 25 degrees above. Beautiful migration of all type waterfowl straight through. —Harry Nicolet

Looks like good - d -bye cabin for this year.—Don

Part III: 1968-72

1964 was the year of the earthquake. The late 60s brought upheaval of a different sort.

Buffalo Springfield was right, "There's something happening here, what it is ain't exactly clear." Far to the West, so many time zones away it was a different day, there was a lot of shooting going on. Not for ducks. At all hours of the day and night. The migration was on, of young men and women, to a place called Vietnam. And like the '64 earthquake, it tipped and tilted tectonic plates, this time of lives.

9 September 1968

Glad to be down here again hunting on the flats. You Don't really know how much you miss it until once again the tree line ends and all you can see around you is the beautiful flats. Jerry Behymer is down here with us. He just got into town on leave from the service (I hate the word) in the Marine Corps. It's the first time I've seen him in four years.

Well!! We had a good night hunt. Dick got 10, Jerry shot 5 - if he had a M-14 he would have Done better - I got 15 - just lucky. Moose steaks tonight - what a life. 11 more days until I go into the service. —Gary Taylor

Names in our Cabin Logs of hunting companions who served their country during those turbulent years:

Vietnam:

Randy Bruce, U.S. Army, 1st Air Cav
Jerry Behymer, U.S. Marines, Forward Air Spotter
Johnny Wheeler, U. S. Marines
Bob Simpler, U.S. Army, Infantry
Gary Taylor, U.S. Army, 82nd Airborne
Mike Taylor, U.S. Army, 7th Cavalry
Mike Noonan, U.S. Navy, Destroyer Hibbard
David Watsjold, U.S. Army, Armor

Korea:

Steve Leirer, U.S. Army
Dick Shellhorn, U.S. Army, Signal Corp

Others from my Cordova High School Class of 1962 who never made it down to Pete Dahl, but served with valor and honor:

Vietnam:

Roger Behymer, U.S. Army, Helicopter door gunner
Bill Henrichs, U.S. Army, Special Forces, 3 tours
David Lape, U.S. Army, Helicopter Pilot, Warrant Officer
Doug Lape, U.S. Army, Helicopter Pilot, Warrant Officer
David Wheeler, U.S. Army

David and Doug Lape were twins, serving in the same combat zone. David was killed by a mortar attack. Bob Simpler survived a booby trap in the Mekong Delta. Mike Taylor was awarded a Bronze Star with "V" for Valor for his heroism in the October 1967 Battle of Ong Thanh, described in the book *They Marched Into Sunlight,* by David Maraniss.

Bob and I were inducted into the Army together in September of 1968, and assigned to separate platoons during Basic Training at Ft. Lewis, Washington. He went on to Advanced Infantry Training, I was sent to Signal School. I eventually served 13 months in Korea, and was discharged as a Sergeant in May of 1970. Steve Leirer and I served a tour at the same Base in Korea at overlapping times, but never realized it until many years later.

Best friend Randy shipped over early in the conflict. Was a hell of a musician in high school, trumpet player. Drafted, he ended up in the 1st Air Cav Division Band. Went to Vietnam on a troop ship. Walked off with a M-16 in one hand and his trumpet in the other. Talked very little about it, other than to say he helicoptered to some places he wouldn't rather be, and played way too many "Taps."

Mike Taylor and I crewed together on seine boats during summers on Prince William Sound. Mike ended up in the Black Lions, 2nd of the 28th, 1st Infantry Division, the Big Red One. He packed a radio and M16 in Vietnam, and ended up carrying messages under hostile fire after the radio was destroyed when the 160 men in his company engaged 1500 North Vietnam regulars. A Spec 4 at the time, he was promoted to Sergeant after that battle, as most of the NCO'S had been wiped out.

Bob Simpler and I were born in Cordova a month apart in homes a block apart. We played together as kids, were the two guards on Cordova High's 1962 basketball team, and were roommates for two years at University of Alaska Fairbanks. He spent a long time rehabbing his neck and shoulder at stateside military medical facilities before resuming careers in teaching and commercial fishing.

In Korea, I received water-stained letters from him for a short time. Then none. He never talked about Vietnam again.

Last year Doug Lape opened up a bit, revealing details about his brother David. The sad irony of flying all those helicopter missions, to be victim of a random round lobbed into an air base compound.

Jerry Behymer enlisted in the Marine Corp soon after graduating from Cordova High in 1964. As kids, we did a lot of crazy outdoor things together in our small little town by the sea. On one early leave, he talked about calling in practice air strikes on a training range in Hawaii. Later, he didn't talk about them at all. Jerry was pulled out of Vietnam in the middle of a heavy firefight when the military discovered his brother Roger was there as a machine gunner in a helicopter and his brother Gene was doing the same on a Navy river boat. Three members from the same family in a combat zone was a no-no since WWII.

Duck hunting stories are one thing; others are not.

There were eighteen in the CHS graduating class of 1962. Fifteen guys.

Eight of us served. Over 50%. One is listed on the Vietnam Memorial.

Many from Cordova served. Some sacrificed ultimately. Along with classmate David Alen Lape, the names Michael Dean Banta, Warren Allen Paulson, and David Henry Elisovsky are etched on the black marble walls of the Vietnam Memorial.

Remembrance

We trickled home, in ones and twos;
No band or banners or thank you's;
Forever changed, several maimed,
And a few not ever again.
Me, I wasn't a Senator's Son,
But somehow one of the Fortunate Ones.

In two years, I had seen my wife less than two months. We returned to UAF.

I finished my Master's degree while Sue did her student teaching and completed an Elementary Ed degree. The following year I taught junior high mathematics in Kodiak, and Sue became a full time sub. In 1972, a high school math job opened at CHS.

We returned home.

Cordova, Alaganik, Pete Dahl. Redux.

Chapter 9

Additions

ADDITION: 1. A wing, room, etc, added on to a building. WEBSTER'S
2. Addition and subtraction are inverse operations. When the
earthquake added 7.5 feet of elevation to Pete Dahl, it subtracted
7.5 feet from the depth of the sloughs we were trying to navigate.

"The times, they are a-changing…"

BOB DYLAN, SONG OF THAT TITLE

Part I: Shrinking Cabin

In the early 70s, the duck cabin began shrinking. Not really. Our families were
expanding, and the 16X24 dimensions seemed to become smaller each year. All
the bunks were full, and the floor was covered patrons sleeping on air or foam
mattresses each weekend night.

Donita and her husband Paul retired from the Air Force in 1971, and came
North to take over Shellhorn's Clothing. Mom and Dad retired in 1972, and the
business name was changed to Cole's Clothing. The new owners had two sons,
Butch and Bobby. Sharon, who had been working in Anchorage, returned to
Cordova, initially to help out in the store.

Our first daughter Heidi was born in 1973; second daughter Gretchen would
arrive two years later. Sharon would marry Larry Ermold, the doctor who delivered
Heidi. His son Brian and daughter Wendy from a previous marriage would arrive,
along with Holly, the new couple's daughter.

In the meantime, Randy and his boys David and John, Merle and his son Ardy,
and countless friends of all of us, became regulars at Pete Dahl. It was a full camp.
And set the stage for Dad's favorite pastime: Projects.

No more counting socks for Mom and Dad, who had pretty much been running Shelllhorn's Clothing solo since the fire in 1963. The Mayor of Pete Dahl counted noses one September weekend, and decided it was time for expansion.

Part II: Cabin Addition, Phase 1

One of Dad's favorite Mantra's was "Gotta get organized." Dad was extremely handy and creative, and would spend hours puffing away on his pipe while planning and designing ingenious Pete Dahl projects such as planters to grow carrots and leaf lettuce; an outdoor clothes line; a retaining wall to prevent erosion in front of the cabin; or a set of steps down to the boat anchorage.

All were based on another favorite pastime - scrounging. In fact, trips to the Cordova burnpile or homes being remodeled around town were routine, and often the source of inspiration. For example, the planters he built alongside the cabin were covered with multi-paned uninsulated windows taken out of a old house that was being made more energy efficient. Dad used them to create a "hot house effect," although you would never know it from the size of the carrots.

So it should come as no surprise that the biggest project undertaken at Pete Dahl took months of planning, design, and logistics. Perhaps that is why Phase 1 began at an odd time.

It was October 1st of 1974 when Dad and Mom began work on the platform for a 16X16 flat roofed addition to the west side of the cabin. Snow was already creeping down the mountains that rim the Delta, and skim ice was forming on the back pond. Closing up the cabin for another season was not far away.

As always, getting the necessary building materials there was a challenge. And another Curran Special. Enter Dean Curran, 25 year old son of Harry, who had captained the first boatload and barge of supplies to Pete Dahl back in 1959.

Dean had already gill netted the Flats for years, and was fishing out of a 24 foot wooden stern picker named the Hopeless. He was also an big time duck hunter, and made several fall trips to the cabin with Dad and Harry.

Dean volunteered to ferry supplies for the addition across the Flats during closed fishing periods. Paul Cole with his sons Butch and Bobby came along as a labor force on his first trip.

14 August 1974

It was another successful voyage of the M.V. Hopeless to the Peed-Al slough after navigating around vicious sandbars. It was a good thing Bob and Butch came along to unload or we probably would have left loaded. As it was it was a beautiful day and the horse-shoeing was fun. —Dean

Dean rendezvoused with Mom and Dad with another load of material late in September.

30 September 1974

Mom and I down to the cabin, nice day and trip, arrived around 1:30 p.m. Dean here, boat almost unloaded - nice kid - left for town around 2:30. Barometer way down, 27.0, might mean a storm, could care less. Steak for dinner - no catsup - but will survive. Weather right, will start Project Addition tomorrow. —Don

Despite chilly weather and north winds, Mom and Dad were up and at it the next morning, and in three days had the platform completed. The Project Superintendent had Mom digging holes, backfilling, swinging a sledge hammer, and slaving away. Raised in a big family on a dairy farm near Lowell, Washington, the youngest of four boys and two girls, she was earning her keep.

Three days of piling, bracing, support beams, joist, blocking, and decking. Plus an oil stove "on the fritz" in the cabin.

"Anita is for sure Number One Pile Buck. I had to take time off while she was tamping the piling - 1st Class Job." Mom, sledgehammer and all, at work on the cabin addition, October 1974.

1 October 1974

Up early (8 AM) Don already banging away. —Anita

Anita is for sure Number One Pile Buck. I had to take time off while she was tamping the piling - 1st Class Job. Weather permitting should get deck down. However barometer now reads 26.9 lowest I have ever seen, stiff wind from north. —Don

2 October 1974

Brrr - woke up to a chilly cabin, 38 degrees inside! 28 degrees outside. I was able to see my breath this morning. —Anita

Project about on schedule, never make it without Anita - pile buck, carpenter, camp cook, etc. What a doll. Now having a B/B, relaxing radio music, warm cabin, a wonderful wife, this is the life. —Don

3 October 1974

Brrrr it's cold outside. Ponds all frozen over, banks loaded with ice at low tide. Les and Jack Keitel have been down for 10 days and never saw any northern flights. It's 7 pm, platform on, and walkway to outhouse relocated. Today "Start early ya got a long way to go" was the word from the foreman and construction boss. —Anita

Now having a B/B, Project Platform complete! —Don

Extra lumber was stored under the cabin the next day. They both "hit the kip" early that night, and stayed through October 14. Dad returned with Randy, Paul, Larry, and I on October 18th. Dean showed up in his gillnetter, and made one of the last entries of that year.

20 October 1974

The last hunt lived up to its expectations between the poker game and the rain gauge it was a close tie. I had a major breakdown of my 12 gauge so borrowed one from Les's cabin. The hunting was kind of slow the last couple days. Now it's time for the trek home after a very good year. —Dean

Part III: Cabin Addition, Phase 2

Dad spent the winter in town sketching detailed plans for completing the addition. Of course, those changed once on site.

11 July 1975

Measured for a material list for the new addition, as always more than you realize. Goofed the rest of the day, read thru the logs - ye gads since 1959 - very interesting!! —Don

Speaking of "ye gads" and "very interesting" (another of Dad's pet phrases), a materials list? Say what? Unbelievable. Lumber and plywood from North Star Building Supply?

This, as Dad would say, was going to be a First Class Operation. On 14 July, he and Mom returned with a load of groceries and tools. The next day, Dad modified his plans, and decided to extend the cabin addition out toward the slough, so more pilings and bracing were installed. The dimensions were now 19 ft 3 inches by 16 ft. Plus a 3 ft by 6 foot woodbox tacked on. On July 18th they ran back to the landing for a load of 2X4 and 2X6 that had been left in the truck.

By July 21, initial wall framing and a hand-made laminated beam had been installed across the 19'3" span. On the following day the duo installed all the roof joist.

22 July 1975

Progress is being made. Time for a B/B. About 8 pm. Yipee. —Don

Beautiful sunset for a change Sat in the new "addition" to listen to the ballgame. Real warm and sunny. —Anita

Hmmm. Dinner and a sunset viewed through studs and rafters, while listening to grandsons Butch and Bobby play Little League Baseball for Cole's Clothing in Kodiak, live on KLAM. Another fine day at Pete Dahl.

Weather slowed things down. On July 24 they headed to town for more framing material, and returned on the 26th with another full load. The Boston Whaler was getting a workout, as were they. The following day they were back to the landing for a load of plywood for the roof. Frank Sherby and Randy hauled down another load of 2X4 in Frank's airboat.

Dad was very meticulous about bridging, blocking, and bracing. Material was vanishing as fast as they could haul it in.

29 July 1975

Cut over 100 pc's of bridging for the roof. Now have to nail it in. —Don

1 August 1975

Finally got the roof bridging complete only 120 pieces (!) of 2X4. Now ready for roof. Have a few more studs to put in place for the walls other than that all set for the walls too. Now 6 p.m. B/B and relaxing. —Don

On August 8th, Dean Curran came across the Flats in his gillnetter with T-111 siding, windows, and a Heatilator fireplace. Due to lack of water, he ran aground a half mile below the cabin, and walked up to holler across the slough for a ride.

8 August 1975

I heard from unknown sources that Anita was cooking dinner so I had to hurry to get here in time. This is an unusual time for me to be here in the middle of fishing season. It was just another ferrying expedition. —Dean

The next day, there was enough water on the tide to bring his boat up to the cabin.

In addition to helping unload all the materials, Dad put him to work installing facia and one run of roof plywood before he departed that day.

9 August 1975

Thanks Dean you're a real pal to have helped out so much. Hope you will be here when the first log get's lighted in the fireplace. —Anita

10 August 1975

Lazy. Up at 8:30 a.m. Got the plywood deck on the roof, ready for nail down. Went up river and picked up the rest of the plywood, siding, etc. in the truck at the landing. All in less than two hours, one of my better operations. Now 6 pm, busy day but much accomplished - now having a B/B. —Don

Had lunch on the "siding" stacked in front of cabin. Nice and sunny. Yahh! Ole Capt. is really getting so he can get by a "bar" without stopping in. Nice quickie of a trip both ways. —Anita

On August 11 and 12 they finished covering the roof with plywood, and then foul weather set in. On August 16 I came down with Chuck Taylor and Merle Hanson, plus more material. We helped move the fireplace into position, and completed roof trim work. Mom and Dad were up and back with more supplies on August 22, and discovered the back window of the original cabin was leaking badly from all the wind and rain. Dad spent two days repairing it. The next day Sharon, Heidi, and I, plus Paul and Donita, showed up with a birthday cake Sue had made for Dad's 63rd birthday. As our second child was due soon, she could not make the trip.

Tucked in the Cabin Log beside the entries for 25 Aug 1975 was part of a brown paper page inscribed: "Long Nose - Happy Birthday, Hook." It was written by Ken Van Brocklin, and you can guess what was in the bag. Dad opened it, and we celebrated with a birthday B&B.

Gretchen was born 3 days later, and Dad wrote this memorable entry regarding her arrival.

29 August 1975

*Yea Man, the men have been running the world **too long** and messing it up!! So we need more gals. Yipee! —Don*

By August 31 all the sub plywood had been installed on the walls, and by September 4 the T-111 siding was up and stained, plus metal skirting around the base complete. Duck hunters were arriving and leaving, adding to the work force when not out chasing birds. Dad would drop his hammer and grab his shotgun when crane or yellow-legs came by.

3 September 1975

Just about the time I had a panel of siding up a flock of yellow legs flew up the slough in front of the cabin by the time I got my gun they were over Maxwells. Then a little

This was going to be a First Class Operation. Dad framing a wall on the cabin addition, July 1975.

later heard some crane, three flew over the pond, I shot twice but - strange they kept on flying - Oh well, you can't be a killer and a carpenter too?? —Don

By September 11 the roof had been covered and sealed with heavy asphalt tarpaper, and all the windows were in. Next came a milestone in cabin history.

16 September 1975

Finished the platform for the fireplace. Then Les Maxwell and John Sellen arrived in Les's airboat. Got the platform for the fireplace lined in, then Les and John came over so with their able assistance got the fireplace lined in, and torched it off. Yippee!! —Don

It was actually a bit more complicated than that, as Mom's entry revealed.

16 September 1975

The Fireplace is in and burning beautifully. Dad so elated you can see by his entry a few B&B's were in order! I had looked out the window to see Les and John sitting on reclining chairs in front of their cabin, drinks in hand and guns ready and natch Les's binoculars. Could not resist grabbing the camera to run over and take their picture. Les asked what we were doing and told him the fireplace was ready to go in and Don was rigging up a deal so the 2 of us could get it up on the platform. Les said God damn I'm going to help and really dashed over and zippo

"The fireplace is in and burning beautifully. Dad so elated you can see by his entry a few B&Bs were in order!" 16 September 1975.

up the fireplace went. He even climbed on the roof to give Don a hand with the flue and top and it was greatly appreciated. John read directions and gave advice. He owns a huge construction co. in Seattle and says he can't even pound a nail. It has been a busy day but a happy one, fireplace is crackling now, light rain on the roof, Don finally tore himself away from it and is snoring satisfactorily in his bunk. One of our hard working dreams has come true.
—Anita

Next Dad framed and poured a suspended concrete hearth in front of the fireplace, complete with flat granite rock from Sheridan Glacier on the surface.

The rest of the fall was spent primarily on building a small inside bathroom in one corner of the addition. It eventually included a motorhome porta-potty, home-made shower and cabinets with a sink, shelves, and walls covered in yellow marlite.

They discovered wood scraps left over from construction vanished in smoke up the fireplace chimney in a hurry, and soon were making expeditions to find driftwood logs to cut up for firewood. And in hindsight, made this amazing observation:

19 October 1975

Anita and I took a walk down to the point, located three small spruce trees, hope they survive the winter. —Don

Survival was not a problem. Thirty eight years later the banks of the slough are lined with dense stands of spruce and cottonwoods forty feet tall, and alder is the firewood of choice. It is much more dense, burns slower and hotter, and can been found in stands fifty yards deep along the riverbanks anywhere around the cabin.

Cabin closure time was right around the corner.

22 October 1975

Gotta go and hate the thought. A big summer's work Done and fun doing it. We shall return. —Anita

Yeah Man. —Don

Part IV: A Masterpiece

1976 was spent finishing the addition interior and exterior, solving poor draft issues with the fireplace by extending the stack higher, building a retaining wall in front of the cabin, repairing leaks, insulating the ceilings, adding more touches to the "bathroom," hauling down an abandoned metal hospital bed for a special ""hospitality" bunk in the addition, building shelves and coat racks, and so forth. Puttering would not adequately describe the pace at Pete Dahl.

Plus there was the demand for firewood. Rare was the night the fireplace was not crackling away prior to bedtime, with Mom and Dad lounging in front of it on a small couch donated by Pete Fridgen. Likely sitting there with a nightcap in hand, Dad envisioned finishing touches to the Heatilator that would challenge his artistic abilities and occupy an entire winter in his garage workshop at home in Cordova.

"Bas-relief is a type of sculpture that has less depth to the faces and figures than they actually have, when measured proportional to scale. This technique retains the natural contours of the figures, and allows the work to be viewed from many angles without distortion of the figures themselves." Wikepedia

About to head downriver with Heidi, age 3, and sister Sharon, packing Pete Fridgen's couch plus other supplies in my riverboat. Clearly, Dad had taught me well about load limits. August 1976.

Somehow Dad decided to create bas-relief duck sculptures mounted on large tiles to encircle the fire place, with a mantle and upper area covered with split driftwood found on the banks of the sloughs.

He and Mom gathered choice pieces of small diameter tree trunks that had drifted down the Copper, hauled them into town, dried them out, and then enlisted the aid of local craftsman and boatbuilder Frank Steen to rip them in half on the big band saw in his shop. The flat sides could then be nailed on to framing around the upper part of the fireplace, as well as onto the mantle.

The sculptures? Well, that was another story. Dad had never made any before, and began experimenting with the process in his workshop. What he eventually settled on was fine-cell blue styrofoam as the form, using a Dremel tool with numerous drill bits to carve and create molds in which he then poured smooth plaster-of-paris type cement. The process took months of experimentation and numerous failures before he finally stumbled onto the right combination.

The end results were truly amazing. Eleven tiles of bas-relief ducks in various stages of flight, painted in a copper-hued blue and green, mounted on pinkish tiles textured with walnut shell, that would encircle the entire fireplace.

In 2012, while cleaning out his old garage, I discovered a stack of blue styrofoam blocks tucked back in the corner of a storage shelf. It was all the forms. The detail, and the time it must have taken to create them, is mind-boggling. And once

Dad had the process perfected, he also created a similar sculpture of his beloved Alaska Flag to be the centerpiece above the mantle.

28 September 1977

Started to make the frames to hold the bird tiles for the fireplace - had to cut them down on three sides to recess them in the concrete. Hope this does the job. Will mix a batch of cement tomorrow - trial run - if all OK just will take a little time. —Don

29 September 1977

Messed around all day getting the frames ready for the tiles. Hope I get them up before the freeze comes. —Don

30 September 1977

Finally, with the able assistance of Anita, got the two sides of fireplace bird tile set in concrete. Looks OK. —Don

3 October 1977

Got the rest of the boids cemented in the top panel, not without a few problems. Maybe will get it finished this year. —Don

4 October 1977

Again worked on the bird panels, walnut shell on glue did not work so mixed some paint we had, plus the walnut shells worked OK on the background. The boids turned out real good, a copper ore green with rubbed copper hi-lites. Dodgers lost to Philadelphia 7 to 5, cost my #1 helper a buck. —Don

5 October 1977

Finished painting the top boid panel, now ready to be fastened on the fireplace. Sawed the split sections of driftwood and nailed them over the fireplace - looks good. —Don

6 October 1977

Yipee!! Got the boid panels in place on the fireplace, plus prop candle-holders, so now except for a few finish touches - Mission Accomplished!! —Don

"Yipee! Got the boid panels in place on the fireplace, plus prop candle-holders, so now except for a few finish touches - Mission Accomplished." 6 October 1977.

7 October 1977

Finished cutting the driftwood for the fireplace and framed the Alaska Flag. All in place now, so project complete! —Don

Indeed. "Looks good" barely scratches the surface of what was a Legacy Project, the centerpiece of our cabin at Pete Dahl, and an enduring symbol of Dad's love of the Copper River Delta.

Thirty seven years later, late in the evening, we still gather around alder blazing in his Masterpiece. Sipping Scotch or Irish whiskey surrounding ice in clinking glasses, the Mayor of Pete Dahl would be shocked at how refined we have become. But the quality of the B.S. would receive his approval. Which leads to the second half of this book.

Fireside Tales.

BOOK II
Fireside Tales

"A good drinking buddy never heard the story before."

Ken Alstad, *Savy Sayin's*

Legends

LEGEND: 1. Traditional story sometimes popularly regarded as historical but unauthenticated. Websters
2. Well-embellished family favorites, told over and over, usually at large, rowdy gatherings, and hence passed on orally from generation to generation.

"Awake sluggards, and waste not life;
in the grave will be time for sleeping enough."

Benjamin Franklin

Part I: Mr Big

September 1931

After scrambling around the backside of the snow-capped mountain on slippery ice- covered rocks, the young hunter plopped down to catch his breath. Below was a clear view of open rocky terrain. He quickly chilled down, sweaty after the effort to get in position for his one chance.

It was early fall on the Kenai, and as far as he was concerned winter had already arrived here on this perch above Upper Russian Lake. Buttoning a wool jacket tighter, he glanced at his watch, made sure his open-sighted 6.5 Styer Manlicher rifle had a good rest plus clear view, and waited.

Well, I hope this works, he thought, as minutes seemed like hours.

Below him, out of view, his father W.R. Shellhorn, and famous Kenai outdoorsman Andy Simmons, were about to make their move. Simmons was one of Alaska's best known big game guides. He arrived in Seward in 1908, and his guiding business was located at Mile 20 on Kenai Lake. Shellhorn had moved to Seward from Seattle in 1915 to install the first phone system in what was then Alaska's major port, and quickly fell in love with the area's fabulous hunting and fishing.

Andy knows what he's doing, mused the 19 year old. Christ, the Territorial Governor gave him his guide's license in 1910. It's one of the first ever issued. Can't get any better than that.

The trio had spotted a nice band of Dall sheep an hour earlier. One looked World Class, according to Simmons. However, the sharp-eyed animals had them pegged.

No way we're going to get close enough, Simmons had said. You have to be above them to have a chance.

Raising his binoculars to glass the herd, he'd muttered, that is one big sheep.

Turning to 19 year old Don Shellhorn, who ran track for Seward High School and hunted anything that moved with young buddy Barton Stanton, he idly hypothesized:

I suppose there is one possibility. We can give you an hour to move down below us out of sight, circle around the backside of the mountain to get above them, and then we'll head up toward them. If we're lucky, maybe they'll turn and go by you within range.

So the race to get into position was over. Time was up. His fingers were getting cold. He scanned the area. Nothing. Crap. Come on guys, make your move.

Suddenly, off to his left, where he hadn't been looking, some motion. What?

And there he was. A big full curl sheep, stepping carefully through rock piles, about 200 yards away, on the edge of a jagged drop off. Completely unaware of his presence.

Quietly shifting position, he found a new rest, took his time, exhaled a deep breath, and squeezed off a round.

The sheep vanished.

With that sick feeling every hunter knows who has worked so long for this moment, and missed, he stood up and thought, Oh - No.

Adrenaline pumping, he grabbed his rifle and ran toward the spot where he had last seen the sheep.

Lo and behold, there on the other side of the sharp ridge line, with a steep fifty foot incline leading to a long sheer drop off, lay Mr. Big.

Wow.

One shot, right where I held, through the front shoulder, he said to himself, shivering now with excitement rather than cold.

He looked at the beautiful animal. Red on white, a tang of remorse. What a set of horns. Had to sit down to catch his breath. Incredible. Turning the horns, he noticed one side was broomed; but despite that it was way over full curl, and the base was massive. This is one big sheep.

He glanced back down the valley where Simmons and his Dad were. No sign of them yet. They had to hear the shot echo through the valley.

Another look at the sheep, a deep breath to settle down. Scanning the horizon in all directions, the lake, the mountains, the colors, the whole thing, he thought: This is a moment I will never forget.

That's what legends are.

In his view of it all, he also realized the sun was well past its zenith. Holy smokes. Enough lollygagging. We've got to bone this sheep out, cape its head, get it on packboards, and hike all the way back down before dark. Dad and Andy aren't here yet; I better get to work.

He quickly gutted the sheep, and started quartering it for packable loads. Left the head intact so they could work on skinning it out together.

The pair of oldtimers soon arrived on the scene. Impressed with the size of the sheep and young Shellhorn's marksmanship, they congratulated him, and then got down to work. Both were also concerned about the time.

And in their haste, Guide Simmons made a mistake.

When telling the story, at this point Dad always paused, perhaps still seeing it in his mind's eye again.

The blood stained front shoulder was laying to the side. Or so they thought. Unnoticed, it was still attached to the head by some of the hide.

No point in packing this out, it's all shot up, said Simmons. So he flopped it out of the way. Or so he thought.

The shoulder started rolling down the incline toward the cliff and drop off, with the massive head and horns tumbling along.

Dad jumped up and started racing after it, the pair above him screaming stop. It was too late. He screeched to a halt at the edge; the last he saw was a blur of white tumbling down, down, down.

Simmons was beside himself. Dad was speechless. They crawled to the edge and peered over. No, it hadn't hung up anywhere in view. And it was at least a thousand feet straight down. No sign of any white patch below. They discussed the possibility of packing the meat out, and then circling around the mountain the next day in an attempt to find it.

Simmons gave that slim odds. Number 1: could they locate the spot; and Number Two: even if they did, by then bears would probably already taken care of it.

Dejectedly turning back to finish cleaning the rest of the sheep, they saw W.R. standing there half way up, with something big and brown in his hands. Look what I found. It broke off while the head was tumbling down the hill.

One horn of Mr. Big

Dad moved to Cordova in 1934 to work with O'Neil Clothing and Hardware; W.R. and Simmons went back to hunt the same area for many years. In 1936 the pair returned with a Dall sheep that ranked third largest in North America.

After W.R. passed away at Cooper Landing in 1944, Dad ended up with the mount of that incredible animal. It hung above the entrance to the old Cordova Commercial Company building on Main Street of Cordova for years. By good fortune, before the entire business district on that side of the street burned down in 1963, Dad had moved the mount to a special finished redwood panel above the mantle of the fireplace in the basement of our home that was built in 1957.

The plaque on the mount reads: "Ovis Dalli, W.R. Shellhorn, 1936, Kenai Peninsula near Upper Russian Lake, Third Largest Head in North America."

And guess what? The single horn from Dad's sheep, despite its tip being somewhat broomed, is bigger than either horn on the sheep that put W. R. Shellhorn in the Boone and Crockett record book.

That very horn sits in front of me now. Dad kept it, and brought it with him when he moved to Cordova. A family heirloom. More than one winter night, with a fire roaring in the "rumpus room" fireplace, and his father's sheep peering down, Dad would tell his story of that unforgettable fall day in 1931. And we would pull the horn out and compare it to those on Mr. Big. Again.

How it would have ranked with Boone and Crockett will forever be a mystery.

Recently we had W.R.'s World Class sheep remounted. The original cape, gray with age from fireplace smoke, was in bad shape. It now hangs in Whiskey Ridge Trading Company near the boat harbor, which is owned and operated by my son-in-law Tom Carpenter.

This fall he and pilot Mike Collins returned from getting very nice sheep deep in the Wrangell St.Elias park. Had the heads and horns drying in the back room of the store. And of course had to compare them to Mr. Big. Always a great conversation starter. Tom was instrumental in having the remount done; mentioned it was quite a challenge finding a cape big enough to fit. Used his connections with the many hunters that come through his shop to finally find one that would work. It looks awesome.

Tom also told a good story about removing the horns from the original mount. It was made out of cross-laid pieces of hardwood, with strange mold material over the top. Had a heck of a time taking it apart. Was inscribed with the name of the Seattle taxidermist that did the work. While telling his buddies about the unusual material, someone asked him if he tried to keep it.

Nah, it's in pieces in the back of my truck, headed to the burn pile.

Gee, said one of the boys, that's too bad. I think the fellow that did the work was the best in the business and world famous. The mount alone would probably be worth quite a bit.

The story of Mr. Big, like all Legends, is worth a lot more.

Part II: The Seward Ponies Ride Again

Winter 1931

W.R. and Meda Shellhorn, along with their three sons, moved to Seward in 1915. W.R. had been a lineman and electrician in Seattle, and continued such work in Seward. He was also quite a boxer; in fact, a well noted Golden Gloves Champion down south.

Back then the railroad ran from Seward to Fairbanks, making it the major port for Alaska. A younger daughter, Wilma (Billie) was born at Seward General Hospital in 1916.

At that time a road ran from Seward to the near end of Kenai Lake, with the railroad following pretty much the same route that exists today. Much of the travel to the other end of the lake and Cooper's Landing was by boat.

The hunting and fishing in those days was fabulous, and the Shellhorn family quickly fell in love with the outdoor lifestyle, especially along the Kenai River. Looking at photos of combat fishing where the Russian River enters the Kenai just below Cooper's Landing, it's hard to imagine what the area must have looked like in those pristine early days. Amazing photos show W. R. Shellhorn holding monster rainbow trout caught on a bamboo fly rod right outside their cabin directly across from Cooper's Landing. Dad's parents homesteaded 160 acres there in the late 1930s. From the deck of the Princess Lodge that now overlooks the Kenai River, one can look down and see the very spot where their cabin once stood.

My cousin Donna Estes Giles wrote a book titled *The Funny River Hunt* based on a 1932 diary written by W.R., and it gives a highly entertaining history of the people and their adventures in those days. While going through old family photos recently, I found a black and white picture of the World Record sheep, laying where it was taken on a surprisingly flat, rocky, snow covered area above Upper Russian Lake. Have often wanted to hike back in and see if I could locate that spot.

W.R. passed away at their cabin in 1944, the year I was born. Grandmother Meda fired three rifle shots to get help from across the river at Cooper's Landing. I remember visiting the cabin in the early 50s. The Shellhorn clan eventually scattered: sons Merritt to Seattle, Willard to Anchorage, Dad to Cordova, Billie to Moose Pass. The homestead was sold, and Grandmother Shellhorn moved to Cordova and lived with us for many years before passing away.

Dad ended up with the 6.5 mm Steyr Manlicher rife with which he shot the sheep. Finding ammo for that unusual caliber was a challenge. Karl Barth, who owned a small hardware and sporting good store here in Cordova, hand-loaded special cartridges for it. Beautiful gun. Short barrel awesome to carry in the woods, incredible smooth action. I bagged my first deer on Hawkins Island with that same rifle.

Dad had many other stories to tell about his youth in Seward. What a time and place to be. One of his favorites was about basketball, a wintertime passion in Alaska.

Seems W.R. was quite a fan. The story goes that one time he was yelling so hard his false teeth went flying from the balcony into the crowd below.

Dad was fast, and a playmaker for the Seward High Ponies. Back then there weren't a lot of teams to play. The college team from the University of Alaska came down on the train from Fairbanks for a game. The whole town was abuzz in anticipation. Seward High wasn't very big; they had only six players on their squad.

Before a packed gym, the college boys came out to warmup. They were big. Clearly, thought the fans, our only chance will be to rely on quickness and guile. The Seward squad entered the court to a big cheer, and then puzzled silence. Only four lads warming up. What is going on?

Well, what WAS going on was this:

Seward's speedy ball handlers Don Shellhorn and Barton Stanton were out shooting ptarmigan to sell on the Red Light District for a dollar apiece, and happened into very good hunting. While counting their anticipated windfall, the happy duo forgot to count the numbers on their watches. It was getting dark as they frantically struggled through deep snow to reach the gym.

Seward's coach was struggling for ways to stall.

Just how long do you warmup down here, asked the University coach?

With a blank look on his face, the Seward coach was searching for a reply, when suddenly the lights went out in the gym.

In fact, the whole town went black.

What's going on, asked the college mentor?

I really don't know, but we have problems with the power down here all the time.

The crowd, already in the dark about their two key playmakers, was now doubly befuddled. But not alarmed.

Ah darn ...the lights are out again. I bet it's all that snow on the power lines. Don't worry, it'll be back on shortly.

More importantly, where in the heck are Shellhorn and Stanton? Those two are always getting in trouble.

The coaches, referees, and administrators huddled around a flashlight.

Well, guys, what are we going to do?

You came all this way to play. The whole town's here. Let's give them time to get the power up and running again.

So they waited. And waited some more.

Finally, the lights popped back on. Out trotted the Seward boys, on cue. All six of them. The crowd stood on its feet and roared.

The Pony Express Rides Again!

And down at the Seward Power Plant, W.R. Shellhorn and his close friend, the plant manager, gave each other a high five after throwing switches and dialing controls to resume the juice that they just so recently shutdown, a call from the gym letting them know that the Dynamic Duo was back.

Already memorable because of these pregame dramatics, the contest itself lived up to its billings. In the first half the teams exchanged baskets twice, and headed to the locker room at intermission with the score tied 4 to 4. The Ponies controlled the tip to start the second half, scored a quick basket, and went on to win by a 6 - 4 final.

"The crowd stood on its feet and roared ... the Dynamic Duo was back." Dad and Barton Stanton relive old glories on the cabin deck, September 1961.

Say what?

Back then there was a jump ball at midcourt after every made basket, and Seward had a tall center who could control the tip. Plus there was no ten second backcourt rule, so when a team gained the lead, it could essentially play "keep away" for the rest of the game.

Which the undersize Ponies did for the rest of the second half, lead by the nifty ball handling of a backcourt duo that became known as the Red Light Boys. Dad also hinted that he and Bart were so tired after hunting birds all day that they couldn't dribble the ball to front court if they wanted.

The Night the Lights Went Out in Seward.

Legendary.

Part III: Never Look Back

Spring, 1931

The slender runner looked up. What the hell just happened? Trying to get to his feet, he brushed dirt out of his face and off his race bib. One knee was bleeding.

He glanced to his right. Someone went zipping by. Up ahead was the finish line. Of the Seward High track.

And here I am laying in the dust.

He became aware of spectators, urging him to get up. And he couldn't.

Two more racers went by, laboring to end their mile long effort.

This is some way to end my high school running career, he thought. He rolled over on his knees, and tried to stand up. Legs like jelly. Crap.

So he started crawling.

Young Don Shellhorn received a big cheer from the crowd as he crossed the finish line.

On all fours, in last place.

Never look back, his coach had told him, you'll lose your stride.

But with no one in front of him, and the twine of victory in sight, he couldn't resist a peek back to see if anyone was closing, meaning he would have to find that one last burst of energy. That little turn of the head had shown he had a considerable lead.

And then he was a runner no more.

Part Three of the Seward Trilogy, Dad's favorite stories of his youth.

Part IV: Love Triangle with a Bear

September 1944

It was a clear day, thank goodness. The plane from Cordova to Anchorage has just flow over, on schedule, at a little after two in the afternoon. John Ekemo, recently arrived from Valdez to work at Bill Leibe's market in Cordova along with his brother-in-law Pete Lovseth, now had his bearings.

John had forgotten his compass, but not his watch, and knew the two o'clock flight was on a straight line from the local airport to rapidly expanding Anchorage, in an almost perfect east-west bearing. After it passed over, he told his newly engaged fiance to wait on a log while he got the lay of the land.

May Hammett, from Valdez by way of Mississippi, suspected her hubby was lost but too embarrassed to admit it. So she stood quietly on the log as ordered, her engagement ring glittering in the sun. John had proposed the night before.

The attractive Southern Belle was dressed in warm woolen clothes she had borrowed from John's sister Lil for her first deer hunt. But it still felt cold. This sure isn't Vicksburg, she thought. The young nurse had flown over from Valdez in a small plane just 24 hours ago.

Pete, whose father worked on the Copper River and Northwestern Railway before it closed down in 1938, had grown up in Cordova. So he had hunted and fished all over the area. The guys borrowed a boat from a fisherman friend of Pete's, and John called May to invite her over, supposedly for a deer hunt. The ring just happened to be in his pocket.

The foursome spent a crowded night on the boat, and were up at daylight to chase Sitka blacktail deer. The plan was for Pete and Lil to go up one side, John and May the other, with a goal to meet on top around noon. John had never hunted the area, the midday rendezvous didn't happen, and by early afternoon all he knew for sure was that they were somewhere above Boswell Bay on Hinchenbrook Island, once again proving the adage about a successful deer hunt: it's when you find your partner.

While John was walking away to gain a clearer view, May sensed some movement behind her. Brown bear were not a common sight in Mississippi, but even she realized what it was. Luckily, she didn't realize how dangerous they could be.

In a calm and relatively soft voice, she called out: John, I see a bear.

John, focused on getting unlost, replied: Oh, I don't think so.

May, as the bear continued its approach: I really do see a bear.

John, humoring this Southern Cheechako: Well, what color is it?

May, with the bear now on the other end of the log: It's brown.

John turned, and was startled to see a very large bruin now standing not more than 24 feet from his bride-to-be of less than 24 hours. Don't move, don't scream, don't holler.

May stood still, John raised his rifle, and nailed it right between the eyes. The first bear he had ever shot landed at her feet. He told May to stay put, took his hunting knife out, and threw it at the beast's head.

The bear didn't move. Neither did May.

Welcome to Cordova.

John told May she could slip off the log. He knew the bear was dead, and brightly observed to his future wife: I shot a bear.

The Norwegian Deadeye wanted proof he had killed a sizable critter, but the bruin had fallen so the paws were under its huge body. He managed to pry one out and cut it off. Using his hands he measured between the bear's ears, and figured it was at least 18 inches.

In the meantime Pete, who was already back at the beach, had been firing shots, waiting for John to respond. John and May, far on the other side of the ridge, hadn't heard them. By now it had started to rain, so they headed down the mountain as fast as they could.

They arrived back at the boat before dark, wet and exhausted. Spent the night in the craft's warm cabin, Dad telling Pete the story again. By then May began to realize just how close a call she had, and confessed later that she had nightmares about it that evening.

It took most of the next day to get back to Cordova. News travels fast in small towns. After freshening up, the foursome decided to take in a movie at the popular downtown Empress Theatre. They happened to run into Everett H. Pettijohn, owner/editor of the *Cordova Daily Times*, and of course Pete and John had to tell the story.

May Hammett was flying back to Valdez to resume work as a nurse when the Saturday, September 30, 1944 edition hit the streets. Back then the daily paper focused on national as well as local news, and World War II items were the lead stories. The following article was to be the only front page non-war news to appear in the Times from the day Pearl Harbor was bombed until the war ended. It ran top dead center of page one.

Cordova Times

30 September 1944

Love Triangle With A Bear

"You Can't Do That To My Girl,"

Says Alaska Nimrod, As His Trusty

Winchester Spits Slug of Hot Lead

It's being whispered around town that there isn't much percentage in being in any sort of triangle with Johnny Ekemo and his best girl, May Hammett - not as long as Johnny packs his trusty Winchester. One fellow tried it. He was big, too - much bigger than Johnny - but, the story goes, he won't be around any more.

It seems Johnny and May were over back of Boswell Bay on Hinchenbrook Island the other day, and May was just standing on a stump surveying the territory while Johnny walked off a short ways examining other points of the locale.

Just about this time the big fellow, afore-mentioned, ambled out of the bushes and set his big, brown soulful eyes on May. He fell in love at first sight.

So, he started walking toward May, possibly just to ask her for a date, when he spied Johnny, and momentarily decided he didn't care for competition. So, he ambled off in Johnny's direction, snorting in a manner Johnny didn't particularly like.

But May's beauty was too much for him. He had forgotten about Johnny. He had to talk with the beautiful girl on the stump.

But May wasn't frightened, even when the big guy snorted up to within 30 feet of her.

"Oh look, Johnny," she said without a tremor, "a big old bear."

Johnny was looking.

He also was raising his blunderbuss, a .270 Winchester, to his shoulder. Johnny didn't like competition either - not that kind of competition. He had never shot a bear before, but like most Alaska boys he'd had a gun ever since the first time he put on long pants, and he knew how to handle a Winchester.

He pulled the trigger and a hot slug smacked Brownie right over the left eye and didn't stop until it had plowed on through to break his neck. Brownie's big powerful front legs curled up under him and he slumped to the tundra right now!

Just for curiosity, Johnny placed a steel pocket tape across Brownie's head. The tape measured off 18 inches - between the ears - just back of those soft brown eyes.

Said May: "The part about the tape measure was ridiculous. John never hunted with a tape measure in his pocket."

Evidently everything else was true.

Part V: North to Alaska

May 1944

From high on the deck of the Alaska Steamship passenger ship, May Hammett and fellow nurses Dorothy Mitchell and Lucile Grice peered through the rain and couldn't believe their eyes. It was the first week of May in 1944, and their journey was complete. They had arrived at Valdez, Alaska. Towering mountains were covered with snow, ice still floated in the harbor, the streets were muddy, there were no sidewalks, and the dock was packed with every bachelor in town, dressed in their finest.

Dutch Harbor had recently been bombed, so they had crossed the Gulf of Alaska with everything blacked-out in fear of Japanese submarines. But obviously communications had not been discontinued. Word had spread with wireless speed that three lovely nurses from Mississippi were arriving, and the single male population was out in force to greet them.

North to Alaska came the Vicksburg Nightingales. Men all over the rugged port city of two thousand had been polishing their shoes and manners, for eligible females were as rare as sunshine. The only single women that came to Alaska were nurses and teachers.

Oh My Goodness, uttered one of the trio, in a Southern version of the English language that would take Valdezians considerable time to translate.

Another of the nurses repeated the phrase, perhaps wondering if they had boarded the wrong ship and just landed in Antarctica. In their black suits with white shirts and dark bowler hats, the mob on the dock did look like a herd of penguins.

Barely twenty one years old, May Hammett had always thought she would leave Mississippi, maybe in the Public Health Service. All three had surmised they might end up in military service.

But Alaska? It was wartime, the whole world was on the move, and here they were.

The gangplank was lowered, a representative of the Valdez Hospital Board greeted them, and the crowd cleared a path as they drove to the hospital.

May Hammett was born on April 30, 1922 in Jackson, Mississippi. When her mother passed away, she was advanced from first to second grade to be with her oldest sister Margie, and consequently graduated from high school when hardly seventeen. She moved to Vicksburg to live with her Aunt Gertrude, who agreed to help her through nursing school "as long as she didn't get married." May worked in Kress's 5 and 10 Store until she was old enough to enroll.

The hospital where nurse's training took place was privately owned by five doctors, and knowing them helped hopeful candidates gain admittance. Guess what? Dr. Knox went to the same Baptist Church Aunt Gertrude attended.

May graduated three years later, and the Nursing School Supervisor, Miss Emma Easterly, mentioned: "Miss Hammett, did you know you weren't 18 when you started training?"

Only 20, May had to wait to take the State Boards, offered but once a year. Dr. Jones, a Vicksburg eye, nose, and ear specialist, needed a nurse in his office, and upon Miss Easterly's recommendation, hired young Miss Hammett. May worked for him a year, gaining invaluable mentoring, and then passed the State Boards.

One day, Jones received a wire from colleague Dr. Armstrong, whom he knew from courses they had taken together in Louisiana. Armstrong was now practicing in Valdez, Alaska, and sent a telegraph saying he was in desperate need of three nurses. Jones gave the flimsy to May, and asked her to post it on the hospital bulletin board, while casually commenting: "I know of no one who would be going to Alaska of all places, but take this over and hang it up."

On the stroll to the hospital, with birds singing and flowers blooming in Mississippi's finest month, she ran into nurse-mates Dorothy and Lucile, showing them the cable. They talked about it and laughed out loud, one asking "Where in the world is Alaska?"

Ah youth. These were amazing times. The whole world was at war. Everyone sacrificed and served their country. The United States had become a global power, its forces were engaged in a battle for freedom.

By the time they reached the hospital, the hypothetical of minutes earlier had become their calling. "Why don't we go?" was the consensus. There was an Army post in Valdez; they had assumed they would go in the service, but hadn't yet been summoned.

Duty, Honor, Country, as well as Adventure, beckoned.

The next morning they informed Dr. Jones of their decision, and he laughed in disbelief. A wire to the doctor in Valdez, who they nicknamed "Army," made it official. All three were astounded by the beginning pay offer of $250 per month.

The trio gave notice, waited until replacements could be found, and left their beloved South in April of 1944.

Taking minimal personal belongings, the threesome chugged from Jackson to Chicago in twelve hours, and took advantage of a short layover to visit the huge Marshall-Fields Department Store. Then back aboard for a trip across America. Destination Seattle, the point of departure for their voyage to Valdez.

The countryside, the universal patriotic spirit, the crowded rails, what an experience. On their own, seeking their destiny, the eternal quest in Carlyle's "glad season of life." And here was our Country, "spacious skies and amber waves of grain, purple mountains majesty". Its spirit, energy, and boundless pride; optimism, hope, and faith in its cause.

By then the Depression was a thing of the past. The entire country was producing war materials 24/7; everything and everyone was on the move. Troops packed every train. Dashing young men in striking uniforms, from every branch of service, surrounded the Southern Belles. Gone with the Wind was undoubtedly their favorite movie.

Oh my. They all fell in love at least once before they had crossed the country. It was the first time they had left Mississippi.

Alaska, here we come.

After a three day layover in Seattle, they shipped north. Already nursing. The Public Health Office had heard of their destination, and enlisted the trio's help in caring for a young girl with TB who was paralyzed from polio and traveling with her family back to their home. They readily agreed. May celebrated her 21st birthday in Ketchikan, Alaska, more than 2,500 miles from Vicksburg.

As they drove from the dock to the hospital, bleak was the best term to describe the frontier-like town of Valdez, dressed in full breakup apparel. Piles of dirty snow, scatterings of dog poop, mud puddles, grey overcast skies, wooden framed buildings with partly shoveled sidewalks, and snow on all sides vanishing into overhanging clouds. No wonder they called Alaska "The Last Frontier." It looked like something out of the Wild West shipped north and covered with water in all stages of solid, gaseous, and liquid form.

The wide-eyed nurses noticed a pair of young men who had forgone the dock scene leaning against the front of the local drug store. One turned out to be Johnny Ekemo, son of pioneer Valdez photographer John Ekemo, a rugged Norwegian from Oslo who had been hauling mail from Valdez to Fairbanks by sled and horse since the 1890s. A lanky 22 year old who was born and raised in Valdez, Johnny graduated from high school there in 1940, and was currently clerking at the enterprise where he and buddy John Gilson were now lounging. In reality it was more of a general store, featuring a variety of goods, including men's and women's clothing.

While being checked out by this pair of bachelors, the trio noticed the women's apparel on display in the window.

War rationing was in full force in "the lower 48." May had never owned a pair of slacks or shoes other than those for work or Sunday. Upon inquiry, to their surprise, they learned those restrictions did not apply in Valdez.

Hmm. Shopping in Valdez. Not quite Chicago's Marshall-Fields, but maybe things aren't so bad after all.

The next day all three went to the Drug Store. May bought slacks, a sweater, a blouse, and heavy shoes. Found out they could get more than one pair, and if the store didn't have what they wanted, it could be ordered from a catalog. Unbelievable. It was a thrill to get shoes, emphasis on the plural.

And guess who sold her the footwear? Young Mr. John Ekemo. Working in the Drug Store because an enlarged heart meant a 4F classification and rejection from military service.

John also worked in a nearby grocery store. And spent much of his down time in the Pinzon Restaurant and Bar flirting with the girls and playing pool with Gilson. Now familiar with May on a foot-name basis, he boldly asked the Southern Belle out to lunch.

This was big small town news. Have you heard that John Ekemo asked that nurse out? With her accent, can he understand what she's talking about?

Did it really matter? Love speaks a language of its own.

A brief three month courtship ensued. Then, sensing a business opportunity, John moved to Cordova in July to take a job in Bill Leibe's grocery store. Word was the owner wanted to sell. John, his younger brother Bill, and Pete Lovseth would buy People's Market. John wrote and called May often, including the invitation to fly over for that infamous September deer hunt that started with her engagement and ended in Pettijohn's "Love Triangle with a Bear."

In the meantime, May was writing letters to Mississippi trying to explain to relatives on a different planet what "the Switzerland of Alaska" was really like. Evidently John had given her the complete tour, for in one of her letters, she mentioned that "liquor flows in Valdez like buttermilk in the South."

May returned to Mississippi in November of 1944 to spend almost two months with her family, and also to find a wedding dress. Bets were placed in both Cordova and Valdez that she wouldn't come back.

She did, riding a bus all the way from Vicksburg to Seattle, boarding Alaska Steam for Cordova, and wiring ahead to Johnny that she was on her way. When the ship docked, John wasn't there to meet her. He hadn't received the telegraph, and was sound asleep. Steamship Agent Frank Burns raced up town to roust him out.

Way to go, John.

Love Does Conquer All.

John received permission from Leibe for a trip to Valdez to get married. Back then a three day wait was required from issue of marriage permit to actual ceremony. Because of travel and the weekend, they waited 5 days. The good news was the wedding dress sent by May's faithful Aunt Gertrude arrived in time.

May Hammett and John Ekemo were united on January 31, 1945. Nine months, and a lifetime's worth of adventures, after leaving Vicksburg.

When telling this tale in November of 2011, May, looking back on it all, said that "I was young and dumb."

We both shook our heads. In awe. Not so.

Chapter 11

River Running

RIVER RUNNING: 1. Guiding a powered boat up or down
shallow Delta waters while avoiding sandbars and other hazards.
LOCAL DEFINITION
2. Decision making is always fun... when you make the right
decision. PETE DAHL ADAGE

"When you come to a fork in the road, take it."

YOGI BERRA, *The Yogi Book*

Part I: Follow the River

The key to success in river running is to "follow the river."

Duh. What else would you follow? Well, there are many possibilities. For
example, a sure way to find the Boxcar was to track beer bottles floating down
Little Arc. Bobbing brown buoys. That was back in the days when nobody was
very environmentally conscious, and there was water running from Scott Glacier
under the 9 Mile bridge to the top of Little Arc. Now that channel is so shallow
it's almost impossible to reach the legendary cabin for a cold one.

Another might be to navigate using USGS maps, which display sandbars in the
major sloughs. Unfortunately, the location of these hazards changes from year to
year. A single log deposited sidewise in a river during fall floods can alter the
gradually increasing flow of rising water during the next spring break up, and slowly
a new sandbar will develop directly below it. Trees and snags aplenty zip down
the Copper following any upriver high water event. They and the inevitable de-
positions behind them are future impeller or prop grinders in the making. Floaters
that make it all the way out the sloughs raise havoc with fishermen's gillnets.

Further, USGS maps are of such large scale to be almost worthless when zig-zagging across broad sloughs braided with bars. The most detailed ones available represent one mile per inch. The width of a thumb represents 1760 yards. Hmm. Plus such maps are revised once every ten to twenty years. Channels change in the course of a summer.

Modern technology, such as Google Earth, is helpful. But even its current scale is deceptive, not showing, for example, enough detail to help in the lower reaches of Pete Dahl, where sharp left and right turns in a narrow twenty foot channel wander through an open flat slough bed 500 yards wide.

Timing is a factor. If the Google maps were generated during big high tides, a slough looks like the Suez Canal. Just wait six hours. Likewise, time of year impacts the amount of water. It will be low early in the spring and late in the fall. But forget seasonal trends. In 24 hours, rainfall and runoff can change what a satellite sees.

Does anyone really think the computer experts at Google Headquarters, sipping lattes while gazing at Planet Earth from thousands of miles above, are aware of these variables? Murky waters more impenetrable to the eye than their mochas might be only two inches deep. Why, the appearance of channels can change faster than Ken Van Brocklin could guzzle a beer after crawling around under the Boxcar jacking up its piling.

On low tide it is now possible to wade across Pete Dahl at almost any point from the cabin all the way up to the cutoff toward Alaganik. One of the first chores each spring is to hike this two mile stretch packing Swede saw, shovel, bright surveyor flagging, and bear shot gun. The saw to cut alder poles which are stuck vertically on the edge of sandbars to mark the channel, in holes dug with the shovel so the shafts won't wash out on high waters; the orange and green flagging to make the dark narrow guides visible against distant backgrounds, using the "Red on right returning" navigational rule to decide which color will be tied on the mast; and the bear shot gun, well, guess what.

A few years ago, in late May, local pilot Mike Collins reported seeing several brown bears cavorting in shallow Pete Dahl water near the entrance from the Ala-ganik cutoff. Intrigued, he banked his Super Cub back to see what was happening. When the tide dropped, sockeye salmon had been trapped between sandbars in a long flat pool, and the bruins were having a field day. Fresh tracks in that area are always evident when marking the channel. Same thing happens in the fall, as Bud Moore and my son-in-law Tom Carpenter discovered while waiting in an airboat for enough water to make it through. Only this time it was silvers, not reds.

But what about this "follow the river" theorem?

Well, it was first presented back in 1959, by Bill O'Brien Sr., one of the original owners of the cabin on Alaganik. Bill was a rotund fellow, florid of complexion, and not lacking in willingness to share his opinion and knowledge on most subjects. He had stopped by our cabin to visit and share a B and B with Dad, who mentioned we had hit a few sandbars on the way down. "We" actually meant me, since from Day One Dad had turned navigation operations over to yours truly. An act of trust and confidence that meant a lot to a 15 year old. It also freed him up to sit with his back to the wind and have a couple cold Lucky Lager's on the way down, but that was secondary.

Bill assumed it was Dad who was grinding his way downriver.

"Why, Don, all you have to do is follow the river."

"Really?" asked a perplexed Old Timer.

"Sure," replied O'Brien. "Just think about where the water has to go, and follow it."

"Right," said Dad, who clearly didn't get it.

"Seriously," said O'Brien. "Think about the water coming downstream. It flows along the cutbank on the outside of the curve, then reaches a bend and point that pushes it across to the opposite side, where it repeats the process. Do you have a map? I'll show you."

The pair set jelly glasses on the table and refilled them with V.O. as I found a USGS map dated 1953 buried in a Blazo Box shelf. Alex Colner's name was printed on the lower corner, with a pencil line trace of the route to our Pete Dahl cabin site. Colner was a short veteran fisherman who always dressed in classic Pendleton whipcord pants and jacket in town, and spoke with an almost indecipherable accent, source unknown. Evidently Dad at one time had asked him for directions, which were lost in translation, based on the results of our first attempt to reach the Promised Land.

Using freshly replenished drinks as paper weights and a Cordova Outboard Shop pencil for a pointer, Professor O'Brien explained Theorem One of Hydrology 101 as if he were Euclid demonstrating Basic Postulates.

It made sense. And worked well, as long as there was significant water running down the wet highway to create a channel, and the river had numerous bends. What about long straight stretches?

No problem. Theorem Two. "Read the river."

Oh boy. Like every other subject, the more advanced the theory number, the more complex, right?

Dad couldn't read a tide book. How in the world could he "read" a river? Yet it wasn't an unheard-of concept. Dad admired Harry Curran, who was great at reading the river. So was his son Dean. As were many local commercial fisherman.

Basically, there are subtle clues to be seen from the appearance of the murky water, especially when it is moving with the tide or flow of the current. Smooth water in one area, with a little line of ripples next door, probably means a sandbar.

Waves that are whitecapping in one area, and rolling nearby, indicate a change in depth. However, windy weather, hardly uncommon on the Detla, often make it difficult to discern these elusive markers.

Boat behavior also provides hints. A sure sign that the water is getting shallower is a sudden increase in boat speed and motor rpm's. The bow of the boat somehow bends downward as the stern comes up, the flat bottom "planing" more efficiently. Always causes an increase in pulse, dry mouth, and hair standing on the back of one's neck, for if a course change doesn't occur immediately, what happens next is usually a screeching halt and lower unit flying in the air, filled with sand and racing at excessive speed as you try to pick your self up and shut things down.

Conversely, if the boat starts slowing down and losing "step," that means you have dropped into deeper water. Which can be frustrating when trying to maintain speed while packing a big load, or maneuvering to avoid bad weather. The lower part of main Alaganik is famous for this latter condition. The channel is directly opposite the storm wind direction. In places, it is impossible to scoot along the edge to dodge big swells and rough chop, as the water is deep right up to the cutbank. A stretch of river that has made many a trip home miserable and dangerous.

Unfortunately, much of Theorem One went out the window following the earthquake. A seven foot uplift in the Pete Dahl area meant there wasn't near as much intertidal water running up and down the sloughs. One would think new channels would gradually develop, but unfortunately a second factor soon entered in: a steady shift of the main Copper River to the east.

Far upriver, the famous Million Dollar bridge crosses the Copper at 52 Mile. Built in the early 1900s during construction of the CR&NW railway, this engineering marvel passes between two glaciers at a location where the entire river is constricted into one roaring flow. Ice bergs from Miles Glacier above come shooting under the bridge, diverted from span supports by triangular cement emplacements that have withstood more than 100 years of battering. Huge pillars of ice tumble from the Childs Glacier below the bridge; a truly spectacular vista. Once beyond the glaciers, the Copper spreads out and begins playing the shifting, random-route game that has created the entire Delta over eons of time.

During the early days of gillnetting, significant flow poured through all the channels below, providing major water from Cottonwood Point in the east to Pete Dahl and Alaganik in the west. Railroad engineers recognized this, and dealt with it by building large steel span bridges similar to the Million Dollar Bridge across large tributaries at 27 Mile, 28 Mile, and 34 Mile. Those bridges are all gone now, damaged by the earthquake, and then rendered useless by lack of water.

Standing on the modern cement and steel bridge at 27 Mile, and looking downriver with binoculars along the western bank, it is possible to see a broad open cutoff to the right a mile below the road. This is the top of sloughs that cut westward and flowed into Alaganik and Pete Dahl. Where Lt. Allen's Expedition, and king salmon that made it past O'Brien-Lantz secret gillnets, struck the main Copper. Today these channels are almost completely dry, except after torrential rains and flood conditions upriver. As late as the 1960s, considerable water passed under the 27 Mile bridge and found it's way down Pete Dahl. Gillnetters could run their bowpickers all the way upriver to anchor just above the bridge during fishing closures. The eastward shift of the main Copper has made that impossible.

And the stretch of "highway" eastward from 36 to 39 mile has become a civil engineer's nightmare. Almost all the ever-shifting flow of the Copper now roars through that area, overwhelming bridges designed for a much smaller flow. Bridge 339, at Mile 36, was finally closed in 2012 as water scoured under the support piers and washed out the far end. A beautiful USFS campground and viewing area near the Million Dollar bridge now sits mostly idle and inaccessible, as State highway designers try to figure out what to do. A Million Dollars won't even cover the cost of blueprints.

Dad always said "you can't screw with Mother Nature." But boy, can it screw with you.

With no water coming down 27 Mile, there is no water coming down Pete Dahl. And with earthquake uplift, there is much less tidal water coming up Pete Dahl. Creating a Perfect River Running Storm at the junction of the Alaganik cutoff and upper Pete Dahl Slough.

It is at this point that water flowing from four directions converges to create a just dandy sandbar and maize. First, the slight flow of silt bearing water coming down from the Copper. Second, the incoming tide from Alaganik flowing past Glasen's cabin and then hitting Pete Dahl. Third, the very slight tide making its way up from the mouth of Pete Dahl. And fourth, perhaps most perplexing, the tide that somehow rushes up from the mouth of Walhalla Slough to the east and pours through a narrow 30 foot wide gutter almost directly opposite the entrance from Alaganik.

Talk about Deposition Central. Currents from four directions meet, stop, and have a field day making sandbars. The weakest is the tide flow coming up Pete Dahl, which arrives an hour and forty-five minutes after the time listed for high water in the Tide Book. Have sat there in my river boat looking at a completely dry Pete Dahl Slough gradually become covered with muddy water pushed up-stream. Lots of time to wade down across the half mile bar trying to decide if there is enough water to make it across while going full bore on the step. My riverboat draws six inches of water at 5500 rpm's, while traveling a teeth-gritting 30 miles per hour. Thirty to zero can happen in a heart beat.

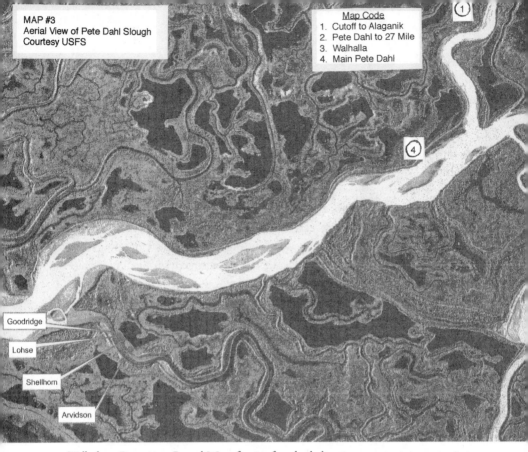

MAP #3
Aerial View of Pete Dahl Slough
Courtesy USFS

Map Code
1. Cutoff to Alaganik
2. Pete Dahl to 27 Mile
3. Walhalla
4. Main Pete Dahl

①

④

Goodridge

Lohse

Shellhorn

Arvidson

"Talk about Deposition Central. Water flowing from both directions converges to create a just dandy sandbar and maize." Cabin locations indicated in the lower left.

Given all that idle time waiting for the tide and pondering options, I've developed Theorem Three for river running this stretch. Which actually contradicts, but strangely, also reinforces, O'Brien's Theorem One.

For this section, don't follow the river, because there is no river. Follow the tide. By thinking of it as a river running the wrong way. Turns out the flow of incoming Pete Dahl tide, despite its relative weakness, is now usually much stronger than any current coming down from 27 Mile, except in unusual flood conditions. Consequently the channel in upper Pete Dahl has shifted to exactly the opposite sides from where it would be if significant water was flowing down stream. Where we used to run on the east bank, now we hug the west. And vice versa.

Perhaps this should be called the Shellhorn Corollary. For it only applies to mid-Pete Dahl. Alaganik still has enough downward current coming from McKinley Lake to obey the basic original O'Brien precept.

As for Eyak River, just ask its most frequent patrons, Randy Bruce and Julius Reynolds, for their theories. Post-earthquake tides have almost zero impact, and flow from Eyak Lake and Ibeck River has diminished. The river is silting in badly. However, they do have one big advantage. Since tides are irrelevant, river running can be done at any time of day or night, and they don't have to be worried about being stranded for 12 hours on falling tides. What wimps. They're missing half the fun.

For trips to our cabin, it now takes at least a 12 foot tide to cross the Alaganik Cutoff -Pete Dahl junction. Plan on being there at the right time. Better have waders and bear shotgun if arriving late. Be prepared for a two hour walk to the cabin, including some serious and spine-tingling bushwacking. At least you can follow your footprints on the trek back to retrieve the boat.

Finally, consider this. The tide is receding in front of our cabin thirty minutes after high tide in the Book, yet it is flooding at the junction two miles up river for another hour and fifteen minutes. Figure that one out.

In fact, Tom almost has it ALL figured out. Acquired an airboat. One of the biggest and best on the Delta, formerly belonged to Gary Weinrick. But guess what? Even it will not travel on sand. In late September 2013, he and Bud Moore waited two hours for two inches of water to cover the junction bar, and barely made it through - in the dark, using a big LED spotlight mounted on top the prop cage to help find their way.

What a guy won't do for a duck.

Part II: Peachtree Point

23 May 1987
The dark blue Ford Bronco XLT was jack-knifed near the end of the boat ramp. A late evening tide was boiling up Alaganik.

"What the hell?," thought the the driver, who had been launching his 14 foot Alumaweld river boat at this very spot for years. It was dusk, 11:30 p.m. in late May. Big 13 foot tides always seemed to occur in the middle of the night or very early in the morning that time of year.

A trailer hitch bolted to the rear bumper was under water, yet somehow the stern of the flat-bottomed boat was not. The bulky red jet unit fastened to a 70 hp Johnson outboard wasn't even touching the water, and engine exhaust from the Bronco's tailpipe was making a gurgling "pop pop" sound as it spit water back out.

Well, this is what XLT stands for, thought the driver, as he confidently shifted into 4 wheel drive. Just pull forward and try again at a different angle.

Except the vehicle didn't move. Double "What the hell?"

Oh. Put it in 4L, you dumbie.

Again, no motion.

By now, the brackish water was up to the running boards on the driver's side. Yikes.

Stepping out with hip boots pulled up, the operator waded back to see what was going on. Something was definitely amiss.

Crap. Winter ice and freeze-ups had lifted several of the interlocking two foot wide cement slabs of the ramp. Steel rebar that held the pieces in place was bent and twisted. The lower part of the ramp, where the trailer wheels sat, was higher than the rear tires of the Bronco. Not only that, the back tires had slipped into an enlarged gap between two slabs, and were spinning on loose sand underneath.

The tide continued to flood in. High water at the landing was an hour after the time listed in the tide book. There was going to be at least another 45 minutes of incoming water.

Holy crap. Goodridge and the Boys better show up pretty quick, or I'll be using my boat to pull the truck out.

Ah, Alaganik Landing Adventures. A staple of every trip to the cabin. Pent up energy and excitement after slaving Monday through Friday in town. Weekend Warriors in a hurry to have fun.

In this case, even wilder enthusiasm. It was the last day of school. Kids aren't the only ones excited when the last bell rings.

A huge bonfire on the gravel banks of Sheridan River, beer chilling in icy-grey fast-moving waters from the Sherman and Sheridan Glaciers four miles upstream. Snacks, burgers, salmon, steaks on a grill over alder coals. Laughter, tales of another school year gone by, eventually crashing in sleeping bags under the stars with Dusky geese honking in the background.

Teacher comrades Al Cave and John Davis always scouted out the precise location several days earlier. Height of the river; biggest pileup of trees, snags, root wads, and miscellaneous firewood built up by flooding waters the previous fall; accessibility from the road; and flat sandy terrain for folding camp chairs and tents among the criteria.

No cell phones back then. A brief All-Points "Out The Road" Bulletin was posted in the high school and elementary teacher's lounges. From there it was head to the Sheridan, stop on the bridge, look up and down river for telltale wood smoke. Signal from an Era past. Only the sound of drums missing. Faces smudged with black from firewood ash and war hoops would follow.

My job was to bring a 3X5 U.S. flag, plus Swede saw, line, duct tape, and grab ties. A tradition that dated back to our first End of The Year Shootout. Stars and Stripes snapping in the breeze. The same flag has flown at Softuk, Cape St. Elias, and Hook Point when we opted to charter small planes and fly to USFS public use cabins at those locations. Mounted on the tallest pole we could find, whose base was wedged upright in the roots of a tangled stump pile, or imbedded deep in the sand. Patriot's Pride, and more than one Salute, before the sun would set. All that was missing was a bugler. Trumpeter swan filled in.

This year's Blowout had started routinely and successfully. Great bonfire, food, frolic, and quality B.S. below the Sheridan Bridge. With more to come. While planning for The Day, someone, while grouching about sleeping on rocks and swatting mosquitos, had pulled out a tide book. Memories of soft bunks at the duck cabin and famous Pete Dahl Snappers the next morning flashed to mind. A Double Down strategy spread like fireweed.

Let's picnic at Sheridan right after school while waiting for the tide. Then go down river and spend the night at Shellhorn's cabin. So what if high tide isn't until 1 a.m. It hardly gets dark this time of year.

Right.

So parked on the roadside by Sheridan River bridge had been my Bronco and riverboat, John Goodridge's big pickup plus airboat, and several other "rigs," as Idaho Spudsters Bob Lenz and Mike McHone called them.

Lenz was high school counselor and boys basketball coach. Hailed from Melba, Idaho. Good luck trying to find it on a map. His CHS Wolverines went 29-1 that year, making it all the way to the State 3A semi-finals, before losing to arch-rival Anchorage Christian in a game steeped in controversy. He had good reason to drown his sorrows.

McHone was the high school principal, also from Idaho. He had gained fame by tackling and bodily carrying off an irate mother of one of Lenzo's top players in the post game melee after the ACS loss. She was chastising fiery Lion's Coach Randy Dunton about the relationship between his religion and his coaching style before McHone intervened. Twenty-five years later, local fans still talk about The Game.

Goodridge's fiberglass-hulled airboat was one of the biggest and most powerful around. Fortunately, as it turned out. Powered by a 350 automotive engine, built from scratch by Cordova High's trio of Voc Ed creative geniuses, alias Goodridge, Morgan, and Trani, this baby could fly, take bad weather, and pack out whole moose.

John and I had run our boats back up Alaganik together in 30 mph winds a year earlier. It was lousy and rough. I would see his airboat vanish in a wall of white spray, and then come shooting out, engine roaring. Impressive. Plus John tended to the more rational side of the Sheridan fire, being a self-proclaimed "Jack Mormon" from Utah.

As I stood at the landing pondering my predicament, the thumping of an airboat bouncing on its trailer over the pothole-filled gravel Alaganik Landing road echoed across the horizon. No need for speed limits on that meandering byway; all three miles filled with reverse speed bumps. John's truck and airboat emerged from the distant timber line, followed by several other vehicles. It would take about ten minutes for them to arrive. This was going to be close.

I braced myself for what was surely going to be quite the show. A line of colleagues spouting out clever one liners before springing into action. They'll be talking about this one for years.

What, you planning on driving your Bronco to the cabin? 4WD doesn't mean "for water drive," Dick. Hmm, if you keep the doors closed, maybe it will float. Look, John brought his air boat, Dick brought his car as a boat, we won't even need the river boat. La de da.

Done savoring the moment, time for rescue. John dropped the airboat off its trailer on the grassy bank. Not by mistake. Standard SOP. Captain G. hopped up in the elevated drivers seat, and fired off the Monster. Its big wooden prop spun merrily. Bugs and hats went flying as he wiggled the large rectangular wind vane rudders, slid across the gravel, and splashed into the slough.

The boys unhitched his trailer, we tied a line from the back of his truck to tow hooks on the front of my rig, and quickly pulled it out. The water was now high enough to launch the boat on the smooth upper half of the ramp.

We were in business. Of what nature was indiscernible.

Loaded all the gear and supplies. Lenz and McHone would ride with me; John Davis, Al Cave, and Jay Beaudin with Goodridge. Off we went. The airboat gang had all donned full-sized red-hued noise-protecting headsets. The engine and prop made an eardrum-popping deep-throated roar.

My crew turned the bills of their hats backwards and unscrewed the cap off a fresh bottle of Peachtree Schnapps. We downed a P & B, and let loose a roar of our own. This was mandatory for the first trip of the year to the cabin. Followups to keep warm while running in the chilly evening optional. Moderation in all things, preached Dad, he of the post-WWII B & B School of Thought. Right. How about Do As I Say, Not As I Do?

Did I ever tell you the story about a 1944 copy of Life Magazine unearthed in the Cordova High School library storage room? It cost 10 cents. Today the same magazine costs $4.00. Used it as an example of exponential growth in Advanced Math class, and challenged students to find the equation for the curve, so they could then predict what it would cost ten years hence. Fun project. The kids and I were equally fascinated with the publication's content. Many reports on the war, of course. But it was the ads that were more revealing. Seems like every third page either had a sales pitch for whiskey or cigarettes.

The back page spread was the capper. It showed a group of doctors in scrubs puffing away from an observation balcony as surgeons and nurses below performed an operation. Bold print proclaimed: "Nine out of ten doctors prefer Lucky Strikes."

John Davis recounted his Dad's story of the Invasion of Europe. Beside ammo, C-rations, and all other kinds of gear, each soldier was issued a carton of Lucky Strikes before hitting the beaches. No wonder years after VE Day, B & B's, plus clouds of cigarette, cigar, and pipe smoke, were still the norm at the duck shacks.

Who could possible question that Generation's preference for a B of highest possible proof?

By switching to Peach, we were clearly the New Breed. Moderation, in deed.

In my small river boat, a bench seat runs from gunnel to gunnel amidships. A steering console is attached to the starboard side, so Mike and Bob were sitting right next to me. Kind of like one big bar stool. Yipee. School is out. No kidding.

We were in the lead, Goodridge following several hundred yards behind to avoid our wake. Cruising. As we approached the entrance to upper Pete Dahl, telltale signs of a potential issue with water level became evident, even in the late evening light. Sand bars, stumps, obstacles not normally visible, clear indications there was no runoff coming down from 27 Mile. What ever water covered the dreaded entrance bar at the junction was going to be tidal.

Back in 1987 the water itself was still having a hard time making up its mind. Since we first began running the river in 1959, the channel at that junction had always been along the far bank of the slough. Where is should have been, based on flow from 27 Mile, the curves of the river, and also the tide flooding in from Alaganik, which certainly couldn't take a 90 degree right turn at the sharp corner on the near bank.

However, nothing ever stays the same, right? Gradually a channel was emerging along the near bank. The downriver flow was splitting around a big sand bar developing right in the middle of the 300 yard wide slough. Which meant there was half the water in each side.

With little light and no wind, aided by Peachtree Night Vision goggles, the whole slough looked flat grey. The stern of the boat picked up, as did our speed. Sure sign of shallow water.

Hang on boys.

Rule One of jet boat operation in shallow water is to pour on the coal. Honestly. It says so on page two of the Manual that comes with the jet unit. The theory is correct. Slowing down reduces speed, which means the stern drops, increasing the likelihood of hitting bottom and sucking up sand in the jet unit intake.

So I pushed the throttle forward, glanced at the tach which now read 6,000 rpm, and gritted my teeth. We were screaming at least 30 miles an hour. And then we weren't. But Lenzo was. Off the seat, over the bow, a full somersault, landing sitting on his butt, bottle of Peach still in hand, surrounded by two inches of water.

I frantically shut down the outboard, its jet impeller screaming at outrageous speed in the air. The wake that had been behind us washed over the sandbar, and there sat Lenz. Who calmly unscrewed the cap, took a swig, and said "Welcome to Peachtree Point."

Had often wondered about all the screwball names on maps of American. Now I knew.

Goodridge and Company arrived. Pulled right up alongside us. Perfect depth for an airboat. By now the crew had the rescue drill down pat. This time it was tow the boat, not the Bronco. Tied my bow line off the stern of the airboat. All of us rocked the riverboat back and forth, prop wash from the airboat spraying crisp invigorating slough water over us as the craft slowly slid across to the deeper water along the far side.

In a testimony to the durability of Johnson outboards, after washing sand out of the jet unit, the 70 horse fired off. We let John go in front of us, so I could use his wake breaking on shallower water to find the channel.

Made it to the cabin. Took down the window shutters, hooked up the propane, fired off the oil stove, and celebrated. We wanted fun, we got it. How long the celebration lasted is unclear. Honking geese woke me up. Rain pounding on the roof, wind whistling around the cabin corners. While making a pot of coffee, I noticed Jay slowly walking out the door. I glanced out the back window. He was sticking his head in the pond.

24 May 1987

Post-school party held here after Hourve Doures on the Sheridan River. Lots of geese, gulls, and snipe nests (with 7-10 eggs each). Lots of beer and Black Queen too. —Jay Beaudin

Good time was had by all… Hospitality was excellent. The weather may have been a little damp but, not matter, a great place to relax… play some cards… drink a brew or 2… and watch the birds. —Al Cave

With school out a much deserved weekend of R & R. As always Dick was a host with no match… had a great time! —John Davis

School's out for another year, but what a year it was. Didn't shoot any bear, but shot a lot of bull. —Bob Lenz

Down at midnight on evening of 22nd, with Bear Slayer McHone and poker players Davis, Cave, Goodridge, Beaudin, and Lenz. John in airboat, me in jet. Came down on the tide after end of year party out the road. Helped navigation immensely. Rained and blew yesterday, so we called Chitina Air (Ken Van Brocklin answered!) and John G. stayed an extra day. Nice today. Finally cleared off. —Dick

Part III: Landing Lu-Lu's

Alaganik Landing has often been the sight of what we call Lu-Lu's. Dandy experiences, also known as Doozies. Something about roaring out the road with river boat in tow, brimming with anticipation of another trip to the cabin, rushing to catch the tide. Creates an atmosphere fraught with potential peril and questionable decision making. Operation Peachtree Point was an illustration. It was a Doozie.

During the years I was off to college, teaching, or in the Army, Randy took up the slack as Dad's partner in misadventure.

Twice they lost the boat. That is, launched the lightweight metal Quachita, and either forgot to toss the anchor on the bank or tie the bow line to a nearby alder. Pulled the Rambler up to the parking area, sat waiting for the tide to come in. Walked back down, and the boat was gone. Out drifting in the slough. Usually under sail due to a stiff southeast wind, which pushed it to the opposite bank.

Not a problem. Patience. Have a stiff B and B while waiting for someone else to show up that was also heading down river. Interpretation #2 of Dad's Time and Tide Mantra.

Prior to launching the boat, gear and supplies were unloaded from the back of the station wagon and set alongside the ramp. Everything was hauled out the road inside the vehicle, after discovering it would bounce or blow out of the boat on the drive out, requiring delays for retrieval.

Materials left on the ramp would also drift or blow away. To be picked up enroute, drifting down the slough. Supplies were sometimes forgotten in haste to get under way. Neighbors from the adjacent cabins would show up with boxes marked "Don Shellhorn, Cabin." Deliver them Freight Collect to the front door. Pete Dahl forerunner of UPS. Guess what the service charge was. Boxes found on slough banks required an added stop and of course therefore a doubled fee.

Randy's shotgun was a victim of Ramp Rush. Everything had been hastily unloaded, wind was howling, the tide was falling. Randy was holding the bow line of the boat, as Dad went scooting back up the ramp, peering through rain splattered windows. Laid a tire tread mark right across the stock of Randy's trusty 12 gage, which had been left on the ramp. Which made for major laughter, a B and B, famous "Horse's Ass" name calling, and a built-in excuse when missing flocks of attacking widgeons the next morning.

I think the barrel is bent. This gun won't shoot straight. Shells won't eject. It keeps jamming. They sure don't make things like they used to. Etc etc etc.

However, no landing story can top events on July 28, 1994.

For two summers, the USFS had been supervising construction of a 900 foot handicap accessible elevated walkway and viewing platform adjacent to the picnic grounds and parking area of Alaganik landing. Volunteers from fourteen different countries spent one month stints camping at the landing while helping build the structure. Lived in tents, prepared meals on site, contributed a total of 4000 hours to build a marvelous wooden path overlooking both the slough and a nearby pond.

Most of the volunteer groups came from Europe. July 28th happened to be a Friday, end of the work week. For the work party, that evening was cleanup time, including a dip in the slough to freshen up for a weekend visit to Cordova.

Late on the tide, I came roaring down Alaganik road with a boat load of supplies, including gas, stove oil, propane, and building materials. Pulled the boat around the turnabout to back it down the ramp for launch in the slough. And noticed several people splashing and swimming in water which was clear on this particular set of tides.

Hopped out to undo the tie-down clamps on the stern of the boat, put in the drain plug, and loosen the bow line. Hollered a greeting to the gang in the slough that I would back in slowly, and be out of their way quickly. They were silhouetted by late afternoon sun.

The response from the bathers was unintelligible, but I chalked it up to my lousy eardrums. After so many years of roaring outboards and blazing shotguns, two alarm clocks are required to make sure we don't miss the morning shoot.

Climbed back in the truck, and slowly eased the boat trailer into the water.

And out of the slough, walking slowly, came several volunteers. Speaking a foreign language. French. The guys had on swim trunks. And the gals? Parlez vous francais? Oh my. They had on scanty underpants. Period. Golden sun glistened off topless dark-haired nymphs, who chattered and laughed as I practically submerged my truck before regaining composure.

They stopped to visit as I peered out the door.

Have you ever tried talking to a topless beauty leaning in your open car window? You know, idle chit chat, dah de dah. Focus, Dick, focus. I'm sure what I said wouldn't have made much sense even if I knew French. Quickly discerning that I was a blathering idiot, they smiled, waved Bonjour, and walked up the ramp. Sauntered might be a better description.

Was it just me, or was the whole ramp swaying from side to side? "Tall and tan and young and lovely, the girl from Ipanema goes walking…" flashed through my mind. Now I knew why the mountains behind Alaganik brought passages describing the Grand Tetons in A.B. Guthrie's *The Big Sky* to mind. Appropriately named by early Plains trappers dreaming of Rendezvous. A word of French origins. Grand indeed.

The landing would never again look so lovely.

11 pm, 28 July 1994

*A **first** at the landing. A flock of naked ladies. No B.S. Forest Service crew from foreign country skinny dipping after working all day in the sun. If only I would have had the case of beer I brought down the night before. —Dick*

Part IV: A Taste of Cordell

The word *cordell* means to use ropes to pull a boat up-river from the bank while others in the boat use poles to hold it off shore. A.B. Guthrie describe the process in detail in his book *The Big Sky*. In the early 1800s it was a standard method of moving vessels all the way up the Missouri River from St. Louis to the Rockies while exploring America's vast frontier.

Lt. Henry Allen and Company attempted to employ the same technique traveling up Alaganik and the Copper River in 1885. So it was not without historical irony that just over one hundred years later I, too, was so lucky to try my hand at cordelling up those very same waters.

Our daughter Heidi was attending Western Washington University at Bellingham, Washington, and invited college friend Jeremy Morace to visit Cordova in July. Naturally, a trip to the cabin was part of the tour. We went down at 10 p.m. on July 15 and spent the night. It was calm and buggy, but we had a good time. Cold beer, fun trying to see who was the best shot with a small .22 caliber rifle, and stories by the fireplace.

Good weather held, and the next day we headed back up river in shirt sleeves. My boat flies when lightly loaded, and also has a tendency to slide on sharp curves, of which there are plenty. It was a great ride. Until we entered the junction with main Alaganik.

Some ungodly clank and grinding sound, followed by a dead 70 hp outboard. Not your typical crisis. Couldn't get it running. So there we were. Adrift at the mouth of Alaganik. No cell phones back then, and no luck with a handheld VHF. Options: wait until someone realized we were overdue; row; or pull the boat to the landing. Rowing was out. The riverboat was built with an extra foot of beam by special request. I tried rowing it once, and gave up. Waiting would mean a long stay. We were early on the tide, which was still flooding in. It would be dark before anyone became concerned. So it was Option #3.

One slight problem. I was the only one with hip waders. My crew was in short boots. Therefore I was the shore gang, i.e. the puller. Walk with the bow line over my shoulder, and pull the boat upstream, while the crew used oars to push it away from the bank. Vector physics, in considerably inefficient form.

It's five miles from lower Alaganik to the landing. In the center of the slough. We quickly discovered paddling across the wide waterway to the opposite side would be necessary in several places because of steep cutbanks. Brush had grown right up to the top edges of the slough, and there was no place to walk under these sheer drop offs.

Despite the zig-zags, it was fair going the first two hours, as the tide was still flooding slightly. By the time we had crossed the slough three times and reached the halfway point near O'Brien's cabin, the current was dead calm. Uh oh. That meant it would soon be ebbing, with an increasing rate. At the three hour mark we reached Snag Point, and the slough was now a river, flowing against the direction of our march. I was developing a great appreciation for what the Allen Expedition must have faced farther up, when the full Copper merged to one huge roaring river racing at a steady seven miles per hour. Wow.

From Snag Point to the landing was only a mile. It took another hour. The current was so swift I had to literally pull and stop, pull and stop. Yet this was not even close to the flow rate of the real Copper.

We headed to town. Didn't even stop at the Powder House for a cold beer. Too tired. Wonder if Allen and the Boys found any pubs on their way across Alaska in 1885.

15 July 1993

Dad & Jeremy and I came down about 10 pm last night. Sipped schnapps and listened to Dad's crazy stories. This morning we got up and shot Dad's guns and I am the best shot in the whole darn world. I put them to shame HA HA. It was a good trip but there are still way too many bugs. —Heidi

21 July 1993 (next trip down after their visit)

If Heidi and Jeremy had known what was in store for them, they wouldn't have been so cheerful. Right after we hit Alaganik slough, $1500 crankshaft I had replaced this spring went out. Me the only one with hip boots. So they pushed with oars, and I waded and pulled boat to landing - took 4 hours. A first, and a last, to be sure! —Dick

Part V: Where's the Slough?

Always looking upward at the banks of today's Delta sloughs, it's hard to imagine a time when those edges would vanish in an overflowing surge of incoming tidal water. Yet during the pre-earthquake era, they did exactly that. Which made for some challenging river running.

Dodging sandbars in a slough was one thing. Trying to stay in the slough when the whole Delta looked like one big murky lake was another. Tides of 13 feet or higher did that. The water would creep over the banks in front of the cabin, and anything that could float would bob about. Building materials had to be stored under the shack, gas cans set on the deck, hip boots worn to the outhouse.

At particular risk were the boats. Allow one to drift over the banks and stay there as the tide receded, and you had a problem. The pre-earthquake rigs were predominately heavy wooden skiffs. They were not designed for portage.

Up until 1964, much river running was done late at night. I mean really late, like pitch black. Spotlights at hand, we would head down river after Dad got off work, catching tides at 8 or 9 pm. Ditto coming back. Otherwise it meant some very short weekends.

23 July 1960

Going home after midnight on high water tonight - real good weekend with Shellhorns. —Julia, Ann, & Nord

During daylight hours it was fairly easy to identify the deeper slough channels during overflowing tides. Remember "reading the water?" However, that was impossible at night. More than once, the long shafts of twin 18 horses on our work skiff would suddenly fly up in unison as I missed a turn and we skidded over grassy banks covered with a foot of water. The good news was immediate action sent the flat bottom rig back into deeper water. But look out for that last step, or end up walking off an eight foot cutbank. Which made for a chilly boat ride home.

Big tides did make for good shooting. The flats vanished, and almost every duck was airborne. Randy and I tried capitalizing on this by hunting the slightly higher grounds of the lower Cutoff. Carefully anchored the boat in the slough, plopped our Deeks in a deep nearby pond, and waited. No ducks. Every theory has its exceptions.

This was back before the days of chest waders. Everyone hunted using hip boots, often overlapped with a pair of rubber bib-style Helly Hansons cut off at the knees. Kept the rear end dry, and made walking a bit easier.

The pond we were hunting almost went over our hip boot tops when we set out the Deeks. When the big tide surge flooded over the banks, the pond became deeper. Duh. We needed to get back to the cabin to begin closing things up. Yet the pond was now over our boots.

No problem. Mindful of little gutters, we carefully waded across marsh grass covered with a foot of tide water, found the submerged bow anchor, and pulled the work skiff over to the bank. And then proceeded to push it across grass into the pond so we could retrieve the decoys. While noticing that the water was beginning to retreat.

Tides run in series, increasing in size to reach a zenith, and then declining. This was the biggest of the set.

Yikes. Talk about scrambling. To move a thousand pound skiff for 12 rubber duckies.

We arrived back at the cabin. Covered in sweat.

Dad: How was hunting? Looks like you had quite a workout.

Yep.

23 October 1960

Closed cabin, had poor hunt, too nice, and us deadeyes couldn't hit our hats. Yesterday tide was so high ran boat into pond we were hunting on to pick up the decoys. —Dick

Had a good time and good steak dinner but no ducks. —Randy

He could have added: And do have boat to go up river.

Chapter 12

Capsized

CAPSIZE: 1. To turn bottom up; overturn. Origin: late 18th cent: perhaps based on Spanish *capuzar*, "sink (a ship) by the head." WIKEPEDIA
2. "Watsjold had a duck hat two sizes too big on."
CABIN LOG, 5 SEPTEMBER 64

"Each man uses his boat in his own way to fill certain needs.
There are as many roads to Nirvana as boats and men."

WILLIAM SNAITH, *On the Winds Way*

Part I: Ballast Man

Given the right combination of wind and tide, lower Alaganik can be brutal. Said Jim Webber, who has gillnetted the flats his entire life: "It can get really ugly out there." And he was referring to experiences in heavy cabin skiffs or bowpickers, both designed to handle rough weather.

Author Jim Harrison agreed. "A strong wind makes all creatures nervous."

Restricted to hunting on weekends due to work obligations, it was not uncommon to push the envelope when trying to reach the cabins. During the pre-earthquake era of larger crafts such as our 22 foot Banta plywood work skiff, it was sometimes uncomfortable but doable.

When by necessity the switch was made in 1964 to a lightweight, low-sided, 14 aluminum Quachita, the waves suddenly became bigger. Going downriver with the prevailing stormy southeast winds wasn't too bad. Match the swells and make sure trailing seas weren't coming over the transom. Slowing down in rough water generated by wind against incoming tides became a necessity, and then freeboard was a concern. Wind would blow spray into the boat. Automatic bilge pumps became the norm.

At higher speeds, the light boat's bow was susceptible to lift from winds. The trick there was to make the heaviest passenger ride up forward. Ballast. If bad weather was anticipated, weight, rather than lack of it, became a consideration when Dad was selecting victims for a duck hunt. Partners with big sea experience were an added plus.

So he and a big, veteran crab fisherman named Tom Jatzeck were at the cabin on a stormy October weekend, and planned to pick Randy up after he finished work on Friday. They contacted him on the CB radio, said the weather was sketchy, but thought they could make it. Told him to bring a case of beer, which as always was somehow in short supply. Randy drove out to the landing, and sat waiting in his truck, which was rocking back and forth in the wind.

No way they are going to pick me up in this, he thought. But looking down the white-capped slough, on the western bank he noticed two figures struggling against the gusts.

It was Dad and Tom. Conditions were so bad they had stopped near Snag Point and started walking. Which meant lower Alaganik was even worse. Upon arrival, they sat in the car, warmed up with a B & B. Why absquatulate? Let's wait for the wind to die down. Which it always does when it becomes dark.

Hmm. Out of sight, out of mind.

Ah, what the hell, let's go for it. Guess who issued the sailing orders.

"I remember it was raining so hard that by the time we walked back down to the boat, the cardboard case of beer was falling apart," said Randy.

How about their ride back?

"Tom road on the seat at the very bow, hanging on," said Randy. "Your Dad's hands became so cold he could no longer hang on to the throttle and tiller of the outboard, so I had to take over and steer. We stopped and bailed the boat out once we were in the cutoff."

Beyond Alaganik, the rest of the run was in smaller more protected sloughs. However, there were stretches requiring dead-on headwinds and waves. Do the math of running 20 mph into a 40 mph wind, and it adds up to a hurricane-type experience. Plus lots of bow ballast.

12 October 1969—7:30 p.m.

Dark - cold - wet. Typical operation. Tom and Don picked me up at landing. Sat in car and drank beer until wind went down? Skipper Shellhorn made fine trip.
—Randy

Up to landing to pick up Randy - little sloppy. Cook Jatzeck got shook - waited
for tide and wind to go down? No problems little dark but made it OK. —Don

Part II: Bottoms Up

Dad often recruited cabin company at Bob Korn's Alaskan Bar, directly across the street from Shellhorn's Clothing. Patrons would scatter when they saw him coming for an after-work cold one, even though tales of survival were a staple of conversation along its lengthy wooden bar.

This beautifully-crafted elbow support of Cordova's prime waterhole had migrated up the coast along with many of its early patrons in 1908. With coal and oil near by, Katella, just 50 miles south, had been selected as the terminus of the Copper River and Northwestern Railway. However, the town of 5000 was quickly abandoned after violent storms in the fall of 1907 destroyed a dock and breakwater that extended out into the Gulf of Alaska. Ambitions and thirsts shifted north.

Dad liked to give everyone in Cordova a chance at a once-in-a-lifetime trip to Pete Dahl, and the lucky winners for this trip were Harry Nicolet and Bob "Moose" Henrichs. An unlikely duo.

Nicolet was a slender lifetime Cordovan; his Dad worked for the railroad. Harry sold life insurance, and had his own cabin down Glacier. A veteran duck hunter and fisherman, perhaps he wanted to make sure one of his long time New York Life policy holders continued paying premiums.

Bob was the son of Postmaster Hollis Henrichs, who was instrumental in the transplant of moose to the Delta. As a youngster Bob had helped raise the spindly calves, hence the moniker. He was a rugged heavy-set fisherman. Clearly a handy guy to have around when high and dry on a sandbar. Plus ideal ballast.

October 12, it was noted in the Cabin Log, was Columbus Day. Before this trip was over, Harry and Bob probably wished they were on the Santa Maria. The cruise down was uneventful. Hunting was slow.

12 October 1965 "Columbus Day"

Hope we get enough birds so Harry can have some. He is a good cook, though he
still lives in the past, all I hear is how well he did last year. Got two snows and
one mallard. Don, one teal, and Harry still didn't connect. —Bob Henrichs

Tomorrow, Bob Henrichs, tomorrow. —Harry

Well, tomorrow turned out to be a day when the whole crew didn't connect. After a dismal morning shoot, in which Bob noted in the Log he "just guided for Harry," Harry replied "That's right. You got zero, I got 2," and Bob added "Right, 2 fish ducks," Dad noted the fresh snow on the mountains and decided it was time to close the cabin.

When they had finished all the chores that entailed, twilight, which happens pretty early in late October, was upon them. Had to wait until the late tide anyhow. As is often the case when closing the front window shutters on another season, several B and B's were in order.

"It was already pretty dark by the time we left," recalled Henrichs. "Your Dad was definitely in top form. We kept getting lost, turning around and backtracking, with him saying repeatedly, "Don't worry, we're almost there.""

As Yogi would say: "We're lost, but we're making good time."

Henrichs: "Finally it was pitch black. We didn't have a clue where we were. Harry and I insisted we stop and spend the night."

They pulled up to the riverbank, took the outboard off the stern, removed plywood floor boards, laid them on the ground, and turned the boat over to "sleep" under it.

Capsized

Actually they propped the rig up with oars to create a lean-to. The boat had a 48 inch beam, so their legs stuck out beyond the edge of their green aluminum shelter. Perfect. By mid-October it stays dark over 12 hours.

Snow fell that night. They woke to the honking of trumpeter swans and a fluffy white blanket on their exposed hip boots. Sunshine, dead calm, and ice crinkling in the slough.

Put the boat back together, and Captain Columbus Shellhorn discovered the landing. Also proved that the origin of the word "capsized" from Spanish *capuzar* was correct.

Although it was not the boat's noggin.

Part III: Load Limit

We never did capsize or sink a boat in Alaganik. None the less, after several hairy Quachita experiences in the big slough, in 1973 Dad decided to switch to the famously seaworthy 14 foot fiberglass Boston Whaler. Brochures describing the craft's unsinkable design undoubtedly caught his eye. Plus its double chime hull cut through the waves, rather than pounding, as do flat-bottomed boats.

However, the Whaler drew more water, and was the absolute antithesis of hull shape for a jet unit. Which of course is what he had mounted on the stern. All 50 horses of it. Compounding the problem was Dad's complete denial of weight restrictions. The Coast Guard required sticker on the transom of this craft read: "Load limit: 3 adults or 500 pounds, power limit 40 hp."

Dad's solution was a narrow line of red duct tape around the sides and stern, indicating maximum tonnage allowed. A visible reminder of load limit. How he came up with the placement of this line is unclear. Why he bothered is also unclear. It was completely ignored.

1 August 1973*

Please note the special asterik on above date. This was a very notable trip down to re-habilitate the Erosion Project of last year, which evidently was poorly engineered - by who? (the Old Timer). I took off this morning to secure material to work on Erosion Control, Phase II and like Nixon got over loaded, that is, took on more freight than we could handle. Anita the Doll worked at the store while I was out getting said material. We left town around 2 p.m. supposedly to catch the tide thru the lower Cutoff. However due to the excessive load of material, had a helluva time launching the boat at the landing. Departed around 5 p.m. so no chance to go thru the lower Cutoff, did lighten the load at the Forest Service cabin (one tank of gas and one case of beer). All smooth sailing until coming down Pete Dahl not paying attention to the channel - then whamho hit a sand bar. What with the load the bow of the boat went down and we were (boat) filled with water. (Mom the Doll kept her cool). Went to the bank and unloaded what was left on the boat. Then bailed out the boat as we picked up the floating items drifting down the slough. Salvaged all except one box of groceries, a horse shoe set and last but not least a chain saw I had rented from John French, will try on the low a.m. tide to locate them. —Don

Yes, after much pushing, cussing and heaving too, the boat overloaded, we crept warily down like 25 minutes to O'Brien's cabin! Then to Forest Service cabin. I was asked to look about for something to bail the boat with, while Captain (?) Shellhorn lightened the load by afore mentioned and drinking one..My trusty bailer turned out to be a paper cup I found in their outhouse! After an hour we reached Dar's cabin okay. Request for beer by Captain denied as I sat atop the light plant. By assuring me we had it made I relented and opened one for him, trusty cup bailing with the other hand. Then some how the boat was tilted at a peculiar angle and plastic bags, boxes of tools etc began floating away. Don after them. After releasing my grasp on the non-sinkable Whaler emptied his heavy chain and sack of spikes and started bailing again. After much retrieving got all but the chain saw and a plastic tied bag filled with canned goods and his new set of horse shoes I suggested we not bring. No lucky horse Shoe for me! Anyhow after arrival at 8:30 p.m. and unpacking, drying out everything we are safe in the cabin and the Captain has been demoted to Cook. Fashionable dining at 10:30.

*Its gotta be better Manyana. **That Shoe Horn did it all by himself** - —Anita*

2 August 1973

Woke up at 7:30 a.m., slept like a (water) log. Nice breeze and sun breaking thru clouds. Went down to bail the boat, thought the tool box was there (gone) - Had breakfast around 10 a.m., then took off on "Mission Impossible" hoping by some chance we could retrieve the tool box and chain saw. Walked up to the approximate location of disaster area, put on waders and walked back and forth, naturally water muddy so only way to find anything was to step on it. Found the tool box, kept on floundering around, kicked something solid reached down to my shoulder in the water - a snag. Just about ready to say to hell with it and then suddenly hit pay dirt - the chain saw! What luck!! Now at the cabin. Just had to have a B/B after that! —Don

Took off for rescue equipped with binoculars, waders, bug dope and rope. Arrived on scene low tide 10:49. Scanned slough for indication of missing chain saw and tool box. Partner with waders on, probing stick in hand, to walk to his favorite (?) Bar. Paced back and forth in front of it fighting the urge to step in. Meanwhile I stand in the mud knotted up rope in hand ready for rescue! He stumbled onto something solid - tool box found. Yipee. The Bar still tempting him, continued his slushing about and with great exultation pulled out the chain saw! Mission accomplished! Ladies and Gentlemen this series of thrillers has been discontinued due to lack of enthusiasm on my part. —Anita

Part IV: Inverse Grounding

Like its Quachita predecessor, the Boston Whaler also managed to land upside down. On land, not water. It was fall in 1974. Randy, Frank Sherby, and I were returning from an trip to the cabin, towing the boat on its trailer behind my red Ford pickup. One of those incredible blue sky, golden hills, breathtakingly crisp October days. Hunting had been poor, but the weather and scenery made up for it. Had frozen hard the night before. Dark sky full of stars and Northern lights; skim ice in the slough and crunchy grass in the morning.

Occasionally, the hunters got it right, and didn't capsize their boat in the water or on the highway. L to R: Chuck Taylor, Randy Bruce, Dick Shellhorn, Frank Sherby, standing in front of the Boston Whaler at Sheridan River, 14 Mile, September 1972

We were at 4 Mile on the paved portion of the road. From 5 Mile on into town, during fall and winter, much of the asphalt is shaded from the sun by Heney Range. We hit a patch of black ice, and the rear of the truck skidded sideways. Having driven in Cordova's ice and snow for many years, no problem. Corrected properly by turning in the direction of the skid. Zig-zagged a bit, and came to a stop on the gravel edge of the highway berm.

Looked back to see how the boat and trailer fared. The trailer looked great. We could see it quite clearly, since there was no boat on it.

Yikes. Scanned the highway. Yep. There she was. Upside down in the middle of the road. Capsized, so to speak.

Boston Whalers are built to last. The only damage was to the fiberglass engine cover of the inverted outboard. We backed up, flipped the craft over, lifted it on the trailer, and drove to town. Slowly.

Went by the Cordova Outboard Shop. Randy worked there, and knew the back room was full of older Johnsons used for spare parts. Al Jardenski's Museum. Found an engine cover from a similar model. Snapped it on, drove up to the folk's house, parked the boat and trailer under the carport.

Dad and Mom were off at the Pioneers Convention in Juneau. When they returned, Dad asked how the hunting was.

Pretty slow. Weather was too nice, but had a good time. Boat ran great, had plenty of water, never hit a single sand bar. He never did learn we capsized the Whaler…on the Copper River Highway.

Part V: Keel Over

Capsized Event #3 was the real deal. Even though it occurred in the middle of the night, and no one was in the boat. Tom, his brother Tim, Bud Moore, and I at the cabin. Bud was a retired City waterworks employee who ran Tom's Whiskey Ridge Trading Company bike and gun shop while Tom was gillnetting; Tim had been up from Illinois for a summer working with ADFG.

We had taken two boats down, my solidly-built 14 foot Alumaweld; and a narrow, lighter aluminum rig Tom had "got a good deal on." Always lots of wheeling and dealing going on at Whiskey Ridge, where B.S. flew faster than canvasbacks zeroing in on decoys.

I had borrowed Tom's craft once when my outboard was in the shop for repairs. Despite higher sides and a semi-v hull, it was tricky to handle. Had to anticipate its next move. Turn the tiny steering wheel, and after a few seconds delay, it might decide to head that way. In narrow stretches of sharp turns, forethought was essential. As if the river itself wasn't enough challenge.

The boat's light weight and high sides proved its undoing.

We had anchored the boats side by side in the slough in front of the cabin. A bow line to an anchor on the beach, stern anchor off the transom corner to keep the boats in the slough, rather than hanging up on the steep banks and rolling over on falling tides.

The weather was deteriorating, winds building, sheets of rain coming down. So much precipitation the slough was rising due to runoff, even though the tide was falling. It was late afternoon when we arrived, too late for an evening shoot. Had dinner, played cards, built a fire in the fireplace, and checked the boats a couple times before going to bed. The bilge pumps were working fine. Listened to the wind howl all night, cabin and bunks shaking. Alarm went off an hour before shooting hours. It was still roaring outside. Opted to forgo the morning shoot, and rolled over in our sleeping bags.

An hour later, we heard footsteps coming up to our cabin, and a knock on the door. It was neighbor Mike Arvidson.

"Ah, hey guys, do you know that Tom's boat is upside down on the other side of the slough?"

We jumped out of the bunks, and sure enough, just a few feet of the keel protruded from brownish runoff water racing down the slough. The stern and outboard were completed submerged. We donned waders and rain gear, and used my boat to cross the slough. Wind and current had evidently pulled both anchors loose; the lines were a tangled mess. It took all of us to turn the craft over. Bailed it out with 5 gallon plastic buckets, and then manhandled it across to the cabin side.

Amazingly, within two hours, the boat was up and running. A testimony to the older Johnson outboards, with less electronics and simpler design, as well as Tom's mechanical prowess and a spare battery in the cabin.

It wasn't long after that before Tom gave someone a good deal on the rig, and purchased a new 17 foot aluminum Roughneck with a 90 horse Evinrude E-Tech and jet unit. No capsizing that baby.

9 October 2006

Wind blew my boat over and sank in slew. Never a dull moment at Pete Dahl. Managed to flip and get started. Unreal. Hope we make it to the landing. —Tom

Tom and Tim did make it to the landing. Bud and I accompanied them with my rig, in case they had problems. I came back down to close the cabin. Mike Arvidson and Rob Brown left the next day, but were back in two hours. After 11 inches of rain in 24 hours on top of all the previous precipitation, the road had washed out in several places on both sides of Sheridan River. Sounded kind of familiar. Will engineers ever figure out the Copper River Delta? The road would be closed for at least a week, so there was no way to get from the landing to town. We were stuck.

Ran upriver the next day in both boats. Runoff at the landing was so high that the water was level with the parking area. The highest we had ever seen it. We put the boats on trailers, and then waited for a plane Mike's father Gus had had lined up to fly us to town. Were a bit surprised when a red and white Cordova Air Beaver on floats came roaring over, banked, and landed in the slough. A slow, massive freighter, it was Alaska's Bush workhorse, and could haul six passengers plus a ton of gear.

"Well," said Mike, "I guess Gus must have thought we brought up a lot of stuff when we closed the cabin."

A week later the road was repaired, and my wife drove me out in her car so I could pick up my truck and boat at the landing. She recognized the washout locations from our famous trip in 1966.

Part VI: Bow Down

Slowly it was becoming apparent that I had quite a find in son-in-law Tom. Daughter Gretchen made a great choice. He was replacing Dad in generating new and exciting adventures at Pete Dahl. Which was no easy feat.

Tom and his moose hunting buddies sank my anchored riverboat right in front of the cabin by running over it with an airboat. While crane hunting below the cabin, he nearly went swimming when a sow brown bear with three cubs strolled out of the brush line and backed him into Pete Dahl slough. He bought and sold boats like popcorn.

And he brought guests that provided new levels of entertainment. Upon discharge from the Coast Guard in Cordova, Tom had gone to work for Dick Groff at Whiskey Ridge Trading Company. Eventually he bought the shop from Groff, who by then had become an annual guest for a fall hunt at the cabin. Groff like stoggies, guns, and Scotch, in no particular order. Carried a huge pistol and big shotgun on every hunt, plus so much ammo the bow of the boat would tip down when he stepped aboard.

When the ladies weren't around, standing on the front deck to enjoy the sights while leisurely relieving oneself was SOP. During daylight hours, there were perhaps migrating birds on the horizon; stars, meteors and Northern Lights, for passing the moments in the night. If it wasn't raining and blowing like hell. Whatever the weather, with age, these interludes seem to occur more frequently and also last longer.

One dark night, Groff headed out to "communicate with Nature." Someone may have heard the door open and close, but ignored it. No one detected a splash. Groff had done a head-first swan dive off the deck into a large metal clothes tub beside the steps that served as a boot wash. Bow down, in nautical terms.

A tough former USFS smoke jumper who eventually became the District Ranger in Cordova, "Groffstein" didn't say anything about it the next a.m. Was a little slow getting his gear on for the morning shoot, but weren't we all.

After a short boat ride up to the slough, we had to walk 500 yards to the blinds. Included crossing one particularly deep and muddy gutter. Groff made it down the near side, but couldn't get back out. S.I.M. We pulled and pushed him up, and he then admitted his side was hurting a bit. Of course we had just the pain killer for that. X-rays in town a few days later revealed several cracked ribs. Groff was dubbed Pete Dahl's High Dive Champ. And became famous as the only duck hunter who had capsized himself - off the front deck.

30 September 2008

WOW!!! Watch that first step. —Dick Groff

Part VII: Truly Capsized

Listening to weather forecasts is a popular duck cabin pastime. Waterfowl somehow seem to also tune in. Appear to sense an imminent weather change, maybe it has something to do with barometric pressure. Often they will make significant moves just before a storm arrives. Or if pinned down by bad weather, shift southward as soon as it breaks.

Local birds not yet interested in heading south also have their own patterns. Randy and Julius swear strong SE winds plus incoming tides produce good hunting, with birds moving up the channel below Eyak River almost on schedule. Foul weather and big tides are normally a sure fire combination on most of the Delta, as wind and water chase fowl inland from exposed mud flats that extend far off shore.

The Big Arc Slayers are blessed with cabin locations at the very mouth of Eyak River, near the former pre-earthquake cutbank edge of the Delta. Most of their hunting is done below that old line, on the edge of sweet gale and marsh grass that has gradually moved further off shore. In a way, they are hunting the newly evolving duck flats, terrain similar to what the whole Delta looked like prior to 1964.

By luck of the draw, the cabins at Pete Dahl are over a mile up the slough from its cutbank entrance. Since Pete Dahl Slough has gradually dried up, access to the evolving marsh lands below the mouth is almost impossible, except on extreme tides.

The original cabin sites were located right in the middle of a series of big, shallow ponds that were outstanding hunting. Now they are too deep for dabbling ducks. Which seems like a contradiction, as the land was uplifted by the earthquake. Credit beavers for that one, as their population has exploded and they have dammed up the drainage systems. Plus, thanks to uplift, saltwater flooding caused by 13 to 15 foot tides that covered much of the Delta no longer occurs. The overflows that prevented brush, vegetation, and trees from growing stopped in that fateful spring of 1964. The ponds are filling in with vegetation, and duck habitat is vanishing.

7 Aug 1974

Took a cruise across the slough to eyeball sand dunes for future strawberry patch. Did not realize there were so many earthquake cracks on that side. Also with glee spotted 2 small spruce trees growing almost directly across from the island below the cabin, first we have seen down here. So named the point "Pete Dahl National Forest." —Anita

Wow. If she could see it now. Stands of forty foot tall spruce and cottonwood extend skyward on every patch of higher ground. A forest indeed, Nord would say. Probably with an unprintable adjective before the word "forest."

None the less, there are still a few ponds near our cabins that ducks "use." They have discovered feed on the surface of weed patches that are encroaching on these waters. One of them, located a mile from the cutbanks, is often frequented by them, especially if the Perfect Storm Combo of weather and tide exists.

So.

Tom and I were sitting in the cabin late in the season, October 28th, 2011, to be specific. We had actually closed the cabin and put away the decoys on October 16th, fearing freeze up. But had marked the dates October 24 thru 28 in red. Sixteen foot tides. Only happen once a year. Waited to see if the warm weather would hold. Which it did. Came back down, re-opened the cabin and blinds. Hunting was slow on Monday, the 24th. Disappointing. We were counting on big flocks of green heads, bands of drakes always the last to leave. The weather was too nice. That was about to change. Be careful what you wish for.

Propane lights were hissing as we ate dinner. Darkness arrives early in October. The little transistor single-band weather radio propped against the glass of the cabin's front window went through its continuous loop of forecasts for various areas near the cabin. Passage Canal, Prince William Sound, Cordova and Vicinity, and then the one we pay attention to, Cape Suckling to Gore Point.

Yipee! Duck weather. Gale warnings, said Hayden's "Clerk of the Weather" in his tinny computerized voice. Which were detailed as winds 40 to 55 mph. We poured a glass of Peach Schnapps and started lining up our gear, loading shell vests with extra ammo. "It's gonna be hot" is one of my son-in-law's favorite phrases.

Kind of tough to go to bed at 7 p.m., so we built a fire in the fireplace, shot the breeze, dah-de-dah. Weather forecasts are typically revised every 8 hours. This Meteorologist was having nothing to do with that. By 9 p.m., he had cranked up Storm warnings. Winds 50 with gusts up to 75. We cranked down a couple shots of higher test Liquid Inspiration, trying to keep up with the escalating wind outlook and rising expectations. Finally went to bed.

Morning shooting hours are leisurely by that time of year. It was still pitch black when we rolled out of the bunks at 6:30 a.m. Made coffee, and turned on the Weather Meister. It was blowing outside, but nothing unusual, probably 25-30.

Perfect. The sight of a long line of four-curl mallards flaring into decoys against that kind of wind is unbelievable. They just sort of hang there. We kept glancing out the window. Still too dark to run upriver.

The weather forecast scrolled to our C.S. - G.P. area, and I almost spilled my coffee when Mr. W, with excitement thought impossible in his computerized voice, uttered "Severe Weather Warning. Hurricane Advisory. Steady storm force winds of 50 to 65 miles per hour, with hurricane force gusts of 75 to 80 miles per hour."

A first in cabin history. Had never heard the word "hurricane" officially used in a forecast while at Pete Dahl. In fact, had to ask the retired Coast Guard Quartermaster sitting across the table just what it meant. Heard a lengthy tale about the local Coast Guard buoy tender Sweetbrier hitting bad weather enroute from Cordova to Hawaii, and only 5 crewman well enough to steer the boat for 3 days while the rest of the gang, including the Skipper, stayed in their bunks or crawled to the "heads." Ever wonder why they have gained that nickname?

But hey, what's going on? It was now light enough to see the boat, and winds remained in Small Craft Advisory range, 25 with gusts to 35.

Despite increasing technology, including satellite imagery, weather forecasting seems to have gone down hill in accuracy. Which creates increasing skepticism. Have cancelled deer hunts and fishing trips based on predictions, only to arise to blue skies and mild winds. Plus "foul" weather equals ducks, right? Like, why do you thing they are called water "fowl"?

"It's gonna be hot!"

Later, as seems oft the case following sketchy decision making, son-in-law would say it was I who lobbied for going hunting. As I recall, when we headed out the door, he had the stern anchor pulled before I even reached in the boat.

We raced up river, anchored the boat, and started walking to the blinds. Our trail follows the grassy edge of an old slough, so the banks five feet above us on either side are thickly lined with alder and willow. Which combine to break the wind, even with most of the leaves gone by late October. None the less, we could hear a distinct whistling sound as we marched single file toward a cut through the brush to the pond and blinds.

As we step up over the old slough bank and trudged through waving barren trees to the edge of the pond, it became apparent there may have been a degree of veracity to the tinny pentameter-like predictions. What's that children's fable about Crying Wolf?

Winds were now a steady 30 with gusts to 40, based on the wave tops on our shallow pond, according to the well-trained eye of my ex-USCG companion. A few birds jumped from the grassy perimeter of the 500 yard wide lake, edgy after being shot at several times. Tide wouldn't be high for awhile; the wind surge would help it cover the outer flats.

Consensus: "It's gonna be hot, maybe."

Followed by, "They ain't gonna fly in the cabin."

Right. A corollary to Captain Olaf Gildnes's Mantra "They ain't gonna jump in the boat" when urging the crew to make another set after three water hauls in a row while seining on Prince William Sound.

My wife once submerged her little Dodge AWD Eagle above the floor boards when berry-picking partner Barb Cave urged her to "go for it" and cross a small gravel stream enroute to huge, glistening blue berries visible to the naked eye 50 yards away on the other side.

Hmm.

We leaned into the wind, and tromped through grass and muck to the near side of the pond. Had two small metal boats stashed in the brush; rowing across the lake was much easier than walking. The gooey bottom was a pain, even though the pond depth varies from only one to three feet.

The near blind was 50 yards out, on stilts, right on the edge of marsh grass encroaching on the lake. Forty or so plastic decoys in front of it were bobbing wildly. Traditionally, being a retiree who can hunt either blind any time, I hunt the near blind when partners are on the scene. Tom, who has to work at his shop during the week, goes to the far blind. Usually it sees more action, especially when birds are heading south in big flights.

Reaching that blind means rowing across the pond. One of the small row boats was a 12 foot Quachita, a bit newer and wider; the other was an older model, 14 feet long, but narrower. It leaked somewhat, but was easier to row. Tom opted for Boat #2. I began walking out to Blind #1, glad for breathable chest waders with attached insulated boots, as the water splashed up to my waist.

Tom rowed by, struggling through weeds in the shallow near shore waters. I hollered Good Luck as he cleared the marsh and headed across the open pond. Predictably, the far blind, 400 yards away, was directly abeam the increasing wind. The boat started a zig-zagging course, Tom trying to head into the wind briefly and then let it spin the bow toward the blind. He was rowing hard and going slow. Memories of steering the USCG buoy tender Sweetbrier enroute to Hawaii probably flashed through his mind.

The wind was increasing dramatically. Blowing so hard it stopped making waves and flattened the water. Had never seen it change so quickly, and scream with such force. Ever. Another Pete Dahl First. Decoys were flipping over, brush was flying off the blind, which was flexing sideways in the wind. Sheets of white water picked up by gusts were racing across the pond. The noise was frightening. Fascinated, I watched a lone mallard fly frantically for several minutes 200 hundred yards out, trying to decoy in. It didn't move anywhere. Finally said the hell with it, turned downwind, and vanished at 90 miles per hour in 3 seconds.

Through watching that show, I turned to check on Tom.

Holy crap. Where was he? Normally it is easy to see all the way across to the far blind.

Tom is an excellent wing shot, and it's fun to watch him stand up, see birds collapse in the air, and then hear the sound of the shotgun as the duck splashes on the pond.

Today the surface had become a white wall of spray, impenetrable as fog. He was out there, somewhere. Nothing I could do but wait. Thank goodness the pond is shallow.

In 30 minutes, the wind dropped back to 40 with gusts to 50, and visibility improved. Looked through binoculars. There was Tom sitting in the blind. The row boat was on the edge of the grass 30 yards below the blind, upside down. Normally we store it several hundred yards above and beyond the blind in the brush, so incoming birds won't flare off it.

Interesting.

28 October 2011

Down with Dick on 24th 13.8 tide. Home 28th 15.6. Crazy weather 2nd morning. SE 80 knots rain so much could not see other blind. That is after rowing across pond, or I should say surfing. The boat flipped on a 70 kt gust, landing on top of me, throwing gun and pack into water. Shot few ducks. When we got back to cabin my boat was across slew, bow anchor pulled out in wind and caught by stern anchor. Me and big tides and wind Don't mix. The next morning awesome hunting all northern mallards. Last night the Cards over Rangers, 10-9 in 11, by far craziest World Series game ever. Headed home till next year. Sunny out, no wind, 45 degrees, is this really October? —Tom

No. But it really was a Capsization.

Chapter 13

Dogs

DOG: 1.*Canis familiarus*, family *Canidae*, probably domesticated from wolf in the Mesolithic period. A domestic carnivorous mammal that typically has a long snout, an acute sense of smell, and a barking, howling, or whining voice.
Wikipedia

2. "There they go. Look at those dogs go!"
P.D. Eastman, *Go Dog Go*, my daughters' favorite bedtime story

"Dog and god are the same word spelled backwards."

Snaith, *On the Winds Way*

Part I: Candy

Our very first duck hunting dog was a small brown and white Cocker Spaniel named Candy. Great house pet, she was part of the family in our tiny little house on 2nd Street. A gentle, tolerant animal that all four of us kids cuddled and loved. She had several litters of pups, fathers unknown, the offspring somehow mostly spaniel-like. Nothing is more amazing to a child than watching and playing with fuzzy little pups as they grow.

Candy wasn't built for hunting on the Flats, but you could never tell her that. She was too small for the tall grass and big ponds, but try sneaking out of the house with a shotgun while leaving her behind. Just wouldn't happen. Even when it was October and there was skim ice on the ponds and marsh that would make her paws bleed. More than once it wasn't only ducks and geese that we carried back from the blind.

Candy had a great nose. Nothing is more disheartening than losing a bird that has come down in the grass. I have spent countless hours cross-hatching patches of tall reeds and marsh to no avail, even after carefully "marking" where the bird plummeted immediately after the shot. Candy would run over and find them in a jiffy, wagging her tail and barking excitedly, even though most of birds were too big for her to carry.

Dad and I watched in amazement when she decided to swim out and retrieve a Canadian goose we had dropped in a pond down Eyak. The big Dusky came floating back toward us on its back almost magically, as we couldn't even see our little Spaniel madly pushing it from behind.

She was a good dog.

Part II: Copper

Dog Number Two was a pure bred male Golden Retriever. Got it as a pup in 1958, the year before we built the cabin. Named it Copper, for both its color and the place it would hunt. Not super original, but it fit.

Golden Retrievers are well known for their gentle disposition, and Copper was no exception. However the species also has a reputation for sometimes not liking the water, especially when it's cold, and our pup proved that quickly. Had a heck of a time giving her a bath, even with warm water. Yikes.

By the time Copper was a year old, he was part of the manifest on every trip to Pete Dahl. Knew how to heel, could do a respectable job of finding birds in the grass, and had some idea of what "fetch" meant. Would even bring birds back - as long as they weren't in the water.

Unfortunately, about half of the Copper River Delta is covered with that most fundamental compound. But hey, it was great having him along. That furry warm spot under his chin made a wonderful hand warmer on cold fall days; and you could count on it always being dry. Like all bird dogs, he could hear, see, and sense things way before me, so I would often rely on him to let me know if birds were coming in, by his suddenly alert behavior.

Plus he made trips to the blind entertaining. I mean, he would run half a mile around a pond to avoid crossing a three foot gutter of water six inches deep, and meet you with tongue hanging out on the other side. We spent many hours together sitting on the 2X12 bench in the blind; he was my faithful loyal companion, and I brought home a lot of birds I would have never found without him.

Strangely, the hunt I remember most with Copper had little to do with ducks. It was on one of those big pre-earthquake tides that flooded the entire Delta, creating a 50 mile lake on its lower edges. On those unusual days, you had to be very careful about tromping about, or could end up over your head in a hurry.

Ditto for navigating and anchoring boats; if they ended up high and dry on a falling 15 foot tide, they could be there for awhile.

These big tides, which occurred only once or twice a month, made for some excellent duck hunting. It seemed like every duck on the Flats would be in the air, scratching his tail feathers to try to figure out what was going on. A dozen decoys stood out for miles, and if you chose your spot carefully, you could sit on a duck stool or bucket knowing you wouldn't need a life jacket, because it was high ground that wouldn't be flooded to more than six inches or so.

Through experience I had found just such a patch of high ground a mile west of our cabin, halfway up the Lower Cutoff. Copper and I headed over there in our big work skiff. I anchored the boat very carefully in the slough, built a makeshift blind, tossed a dozen Deeks in the nearby pond, unfolded my wooden-canvas duck seat, and waited for the action. It was midday, little wind, mostly cloudy, visibility was good.

As expected, more and more ducks went airborne as the tide started boiling in. Bands of birds were visible in every direction. Copper was increasingly agitated. I was watching the waterfowl, his attention was on the water rising around us. Oops, I had somehow forgotten my faithful companion didn't like to swim. And it was already too deep for us to get back to the boat. Oh boy. I could see a plane flying over and spotting me in the middle of the Copper River Lake, with a big golden retriever sitting on my lap. The gang at the Alaskan Bar would be laughing about that one for a long time.

I reached over to pet and reassure my jittery companion, and realized he was stirred up not only by the incoming tide, but by what was on its surface. Swimming at us from every quarter of the compass were shrews, voles, and mice of every imaginable shape, color, and size. They had been flooded out of their holes, and were headed for the only high ground available. I glanced up and noticed many of the birds zooming around were not ducks; they were hawks, harriers, owls, eagles, and any other airborne predators on the Delta, having a field day diving and catching a cornucopia of food.

To my surprise, Copper decided to join the fray. In his excitement, he totally forgot his fear of water, and started racing around outside the blind, catching the invaders and wildly tossing them in the air. Defending our tiny island and his Master from the invading hordes, and scaring away every duck within sight. I felt bad for the little critters, but what were the options: me, my dog, and 500 rodents sharing a duck stool?

By the time the water started receding, I hadn't fired a shot, Copper was exhausted, and the tide shoot was history. We had shared a unique experience. For one golden day my retriever had raced around in water and fetched several hundred critters. We called it quits, used the long anchor line to pull the boat close enough to pile in, and headed back to the cabin.

The next day on the way to the blind, Copper pulled up to halt on the edge of the first little band of water.

I picked him up and carried him across.

Part III: Julie

Julie was a female golden lab. Member of the Lenz family, or should I say tribe: Bob, Deb, and their three boys, who could have worn war paint most of the time, based on their brotherly interaction.

The Lenz gang came to Cordova from small town Melba, Idaho, via Bethel. Bob was a standout high school athlete there, went to college in Spud Country, and then took his first teaching job way up north at Bethel, Alaska. Built a small school state basketball championship team in no time, and was recruited to come to Cordova by fellow potato head, aka High School Principal, Mike McHone. Taught some junior high classes, became counselor, had wonderful rapport with all the kids, and went on to build one of Cordova's finest roundball teams under a new 3A classification system. That 1987 squad lost only one game the entire year, unfortunately in the State semi-finals.

Lenzo, as he was known, had a great sense of humor. Had to, looking at some of the early squads he put out on the court. I refereed his games, and could always tell when he was a bit unhappy with my interpretation of the action on Cordova High's sparkling floor: he would send out a team captain during a break in the action, with specific directions to "Ask Mister Shellhorn if he could…," with the emphasis on Mr.

Bob also had a way with visiting coaches, creating friendships where hostility had existed before. He and Dan Eide, the latter of legendary Valdez volatility, became best of friends, and in the long term even had the cross-Sound mentor saying an occasional positive word to the Zebras, when not bellowing like a moose at certain calls.

Lenzo's early Cordova antics while sport fishing and hunting were the topic of much laughter during teacher lounge lunch room breaks, and led me to believe he might be duck cabin material. So I invited him to come along for a shoot at Pete Dahl.

Bob asked if he could bring along his dog, and I said sure, why not?

Taking a newbie on a duck hunt is always entertaining. They don't know the area or the drill, and you don't know what to expect. Plus adding a dog is often like putting a little extra Tabasco in your post-morning shoot Pete Dahl Snapper; it can increase the zest factor considerably.

We piled in my 14 foot riverboat and went roaring down Alaganik. Julie seemed pretty tranquil in the home setting, despite cowering in fear of random arrows and flying tomahawks from the trio of young descendants of Melba tribes who likely ambushed early white explorers. Now free from The D Team, aka as Dennis, David, and Daniel, she was all over the boat, racing from side to side as snipe zipped along right in front of the boat at 25 miles per hour. I had to constantly adjust course as the flat-bottomed rig tended to shift direction with the shifting weight, but Lenz didn't seem to notice, so what the heck, we had another cold beer.

There has never been a trip down river that hasn't been a big part of the joy and adventure of going to the duck cabin, and this was no exception. It was fun watching the dog, nostrils sniffing away, senses on full alert, countless eons of genetic change and adaptation for this type of moment. She was one happy animal, and so were we.

It was late afternoon by the time we pulled up in front of the cabin at Pete Dahl. We unloaded the gear while Julie went racing around to check out the area, tail wagging 90 miles an hour, nose buried in dozens of scents she hadn't smelled in years.

Evening hunts never have been much as the brush and habitat have changed on the Delta, so we settled in, fired off a small portable propane grill, tossed some ice in the glasses for a tonic, tuned in a ball game on the radio, let the dog run off more energy, threw a couple steaks on the barbie, sat on the deck watching for birds, and enjoyed the sun going down. A classic evening shoot at Pete Dahl.

Anticipation is half of hunting; we had a nice dinner, then a touch of Peach Tree Schnapps in some weird glasses given to my folks from some dry cleaning business that actually showed the ounces contained within, while enjoying an alder blaze in the fireplace, and headed to the bunks.

Only to discover one of the bottom ones had already been staked out. The back wall of the original 16X24 cabin has two tiers of 3 metal framed, canvas covered Navy surplus bunks, with the lowest ones only about a foot off the floor, designed intentionally for those having difficultly navigating to sleeping quarters. Julie had decided she liked the one on the lower left with its soft foam mattress and double layer of sleeping bags. Bob pulled her off, turned around, and she was already back in the sack. Hmmm, thought I. Wonder where she sleeps at home. Maybe under the bed to keep away from the prowling young Nez Perce wannabes at Camp Lenz.

The cabin addition also has a couple nice bunks, one, of all things, a metal hospital bed that Dad salvaged from the dump. It even cranked up and down.

More than one hunter recovered from the Evening Shoot there. I crawled in after setting a pair of alarms and turning off the propane light. Julie and Lenzo already had a snoring contest going in the two lower bunks.

The alarms rattled us awake an hour and a half before shooting hours, which is a half hour before sunrise. Had the standard pre-hunt breakfast: coffee, sweet roll, and a couple advil or aspirin; hopped in the boat, and went racing up the slough above the cabin until it became so narrow we couldn't go any further. Anchored the boat and started the 30 minute tromp to Walhalla. Arrived there right about legal shooting hours, with everything set up. Julie had been a model of decorum, even "heeling" on the walk over, maybe because she was exhausted from the day prior.

A nice morning, not much wind or cloud cover, mid-September, mild; I didn't anticipate a lot of action. I dropped Lenz off at the blind I usually hunt, dead center on the upper edge of Walhalla Pond, which is about a half mile across. When the wind blows southeast, the birds zero in on it. Over the years the blind had evolved into a mini-cabin; plywood roof, back, and sides on a creosote 2X4 frame, with a 2X12 bench, wide enough to seat two hunters. Now a couple weeks into the season, the local birds had become rather wary, so I had spent a lot of time camouflaging it, especially in the front facing the pond, since that was the direction for in-coming birds drawn by a spread of sixty plastic-molded decoys carefully arranged with a hole in the middle where the birds would hopefully be attracted into range. It blended in well, covered with loads of brush and grass matching the surrounding vegetation, the end result of hours of work, often out of boredom when hunting was slow. A labor of waterfowling love, it was a thing of beauty, a prize winner if they ever had a Pete Dahl Blind Decorating Contest. One time I had walked right by it in the early morning light, it was so perfect.

Often you can tell a lot about a duck hunter by his shotgun. Lenz was totting a pretty, well-maintained pump 20 gage. Maybe not big enough for geese, but obviously the guy must know what he's doing to bring that along, thought I. After all, Dad and I were about the only guys on the Delta who shot 16 gage Model 12 Winchester pumps until they both literally wore out, so who was I to judge a hunter by his barrel size.

I gave Lenzo a few suggestions on usual bird flight patterns, and said I would be on the far edge of the pond about 500 yards further away. Said just to blaze away, but please don't shoot the decoys, and that I would wander back through in a couple hours. He and Julie eased into the blind through the carefully concealed side entrance. I noticed the dog was on the bench before Lenz even got in.

I hadn't even made it to the far blind before I heard a three shot volley. Turned to see Julie swimming out to make a retrieve just as daylight was breaking across the pond. Awesome. Way to go, I hollered to Lenzo.

I slogged over to the far blind, it needed a little brushing up as it had't been used too much. Glanced up at the sound of another three shot volley to see Julie splashing merrily out of the blind and leaping into the pond again. All right!

Duck hunting from adjacent but well spaced blinds is a lot of fun. Sound travels much slower than light, and regardless of how many times you have witnessed it, seeing birds fold up in mid-air and start tumbling down before hearing the report of the shotgun is a fascinating sight. Almost as entertaining as watching a flock of birds decoy in, flare, and fly away unscathed, and then hearing shotgun blasts and verbal epitaphs. Plus sometimes birds missed from one blind will decoy to the other, if they haven't been shot at too many times.

Today all the birds were decoying into Blind # 1, manned by the Idaho Kid, who I was beginning to recognize was one hell of a shot. Every time he pulled the trigger, Julie was out retrieving. Very impressive.

This went on for more than an hour. I hadn't fired a shot. Lenz was blazing away, and by my estimation, had not only have his daily bag limit, but was probably running low on ammo. There were a couple extra boxes of shells left in a dry shelf in the blind, but they were 16 gage, which would be of no help to Little Big Man, i.e. Big Shooter with Little Gun. Lenzo did look like he had a little Nez Perce blood in him, it dawned on me.

So I decided to wander back and see how things were going, plus maybe provide some backup. For some reason Lenzo didn't hear me approaching the blind, maybe his ears were still ringing from all the shooting.

Hence he was startled when I peered around the entrance to the blind. I was very startled by what I saw. Lenz was scrunched over against the far side of the blind. Julie was perched in the middle, tongue hanging out, peering through a shredded stand of brush that used to be the front of my blind. And beside her sat a pile of decoys.

I was speechless, but Lenzo was quicker with quips than with his trigger finger: "I'm not shooting worth a damn, but Julie is sure retrieving great."

What?

On the duck strap hung one unfortunate little diver, a immature golden eye, which undoubtedly had made the mistake of swimming into the decoys.

Julie, loyal, faithful, confident, and even sensitive to ineptitude, had leaped off the bench through the brush and fetched a duck every time her Master shot. Unfortunately, the only ducks floating after Dead Eye's volleys were decoys. So there sat a pile of my finest widgeon and mallard look-a-likes, neatly arranged, with numerous teeth marks to memorialize her efforts.

Still trying to comprehend it all, I glanced through a wide open view of what was left of my blind to what what was left of my decoy spread. Several of the plastic survivors were canted left or right, more than one slowly sinking bow or stern first. I was about to ask the Idaho Kid how far you lead a swimming duck when Julie leaned forward and nuzzled my hand.

I realized here was a happy dog that had worked her rear end off, had a great day doing what she was bred to do, and wanted a little petting and reward for her efforts.

So as I stroked her head and rubbed her ears, I muttered to Lenz the Pete Dahl phrase that communicates recognition of a memorable performance and also a degree of endearment, "You Horse's Ass."

7 October 1984

Great time with wonderful company. Dog did better than the shooter.
—*Bob Lenz*

Part IV: Pride

The early evening shoot was in full swing at Maxwell's cabin on Pete Dahl. Glasses of golden liquor tinkled amongst ice cubes as Master Chef Les began cooking up dinner for the crew: Nord, Pogey Paulson, John DeLeo, and young Jerry Behymer.

"Copious quantities of booze were being consumed," recalled Behymer, a teenager who had spent the summer crewing on Les's seiner the Bear Cape, and had been invited down for a weekend with the Boys.

"We had finished hunting, and were sitting around the cabin when someone noticed a flock of ducks approaching. Les was a great wing shot. Grabbed his gun, stepped on the porch, pulled up, and dumped a big mallard right in the slough."

"The river was running strong. Les had a beautiful, faithful Chesapeake Bay retriever name Pride of Swinomish who saw the bird go down. The dog leaped off the porch, jumped in the slough, and went swimming after it. The current was so fast we all watched him vanish from sight around the river bend below the cabins."

Dusk was falling, and despite considerable hollering and efforts, Pride did not return.

"The mood was quit subdued as Les let his heart hang out about losing his dog. In fact, his love grew stronger with each drink proffered by his cabin mates to drown his sorrow."

"Some five hours after the incident we were getting ready to hit the rack, and heard a whine at the door. There was Pride, duck in mouth, and very tired."

"Lord knows how far and what hardships that dog must have gone through to get back to the cabin. But all was well with the world as we again hit the sack, Les with faithful Pride on a special mat beside his bunk."

Chapter 14

Swans

SWAN: 1. *Cugnus Buccinator*, a.k.a. trumpeter swan; mature
length 65 inches, wingspan 6-8 feet, recognized as the largest of
the 7 swans found worldwide and is one the heaviest flying
birds at 25 to 35, and occasionally 40, lbs.
R. H. ARMSTRONG, *Guide to the Birds of Alaska*
2. Swan dive: a particularly graceful fall into a pond, or off a
duck cabin porch. PETE DAHL DEFINITION

> "A thing of beauty is a joy forever."
>
> JOHN KEATS, *Endymion*

Part I: John, Ed, and Dan

Having a Chapter about swans among stories about duck hunting might seem
strange. After all, swans are protected. Shooting them is a no-no. Thank goodness.

The haunting call of these huge graceful birds resonates across the Delta and
Eons. Trumpeting together, their peal symbolizes lifetime mating, as well as a
gathering signal to young grey cygnets.

How anyone could confuse trumpeters with snow geese is beyond me.
Snows are much smaller, have shorter wings with district black tips, a much
faster beat wing beat, shorter necks, and usually travel in large but often disor-
ganized flocks, issuing a noisy high-pitched squeaky yelp. Yet more than once
hunters have mistakenly brought down trumpeters thought to be geese. What
a shame.

One veteran hunter who could tell the difference was my father-in-law
John Ekemo. He and I were trudging to Walhalla early in a grey, winding,

"It's been quite awhile since I got a snow goose," said my grinning father-in-law. John Ekemo, Dick Shellhorn, & Don Shellhorn heading out for an afternoon shoot, October 1979.

October morning. I was in front. A flock of seven trumpeters came floating by, battling a stiff southeasterly. In their signature single file, light just breaking on the horizon.

I hear a bang.

Oh no.

I turn around.

It's been quite awhile since I got a snow goose.

Really.

Yep, says John.

We walk to where white lays on tan. He picks up the bird. Black wing tips and that sly Norwegian grin under cockeyed glasses.

The last bird in the row had been a lone snow.

Almost as good as the time he dropped a nice bull moose out of a swaying fifteen foot cottonwood. Three hundred yards shot. We were in thick brush, John had climbed the sapling to see if he could spot the bull pilot and close friend Cliff Collins had spotted a day before while returning from Long Lake in his Super Cub.

Asked us to hand up his old Winchester Model 70 .270 caliber rifle and steady the tree. Say what? One shot later it was time for him to put his butchering skills to work and then head back to open the meat market at K & E Foodland on Cordova's Main Street. While his son Johnny and I tried to figure out some way to get 800 pounds of meat half mile back to the road and then to the grocery store's basement cool room where it would hang and age for several days amidst stacks of eggs, milk, and produce. Often wondered if dinner salads around town had a gamey ambiance during moose season.

Swans trigger memories.

Once close to extinction from market hunting for meat and feathers in the 19th and early 20th centuries, trumpeter swans have made a comeback. They seem to be thriving on the Copper River Delta. Many now forgo migrating south and winter here, especially at the end of Eyak Lake and the mouth of the Eyak River. Makes for a tough time during a really bitter cold spell, swans hunkered down in white humps on clear ice with a strong north wind ripping across the lake to ruffle their feathers. But most of them seem to make it through.

From 1977 to 1987, oldtimer Ed King helped the swans along, feeding them barley from Kenny Lake that was brought to Cordova in bags on the ferry from

Valdez. Toni Bocci of the local ferry office and the crew of the *F/V Bartlett* helped with the project. Ed used a wicker pack-basket and toboggan to haul the grain to a spot directly above the far side of the Eyak River weir, and the swan would come up and eat right out of his hand. One year 260 stayed over. Jack Stevenson was plowing snow for the Department of Transportation back then, and asked Ed to put up a flag on the far end of the Eyak Bridge when he was feeding the birds so he wouldn't bury him with a flying mass of snow when he was clearing the roads early in the morning. In the summer Ed would stop at Mile 30 on the Copper River Highway, and swan would climb down off their beaver house nesting sites to paddle over for a visit.

Trumpeters were also Dan Traub's favorite. A quiet, soft-spoken gentleman amidst the rowdy Pete Dahl bunch, Traub was a teller at the First Bank of Cordova, and hunted with his boss, Dick Borer, out of the cabin furtherest to the west. When everyone else was raising hell during the evening shoot, he would take a walk outside at dusk to listen to the swans calling each other while settling in for the evening.

Dan and his beloved birds had a sense of tranquility and grace about them that I deeply respected and admired. There was a lesson there.

Since Dad first took me to the bank to open a savings account, I always enjoyed going up to the teller's window, being politely greeted by Dan as I slide a bank book and proceeds from my paper route across the glass counter under polished brass bars, usually with some conversation about bird hunting or local events. Dan also kept score at the high school basketball games. He and clock operator Charlie Simpler sat crammed behind a tiny plywood scorer's table on the third and highest row of wooden bleachers in the crackerbox City Gym. They were there when we pulled off a stunning upset of East Anchorage, the high flying Thunderbirds from one of the biggest schools in the state. The crowd went crazy, while Dan calmly finished the scorebook in his best meticulous bookkeeping style. He was a good man.

Part II: Swan Shows

Swans are one of my favorite decoys.

Say what?

As it turns out, their white color and size makes these huge birds extremely visible from long distances, a plus when trying to pull ducks in on on a blustery waterfowl day. Swans are popular with many ducks, widgeon and mallards in particular. Because of their long necks, the big birds can reach underwater several feet when feeding. In the process, they stir up goodies that dabbling ducks cannot reach. Invariably, amongst feeding swan you will see ducks busily zipping around, merrily chowing down on leftovers that have floated to the surface.

Consequently, swans make excellent "confidence" decoys; i.e. non-hunted species that attract ducks to decoys.

More importantly, at least to me, swans make for high entertainment, especially, it seems, on those days when there aren't a lot of birds moving. Some of my most memorable hunts have come when I didn't get a bird, yet sat back for a Swan Show.

One time, while sitting in a blind on the upwind side of Walhalla pond, I heard some trumpeting behind me. It was late September, the half mile wide lake was flat under skies blue. I was admiring snow on Heney Range to the west, day dreaming about the great spring skiing we had on 2900 foot Mt. Baldy, dead center in my binocular view. There were about 50 plastic molded decoys in front of me, split in half, mainly widgeon and mallard look-alikes, with an open space in front of the blind to lure the real guys into range. Plus a pair of sparkling white plastic swans. The only action was sight seeing and hot coffee from my thermos. Sitting there with no motion from the wind, the colorful decoys looked unrealistic, and no birds were moving anyhow.

Suddenly, from over my back, came the whistling sound that gives every duck hunter chills. With coffee spilling, a quick reach for my Baretta. There they were. Two huge adult swans, all the feathers in those incredible eight foot wing spans, gracefully tearing through the air, about ten feet above me, seeming in slow motion due to their size, banking to land as close as they could to the pair of swan decoys. Wow.

Watching swan land is quite a sight. Poetry in air, panic in landing. Huge black webbed feet extended like landing gear, they just sort of crash to the water. With a lot of honking.

By the time they splashed to a halt, this pair was 50 yards beyond the decoys. The post landing check list included regrouping, checking to see all feathers were intact, re-establishing eye and verbal communication, several dips in the pond to check depth, and then a scan of the airport.

Glancing toward Duck Concourse One, they eye-balled the two swan decoys. Which looked like the real deal. One had a longer neck, just like the big male; the other a little shorter, like it was preening. I had them set toward the middle of the left group of decoys, with several widgeon and mallard around them. Attractive arrangement, based on years of watching duck-swan interaction.

In late September and throughout October, swans start banding together to migrate south in long orderly rows of white. After splitting apart into aggressively defended areas for nesting and rearing young throughout the spring and summer, it's time to get ready for the Big Move. This pair was intent on finding some traveling companions.

With the dominant male in front, they started trumpeting while swimming toward the decoys. Wiping cold coffee off my face and lap, I picked my thermos cup out of the blind brush and refilled it from my neoprene-insulated bottle. This might be interesting.

As they reached the edge of the decoys, both started honking a little louder and more frequently. Not much response from their brethren. So they started maneuvering through the duck decoys to get closer.

The widgeon and mallards were not behaving as they should. In fact, they were not behaving at all.

These ducks are such a nuisance, usually they get out of our way, I could sense Mr. Big thinking. After all, we give them all the leftovers. Come on, give us a break.

Plus louder calling to the white duo up ahead.

Hey guys, at least talk to us. We're going to be heading south on the same flight.

Finally, about five feet from the swan decoys, Big White had enough. A green head mallard sat dead in his path. Pausing, arching his long neck back to its full length, he struck forward as hard as he could, creating a loud thunk as he hit the mallard's rear end with his big heavy bill.

The mallard, of course, didn't go anywhere. It bobbled up and down wildly, while both swan looked on in astonishment.

What the hell, they honked loudly.

Now what do we do? That is one dumb duck.

I'm already telling myself this is a great morning shoot.

Glancing ahead, they noticed the swan decoys were placidly watching the show, while bobbing a bit in the now choppy water.

Well, they don't seem to be upset, so it must be OK. Let's go talk it over, and then get out of here.

So the two swan steered around the remaining decoys, and Mr. Big cruised right up alongside his white counterpart.

I wish Ed King was there to translate.

The tall swan decoy was life-like in fine detail. Black eyes, well-shaped bill, long graceful neck, patch of black on tucked-in tail feathers. A mirror image of its visiting counterpart.

Now honking in a polite, subdued tone, Big White actually bent his neck down, and looked Decoy White in the eye, only inches away. No response, not even a blink.

Bemused, Mr. Big straightened up and looked at his spouse, who was watching the whole show.

She trumpeted what must have been the equivalent of: Hey, if they don't want to be social, screw em. How rude. We'll find more friendly folks to fly with.

The pair maneuvered out of the decoys at a rapid pace, made sure the runway to the west was clear, and took off. Which takes awhile.

While watching swan land is entertaining, seeing them struggle to become airborne is remarkable. Those big landing gear are also a key ingredient to take off. With massive wings flapping and wingtips hitting the water, their feet do a 30 yard dash across the water to assist. It's a frantic foot race against gravity, with a splashing plop-plop-plop sound until it's finally gear up time. On a calm day, the noisy pattern can be heard from invisible ponds a mile away.

No ducks that day, but so what.

Part III: Swan Song

Another swan story. Late season. Ice on the pond, frost in the blind. Miserable conditions. Drake mallards and swans are the last birds to head south. Green and white, summer and winter, side by side.

Hoping for long lines of four "curlers," green heads with bright reddish-orange feet dangling as they bomb into the decoys. Sometimes spectacular shooting. Not this day. Swan Song Time. Toe warmers tucked in wader bottoms, feet tingling. Pouring hot coffee from the thermos over boots to warm them up after breaking decoys out of ice.

Everything grey, brown, or black, no leaves on barren alder and willow, horizon and contact lenses full of gritty dust blowing down the Copper. Time to close blinds and cabin. Sloughs already skimmed with ice; any thicker and outboard jet units won't work, then how will we get out of here?

While pondering all this, a pair of young swans land beyond the decoys in what little open water is left, and begin paddling toward the big white decoys. Both birds a mix of grey and white, with reddish-pink still visible on their bills, obviously this year's hatch. Small. Somehow separated from their parents, they are in trouble. Need to find some company to show them the way to warmer climates. If they freeze in, it's over.

These guys are so immature they can't even honk. They squeak. Not good.

The duo swim closer and closer through a patch of ice-clogged open water where I had broken through to set the decoys.

Speaking of freezing in, if I sit much longer, my wet neoprene waders might stick to this bench.

I squirm around, taking stock of what is in the blind and everything that needs to be packed out. When I look up again, there is only one cygnet, appealing to the decoys for advice. Then I hear some crunching. I shift around, not noticing that with every movement, my wader bottoms are making a soft squealing sound on the wet wood.

Like all good blinds, this one has only one exposed entrance, off to the right. A small opening to step through, with cover everywhere else so the birds won't flare. Still looking through the brush in front of me for the second swan, I sense motion to my right, and peering down, see a pink-black bill and long grey neck, topped with a black eye, looking right at me through the blind entrance. When I shift slightly, my waders make that little sound, and the bird squeaks right back.

The thought crosses my mind to reach out and pick this little guy up. Even if I could, what would happen next? We eyeball each other for a bit, he decides I wasn't white and can't fly, and crunches back through the frozen grass to the pond. When I start picking decoys up, the pair swam off, vanishing in blowing snow and dust.

To this day I wonder if they made it.

Part IV: B-52's

It might seem a contradiction, but because of their size and lumbering grace, swans remind me of B-52's.

Remember that monstrous Stratofortress of the Cold War Era, and later Vietnam and Gulf War fame? Built by Boeing from 1952 through 1962, and then continually modified and upgraded, this eight engine, 159 foot long bomber had a wing span of 185 feet, maximum speed of 650 miles per hour, and took two miles of runway to take off.

A high school basketball court is 84 feet long. Half the fuselage and one side of the wings wouldn't fit in Cordova High's gymnasium. Incredible. Getting this thing airborne had to be as heart pounding as watching a swan frantically splash its feet across a pond in hopes it would clear the brush line at the far edge. Much shorter airframe but similar takeoff and landing style.

Born in 1944, I was a child of the Cold War. Remember vividly Cub and Boy Scout meetings in the tiny gymnasium on the bottom floor of the old Baptist Church right across from our house. The part we liked best was eating stale popcorn leftover from the North Star Theatre while watching Army Airforce black and white movies of fighters and bombers blasting their way through Germany in World War II.. Even recall air raid drills during the Cold War. One time a bomber from Elmendorf AFB in Anchorage flew over Cordova in the middle of the day and showered the city with leaflets saying "You have just been bombed" or something to that effect. Surplus Army helmets strapped on tightly, we raced all over town gathering them up. What a thrill. Russia wasn't that far away. Maybe the paper said we should have been in our fallout/bomb shelters.

Flash forward to the 1990s.

At the end of each school year, most the male teaching staff in Cordova would head 15 miles out the road for a big bonfire-picnic-blowout-celebration below the Sheridan River bridge. By then, kids weren't the only ones ready for summer vacation. The river's water level from its Sheridan Glacier source four miles upstream would still be low but the temperature would be perfect for chilling beer; banks were littered with firewood carried down by fall flooding and winter ice; daylight lasted forever in late May; and if we were lucky the mosquitoes wouldn't have started hatching out.

A chance to blow off steam, drink some really cold ones, relax, tell stories, make summer plans, and spend a refreshing night outdoors. Sleeping bags and tents optional, some nights we didn't bother going to bed. The sun was down for only a few hours.

School was out. It was a race between kids and staff to get out the door after the end-of-the-year picnic and baseball game. So here we were, on the banks of the Sheridan, firewood piled up, all having a grand time. Beautiful evening, good food and company, hot fire, although a light breeze kept shifting direction as it often does late in the evening, meaning we had to keep reshuffling to stay out of the blaze's smoke. B.S. was shifting into high gear, interrupted by trumpeters flying by on deployment across the Delta to stake out their nesting sites. When it was my turn, triggered by their passing, I opted for swam stories. Including the B-52 analogy.

Funny how one tale leads to another. What followed was one of my all time favorites. With the river and Alaska Amber flowing, the fire snapping and roaring, a Classic involving the big black bomber. Lest this cost me a treasured friendship, no names will be used.

The story teller was a Cowboy turned Teacher. In the Days of his Youth, prior to becoming educated and civilized, Living the Dream. "A Lariet Proletariet" working for "thin coin," in the words of Ivan Doig. Riding the northern plains, poking cows, singing yipee-ky-yay, raising hell at the local bar on weekends, doing all the things Willie Nelson counseled against in his song "Momma, Don't Let Your Babies Grow Up To Be Cowboys."

Tall tales around the campfire are part of Cowboying 101, and he was good at it. The sun was setting, so we all scattered in search of the biggest piece of log drift we could carry to toss on our ten foot high blaze before it became dark. Then settled into our collapsable camp chairs, had a shot of really good 80 plus proof, and kicked the story telling up a notch.

It was CowPoke's (hereafter CP) turn.

Seems the cow crew had a regular watering hole - you know, ramshackle place in a nearby little town, bar, stools, mirror, pool table, juke box, wooden floor, ladies looking for a good time, perfect setting for blowing a week's wages in a couple hours. No six shooters, thank goodness. I envisioned horses tied up outside and spurs jingling on cowboys boots, ten gallon hats, straights shots in those stubby clear glasses.

Howdy, partner. Hit me again, barkeep. And leave the bottle. Etc.

CP and Crew hit the scene, ready to quench a six day thirst, also perhaps a bit tired of each others company in the bunkhouse for a week.

After a couple quick ones, CP surveyed the scene. Accustomed to scanning the wide open spaces for missing head, his eyeballs just about jumped out of the same when he focused on the pool table.

Leaning over the table in tight leather pants, low cut tank top, and cussing loudly at every shot missed in a language every cowboy understood, there she was, the New Girl (hereafter NG) in town.

Hot damn.

Here, by the Sheridan firelight, CP always paused, took another sip, smiled, and then said: "Boys, it was love at first sight."

Courtship and romance, Cowboy Style, quickly ensued. CP giddyupped into action, and had NG lassoed before the other boys could even get ropes off their horses.

Turns out NG was from Back East. Detroit. Like many before, her family had migrated West. Perhaps NG was unhappy to leave the Big City, but she was certainly up for Adventure. Which CP was eager to provide.

NG wanted to learn about the Cowboy Style. CP couldn't wait to oblige.

Envision a clear, hot summer day out in the middle of the plains. A.B. Guthrie *Big Sky* country. CP stuck with the job of mending fences, and making the best of it by inviting NG along.

Another sip. Then CP continued his tale, the audience's faces aglow in rapt attention.

It was hotter than hell. I was stripped down to the waist, sweating like a stuck pig. We were in the middle of nowhere. NG was bitching about the heat, so I said What the Hell, there's no one around for as far as you can see, take your shirt off and cool down.

Which she did. I'm thinking, Wow, these plains are starting to look a lot better.

NG was starting to get the hang of this wire stretching thing, but still complaining about the weather. So standing there bare-chested, I said Well I feel pretty cool myself.

So NG decided to join the crowd. The next thing I know she's also topless.

CP here confessed he was having a hard time focusing. On the fence wire.

The barbs were the last thing on my mind. I knew Willie blew it with his song. It should have been Mamma, I Want To Be A Cowboy Forever.

It was the best day of Cow Poking in all my life, said CP, with a far away dreamy look in his eyes.

And, of course, another perfectly timed pause and sip, to let the boys visualize the scene in greater detail. CP was painting a Masterpiece.

Remember the part in a Hemingway novel where the earth moves?

Suddenly, said CP, I was having a hard time keeping my feet solid on the ground; it literally started shaking.

What the hell is that, screamed a terrified NG.

Holy shit, I think it's an earthquake, shouted CP.

The vibrations became worse.

And then, with a thunderous roar, at under 500 feet, a huge B-52 came blazing over the horizon. On a low altitude, radar-evading training mission from a nearby Air Force Base.

The couple looked up, which from above, must have been quite a sight.

As the black bomber went screaming by at 500 miles per hour, CP, to this day, swears he could see the pilot looking right back, and caught a flash of a smile in that 3 second interval before it was gone.

A pause, to let us all envision that sight.

Then CP: I really thought they might turn around and come back. And I always wonder what they said over the intercom.

Logs crackle and bonfire sparks shoot skyward into starlit sky.

No Northern Lights, but dancing eyes around the blaze.

It started as a hum.

And then the Boys were serenading CP: "Mamma, don't let your babies grow up to be cowgirls…"

Chapter 15

Eagles

BALD EAGLE: 1. "*Haliaeetus leucocephalus.* Length: 30-43 inches, Wingspan: 6.5 - 8 ft. Adult with white head and tail is unmistakable. They are scavengers more than predators and subsist mainly on dead and dying fish. When fish are not available, they will kill birds and sometimes small mammals." *Guide to Birds of Alaska,* ROBERT ARMSTRONG, 1984
2. Evil Eye: the look most duck hunters receive upon returning home after a weekend at the duck cabin and an Eagle Eye inspection by their spouses.

"I want to fly like an eagle, To the sea,
Fly like an eagle, Let my Spirit carry me."

STEVE MILLER, "FLY LIKE AN EAGLE"

Part I: Decoys

Despite a meticulously arranged spread of life-like plastic GHG Pro-Grade wigeons mixed around a pair of shining Cabelas white trumpeter swan confidence decoys, and a dozen Flambeau Classic mallards on the other side, with an inviting open space in between, the ducks weren't interested. In fact, there were none in sight.

Mid-September, Walhalla pond. Ducky weather too. Stiff southeast wind whistling through alder and willow against the back side of the blind, yellowing grass waving alongside the upper edge of the big lake, clouds zipping by, rain dappling the water, decoys bouncing realistically on the choppy surface.

Can't shoot what ain't there passed through my mind, as I reached for a thermos of hot coffee, struggling to stay awake. The midseason lull between nesting locals and soon to arrive Northern birds must be here.

From behind, a sudden loud whoosh over the top of the blind followed by an even louder thunk in the decoys. A large bald eagle skimming ponds from the upwind side had scored.

Or so he thought. Up from the spread rose America's Emblem with a greenhead mallard in his talons. The lead anchor attached to decoy line trailed behind. For about three seconds and 100 feet, until Mr. Big realized his mistake, and unceremoniously let go.

Decoy, weight, and string tumbled into deeper water 100 yards out. Wind and waves would carry it to the opposite side of the half mile wide pond. Retrieving of a different sort ahead.

Wow.

A terrain-hugging low altitude down-wind attack. No classic plummet from high above. Just a sudden appearance from nowhere. Eagles on the prowl often zip by and then flare, realizing they have been duped.

Others mistakenly finish the ambush. It happens very fast. The winged versions of Top Gun uses their front talons not to grab the bird, but to strike it as knuckles, and then sinks the lone back lone claw in, using forward momentum to grasp the victim. An examination of the decoys assaulted in this manner reveals only one scar in the plastic.

Every now and then a duck that has flown into my shotgun's pattern will drop into the pond. If a stiff wind is blowing, it quickly begins to drift across the vast pond. More than once, an eagle has come cruising by to retrieve the bird before I can even leave the blind. They do not bring it back and drop it at my feet, nor are they well known for having a "soft mouth."

Whenever eagles are skimming about, it's a good time to be alert. For both hunters and ducks.

Part II: Snow Angels

My four year old daughter and I were down on the beach in front of our home on Odiak Slough playing in the snow. The white stuff had been coming down hard for several day. After shoveling out our stairway to the road, it was time to take a break.

Heidi was in a bright red snow jacket, complete with hood, plus an oversized pink knit hat her Aunt Lil had made, and blue snow pants. I wore wool bibs, a camo fleece jacket used for deer hunting, and wool hat. We had been riding an orange plastic sled down the small hill alongside our home. Perfect gentle terrain, flattening out at the bottom, no car traffic to worry about as the ice-choked slough fronted our home. Great snow. A solid base with six inches of light powder on top. It would soon be time to put up Christmas tree lights on the nearby 25 foot spruce I have been pruning for years.

Two hundred yards across the intertidal waterway is Whitshed Road, plus a steep hillside covered with spruce and hemlock, rising up toward rolling meadows in front of 2200 foot Mt. Eccles. The timber is a favorite place for eagles to hang out year round, with several nests on the taller trees. Their white heads stand out against the dark green background. With salmon spawned out for the winter, eagles will make periodic dive bomb attacks from their lofty perches hoping to score on teal, widgeon, gadwall, pintail, and mallards that feed in the intertidal zone. Rarely are they successful against the quicker waterfowl, who seemed to keep one eye skyward at all times. We always root for the ducks.

The two of us were having a grand time. Slide down together, powder flying in our faces, usually crashing into soft snow at the end. Gradually making a packed runway that gave us more speed. Plus she, of short legs and rosy cheeks, receiving a free ride back up every time. Blue sky, white snow, twilight sun, laughter, father and daughter. Is there anything better?

After half dozen trips, I was ready for a break. Four year olds don't understand the concept, so part of early childhood parenting involves proposing alternative activities. How about Snow Angels? Fall backwards into untracked snow, look straight up at the sky, slide your arms and legs back and forth, then carefully stand up.

Wa La, Hark the Heralds in Pure White.

So there we were, side by side, just a finger tip apart. Busily waving our arms and legs in horizontal motion.

Suddenly, this loud rushing noise, a flash of white, black, and yellow. Three feet above our heads.

"What was that, Daddy?"

Holy Crap, pardon the expression. Now I knew what the ducks felt like. A bald eagle had mistaken us for an injured animal floundering in the snow, and luckily veered off at the last second.

"Oh, it was just a bird out flying around."

As was my heart, with a deeper belief in Angels.

Part III: Duskies

Perhaps no single species has been impacted more by the 1964 Good Friday Earthquake than the Dusky Canada Goose. A smaller, brownish-tinted subspecies of its much more well-known larger relatives, this unusual bird nests almost exclusively on the Copper River Delta and winters in Oregon's Willamette Valley.

At one time the population of Dusky geese numbered more than 25,000. By the 1990s it had fallen to 16,000, and sank to a low of 5400 in 2009. Reasons for the decline are numerous, but clearly habitat change is a major factor. Higher ground as a result of earthquake uplift has produced thicker vegetation, which has choked out nesting habitat, while also inviting a broad array of predators further out onto the Delta.

Mink, weasel, coyote, and bear now routinely roam a region wooded with tall spruce and cottonwood. Willow, alder, and sweet gale provide further cover for their predation, which naturally includes eggs on nests, newly hatched chicks, and geese in flightless molt stage in early August.

The incredible change in habitat is hard to describe. A picture is worth a thousand words. Nothing illustrates the earthquake uplift impact more than the following photos.

If you go back and examine the background of many of the photos elsewhere in this book, you will see the same astonishing change in the horizon.

Human measures to help the Duskies survive have included an elaborate nesting island strategy. In a collaborative effort between Ducks Unlimited, the USFS, and multiple other state and federal agencies, more than 500 such islands were installed in 1983, mainly in the Alaganik area. Evidently land-based predators haven't figured out eggs are a short swim away, as nesting success is considerably higher on such mini-hatcheries.

Keeping these brush-covered havens intact has been a challenging task. The early styrofoam and sandbag models deteriorated. Pond ice shifting in high winds during breakup pulled out anchors. Gradually newer fiberglass replacements have been installed. The number of islands is now around 400.

Their locations have been expanded to include the Eyak area, because another factor in the declining number of islands is available water area. Encroaching vegetation is causing all the ponds on the Delta to shrink.

Additionally, most of the remaining ponds are now much deeper than they were before the earthquake, which certainly runs counter to what one would expect from an uplift. A major culprit in this dynamic is none other than the beaver, who with an abundance of brush along every gutter and small slough, has built an unbelievable system of dams that have clogged up the vast Delta drainage system.

Most of the ponds on the Delta are now too deep for dabbling ducks, who rely on tipping to reach feed on the bottom. More and more birds are spending most of their time on salt water marshes and intertidal zones beyond former cutbanks that lined the edge of the pre-quake Delta.

Numerous State and Federal agencies have done countless studies on the impact of the earthquake on the Delta. It is a unique opportunity for research.

August 1966, two years after the earthquake. Dad struggles to get the Quachita running in main Pete Dahl Slough. Note the treeless Delta. The four specks on the horizon are the Pete Dahl duck cabins.

October 1977, 13 years after the earthquake. Dad in front of our cabin, with the exit tributary to main Pete Dahl directly behind him. Low alder and willow just beginning to show up on "the Point."

September 2009, 45 years after the earthquake. Tom Carpenter arrives at the cabin in his river boat. This is exactly the same view down the slough as in the photo of Dad shown to the left. Notice the cottonwood and spruce on "the Point."

And some of the results have been surprising, as well as confounding. Especially for these geese.

Guess what species is the major cause of egg and gosling losses? Using various tools, including stop-lapse cameras, the winner is … the Bald Eagle. In a landslide. Our National Emblem is responsible for about 80% of the predation.

Wow. And what to do? Reinstate the bounty on Bald Eagles that was originally started in Territorial days to protect spawning salmon, and discontinued in 1953? Remember Bill O'Brien Sr. buying provisions for his first winter in Alaska during the 1930s at Cape Yakataga on a 50 cent payment per eagle?

Other research revealed that big hooligan runs in the spring when Duskies are nesting seems to correlate with diminished eagle predation. So hope for lots of dead ripe hooligan lining the banks of Alaganik? Sadly, hope is not a strategy.

Some unusual ideas surfaced to counter poor hooligan runs. Such as fake goose eggs poisoned with just enough drugs to make eagles sick but not kill them, teaching Mr. Baldy to alter his breakfast menu. Right. But what about goslings? And how many bogus eggs would it take to condition all the eagles on the Delta?

Wait. How about blocks of tasty old frozen salmon dispersed on the cutbanks of Alaganik? We all know eagles love salmon, and canneries are try to get rid of their surplus. Hmm. Wouldn't this just whet now well-fed eagle appetites for an egg or gosling dessert?

Another tactic was transplanting brown bears, who were having a field day with nests and goslings. In May of 1987, nine bruins roaming in prime goose nesting habitat were darted from helicopters. The tranquilized brownies were tagged with monitors and then rolled into cargo nets. From the cabin porch we watched them fly by suspended under helicopters, enroute to new homes on Hinchenbrook and Montague Island.

24 May 1987

Nice today - finally cleared off. Lots of geese but no bear for bear slayers. Fish & Game has darted and transplanted nine brown bear from this area (Castle to Alaganik) in past week trying to help geese. —Dick

Within two weeks almost all the flying bears were back.

Huge tankers bound for the Trans-Alaska oil pipeline terminus in Valdez ply the twelve mile wide 160 fathom deep ocean entrance between these two islands. Its heavy currents and rough seas are notorious. Wonder if any 1000 foot behemoth had to alter course to dodge a brown bear headed back to the Copper River Delta for a Dusky Egg Omlette. The geese were probably hoping it was Captain Joseph Hazelwood at the helm.

Fortunately, human hunters are a bit easier to regulate than eagles and bears, so the season on the Delta's small subspecies has been severely restricted. While duck season opens on September 1, Duskies cannot be taken until late September. By then, most have already departed for Oregon. Where they raise havoc in farmers' fields, intermingling with other goose populations, which honk and cackle their thanks for bring protected status south.

It's a management dilemma that has cost at least one local USFS District Ranger his job for stating the painfully obvious: the geese will figure it out. Which they have begun to do, by nesting on nearby barrier islands, as well as Middleton and Hawkins. Oh, I know, experts point out these birds are a bit different genetically, and not pure Delta Dusky. Who the hell is 100% anything these days?

The whole scenario reiterates another of the Oldtimer's sayings: You Can't Screw with Mother Nature.

Personally, I give these geese a free pass to Oregon.

Part IV: Harriers

While this is a Chapter about Mr. Big, I can't resist tossing in an anecdotes about a smaller bird of prey that abounds on the Delta. If Eagles are dive bombers, these guys are fighter jets. Can they ever maneuver in their hunt for voles that scurry about in the grassy marshes.

The other day I'm in the far blind enjoying a cup of hot coffee while gazing at Sheridan Glacier off to the north. Blue bird day, which means, for duck hunters, a no bird day. Even the decoys looked bored and completely unrealistic. Who cares. Late September, and still a warm sun. Good grief, even a few bugs to swat away. Enjoy the moment. Won't be long before toe warmers are part of the daily get-up.

Two hundred yards across the lower arm of the pond, a Northern Harrier comes zipping along, looking for lunch. Gliding gracefully, then darting and turning. Suddenly wings fold, and it vanished into tall grass. Hmm. I grab my binoculars to see what's happening. Up it pops, climbing almost vertically, with an unfortunate vole in its bill. Delta Drama. Still accelerating upward, it drops the prey from its beak. The unlucky meal slides down the harrier's chest, and is grasped by its talons, without a single change in wing beat.

Without 'binos, I would have never seen what happened, it was so quick. And so casual. Ho hum, it's a ways to the perch where I'm going to have lunch, so maybe I'll let the freight fly in the lower cargo bay. Wow.

Chapter 16

Moose

MOOSE: 1. *Alces alces.* largest extant species of deer family, distinguished by palmate antlers of the male. Name derived from ancient word "moosu," meaning "he strips off," referring to browsing style of feeding. WIKEPEDIA

2. Moose Milk: a creamy holiday punch flavored with dark rum and coffee liqueur served at Gary Weinrick's Xmas Party and guaranteed to make even a moose call it a night.

"You won't know if you don't go."

JAY BEAUDIN, BACKCOUNTRY SKI PARTNER;

REFERRING TO SNOW CONDITION UP HIGH.

Part I: Airboat Moose

5 p.m., September 1, 2006

Leonard and I looked at each other. It had already been a long day. Uh-oh, oh boy, holy crap, you've got to be kidding, and several other phrases were exchanged in that glance. Ardy stomped on the throttle and flapped the tail rudders back and forth. We inched forward slightly, bending the fiberglass gunnels inward against the forty foot tall rock-hard dead hemlock trees on either side.

It was an air boat, but we were firmly grounded.

Airboats have become the *modus operandi* for hunting moose on the Copper River Delta. Most of the huge ungulates simply cannot be reached otherwise. One would think the Good Friday earthquake of 1964, which uplifted the Delta anywhere from six feet at Eyak to nine feet at Cottonwood Point, west to east, would make it easier to harvest the moose that were transplanted to the areas in the the late 40s and early 50s.

As it turns out, just the opposite is true. All the sloughs have become less navigable with traditional outboard driven river boats. Brush has sprung up everywhere, and the preferred habitat of the moose has gradually moved closer to the edge of the ocean and further away from the Copper River Highway. Road hunting has become less and less productive.

Habitat change. Prior to the earthquake, much of the area below the road was a vast intertidal plane of grass and great duck hunting. Now it is thick alder, willow, cottonwood, and spruce. In recent years at Walhalla Pond on the edge of the Delta cutbank, it's not unusual to see more moose than waterfowl on a sunny September day.

And of course there are the beavers. Surrounded by dam building material on the edge of the banks of every slough and gutter, my Oregon State Mascots have gone on a dam building spree, plugging up ponds and waterways, further hastening the growth of encroaching vegetation in the standing water.

Aerial views of the Delta show a maize of dams, and vanishing ponds filling in with a variety of plants. Most are now too deep for dabbling ducks, and without the attractive feed created by brackish intertidal water that used to flood much of the lower Delta on big tides. The same barriers also make it impossible to walk any distance without encountering a gutter well over a hunter's head in depth.

A few lucky or hardy permit holders score on moose close enough to the road for canoes or four wheelers as retrieval apparatus, but it has been a long time since many have been hauled out on pack frames.

As many other Cordovans, I grunted and groaned under the weight of a quarter of moose on a packboard several times back in the 60s and 70s, but like it or not, the days of that hunting style are pretty much gone.

So here we were. On my first airboat moose hunt. Not between the veritable rock and and hard place, but awfully darn close.

A couple miles above the road at Seven Mile. A hot sunny afternoon. What little water there was in the shallow sandy creek we had been zigzagging up was vanishing before our very eyes.

Well, I thought, I guess I shouldn't be surprised. Leonard, a wiry outdoors guy, gillnetter, assistant hunting guide, and trapper, just rolled his eyes when we pulled up to Ardy's place at 5 a.m. to begin this adventure. Our airboat operator was not known for getting things done in advance. Several parts plus two plastic bucket seats that sit securely fastened to the floor just forward of the elevated driver's chair, important for passengers to sit and hang on to when crashing through brush, lay strewn about. An aluminum hoist used for lifting moose quarters into the boat lay in disarray on the ground.

"Looks like we'll be hanging on to the bow cover and ducking," muttered Leonard. "And doing some heavy lifting."

Captain Ardy is quite mechanical and crafty. Sitting before us was one of the biggest and most powerful airboats on the Delta. Local Ron Trumblee had made a 16 by 6.5 foot fiberglass airboat hull several years earlier. Ardy bought it, and had fiberglass specialist Tim Miller cut it in half and widen it midships by ten inches. Then he went to work mounting a big 350 Chevy automobile engine to swing a 78 inch two bladed wooden prop, and covered the bottom with a sheet of Teflon for sliding over rocks and hard stuff. This baby could fly and pack weight.

The year before, on a sunny September 1st morning, Ardy, Leonard, my son-in-law Tom Carpenter, and local pilot Mike Collins, plus a whole bull moose, with head and 72 inch rack protruding over the bow, pulled up to the mucky beach in front of our Pete Dahl cabin. Estimated load: 2500 pounds. Bagged by Tom, and hauled out in one trip from thick, brushy terrain near King Salmon Slough to the east. Now that's impressive.

Ardy had several years operating a smaller airboat under his belt. That hunt was his first in the new Panzer Tank of the Delta Airboat Fleet. The day before, he had discovered the new rig could not only fly, it also had a disconcerting habit of sliding with reckless abandon on greasy mud. No keel on the flat bottom of airboats.

Leonard and I were sitting at the cabin table looking out the window while waiting for Ardy, Tom, and Mike to return from an spotting mission in Mike's Super Cub. Moose season opened the next day. We could hear the airboat down river, returning from the mud flat where they had just landed.

I was startled when Leonard jumped up, knocking his chair over, and yelled: "Holy crap. Ardy just fell out of his airboat into the slough."

Not really. We raced out the door. Ardy was standing armpit deep in the murky narrow channel, my 14 foot Alumaweld riverboat with 70 hp jet outboard no where in sight. It had been anchored in the middle of the slough, which is 30 feet wide at low tide. Captain Airboat was going to swing past it so he could pull up on the bank in front of the cabin for the night, and not have to worry about falling tides.

The only force that guides airboats is wind generated by the prop and vectored by tall vertical rudders. Ardy tried to pass the riverboat by pulling up on the sloping mud on the far bank. The craft skidded sideways, hit the water, and proceeded to run over my anchored boat, from motor to bow, before it could be stopped.

Ardy hadn't fallen out of the airboat. He had jumped out and was reaching underwater, struggling to pull my invisible boat off the bottom.

We raced out the door, not bothering with waders. Helped pull the submerged craft to the surface. Bailed it out with plastic 5 gallon buckets, and pulled it up on the bank. A quick survey of the damage revealed I wouldn't be going up the slough at daybreak for the traditional opening day duck hunt at Walhalla while the boys were off chasing Mr. Bull.

Put a damper on the evening's dinner, but nothing a little Peachtree Schnapps couldn't cure. Meat from eight skinny early season ducks probably wouldn't weigh as much as the moose's tongue.

And guess what? The next year, when I was drawn for a cow moose permit, who was right there to offer his airboat services?

I, of course, wisely accepted.

One thing about hunting with Ardy. Not only do you always get your game, you can also be assured of a rollicking unpredictable hunt.

Ardy was a chip off the old Scandinavian Block. His dad Merle taught junior high science in the next room over from me at Cordova High. Every now and then through the wall I would hear a loud "Hey!" which sounded like a moose bellow, but really was just his way of getting the class's attention.

Merle hailed from Choteau, Montana, and can you believe his high school English teacher was A.B. Guthrie, who won a Pulitzer Prize for his novel *The Way West*? Guthrie's *The Big Sky* is my favorite: Mountain Men, Indians, beaver, buffalo, and Rendezvous. Maybe A.B. taught Merle and his classmates how to whoop and holler like they did in the real Wild West, and the habit came North with Educator Hanson.

Merle valued the importance of proper preparation when heading outdoors. Consequently we had many great adventures together. My favorite was when we decided to supplement our meager teaching salaries by digging razor clams. Local private pilot Karl Steen dropped us off down the coast 40 miles at ocean beaches near Katella during a set of big minus tides early one May. The plan was to camp, dig clams for a couple days, and fly home rich.

Merle indicated he had a tent that would be just the ticket. Perhaps for A.B.'s gang, as it turned out. We landed late in the day. It was chilly. Few clams were showing on the evening hold-up tide. No problem, they'll be everywhere on low tides in the morning. We decided to set up camp. Merle pulled out the tent. It was Ardy's, who at that time was a tyke. His pup tent was four feet long, three feet wide, and three feet high, with two small poles to hold it up. The sun was heading down and the north wind was coming up, blowing biting sand along the long flat beach, as the Gulf of Alaska surf crashed nearby.

We found a couple wet logs to anchor the tent down, and started looking for firewood, without luck. Everything was waterlogged. Finally discovered a creosote piling stub that had washed ashore. It burned well and brightly, with a nice odor and pleasant ambiance. We broke out the Blackberry Brandy to toast our good fortune. Anyone for a tar-flavored hot dog?

My partner was six foot, I'm six inches shorter, his head was six inches away. Very cozy. I remember waking up the next morning to the sound of Merle snoring away. My head and shoulders in the tent, thin damp blue nylon above, and the rest of my wet sleeping bag sticking out, covered by snow.

Only way to get warm was to get moving. We crawled out and started looking for clams. None were showing. It was clear and cold with a stiff wind. Even the razors had figured they should stay in bed.

Karl arrived a couple hours later. We returned to town with 11 undersized clams and a distinct creosote fragrance. Shares in the Katella Klam Korporation never made it to the stock market. But a typical Hanson Safari.

Now here we were. Surprised? Nah. Ardy was just following in his father's footsteps.

So just how did our 5 a.m. start leave us mooseless and stuck between two trees twelve hours later?

Well, with early morning sun shining brightly in our faces, we had headed out the road to the far side of the Sheridan River bridge at 15 Mile. Met up with Rob Maxwell and Ron Goodrich. Two airboats always better than one. Rob has a nice rig; Ron had been drawn for a bull.

Several moose had been spotted below the road late the prior day. Simple. We'd race down, get our moose, and be back to town in time for Doreen's famous sourdoughs at the Coho Cafe. Might even have a quick cold one at the classic old wooden bar patrons must bypass enroute to the popular eclectic backroom diner. No problem.

Sheridan is a swift glacial river, filled with stumps, protruding sweepers, and coarse gravel bars. Rob led the way; we followed.

All right, this is kind of fun, I thought, as we dodged obstacles and skidded over a shallow bar of round, granite boulders.

We came roaring around a bend and startled several moose near a stand of alder. They turned and headed for the brush. Rob veered to the left, we thundered downstream to loop around. Ardy dropped Leonard and I off on the riverbank and turned down river. We started thrashing through brush over our heads, couldn't see a thing. Heard Rob's airboat stop, a long pause, and then a single shot. Ron had his bull down.

Leonard and I continued crashing through sweet gale and willow for several hundred yards. It finally shortened to eye level, but no moose were in sight. We could hear Ardy roaring around to the east, looking for a way back. Decided to angle over and help the other crew while waiting for our Captain.

Ron had himself a nice medium size bull with a 50 inch rack, prime eating. Gutting and quartering a thousand pound animal laying on its side in brush, mud, and water, with bugs of multiple species swarming everywhere, is no easy task. We all went to work, Leonard diving in to help roll out the big gut sack.

Rob's airboat was close by, but there wasn't much water around. He had pulled up near the moose by sliding over wet grass and brush. Sun was already starting to dry the dew. Vegetation that is moist and slippery under the bottom of an airboat can become dry and grippy in a hurry. So we were scrambling.

Behind us, we heard the growl of Ardy's airboat pulling up. Leonard, arms soaked in moose blood, pulled his head out of the belly cavity, glanced over his shoulder, jumped up, waved his arms wildly, and screamed: "Jesus Christ, turn it off!"

Ardy, wearing ear protectors, sitting on the elevated driver's seat in front of the huge engine, couldn't hear what he was saying, but got the idea. He shut the engine down. Still deaf from all the noise, hollered: "Christ, Leonard, what are you so excited about?"

With red arms, Leonard pointed and said: ""Turn around."

By now we all wondered what was going on, and stood to see what was up.

The tips of the two-bladed wooden propellor were now at least two inches shorter, having shredded themselves against the metal cage that surrounds it. Four bolts attach the powerful automotive engine to its elevated mounting bracket. The two back bolts had sheared off, and every time Ardy accelerated, the engine pivoted upward on the front two bolts, with the propellor shearing itself off against the cage.

Wow. Ardy, with ears muffled and facing forward, hadn't even noticed it.

Replacement engine mounting bolts are spare parts airboaters don't normally carry. Ardy did have a come-along tucked under the bow, standard equipment for extricating stuck craft. It seemed clear Ardy's airboat was out of commission, so the gang went back to butchering the downed moose, assuming two trips to haul it back to the road. Then another to somehow tow Ardy's airboat up the swift Sheridan.

By now it was midmorning. Warm and the temperature rising. Mosquitos and horse flies chomping away on man and moose, grass and brush now dry with a light coat of friction-generating Copper River dust. Getting the moose to the river in the healthy airboat was going to be a challenge.

We had a problem.

Ardy kept eyeballing the damage. And to his thinking-out-of-the-box credit, came up with a solution.

The come-along. Its strong cable could pull out a stuck airboat, so it should hold down an engine. He wrapped the cable around the back of the engine and the rear of the mounting frame, and then cranked it down tightly. Stability obviously a concern.

With us watching carefully, he fired off the engine, which remained securely on the frame, even when throttled up. The shortened prop was noisy, but cleared the cage nicely.

Next a trial run. Wiggling rudders while adding power, Ardy got the airboat moving, and went off on a trial spin through the grass and brush. Despite the shorter blades, it worked fine. We were back in business, albeit less than 100%. Something to be said for horsepower. And innovation.

Finished cleaning the moose, loaded a half in each airboat, Ardy taking the heavier front quarters. Had a tough time getting Rob's smaller and less powerful rig going. Push, rock the bow, roll in as it moved by or just get out of the way. Cut and lay alder over a sandy spot. Found a 50 foot narrow gravel gutter filled with a foot of water. Cut more alder so we could jockey the airboat to it, and then clear overhanging brush so it could pass through. Trailing behind, Ardy's airboat powered over the path easily.

This was my first airboat moose hunt. Nothing to it. Easy. Right. And I thought packing quarters out was fun.

Finally we busted out on the edge of the Sheridan. From there it was smooth sailing back to the road, despite bucking the current. Loaded the moose in Rob's truck, the airboats on their trailers, had a cold beer, and did a brief post-mission analysis. It was midday, time for Rob and Ron to get their moose into a cool room, skin the hide off, cleaned it up, and begin the hanging and aging process. They bade adios and drove off toward town.

Being naive in the workings of the Scandinavian mind, I assumed we were out of commission and would follow. Envisioned tranquil days in the duck blind at Pete Dahl before we could resume our Merry Moose Harvest. Teal are much lighter quarry.

Ardy and Leonard began to banter. Which they love to do, though they would never admit it.

Whadda ya think?

What do you mean, whadda I think?

It seems to be running pretty good.

Are you kidding me?

No. We just hauled the front half of that moose out, no sweat.

You can't be serious.

Take a look at the come-along cable and the engine. It hasn't budged a bit. And we haven't lost much power, though it is a little louder.

I just stood and listened. An airboat novice, what did I know?

OK, how about if we try road hunting. We'll drive the highway, scope from high spots like the cliff above McKinley River. Maybe get lucky without having to go far off the road.

Well, I guess we could do that, since we're already out here. Plus I need to catch the next gillnet opener day after tomorrow, so we need to get this moose now.

Yikes. A chill went down my spin. Me, the airboat novice; and Ardy, the Flying Norwegian, roaring around without the veteran Leonard?

So out the road we headed. It was now early afternoon, hot and sunny, so no surprise, we didn't see any moose. Highway hunters passed us going both ways. We even stopped, dropped the airboat, and Ardy hauled a moose to roadside for some nimrods that had downed a critter in deep, swampy brush half a mile away.

By 2 p.m. we were discouraged, tired, and ready to call it a day. On the way to town, Ardy brightly recalled reports of several moose up Ibeck River north of the road at 7 Mile.

Plus we'll be above the highway so if we break down we can always drift down. What a sales pitch. We bought it.

With no place to launch the boat off the elevated rocky road berm at 7 Mile, we put in near a sandy flat at 8 Mile called the Golf Course because local duffers would occasionally go out and slice or hook balls into thick alder off the fairway while polishing their game for winters in Palm Springs or Hawaii. A band of water two inches deep and the width of the airboat meandered through sand alongside the road from the Golf Course to the Ibeck bridge.

Early September happens to be the peak of the silver salmon run, and combat fishing has come to Cordova. Sixty cars crammed the roadside, and both banks of the clear river were elbow to elbow with a mix of plaid-shirted locals and nattily attired out-of-towners proudly displaying Cabelas latest from head to toe. Most pounding the water with Vibrax or Pixie spinners. Several went straight to the chase, with big globs of eggs hanging off bobbers. A brave few purists cast flies about.

So congested was the scene, the USFS added a lovely plastic Porta Potty. Every now and then brown bear would chase fishermen off and gobble up salmon left behind. They did not bother using the Facility after dining. Terrified piscators did, if they hadn't enroute.

A speed zone had to be created on the highway, as anglers would wander back and forth across the road, ignoring on-coming traffic, or sticking out long fly rods to slow down vehicles. Dropping a lure off the bridge on top of unsuspecting silvers visible in the clear water ten feet below was a sure fire strategy until ADFG banned the practice. Undercover enforcement agents in fishing garb mingled with the crowd. Locals recognized their faces; visitors would be stunned when the imposters dropped their pixies and pulled out their badges to check licenses and limits.

Oh well. Nothing ever stays the same.

We roared down the shallow roadside stream, and popped out into the Ibeck. Right above the bridge, in the middle of a wall of fishermen, the shredded prop roaring and spraying water. Anglers frantically retrieved their lines, scattered, and waved their arms. And tongues.

This day has already had quite a bit waving, I mused.

Wearing noise protectors, we couldn't hear what they were saying, but you didn't have to be a very good lip reader to get the idea. This day is turning out OK, thought some devious part of my mind, remembering the good old days when if you even saw a fisherman, you moved elsewhere so as to not crowd his space.

By the time we were 200 yards above the road, the fishermen had vanished. Not easy packing a limit of silver salmon to roadside much further than that.

The area above Ibeck is sandy, with big stands of tall, white, brittle dead hemlock and spruce drowned out by shifting waters from the mountains and Scott Glacier to the north. Plus, like every where else, alder and willow have gone wild.

We followed the clear, meandering Ibeck for a mile. The terrain opened up and started looking like moose country. Ardy pulled up to a soft, moss-covered sandbar and shut down the engine. We grabbed our rifles, hopped out, and walked 300 hundred yards, stepping in several sets of brown bear tracks, size L, XL or bigger.

Hmmm.

Leonard, who has sharp facial features, equally incisive manner, and considerable sangfroid, came to such an abrupt halt that Ardy and I almost bumped into him. He turned, fixed his gaze on the Norwegian, and growled: "What are we hunting for?"

Ardy, puzzled, "Moose."

Leonard: "Do you see any moose tracks?"

Ardy: "No."

This duo should host a talk show.

Leonard: "If you want to eat brown bear this winter, we're in the right spot. If it's moose you prefer we need to head that way," waving his arm like Patton toward the brushy country to the east.

Ardy: "Not a problem. There's several little creeks we can follow to get over there."

So we dropped back down the Ibeck a ways, took a left, and headed east toward all those dead trees, and our destiny.

Ardy was doing a masterful job of maneuvering though the white dead stands but the stream we were following kept splitting and shrinking. We came around a bend with a big tree on each side. Airboats are hard to slow down. Our Navigator made a snap decision to go for it. Airboats don't have reverse, he really didn't have much choice.

We slid halfway through, and then came to a quick halt. Petrified tree trunks had grabbed us amidships on both sides. Ardy stopped the engine. Quiet descended upon the scene, interrupted by the slight trickle of water running under the boat.

A silent pilot and speechless crew pondered the situation.

Oh my. To put it politely.

Options, anyone?

Maybe we can push the boat out backwards? The three of us hopped out and tried. No luck.

How about forward? Can we squeeze through? Ardy climbed back in the pilots seat, fired off the 350, and gave her the gas. Jammed us in even tighter.

By now Leonard's face was scrunched up like a prune. I almost laughed, but sensed little humor left at the late hour.

How about the trees themselves? Can we do something with them? Leonard looked under the bow. A small bow saw for splitting moose. Some airboaters pack a chainsaw lubricated with vegetable oil for that task; no such luck for us. I had a small folding saw in my backpack. We all had knives for butchering.

And, of course, we did have a come-along, which we could have used to pull the boat out backwards. Oops. Already occupied.

Leonard and I set to work, endeavoring to cut notches at gunnel level in the brittle trees. It was brutally slow going, and hard to maneuver the coarse lightweight saw blades under the edges of the hull. We tried three times, carving out gouges, and then standing back as Ardy wrapped up the throttle. Each attempt wedged the hull in tighter. The fiberglass sides were now bowed inward. Considerably.

The only answer seemed to be a chainsaw, for cutting big notches or falling the trees. Speaking of falling, what little water there was in the tiny stream was drying up before our very eyes.

"Well," said Leonard with a sigh, "I guess we're going to have to hike out and get a chain saw. Maybe we can get another airboat to run us back up."

Oh boy. Wouldn't all the sports fishermen by the road love to see us obnoxious airboaters trudging by in absolute silence. They'd better be quiet, or Leonard, who could be feisty when provoked, would at a minimum be snapping poles as he passed.

But wait. Looking at our towering white adversaries, I noticed both slanted outward. Yes, the water level was dropping. What would happen if we could cause it to rise?

"A dam. We need to build a dam. Behind the boat. If we can get it to float upward a few inches, it will free itself."

Leonard and Ardy looked at me like I was crazy. Weren't we all by that juncture? But also desperate. And we all know that desperate times breed desperate measures.

Using the two hand saws, we cut alders and laid them flat behind the stern. Gathered logs, stumps, scattered dead sticks and branches. Patched the small rudimentary dam with clumps of grass and mud. I should have been wearing my Benny the Beaver T-shirt, and singing the OSU Fight Song: "OSU our hats are off to you, Beavers, Beavers, fighters through and through..."

We scouted upstream, kicked channels in the sand, and built gravel dikes to divert rivulets toward our project. Slowly, the water level under the boat began to rise. Unbelievably, it worked. Within an hour the airboat had popped up of its own accord and was floating. Hydraulic pressure had freed it from the trees. Oregon State has had many difficult football seasons. Unlike the Orange and Black clad Corvallis Beavers, the Cordova Broad Tails had rallied late in the game.

We pushed the craft out backwards, and rotated the bow around. Captain A fired off the engine, and downstream we raced.

Definitely done for the day. Or were we?

Roaring by our happy fisherman friends, we pulled up alongside the Ibeck bridge to head up the shallow sandy creek to our vehicles at 8 Mile.

Oops. What creek? The water had vanished. Airboats do not slide on sand. Pilots have gone flying from their lofty perch when rounding a corner and coming to a screeching halt in the grasp of its coarse surface.

A smirk crossed more than one sport fisherman's face when they realized our predicament. Wouldn't have been surprised if they had all dropped their poles and started clapping and cheering in unison. No point in asking them for help.

By this time, our helmsman was done screwing around. A truck, driven by the same hunters whose moose he retrieved what seemed like days ago, just happened to be idling by. We flagged it down.

"Give us a hand, could you?" asked Ardy.

"Of course. What's up?"

"We just need the bow pointed up on the bottom edge of the rock berm," replied our Captain.

Which with their help, we accomplished.

Ardy hopped back at the controls, hollered stand back, and gave the airboat full throttle.

Everyone was astonished to see his Uber Machine climb up the 40 degree granite boulder road side grade, rise airborne, and plop flat on its teflon bottom in the middle of the Copper River Highway.

"One more favor, guys. Spin the bow so it faces down the highway."

Leonard and I piled in, and we skidded down the pavement to our truck at 8 Mile. Vehicles coming the other way stopped, drivers wide-eyed, to let us pass.

Mooseless, but certainly not adventureless.

Three days later we did get my moose, Ardy at the helm, two miles below the road on the east side of the Sheridan. We all ended up with several boxes of steaks, roasts, ribs, burger, and sausage.

Cheap, easy, airboat meat.

Part II: Swamp Buggy Moose

August 1962

Fred Pettingill hailed from Elba, Idaho, a small settlement south of Boise. Was raised in a family of staunch Mormons, which most Cordovans who knew him would never guess.

Fred and his brother Kent came north to log on Montague Island in the 50s. "Wearing an earring, if you can believe that," according to his daughter Rene.

In the local parlance, Fred was immediately dubbed "a goer." Arrived in the Last Frontier mostly recovered from a broken neck suffered while riding broncos in Idaho. Everything was done "full bore." A jack of all trades: logger, pile buck, carpenter, equipment operator, construction worker, commercial fisherman, among others. That first winter he was seen skiing down " The Lady," a extreme snow face on Mt. Eccles. Wooden skis and non-release bindings were the equipment of the day back then.

Fred tied in with George Date, who owned a small local construction outfit. George was also known as a "goer"; which made for an animated and entertaining combination.

Back then extending the "Copper River Highway" over the old Copper River and Northwest Railroad grade was in full swing. George's company was in on the work, tearing up railroad tracks, trestles, and bridges; slapping down gravel, installing culverts, and building replacement spans here and there.

At that time everyone in Cordova was pro-road; Chitina Here We Come. From there Cordova would be connected to the Alcan Highway and the Lower Forty Eight. The railroad had been closed less than twenty years. Many locals remembered riding the train to Chitina and the mines at Kennecott.

Superintendent Date's management style was predicated on driving around wildly in a red pickup, chomping on a cigar, shouting orders, spurning the boys on. Double full bore.

The story goes on one occasion George had the gang tear out a short bridge, and then realized they need more equipment and supplies still in town to continue the project. Hopped in his truck, turned around, went tearing off with gravel flying, and drove right off the bank and into the river. Where the bridge had been.

Go George, shouted the Crew, before they plucked him out the waterway. That evening, over a cold one at the Alaskan, they renamed it George Gorge.

Fred eventually bought out George. The proud new owner of Eyak Construction, he was the perfect replacement, running things in similar "balls to the wall" style.

One of his key employees was Kelly Lape, a talented equipment operator. Kelly's twin sons Doug and David were my classmates at CHS.

Soon after Fred took over, the Eyak Gang was tearing down a massive wooden railroad trestle far out the road. Fred was a hands-on leader, and while standing high atop the structure, found the need for an ax. Being a logger, and not wanting to waste time, he hollered at Kelly to toss one up.

It came zinging along in cartwheeling fashion and clipped the tip right off Fred's nose. When I first came to know Fred, as my little league basketball coach, I always wondered why his nose was crooked. Seems he and Kelly found the missing part, picked it up, drove to town, had it sewn on, and headed back to work.

Undoubtedly finished the day talking about it at the Cordova Elks Lodge, where Fred worked his way through all the Chairs and served as Exalted Ruler. Both the Elks and Moose were going concerns back then. I can still remember Fred, Louie Hasbrouck, Kenny Van Brocklin, Jimmy Iliff, and others in their sweat soaked purple Elks uniforms during winter evening City League basketball games at the old City Gym, now the Bidarki Rec Center.

When the Elks played the Moose, time outs were often taken to wipe down perspiration that turned its slippery wooden surface into a ice rink. Especially along the free throw lanes, where everyone hung their heads down, hands on knees, gasping for breath, and dripping sweat. Not much doubt about where the boys did their pre-game, and their post-game, for that matter. Not infrequently injured members of both Antlered Squads were carted down the stairs from the second floor gym and up the stairs to the E.R. of the hospital, conveniently located right across the street. Always had an extra nurse on call during City League games. Maybe that's how Fred met his future wife.

Fred gave a great deal of time to the Elks Youth Program and kids in general. I remember the first time we went out on an overnight campout with Fred as Scoutmaster. We were spread out in two-man tents near the campground at the end of the Sheridan Glacier Road. Fred and his assistant claimed the old log cabin that sat partway down the trails that connected to Cabin Lake. They took great delight in scaring the bee jeesus out of us by sneaking up to our shelters in the middle of the night, growling like bears or screaming like Indians, and then racing off. We repaid the favor by stuffing moss in the cabin's chimney. Not sure what Merit Badge we earned out of that one.

I came to know Fred even better when he bought our family's little house on the corner of A Avenue, across from Mt. Eccles. Newly arrived nurses and school teachers have always been prime courting grounds for small town Alaska bachelors, and Fred had charmed a cute nurse from Maine named Betty Gamble into marriage.

Fred and Rod McDonald had helped build our new home right next door on Second Street, and by the time we moved in, two little Pettingills were roaring around, and number three was on the way. Fred had additions to the tiny house going up both to the east and west before we had even finished unpacking in our new place. We all came to know Fred, Betty, and family even better now that they were neighbors. I babysat the kids, Fred whomped me at chess. Evidently bunkhouse cowboys practice many unheralded intellectual activities when not in town raising hell on Saturday night. Or perhaps while bedridden with broke bones.

Fred was one heck of an outdoorsman. He loved to hunt, trap, and fish. In the winter of 1961, he invited me to go trapping out the road. See if we could catch a few lynx and wolverine along the base of the Queen's Chair. Back then it was possible to drive down a newly completed mile long dike road this side of Ibeck River that ran north to the bottom of the mountain. We would motor out in Fred's old truck, park at the end of the dike, and then hike toward Eyak Lake. A natural game trail followed the base of the mountain, and made for good trapping. At that time there didn't seem to be many coyote around, but lynx and wolverine were common.

Fred spent more than one late Saturday night at the Elks. Lodges were a going concern back then. So it was no surprise that he was a bit under the weather one Sunday when we headed out to check our sets. Maybe he and Betty danced til dawn to live music provided by Jerry Ware and his Magic Organ. No kidding, that was the solo artist's appellation. His raspy voice, talented keyboard skills, and mechanized percussion beats kept the crowd rocking. The bar too.

One of the most frequently requested songs was about airboating. The early models were small metal hulls powered by airplane engines, and prone to going airborne, flipping sideways, or sinking. So of course, Fred and several of his bar mates had to have them. Ware would crank the volume of his electronics up full bore, and croon "God dam, God dam, jump another beaver dam, going as fast as I can," along with "A tisket, a tasket, Webber blew a casket" and "I'm just glad to be alive, in my 185."

It was snowing lightly, with not much daylight that time of year, but the trail was easy going. We hadn't even reached our first set when we heard quite a commotion. Were greeted upon arrival by a hissing, agitated lynx with one foot in the long spring trap, glaring and leaping at us every time we approached. He couldn't have been in the foothold that long.

I had never seen a lynx up close before. The trap chain was cabled to a nearby tree, and seemed to be holding. Fred carried a small 22 pistol in his pack for such situations. Reached in to get it out, paused, looked at me, and said "Oops. Took the pistol out to clean it last week, and forgot to put it in the pack this morning."

Mr. Lynx took another leap at us, cable taut, chain rattling. Yikes. I jumped away. Before I could say anything, Fred, quick thinker at all times, had already come up with a solution. Actually solutions.

"Well, we've got two options. We can hike back to the truck, drive to town, get the pistol, come back out, and hope this guy is still here. Plus it might be a bit dark by then."

"Or we can go with Plan B."

Even at a tender young age, I had become wary of Plan B, also one of Dad's specialties.

"And what would that be?," asked I.

Fred looked around, walked a couple yards, and picked up a large stick.

"You distract him, and I'll get him with this," he stated. With a grin.

Yipee. I remembered thinking about one of my favorite childhood books, *Little Black Sambo*. These days it's banned from the shelves.

Ah, the Days of Our Youth. Dick be nimble, Dick be quick, As Fred kills the lynx, With a nice big stick.

"Ah, what the heck. Let's go for it." One way or the other, I was about to enter the Kingdom of Goers.

The rest was a blur. Time does fly when you're having fun. Some serious feinting, jabbing, jumping, acrobatics, and finally a lynx to pack home. A story to tell my folks, a day to remember.

Fred skinned and tanned the hide. Gave it to me as a keepsake. The soft, plush fur was beautiful.

By now, you're probably wondering what this all has to do with a Chapter about moose.

Well, with all this background in mind, now comes the tale of my first moose hunt. With Fred, of course.

The year was 1962. Doug Lape and I had both graduated from high school that spring. It was only the second moose hunt on the Copper River Delta, following the transplant of the big animals as calves from the Kenai Peninsula beginning in 1949.

As fates would have it, the Sheridan bridge had washed out again, so a modern span was being built across the problematic river at 14 Mile of the Copper River Highway. Sandstrom Construction was in the final stages of finishing the bridge, with inspections and approval right around the corner. The last thing Dale and his Crew wanted was a bunch of moose blood on the shiny new concrete. Nor did they want to deal with liability issues involving a bunch of crazed moose hunters crossing a structure that had not been certified. No traffic was allowed, severely restricting the harvest area to Miles 5 through 14, less than half the west side of the Delta. Moose beyond Sheridan had to be chuckling between bites of willow.

They hadn't reckoned with Fred P.

Eyak Construction had an area out Whitshed Road near the shipyard for storing all their equipment. Parked sitting among trucks, bulldozers, front end loaders, cranes and other gear were twenty swamp buggies. Atlantic Richfield had been doing gas and oil exploration work on the Delta, mainly on the other side toward Katella, which at one time had a functioning oil well.

The swamp buggies were stored there, waiting for a barge to haul them out. Before Fred and Kelly's very eyes. Goer Fred thought, what the hell, letting equipment sit idle is the best way to let it go to hell. In fact, he told Atlantic Richfield part of his storage fee might be the use of one of the machines.

So it was no surprise when Fred turned to Kelly and announced: "Let's fire off one of these puppies and go moose hunting." The duo decided to invite Doug and I along. Moose are big animals, having a couple eager young high school lads along might prove helpful.

The plan was to pick the swamp buggy up after work the evening before the season opened, head out the road, cross the Sheridan, spend the night camped out, and then have half the Delta all to ourselves.

I had never seen a swamp buggy before, neither had most Cordovans, many of whom almost drove off the highway when they saw Fred driving this contraptions out the road, with Doug and I riding directly behind him in the small equipment bin. Four huge "V" threaded tires, taller than us, about six feet in diameter. Independent suspension, four wheel drive. Air cooled 40 horsepower combine engine mounted high above the front axle, with a metal bucket seat directly behind for the driver. Long gear shift lever, 20 speed transmission. The metal bin box was four by six feet with solid floor. When Atlantic Richfield used the rigs for their exploration, each one towed a small barge behind it holding a trailer-like structure for housing and equipment.

These rigs were not designed for speed or comfort. But were they ever eye-catching. And incredibly mobile in the wet, brushy, and gutter-filled terrain of the Delta. Doug and I were having the time of our lives waving at passing vehicles as we chugged along; clearly Fred was enjoying the moment too. Kelly followed in a pickup with a flat bed trailer for hauling the moose back to a warehouse at Eyak's storage yard, where a crane would be used to lift the animals to be skinned and then hung to age.

We pulled up to the town side of the closed Sheridan River bridge. The road was crammed with vehicles, hunters scouting for nearby moose and trying to figure out their options.

We motored up to an awestruck crowd. Fred had just completed his initial operating time on this hummer driving out the road. In typical Pettingill fashion, he hollered to Kelly, "Well, let's see what these machines can do."

The onlookers parted and rushed to the river bank, waiting to witness The Show. Multiplicity of possibilities. Side bets quickly placed. Man and Machine versus The Elements. This was as exciting as a Rodeo, not standard Alaska Fare. Fred riding the Big Mechanical Bronco, Kelly, Doug and I hanging on. No PFD's, of course. Down the roadside berm directly below the bridge we went, crashing through low brush, and plunging in the river.

We quickly entered water deeper than the wheels. Icy cold, grey, rippling, noisy, racing downstream. Covered the tire rims; Fred's feet were getting wet as he shifted gears. The big tires floated the rig, and the forward spin of their treads gradually pulled us across until grabbing rocky bottom on the other side. We landed 75 yards below the bridge. Luckily the current hadn't been swifter.

Crawled up on a gravel bar, drove back to the lower edge of the road, eased up the berm. The crowd on the other side cheered. We waved our hats and headed down the highway to our Private Happy Hunting Grounds. It was a sunny evening, and the Hunt was off to an adventuresome start. We bounced along to what is now called One Eyed Pond, originally a gravel pit for road construction. Parked the rig, dug out our sleeping bags, built a fire, shot the breeze, and called it a night. Spawning salmon splashed in a nearby stream, and the bugs were fierce. It was a restless night, anticipating the hunt and wondering if any bears were about.

Up at the crack of dawn, coffee on a coleman stove. Chilly, everything covered with dew. But it was going to be a nice day. Uncertain what the buggy could do, and if it would scare off moose, the plan was to hunt on foot, and use the machine for retrieval.

Off we trudged. Thick brush hampered our visibility. Fred climbed a small tree to scan the area, couldn't see much. Decided we needed to veer off and head toward the many timbered humps and "haystacks" surrounded by more open terrain. We could climb up their spruce and hemlock to spot our quarry. After slogging for several hundred yards through watery muck, tripping over hidden roots, stumbling in low brush, and falling in brackish gutters, Fred and Kelly had enough.

"You young bucks go on ahead to that first knob, climb those big trees, and spot us some moose. We're going back to get the swamp buggy, and see what it can do. We'll rendezvous at the near end of the stand."

So Doug and I clamored ahead to the island of tall timber. It was surprisingly good going under the trees once we arrived. Moss-covered firm sod loaded with moose tracks and droppings. We found two tall spruce trees, leaned our rifles against their trunks, and climbed up through the thick branches as high as we could get, at least thirty feet up.

Quite a vista. Sun was up, a nice breeze at the high elevation kept the bugs away. Could see for miles, and spotted several moose, including a pair bulls, less than 500 yards away. We were whispering back and forth, and noticed motion directly below us. Through the thick brush, a white rack of at least 60 inches silently passed under the trees we were perched on.

Oh man. We could have practically jumped on the bull's back. We climbed down as quietly as we could, and then struggled back up, working our rifles through the limbs. Seems like it didn't take very long, and we had been stealthy.

Evidently not. Doug pointed off to what seemed like the horizon and Mr. Big trotting away.

Behind us we could hear the swamp buggy coming. It pulled up just as we stepped out of the timber. Had absolutely no problem blazing through the brush and water. Fred and Kelly laughed at our story,

"That's it, boys.," said Fred. "Hope in, we're going moose hunting."

We quickly encountered a deep, six foot wide gutter. "Hang on, here we go," hollered Fred. The front wheels plunged in, the vehicle pitching forward and down at a steep angle. Fred shifted some gears, the front tires pulled us across, and grabbed the opposite bank. The back tires plunged in, as the front of the machine pulled us up and out. Amazing.

The hunt was on. Moose seemed baffled by the swamp buggy, not racing off like the bull that had walked under us. Shortly we had our first bull, a midsize animal downed at 200 yards. Gutting and quartering game of that magnitude for the first time was quite an experience. Then the question was how to get the quarters in the swamp buggy bin, whose upper edge was six feet above us.

Fred the logger to the rescue.

"Tie a rope around its leg," he ordered. "Now lets try this." He carefully threaded the line through the "V's" in a rear tire, told us to hang on the end, hopped up, and slowly pulled the machine forward. Lifting the quarter to the top of the tire in the process. From there we flopped the it into the bin. Cool.

We were in business. By early in the afternoon, we had three moose. Two quartered and piled in the bin, the third gutted whole, being dragged behind. Honestly can't remember where Kelly, Doug, and I sat, or if we even rode. Neither could Doug.

I do recall the astonished audience back at the Sheridan Bridge when we forded the river, towing that third moose behind.

No, it wasn't the most sporting hunt in the world. But almost every moose hunter on the Copper River Delta will tell you the fun ends the minute you pull the trigger, and it's really a harvest, rather than a hunt.

I have taken moose on foot, by canoe, riverboat, airboat, and swamp buggy. Each hunt had its special moments. But only Ardy's Airboat Special came close to matching that crazy first hunt with Fred, Kelly, and Doug.

Part III: Horny Moose

September 2002

Exhausted and soaked with sweat, the duck hunter flopped into his river boat. As a teenager, he had played a fleet center field for the City team when they putted out Mile 13 way to face the FAA squad in slow pitch softball on the spacious diamond opposite across the road from the airport.

But that was a long time ago. A really, really, really long time ago. Like the 1960s.

Holy crap, this is supposed to be duck hunting, he gasped, not a half-mile race with a bull moose.

Say what, a track meet between Man and Beast?

Yes, times have changed on the Copper River Delta.

When moose are in the rut, they think about as well as adolescent males in the midst of mini-skirts or low-cut halter tops. There is only one thing on their minds, and it ain't ducks.

By mid-September, any loud noise seems to attract The Boys, big or small. Inadvertently bang an oar against the side of a metal boat when rowing across a pond, holler obscenities after flock shooting and missing two hundred widgeons attacking your decoys, or just blow your nose. Flashing moose antlers pop out of the brush, usually headed your way. In a hurry.

More than once I've had to pepper obstinate bulls with #4 shot at 100 yards. The pellets rattle off their horns, the moose shake their heads, and on they come, lust on their minds.

It's fall, and male moose are in a hurry, gathering a harem and chasing competition away. Younger bulls with smaller racks wisely shy off. Not so for bigger rivals.

Moose drop their antlers over the winter. It is legal to gather the abandoned headgear, which can be used for carvings, knife handles, decorations, souvenirs, and so forth. Early in the year, before the brush leafs out, small plane pilots fly the Delta, searching for racks. Either landing to gather them or marking the location on their GPS units for retrieval by foot, four wheeler, riverboat, or airboat.

One of the most spectacular finds in years was not one big rack, but a huge pair that were interlocked.

"Thad Richardson spotted them while flying the Delta one spring," said Don Scutt, who runs North Star Lumber, Cordova's local building supply. "Retrieved them with an airboat. Never could have got them in his plane anyhow. One rack was more than 60 inches, the other just under 70. Took two guys to lift them."

"He didn't have anywhere to store them, so they ended up down here in the lumber bay for almost two years. People heard about it, and would drop by to see them."

"Including a lot of tourists," he added, reflecting " Gees, maybe we should have charged admission."

"We talked about hanging or mounting the racks out at the Alaska Airlines terminal at Mile 13, but that never happened."

Would have been quite a conversation piece while waiting for planes arriving late, which is a common pastime in wild-weathered Cordova. Gaze at the interlocked antlers. Visualize two huge bulls butting heads over a nearby cow. Trying to back off, and discovering they are intertwined and inseparable. Then imagine what happened next. Struggling, fighting to retain their footing. Sooner or later, exhausted, one or the other must have fallen to the ground, taking the other one with him. Panting, kicking, wild-eyed, demolishing brush around them, how could they stand back up?

What followed couldn't have been pretty. Starvation, bears, wolves? We'll never know.

However, in their quest to propagate the species, the racks serve as a reminder of how intense and single-minded bulls can be. Which is not good news for duck hunters.

As post-earthquake moose habitat expanded further out on the Delta, more and more of the big animals could be seen wandering around brushy ponds, with bulls not the least bit intimidated by the banging of shotguns. Close Encounters of the Moose Kind were inevitable.

The hunter who staggered into his boat, winner of the first ever race from Center Slough to the Eyak River, was Randy Bruce.

"I had anchored the boat on the west side of the Eyak, and hiked over for a morning shoot. This side of Center Slough is good hunting, and we had a blind built on a pond there upriver from the timber line. But the trail to the spot is also a natural moose path."

"It was rutting season, and this young mulligan bull on the opposite side of the pond must have thought I was a cow. It came right toward me, grunting as it splashed across the pond. I fired 9 shots over its head, and was down to 3 shells in the gun and 3 more on the pallet boards on the floor of the open blind."

"I actually laid down in the bottom of the blind, hoping it wouldn't see me. It came all the way across the pond, and walked within 5 feet. I froze, and just wanted to let it get by me. I could hear it splashing, and thought it was going to stop and start eating the willow in the blind."

"When it had moved off about 100 yards, I stood up. The dang moose saw me, turned, and came my way. I took off running toward the cabins with my shotgun and a bag limit of ducks."

Made the 15 minute dash back to the riverboat in record time, leaving Mr. Moose in the dust and sweet gale.

He pulled across Eyak River to the cabins, looking for a cold beer and someone to tell the story. Hunting partner J.R. Reynolds, former Game Biologist for the local ADFG, and hence manager of the Delta moose herd for years, was on the porch of his cabin enjoying the sunshine while cleaning ducks.

"I remember it was a Sunday, because he was listening to NFL football on the radio," said Bruce. "I also realized I had left my hunting coat in the blind. He found the entire story quite entertaining."

Later that afternoon Julius showed up at The Last Resort with the his partner's coat. The next time Bruce went to that blind, there was a sign posted.

It read: "Moose Crossing."

Part IV: Flossing Moose

Until retirement from teaching math at CHS in 1999, I was a weekend warrior at Pete Dahl. The folks would give me grocery and supply orders on Sunday, which would be delivered the following Friday or Saturday. Dad loved ice cream and the Anchorage newspaper, which came down with each trip. They had a small propane refrigerator, but the ice cream always arrived very soft and was gobbled up immediately.

One thing they didn't need from town was laundry service. Mom washed their clothes by hand, and Dad built a 40 foot clothes line system near the east side of the cabin, extending out parallel to the slough, facing south to catch the most sun.

Dad believed in building things "skookum." The drying apparatus was made to withstand gales roaring in from the southeast and constant sand-laden winds screaming down the Copper all winter long. Pairs of creosote 2X8 planks nailed together for six foot tall support posts were embedded deep in the ground, and braced with creosote piling and logs. Three foot long cross bars were mounted to the top of each post, for not one, but two, clothes lines stretched across the span. Dad evidently liked clean jockeys and socks.

They could have opened up Pete Dahl Laundry, Inc., if there had been enough customers. Built in the first years of their retirement, it still stands today. We use it to dry hunting clothing on rare sunny days. Also apparel from visitors who inevitably fall in the slough, pond, boot-wash bucket, or other available swimming holes.

The only thing that has required occasional replacement are the clothes lines. Both were originally plastic-coated antenna wire, which seemed to survive the weather longer, and was in big supply in our constant quest to obtain better AM radio reception for music, football, and especially the World Series.

Perhaps more amazing in durability were the wooden clothes pins, which we often forgot and left on the lines year round. Winds pouring down the Copper's main channel routinely sandblast inches off the weather sides of 6X6 treated wood posts that support bridge guard rails from 27 to 39 mile. Tired of replacing the posts, the Department of Highways finally switched to steel supports in recent years.

Somehow the Pete Dahl clothes pins survived such scouring for years. Every now and then I'll toss one away that is about half its original width, but still works for today's lightweight poly under gear.

The clothes lines are popular with swallows that nest under the cabin eves. Great bug eaters, these fork-tailed aviators dart and dive about, and then take rest breaks on the lines. On windy days they hang on for dear life as the lines bounce about only 15 feet from a window above the cabin's ancient porcelain kitchen sink.

Late one fall day, hands deep in suds, scouring pots and pans, I glanced out the window to see a cow moose crossing the slough in front of our cabin. Fifty yards upstream, heading our way. The tide was low; it didn't have to swim at all.

The 100 yard stretch of bank and flat silty ground between our place and Arvidson's cabin has been carefully maintained. Gas-operated weed wackers, brush cutters, and lawn mowers have been used to keep the vegetation down. Otherwise it would be the same thick stand of alder, willow, cottonwood, and spruce that has popped up everywhere.

We left four cottonwoods spaced evenly across the clearing. In unison their leaves flash and rustle softly in the breeze. All are now more than thirty feet tall, and in the early fall bull moose come by to rub velvet off their racks against their soft trunks.

Moose are notoriously slow movers, so I leisurely finished the dishes and watched. Wonder what this one has in mind? She eased up over the bank, eyeballing our cabin and Arvidson's, showing zero concern about man-made structures. Paused to study carefully shaped spruces scattered about the opening. I have taken to giving them an annual pruning, a hobby picked up after seeing cleverly designed Banzai trees at Disneyland's "Small World" attraction. We rode the little boats three consecutive times on our daughters' first visit to the Magic Kingdom, so I had considerable time to study their designs. Forty years later, the tune "It's a Small World after all..." still rings in my ears.

The moose's gaze turned to the clothes lines. Hmm, wonder what that is? The line furtherest from her was white plastic coated antenna wire; the closer was quarter inch green poly which had been used to replace a frayed cotton cord. She ambled up, feet sinking slightly in the soft dirt, head just above the lines, long legs taking easy strides

Looked at the green line directly in front of her. Perhaps confused it with willow, right at mouth level. Chomped on it, and then slowly moved her head back and forth, sliding the strange item between her jaws.

Moose Flossing 101

The motion put tension on the slightly sagging line, but it didn't break, and the support posts held firm. Dad had built a clothes line system to survive more than just the weather and a week's worth of underwear.

Madam Moose evidently found the flavor and texture of polypropylene line lacking. Stripped from an old gillnet, it was chewy with a slight salmon ambiance. I figured that's it; she's going to get tangled up and pull the whole thing down.

Nope.

She ducked her head, took a step forward, and tried the white line. Which she liked. I peered out the window equally open-mouthed as she slide the plastic-coated wire back and forth between her teeth, repeatedly. Perfect diameter moose floss. She began pulling on the line so hard I was concerned it might topple the entire structure, so I stepped out on the porch, leaned around the corner, and quietly asked her to leave.

Not the least bit alarmed, she looked at me, dropped her head, walked under the line, and strolled around the corner. The last I saw she was wading across the pond behind the cabin, bending to browse on aquatic plants, with the cleanest moose teeth on the Copper River Delta.

Longtime local dentist Dr. Gilbert Urata was pleased when I told the story on my next visit to his office.

17 September 2007

Watched a cow moose chew on both clothes lines at dusk three days ago. Went out and shooed it off so it wouldn't tear them down. Bull moose grunting behind cabin last night. Tom looked out window and saw nothing but horns. —Dick

Chapter 17

Bears

BROWN BEAR: 1. *Ursus Arctos.* Large bear distributed across much of Northern Urasia and North America. Costal Alaskan bear, living on a steady, nutritious diet of spawning salmon, can weigh 1500 pounds, with adult height range of 5.2 to 9.2 feet. Wikipedia

2. "It was a bear," a polite way of referring to a particularly challenging situation. Local Idiom

"The third time's a charm."

A Phrase of Shakespearean Origin

Part I: Bridge Bear

7 August 1996

Dreams of past glories die hard. Jane Leavy, in her book *Sandy Koufax, A Lefty's Legacy*, wrote: "Myth-making is a collaborative process, a collusion between recollection and fact."

Walhalla Pond was a Myth Maker. Pursuit of its pre-earthquake duck hunting renown led to improbable efforts against inevitable change.

"You can't screw with Mother Nature," Dad would say.

But oh did we try.

Slowly at first, and then at an accelerating rate, willow, alder, sweet gale, and cottonwood on the trail to Duck Hunter's Heaven grew taller and thicker. Just getting there became a Bushwacker's Delight. By the early 90s, what had once been a relatively easy twenty minute walk through short grass on fairly solid ground had become an hour long hump through boot-tangling shrubs, deepening marshes, and expanding brush lines. Prickly spruce spiced up the trek. Even beavers wanted nothing to do with them.

Armed with Swede saws, axes, shears, shovels, pruners, lopers, and gas-powered brush cutters, days were spent each July and August keeping a rudimentary path open so we could reach our Golden Pond. In several places, "tunnel" would be a better description. Stretches of alder and willow reached heights of fifteen feet, and combined with even taller cottonwood and spruce, formed an overhead canopy that blocked out the sun.

Moose quickly discovered and appreciated our efforts, and helped keep the brush down by tromping on our trail. In some places the big browsers turned it into a muddy quagmire. While hiking to Walhalla at early dawn, headlamps strapped atop duck hats, we cursed when tripping in deep hoof prints. But hey, it was their Delta too. Plus our X-rated racket likely gave us a passing lane through waving antlers.

So. One sunny August day in 1996, armed with bug spray, candy bars, saws, pruners, a gas-powered Sears Craftsman brush cutter with 4 tooth blade and harness, 2 gallons of mixed gas, and a 30-06 rifle with 4X Leopold scope, I'm having a fun time working on the trail to Walhalla. Duck season is only three weeks away. It's time to get organized.

Cutting sweet gale and willow is a nightmare. Their branches start right at ground or water level, and shoot out in every direction except up. Brush falls on top the cutter shaft, so you have to physically swing it out of the way. Stems bind between the blade and guard, which means stop the engine, detach it from the body harness, lay it one the ground, pull out the jam, re-harness the engine, crank several times to get it re-started, and try again. Bugs swarm inside the face guard necessary for protection from flying sticks; insect repellant mixed with sweat drips in your eyes; ears ring despite noise protectors; hands in heavy gloves become numb from vibrations; and the brush grows back thicker every time it is cut. You know it will be worse the next year.

Like I said, a fun time. Remember G.O. Young's description of guides' invective in *Alaska Yukon Trophies Won and Lost?* A refresher, with one early 1900s typically polite phrase: "Well, this is just one continuous round of pleasure; if it ain't one d---thing it's another."

Classy.

How the English Language has changed. Our utterances were not. Even though we too, were on the hunt for Trophies.

Ducks.

Half way across a 300 yard opening of low brush, the wacker and I ran out of gas. Removed the harness gear, time to let the machine and I cool off.

Grabbed a Nalgene bottle of Crystal Light iced tea mix, Milky Way candy bar, and Swede saw. Decided to walk 100 yards up the trail to a thirty yard band of tall alder and willow on either side of a deep gutter. Take a break in the shade, and then knock down a few larger trees by hand. Mr. Weedwacker was giving me a headache.

Also slung the 30-06 over my shoulder. Had frequently encountered moose in this area. Wanted the rifle for self defense, but mainly as a noise maker. This time of year, the hefty ungulates usually take off as soon as they see or smell you. If not, a shot over the head typically encourages the thought process.

The biggest gutter we had to ford in order to reach Walhalla had been a challenge for years. Pre-earthquake tides made it too wide and deep to cross; post-earthquake beavers had done the same. We tried tearing down their dams and going to war with my Oregon State Mascots, but discovered it was like fighting the Chinese during the Korean War. They just kept on coming, in more and bigger divisions. The sound of running water seemed to be their bugle call to arms; they did their maneuvering and construction under the cover of darkness. It was a losing battle, and took us far too long to figure out that they could build more and bigger dams faster than we could tear them out.

Eventually the Beaver Wars ended in a stalemate. A cease fire similar to that in Korea, although we never did sign an armistice. The gutter still created a barrier. So we decided on a bridge. My two years in the civil engineering program at UAF before switching to a math major at OSU were about to pay off.

The first span was simple and elegant. In the winter of 1992, a sixteen foot flat-bottom aluminum river boat with a bashed-in side drifted up Odiak Slough on a big tide, and landed on the beach in front of our house. I tied it off, and the following spring we pounded the hull back into semi-shape, loaded in cross-ways on my 14 foot riverboat, and hauled it down river. MacArthur would have been proud; an amphibious assault behind enemy lines. We dropped our prize off at the trailhead, waded it across a big lake, cut an opening through the alders, dragged it through the brush, and stretched it across the gutter. The bottom leaked like a sieve, but so what. Turned it upside down, and had ourselves a bridge. Styrofoam sealed within the seats provided buoyancy.

Unfortunately, neither bow nor stern quite spanned the gutter, so the end of the floating catwalk you stepped on had a disconcerting habit of sinking, while the opposite extremity rose ominously out of the brown aqua. A water totter. Something to eagerly anticipate on those early morning hikes with a thirty pound pack full of ammo, decoys, thermos, duck calls, binoculars, extra clothing, snacks, and all the other essentials for a successful hunt. Its quirky behavior increased the pace for that 20 foot stretch. Ready, set, go.

Meanwhile, beavers sat on the banks, scratching their heads while looking on in amusement. Those crazy human beings; why don't they build a dam?

We actually hoped they would jump in to help out by building their trademark masterpiece nearby. Instead they went down stream 500 yards and put up a Hoover-like obstruction which raised the water level for miles upstream, making our pontoon bridge even more unstable. Like the North Koreans, constantly agitating at Panmunjom, were these furry little engineers.

However, the bridge continued to work, if your remembered your preschool nursery rhyme about "Jack be nimble, Jack be quick…" Despite its deficiencies, Bridge #1 served in entertaining fashion for two years.

When the maintenance crew arrived in the summer of Year #3, the bridge was still in place, albeit with a new inverted "V" shape. Unlike any suspension bridge I had ever studied. A heavy snow and ice load had collapsed it over the winter.

Undaunted, we manhandled a 16 foot 2X12 plank across the half mile trail, nailed it to both ends of the upside down metal boat, and tried tiptoeing across. It was like walking on a rubber band. So we packed in 2X4's, nailed them down amidships as supports, scabbed on a few braces here and there, and had ourselves a new, improved span.

Which I was now eyeballing while taking that break from brush cutting.

The first trip across every year was for the intrepid only. Were the supports still solid? Were the ends still tied in place? It was easy to check the near end physically; the other end, only if you got there. It was a warm, sunny day. The worse that could happen would be taking a dip, which might be refreshing. The beavers were lined up atop their nearby house, munching on saplings, waiting for Show Time. As my wife's friend and co-pilot Barb Cave said to Sue just before she submerged our Dodge Eagle trying to race across a river to get to Barb's secret blueberry hot spot, "Just go for it!"

So I hit the accelerator and went hot footing across the plank. Jumped off on the other bank, and to my pleasant surprise and tail slapping applause from nearby fans, noted the bridge had barely budged. Awesome.

I glanced down the gutter to see if any flat -tailed friends were joining the crowd to watch the return trip. Nope. The Show was over, and they were all cruising down stream.

I had raced across the bridge with my rifle at port arms, not wanting to go swimming with it strapped across my chest.

Lucky for me.

I caught some motion out of the corner of my eye, and glanced back across the bridge.

Holy crap.

Twenty feet up the trail, through the alder tunnel I had just traversed, a brown bear stepped out. Not Mr. Big, probably a three year old. But big enough. Maybe looking for a beaver lunch. Perhaps the splashing sounds made when I crossed the bridge had attracted his attention.

Who knows?

I do know what happened next.

He dropped his head and came running right at me.

I spun around, and as his front legs hit the far end of the bridge, shot.

Talk about a blur.

He slid across the 2X12, splashed in the water, and landed right at my feet. I jacked in more rounds and shot him twice, with the barrel of the gun literally touching his back, before sitting down and shaking. Adrenaline pumping, I can't say I even remember clearly doing that, until I noticed three shells were gone when I reloaded.

It was the first bear I had ever shot.

I'm a big Sinatra fan. Frank sings "Luck Be My Lady Tonight" daily on our cabin radio. KHAR in Anchorage, AM 590, Oldies but Goodies.

I'm glad to be older. And Luck was My Lady that day.

Number One, to be standing there holding the rifle. If I had been sitting on my pack sipping ice tea and eating a candy bar, the 30-06 would have been leaning against a tree, and I would never have had time to shoulder it.

Number Two, to hit the bear at all. A scope at that range is useless, actually a hinderance. It was point and shoot. I caught a break. When the bear came down the far bank full bore, he was running slightly down hill, with his neck and back exposed. The first shot went through his neck from above, just beyond the base of his head.

Maybe all those years of instinctive shotgunning, using the barrel as an extension of the arm, paid off. My worst duck shooting occurs when I start thinking and analyzing. There was time for neither in this case.

To this day the thing that puzzles me most is why the bear was even there. I had been operating a brush cutter that sounds just like a chain saw only 100 yards away for more than an hour. Plus I had walked through that side of the trail making all kinds of noise just five minutes earlier.

So much for those hikers who tie a bell to their pack to alert bears they are coming.

7 August 1996

Back at cabin having a B & B, Oldtimer! Brown bear charged me on trail at bridge - killed with 1 shot at 15 feet. —Dick

Part II: Power Creek Bear

12 July 1998

It had been long day, but we were almost there. A truck plus cold beer in an ice chest awaited us by the spawning stream near the end of Power Creek Road. Descend through thick brush on a moss-covered sixty foot drop, cross a shallow braided glacial flow, and a sunny July day trek would be complete.

Dr. Larry Ermold was in the lead; his daughter Wendy, a slight five foot blonde twenty year old home from college was in the middle; and I was bringing up the rear. We were bushwacking it straight down from the Hut, a small cedar shelter the USFS had built at an elevation of 1800 feet midway on the ridge line trail between Crater Lake and Power Creek. This shortcut wasn't unfamiliar terrain. We had hiked up and down it loaded with ski and bivy gear several times in the winter for amazing backcountry skiing and overnight stays in the cozy yet often completely buried shelter. Several times we had to use ski poles as probes to find the metal roof of the hut, and avalanche shovels to dig down to the entrance.

In fact, one of the reasons for the hike was to install a small plywood swing-down table on a wall of the hut, so when we camped there overnight in its cramped quarters we could get some of our gear off the floor. A place for the bivy stove to melt snow for water, as well as cooking gear, candles, dry food, and sundry items. High test Scotch for watching stars that seemed feet away was tucked in Nalgene bottles right outside the snow-banked door.

I had carried the plywood to the Hut by lashing it to a day pack. The engineering had worked perfectly, just some hinges, eye hooks, and a little chain. We would drink and dine in style buried beneath the snow next year.

Our first winter trek to the shelter had followed the same route we had hiked today: up the 2.4 mile Crater Lake trail built by the CCC in 1938; then traversing the Ridge line 3.5 miles to the Hut. It was a hump. After six hours of climbing, including post-holing in several steep places, plus up and down skiing with climbing skins, ski crampons, and ices axes to traverse several glazed sections before gaining the shelter in falling light, we had vowed to find an easier way. We finally settled on just going straight up from the Power Creek road, which meant wallowing in waist deep snow in the upper 50 degree pitches, plus using ropes to climb over rocky faces, but it was quicker and shorter.

In the summer, this route was very brushy with both thick alder and devil's club on open faces, but the going wasn't too bad in the lower timber. It was also clearly bear country. We constantly ran into sign, especially early in the spring when both black and brown bear were coming out of hibernation.

Wendy seemed a bit out of gas after we reached the Hut, so after doing our modifications plus having a lunch that included hot soup cooked on a pack stove, we decided heading straight down seemed like a much easier choice than retracing our steps over the six mile trail. With all the switchbacks and elevation changes involved in trying to locate rock cairns marking the open upper ridge path, the long route was at times demoralizing as well as exhausting.

So down the shortcut we went, on full Bear Alert. Larry and I were carrying 44 magnum pistols on shoulder holsters, plus making considerable noise using Fox 40 whistles from my supply for refereeing high school basketball in the winter.

Fox 40s are very loud. In fact, they had been developed by Ron Foxcroft and Chuck Shepard after an incident in the Olympics. Foxcroft witnessed an obvious foul, but the pea in his whistle jammed, and he could not stop play. Needless to say, the referees were booed. These computer-designed puppies do not have a pea in them; and the harder you blow, the louder they get. Foxcroft introduced the Fox 40 at the 1987 Pan American Games. Before the end of the games, he had orders for 20,000 whistles.

When not tooting on the whistles, we were hollering loudly. Hey bear, coming through!

So here we were, merrily descending through tall shady timber, five hundred yards to go. Great day, mission accomplished. Could almost taste that cold Alaska Amber.

Then all hell broke loose.

Larry had just crested the top of the last drop off, which was covered with spruce and hemlock, plus low underbrush of blueberry, alder, and more devil's club. He hollered, "Oh shit, it's a bear. With cubs."

Remember the saying about the joys of decision making, i.e Decision making is fun when you make the right decision? Sometimes you just don't have much time to ponder your choices. We had three alternatives: stand our ground and hope the sow would make a bluff charge up the cliff; try to drop her with our pistols if she didn't; or retreat and head up a tree. With thick cover, chances were the bear wouldn't even see us until ten feet or less away, and the noise below told us an angry bruin was already coming, although we couldn't see her. Trying to hold our ground and shoot at close range with pistols would clearly be a one shot option. It wasn't a very lengthy discussion. We turned and scrambled back up through our rough trail. The racket behind us was certainly an incentive to act. Quickly.

Things were a blur, which I discovered was a common denominator of all charging bear incidents. I remember grabbing Wendy and pushing her off toward a stand of stumps and trees to the right. I veered left toward a spruce tree that had very few branches the first eight feet or so. I was wearing hiking shorts and knee high socks plus my skiing day pack. It felt like my legs were in wet cement even though I was racing uphill as fast as I could, with the sound of crashing brush and snapping branches behind me. Am sure when the bear crested the cliff the first thing she saw was me running away, absolutely the worst scenario. Made it to the tree, and started shinnying up frantically. Got to the first branches, a bare leg over one of them, and heard a noise no one wants to hear. Turned to look, and there was the bear, or should I say the mouth, teeth, saliva, head, eyes, rage, and roar of a bear, her body wrapped around the tree, about to grab my other bare leg, hanging below the branch.

Holy christ.

I jerked the leg up just as her jaws snapped shut with a distinct clack. She missed. At that point, you like to think you are congratulating yourself on escaping; in reality, I was trying to breath and scream at the same time, fear and adrenaline surging, frantically trying to pull myself up over the branches to get as high up that friggin' tree as I could.

Without success. My body, arms, and head were facing the trunk, and believe me I would have climbed 30 feet to the tippity-top of that spruce if I could have. Forget the scratches on my arms, leg, and face; forget everything, just get higher. Later, I would tell people that I thought maybe I had it made. Bull shit. There isn't a lot of rational thinking going on in moments like that.

The next thing I remember is pain and screaming. Unbeknownst to me, the angry sow, who had left her two tiny cubs behind, in a Perfect Storm of Female Bear Defensive Instinct, had dropped down, moved back several feet, and then charged again, getting a running jump that gave her enough height to reach my leg. I had been bitten once by an improperly leashed German Shepard, but that was nothing in comparison. Hot, burning, stinging, terrifying; maybe that's where the term grisly comes from.

Oh shit, oh shit, oh shit, she got me. Aughhh, shit.

Yet by some strange luck, that was it. Mrs. Bear could have easily ripped me out of the tree, there is no way I could have hung on to the branches if she had pulled. Instead she sunk all four major teeth into my leg, and then let go. Believe me, I wasn't watching, but could tell she had released.

Then a loud roar. Of a pistol.

Larry, who had been waving his weapon and trying to decide whether to shoot or not, concerned about hitting me instead of the bear, blasted at the sow as it went racing by he and Wendy, who were standing on a stump 30 feet away. The little cubs had arrived on the scene, and the sow was so busy chasing them off she didn't notice either of my companions.

Luckily. And equally lucky, he missed.

Larry hollered stay in the tree in case she comes back. So I hung there for how long I don't know, probably a much shorter time than it seemed, before I couldn't hang on any longer, and dropped/crawled/fell out of the tree.

Larry and Wendy came over. Weapons in hand, we sat there, listened, and waited. The bear did not return. Just as well. I know my shooting wouldn't have been very accurate.

Time to check out the damage. Nice to have a doctor around.

I peeled down the torn wool sock, and we looked at four deep puncture wounds on the front of my left leg, two on each side of major bone, about halfway between my knee cap and ankle. Stung and ached, but barely bleeding. Wow. Of all the places to be bit, I guess that was the best. No knee damage, no rips or tears, no major blood. Just a kind of numb overall sensation, a "what the hell just happened" feeling.

Not much we can do here, said the doctor.

We waited a little longer; gathered ourselves together. Wendy was obviously frightened and trembling. Time to get out of here.

Larry helped me to my feet, offered to take my pack. I put weight on the leg, it didn't hurt that bad, so I swung the rucksack on my back and said let's go. We did tread very lightly, with sidearms out, the rest of the way, in case the bear had veered back in our path. The noise of the milky glacial river made us realize the sow had never heard our whistles and hollering.

Crossing the stream felt good, cold water numbing my leg. We hopped in the pickup and headed to town and the hospital.

Strange the things you remember. Power Creek road is one lane gravel; hilly, curvy, right along the edge of Eyak Lake. Passing vehicles is impossible. And wouldn't you know it, in front of us was another truck driven by a local oldtimer chugging along at about 5 miles an hour, enjoying the sights and completely oblivious to us tailgating him and honking. It was six miles to town, and we were unable to get by him until less than a mile from the city limits.

But hey. I was doing fine. The good doctor had prescribed a cold beer.

We went straight to the emergency room at the hospital, which is six blocks from our house. The physician on call was visiting from back East. He was excited. Had never seen a bear bite before. Nurses did all the usual stuff. I didn't ask what my pulse and blood pressure were.

Larry went to call my wife. No cellphones back then. She was at home with my mom and sisters, waiting for us to show up for dinner. A bit exasperated when answering the phone, anticipating a call from the Powder House saying we were having a cold one and would be home shortly, while dinner was chilling down on the table. Can't say I blame her; over the years that has been SOP for us thoughtful husbands.

Larry gave her this cryptic message: "Sue, we're at the emergency room."

Sue: "What happened?"

Larry: "Dick had a little accident. Everything is OK, but don't bring your camera."

Say what?

She came racing down, and there I was laying on the emergency room table. Almost had to elbow her way in to see me. By then everyone in the hospital had heard about The Bite, and wanted to see what one really looked like. Nurses were coming in and out like it was Code Blue. The bear had ripped holes in my left hiking sock. Could have paid for a new pair had I been charging admission.

Exam went fine; one wound was much deeper than the others. Infection was the main concern. Mrs. Bear had probably been dining on Salmon with Eggs before it sampled Leg of Me. Tetanus shots, antibiotics, pain pills, lots of fluids, and keep it elevated, plus change the dressing often.

For some reason the Back East doctor kept calling me a hero. Why I'm not sure. In reality it was helter-skelter, and anyone who tells you elsewise in a situation like that is full of it.

We headed home. It was a sunny day. Had a nice dinner. I hate pain pills and their side affects, but went with the flow.

Cordova rumors fly faster than canvasbacks.

By dawn the next day my leg had been torn off. My left buttock had more holes in it than my duck decoys. Doctors ran out of suture material, and had to borrow gill net twine from Redden Net. I was in intensive care; and couldn't have visitors yet.

In reality, by afternoon the next day I was sitting on our house deck overlooking Odiak Slough, leg propped up, enjoying the warmth of the sun and a chilled brew. The doctor said drink lots of fluids.

Daily visits to the hospital to have things cleaned out and checked ensued. Nurse Sue, whose Mom was a real, bonafide nurse with some great stories to tell about her early days in Valdez via Mississippi in the 1940s, would later tell me that she could see some pretty interesting stuff deep down in the Big Hole while changing the dressings.

Meantime, everyone in town was at the local hardware or sporting goods stores buying bear spray or short-barreled shotguns. Wish I had told son-in-law Tom, down at Whiskey Ridge Trading Company, that I wanted a 50% cut on all bear-related sales. Surprised he didn't call and ask me to recover in a wheelchair by his checkout counter.

Finally the rumor curve reached its apogee. Then Cordova Humor stepped in. Friend Bob Lenz, boys high school basketball coach, dropped by. We had shared many fun times together. Remember Peachtree Point? He brought along a quart bottle of the Golden Elixir, with a revised label on the front that said "Old Brown Bear," replete with upright bear image, and subtitle, "Bear Repellent."

The empty bottle is a dusty keepsake recently discovered in our attic. Had forgotten the best part. On the back, Lenzo Verse: "When you really want to git, But your pants are full of shit, Take two colossal swigs, And kiss your sweet ass goodbye!"

Not much of a Poet, but knew the Powers of the Potion. It surely speeded his recovery after tumbling off the bow of my river boat. And mine eleven years later.

Some of the local good-natured humor arose from basketball, a small town Alaska wintertime passion, which I've refereed for more than forty years. Samples: "White men can't jump, but brown bears can." "Cordova's refs are so bad even bears won't eat em." "Bite and release," a play on the catch and release of sport fish. But all in jest. In Cordova, being the butt of a joke is the highest form of flattery.

A week went by. Infection was no longer a concern. It was time to stitch things up. Deer season was two weeks away. I wanted to be on top Hawkins Island on opening day.

It is always disconcerting to watch doctors with needles and thread putting your body parts back together, especially when the impacted area is numb, but crunching sounds are audible, and the process is visible before your very eyes, if you so desire.

One of the shallower bites required no stitching; two others took maybe a dozen or so. The top right one was a dandy. Must have come from the upper canine of my Angry Antagonist. Closing that one took all three doctors. Two to push the hole shut, and the other to work from deep down, up and out. Fifty plus stitches. I was really skeptical about the needlework holding, but they guaranteed their artwork, and gave me the get- go to start rehabbing right away.

Which I did. Daily hikes up to the base of the Mt. Eyak ski hill parking lot to start; then to the top of the ski area, known as the Tripod; and finally to the Eyak ridge line, about a 3 mile trek roundtrip, with an elevation of a couple thousand feet. Carried the same day pack from that fateful day, wore the torn sock my wife had mended back together. A few days before the season opened, lounging in sun on The Ridge, spotted three deer in the basin toward Hippy Cove. Stitches came out on July 28th. Shot a nice buck on the second highest peak of Hawkins on August 1.

Bear stories seem to enthrall people. I discovered early on that asking about my encounter was really a lead-in to telling their bear adventures. Which is fine. Many people wanted to know if I was haunted by the experience. Do you have nightmares, are you afraid to go in the woods, etc?

No.

I live in Alaska for the outdoors. This was an unusual encounter where things just happened to be perfectly wrong. We were making lots of noise and were armed, but startled a sow with little cubs. Mamma Bear did exactly what could be expected. The terrain just didn't give us options.

Bear stories seem to die hard. People love em. Check out the Alaskan Reading section in any store that carries books, and I guarantee you will find shelves full of them. At least one book cover will display exactly what I saw when looking down out of that tree.

In early September, the Alaska Governor was in Cordova. Among his stops was a visit to our Blue Ribbon Mt. Eccles Elementary School. A state trooper in full uniform was along as his escort. While standing outside the auditorium waiting for students to file in for an assembly, the trooper was telling the Governor the story about this Cordova guy that was recently mauled by a bear. My wife, who was teaching third grade at the time, just happened to be standing there as her class passed by.

She tapped the trooper on the shoulder.

"Excuse me, that was my husband, and he was not mauled."

In fact, I sometimes tell people I was vaccinated. I feel immune. After all, I'm a retired math teacher. One of my courses at Oregon State was titled Probability and Statistics. What are the odds of being bit by a bear twice in your life?

Not very likely, although I did start carrying a short-barreled shotgun whenever tromping through obviously bear-prone terrain.

But maybe not as unlikely as thought.

Just ask Vern Kuder, a local hunting and fishing guide.

He's been chewed on twice.

July 18, 1998

Dick is not here. He is at home recovering from his bear bite. Yes that is right a bear bite. Has quite a story. I Don't have time to tell it. Tide is right. —Larry

Part III: Outhouse Bear

13 June 2007

Other than a cabin, an outhouse is the highest priority structure at Pete Dahl. For obvious reasons. Can't have one without the other.

Ours is a beauty. Built of scrounged 2X4's and 3/4 inch plywood from concrete forms, covered with heavy gage roofing metal full of nail holes, and soundly anchored to four creosote pilings that would support the Empire State Building, it is there to stay.

Our privy was so plush and popular that everyone in the neighborhood used it. Maybe it was the pink interior. Or the great view of the slough and quacking passer-byes. Mom put a little plastic piggy bank alongside the seat that says "Pay toilet 25 cents." Has been there since 1959. At latest count there was 43 cents in receipts. Maybe the outhouse door needs a combination lock.

Mom soon added a small 8 by12 inch wood sign, tracing her hand on it, with the caption: "All (hand outline) keep this outhouse clean." In the upper left corner she drew a winking bull, under it a sales pitch: "Hit the Bull's Eye, 10 cents a shot." Evidently some of the late evening shooters weren't too accurate or tidy. Cleanliness did improve, but there was no spike in revenue.

Over the years various improvements have been made. A thermometer is mounted in one corner, to determine if the temperature really is below 32 degrees while you turn blue on the seat. Backup rolls of TP and various containers of treatment chemicals are stored on nails and shelves.

One wall is adorned with a very special calendar. Being a graduate of Oregon State and loyal alumni, I have taken merciless grief for countless decades over their hapless football program. I was a student at OSU when the Beavers last went to a Rose Bowl. Rode a bus from Corvallis to Pasadena to watch them get thumped by Michigan. That was in 1965.

Oh my Beavers. Tacked to one of the cabin's kitchen cabinet doors is a page from Penthouse magazine, that noted sports publication. Photo of a lovely Pet of the Month, clad in skimpy OSU t-shirt, holding a football in one hand and pinching her nose with the other. Not because of my cooking. A friend had noticed the Beavers made Penthouse's annual Football Edition as one of "America's 20 Worst College Football Teams." Each year I tack their football schedule beside Ms. Pet. The Beavs are now much better, but it is still an Outhouse Tradition to post my annual Alumni Association Calendar on the crapper wall, for obvious historical reasons.

In 1996, we did make one major improvement. That spring, Jay Beaudin, John Davis, Larry Ermold, and I had flown to the Don Sheldon Hut at the Ruth Glacier of Mt. McKinley for four days of incredible glacier skiing. We also partook of one of the most famous outhouses in Alaska, perched on a sheer cliff with a truly breathtaking view of the surrounding mountains. Fitted with a styrofoam seat, which was awesome in the cold weather. In the fall, we added a similar quick-warming soft foam seat to our sea level Edifice. Only took 37 years to figure that one out.

The outhouse plays a crucial role in the first stages of our daily hunting routine. No one ever, with a capital E, wants to do what the wild bear does in the woods, if it can be avoided. Folded TP in a plastic ziplock is an essential commodity in the duck pack, but avoidance of usage is paramount. The morning shoot alarm clocks rattle, followed by several cups of coffee while it's still pitch black out. An unspoken game of Outhouse Roulette begins, hunters squirming after Cup #4 while waiting to see who will go out and warm up the Throne. Finally someone caves in. Holy Crap has multiple meanings.

Visitors provide invaluable data. No one has to ask; returnees automatically recite a checklist of info. Temperature, precipitation, wind speed and direction, birds heard or seen, whether there is enough light to run the slough, what apparel to wear, how fast everyone needs to suit up, how much ammo they should take. But not in U.S. Weather Bureau language.

Christ, it's cold out there. Man, it's coming down. Wow, I almost blew away. Did you hear those geese? Why did we get up so early, I can't even see the slough yet. Better dress warm, we might need toe warmers today. It's getting light out, what are you guys doing sitting around? It's gonna be hot!

Rituals are such an important part of duck hunting.

At various times the outhouse interior has been painted pink, light blue, and mint green. The exterior is standard Forest Green XO rust, descendant of the original Rustoleum of similar hue.The door, also green, is decorated with a lovely yellow crescent moon. Situated facing the slough, one has a very nice southerly vista and often sees ducks or geese pass by. Waterfowl that have been elusive for endless hours in the blind fly by at close range, quacking or honking in delight. It is amazing how birds can detect when you, rather than they, are in a vulnerable position.

Somehow, perhaps because I was an eager 15 year old, it was my privilege to dig the original outhouse hole. Evidently it was a top notch performance, as I've been doing it every since then. At last count, we're on hole #6, which if you consider 53 years of B.S. at Pete Dahl, is remarkable efficiency. The key component to outhouses in our particular subdivision is a 55 gallon drum with the top cut off, sunk to full depth so the rim barely protrudes above the ground. We discovered early on, the hard way, that poking holes in the bottom of the barrel is crucial. The water table on the Delta is only a few feet down. In the winter, when everything freezes, expansion will cause the drum to rise, with dire consequences.

By now, you are probably wondering what in the world this all has to do with *Ursus arctos.*

Bear with me.

When the outhouse barrel reaches its carrying capacity, it is fragrantly obvious something has to be done. Options are limited. I've tried both. Believe me, moving the outhouse is the better choice.

We quickly learned that digging a hole and putting new piling around the sunken drum was the easiest part of the operation. Tipping the outhouse over and moving it to a new location is the challenge. The darn thing must weight a 1000 pounds. In the early days, everyone in the neighborhood was using it. With so many patrons around, an Outhouse Party turned work into play.

Have a few cold beers, try not to fall in the new barrel while tipping the Colossus over, slide it over to the new foundation, tip it up into position. Wa la. Have a shot of V.O. or Peachtree, and draw straws to see who wins the honor of sighting it in. By Pete Dahl standards, a good day's work. Just be careful not to step in the recently exposed other barrel, which will soon be filled in with dirt and covered with transplanted grass.

The first three re-locates were somewhat uneventful. Learned one had avoid digging in a previously excavated site. Which was getting kind of tricky in such a restricted area. But could usually identify former Glory Holes by the extremely tall verdant grass waving amidst shorter vegetation.

Time marches on. When the need for Move #4 arrived, Larry and I were the prime hunters out of our cabin. Borer's cabin now belonged to John Goodridge, who often came down with his twin sons. That was about it. As hunting declined, the labor force was shrinking. So was outhouse usage, but everything reaches its limit. We went through the drill; tipping The Behemoth over was easy, but raising the Titanic just about did us in.

Thank goodness for the strength of those Goodridge boys, both outstanding high school wrestlers. One was born in Cordova, the other in Anchorage. Dr. Ermold delivered the first; the second arrived after a medivac flight to the Big City. Of such interest it even made the Paul Harvey News. Both went on to become engineers. Perhaps moving outhouses a factor in their career choices.

Move #5 took place in August of '97. Employing a revised strategy. Invited a couple big, strong teacher friends, Paul Bednarz and John Davis down. Plied them with food and booze, and then casually mentioned that there was a little building out back that needed to be moved. Already had the barrel and new foundation in place, directly adjacent to the outhouse. Pulled a few nails, lift its edge on to the abutting footing, slide it over, that was that. Too easy. Simply physics. $W=fd$. A short distance, multiplied by some High Octane force, equaled elegant Work.

By the time for Move # 6 arrived in 2007, John Goodridge had retired from teaching and moved south. Larry was now my ex-brother-in-law and ex-hunting partner, also off south somewhere. With a former local nurse who "liked anchovies on her pizza." Right. Life marches on.

Due to the plethora of existing holes, the new site had to be almost 12 feet away from the existing location. Uh oh. The d in $W =fd$ had become much larger.

So here it was. The Ultimate Outhouse Moving Challenge. Perfect. A chance to match wits with Mass and Inertia. Come on, how did they build the Pyramids? Pulleys, levers, inclined plans. Logic. Physics. Engineering. Yes!

Again, the trick would be to NOT tip the structure over. Once sideways, it might as well be a downed moose. I spent the whole winter scheming and diagramming, waking up at night with brilliant new ideas. A Cabin Project. Is there anything better? No building codes, nor behavior codes. Just let it flow. As it had, and always will.

Early on it became obvious I would again need help. How do you politely ask someone if they would like to help you move an outhouse cross-country? This took some serious thought. But I found the perfect guys. We hunted deer and ducks together, soaked halibut lines and caught a few big ones now and then; shared a love of sports and fun times at the Sheridan River and McKinley cabins. Plus both were big and strong, one with a brief background in logging down in Washington before moving into education; the other a fellow math teacher with lots of carpentry and problem solving experience. Both likely to help. In short, good guys John Davis and Al Cave. And one already had his Outhouse Moving Merit Badge.

So, an April eve, sipping fine scotch after a hot tub.

Hey guys, how would you like to move an outhouse?

Sounds like fun. Sign us up.

Game on.

Phase One of the project would involve digging a fresh hole and setting new pilings. Rather than having buddies do the dirt work that was my specialty, I headed down river solo for this endeavor. Had four lovely treated eight foot 6X6 for support pilings, plus 2X4's and 2X6's for the platform, along with a breakthrough in Pete Dahl Outhouse Technology that I had been dreaming about all winter long. Instead of a 55 gallon barrel, which rusted out from the corrosive action of you know what, a 5 foot piece of plastic culvert pipe just a little bit bigger in diameter than a barrel. Light weight, with no bottom. Material wouldn't decay, and the winter freeze wouldn't push it up. Outstanding.

Six a.m, June 13, 2007. After arriving at 11 p.m. the previous evening in Alaska's around-the-clock daylight that time of year, I was up and at it. Cool, a bit overcast, not too many bugs, great digging weather. The Delta river banks are accumulations of thousands of years of Copper River silt, and easy going. The fun starts when you get below the water table, about three feet down this time of year. Every shovel of muck out is replaced by another one sagging in. But hey, I was used to that by now. Also had learned to make the hole at least a foot bigger on all sides than the barrel, so I had a dandy dig going. I'm 5 foot 5 inches tall on a good day, the culvert was 5 feet long. Arctic terns nest near by, and aggressively dive at intruders. If any try to strafe me, my foxhole is ready. They also serve as a good alarm should any bears wander by.

Things were going quite well. It was noon, I'd taken a couple coffee breaks, the weather was improving. Getting in and out of the hole was becoming a challenge, so I stuck an inverted 5 gallon plastic kelp bucket in the bottom as a footstep.

Finally, Show time. Rolled the culvert over, set it vertically in place, climbed within, and using a shovel in cramped space, began leveling its top edge while constantly pulling my wader boots out of mud sucking at my feet. Would be rather embarrassing if a small plane flew by and saw me frantically waving for help.

USCG Cordova. This is Whiskey Bravo 279. I'm in a Super Cub over the Pete Dahl cabins. We have an emergency. Man trapped in outhouse hole. Please scramble your rescue helicopter with an Extraction Team immediately.

Right. Would never hear the end of that one. Had considered tying a rope to the nearby outhouse just for that possibility. Recalled you are supposed to lay flat to get out of quicksand. How would you do that in a three foot diameter hole??

Progress was slow. I paused to regroup.

Have you ever had that feeling that something is going on, of which you need to be aware? Maybe after Bear Encounters 1 and 2, my Sixth Sense was a bit keener. Can't say what I heard or felt, but stopped what I was doing to peer out of the hole.

The ground was at chin level.

Down wind 25 feet away was a brown bear. Broadside. Sniffing at our burn barrel, which is located just below the top edge of the slough bank.

Crap. I'm in this hole with a shovel, so making the mistake of trying to run sure isn't an option.

Another one of those heart pounding moments when things are racing but really going slow at the same time. I don't know if the bear smelled me or heard noise from movement of my feet in the water at the bottom of the hole, but it slowly turned to looked right at me.

Not a huge bear, likely another three year old. But bigger than the Plank Bear, and much bigger than me.

I've heard the theory that in close quarters, don't look a bear in the eye, such behavior is perceived as a challenge or threat. What? Just close your eyes and kiss your _____ goodbye? In fact, since the Hut Bear encounter, almost everyone seems to have offered personal postulates about the ideal relationship between Man and Bruin.

Whatever. We were eyeball to eyeball, just like that. And I'm wondering, among other things, what in the world does this bear think he's looking at? Some sort of weird ground hog, marmot, rabbit, or other juicy tidbit there for the taking? I'm also pondering, if that is the right word, my options:

a) duck in the hole, which might bring him running;

b) holler, wave the shovel, try to make myself big, which might

    1) chase him off, or

    2) piss him off; or

c) just freeze and hope for the best.

Anything to avoid self-defense with a Number 2 shovel, please.

To this day, I don't know why the bear did what happened next. Maybe the theory that I had been vaccinated against bears in the Hut encounter worked. Or maybe I was just pretty damn lucky. Sometimes, it appears, inaction is the best action.

Mr. Brown turned, walked parallel to the front of the cabin, and dropped over the bank out of sight.

I waited a minute, honestly thinking about jumping out of the hole and locking myself in the outhouse 12 feet away. Finally I crawled out, eased my way into the cabin, took the bear shotgun off the gun rack, and scanned things from the front deck. If there was ever a bear that deserved a free pass it was this guy. I had no intention of shooting him, but wouldn't hesitate to encourage a speedy departure with a volley over his head.

Climbed up on the cabin roof. Watched for ten more minutes. He was clearly gone.

And the outhouse hole had been baptized before the building had even been slid over it.

Later that day I finished setting the 6X6's, and at midnight took advantage of a big tide to run up and get the boys at Alaganik Landing. Sun barely sets that time of year, no problem.

Wouldn't you know it, Al's new rig had mechanical issues. Had to tow him back to the launch site. Rather than abort the mission, we loaded all the gear in my boat, and John came down with me while Al went back to town.

We arrived back at the cabin around 2:00 am. It was already getting light. Pretty dawn. Took a six hour nap, up at eight, fresh coffee and rolls, Hi Ho, Hi Ho, It's off to work we go.

Beautiful day. Made an elevated ramp to slide the outhouse to its new foundation.

Used jacks, planks, pry bars, and broom handle rollers (John's idea) to get the outhouse over the hole. It was the first year of XM satellite radio at the cabin, and we listened to Ron Santo do color commentary for a Cubs game on a little portable radio sitting nearby while we worked. To this day, every time we recall that day we laugh at a broadcast that will never be forgotten. Not because it was a great

"A true lesson in physics and mechanical advantage." Outhouse Move #6, starring John Davis, June 2007. The new location is to his left.

game, but because Santo and his partner talked for two full innings about their golf game and didn't even bother giving the score. Santo, a former All-Star third baseman for Chicago, would eventually be voted into the Hall of Fame. Every now and then between hooks, slices, and Mulligans, he would moan something like "oh no," or "oh man," which we assumed meant things weren't going well for his beloved Cubbies.

Broadcasts from the Windy City became one of our favorites.

And two days of "outhousing" became one of our favorite cabin memories.

June 14th 2007

Came down on a 1:00 am tide Wed. morning. Wed. we moved the outhouse. A true lesson in physics and mechanical advantage. Great weather but still cool for summer. It's Flag Day and the Flags (wild Iris) are far from being ready to bloom. Watched moose across from the cabin this morning at breakfast. We're heading back at 2:00 am tomorrow morning. Another great time was had at Pete Dahl Slough and the Shellhorn's cabin. —John Davis

Chapter 18

101's

101: 1. Beginning level college course in almost any subject.
Wikipedia
2. The number of shots it take to bag your first teal on the wing.

"Learning is a change in behavior. If you keep doing the same thing
and aren't catching any fish, you ain't learning."

Conversation overheard between two commercial fishermen at
Seaman's Hardware in Cordova

Part I: Psychology 101

As with many sports, much of duck hunting success depends on mental approach. Which pre-supposes some degree of intelligence. IQ tests to evaluate and compare human brain power were developed by psychologists including Stern, Terman, and Binet in the early 1900s. Most duck hunters probably score somewhere between spoonbills and widgeon on this scale.

As Snaith pointed out, "A sport is something special in order to offset an image, which, to the uninitiated, must appear to be an idiot's delight."

That sums it up rather nicely. After all, what rational individual would spend thousands of dollars and countless hours freezing his buns off in horrific weather to shoot a hapless bird which yields perhaps 4 ounces of meat which his wife refuses to cook or eat.

Therefore, trying to apply findings of Giants in Psychology to waterfowlers is likely as folly-prone as trying to knock down crane 2000 feet high with #2 shot blasted from a $2000 Benelli shotgun.

However, idiots are often the best true test of hypotheses regarding homo sapiens.

B.F. Skinner was a famous psychologist who pioneered many theories of behavior using rats and mice as experimental subjects. He could have learned just as much by observing duck hunters.

Skinner studied the success of his rodents in traveling through intricate maizes based on positive reinforcement in the form of food. He postulated that rewards are what condition behavior, and developed the corollary that partial reinforcement was the most effective. In other words, don't give the little guys a pellet every time they turn the correct way, keep 'em guessing a bit. Seems rodents like to gamble just as much as anyone else.

Which is one of the founding principles of duck hunting. If the sky was full of ducks from dawn to dusk, and bag limits were filled in ten minutes, what fun would that be? If a bird fell with every pull of the trigger, it would be almost boring. To quote Yogi, "If the world were perfect, it wouldn't be." Plus how to justify spending all winter mulling over new guns, ammo, decoys, and apparel?

Just this fall, Randy, on the evening VHF Duck Report from Eyak, complained about that day's particularly hot shooting. It was so ridiculous he had his limit in 15 minutes. Now what to do? Three years ago Tom and I happened to catch a morning of spectacular mallard hunting in late October. Son-in-law opted to shoot only drakes with three curls or more on the second day. His eye sight and shooting skills are far better than mine, but we both limited out in short order and shook our heads watching birds by the thousands pour through.

What do you remember more: the shots you made, or the shots you missed? Why is ranting and screaming common behavior when a flock of greenheads comes roaring into your decoy spread, you stand and blast three shots from your semi-auto in less than 3 seconds, and they go flying off, quacking raucously while depositing airborne fertilizer on your hat?

Perhaps B.F. chased ducks when he wasn't playing with mice. He surely would have loved a maize called the Route to Pete Dahl. A BXB upon successful traverse was our operant condition reward.

Others developed their own behavioral postulates. Mae West might not have had a Ph.D, but she clearly understood human nature: "To error is human, but it feels divine."

Ms. West was, in a way, verifying Skinner's theories. And would she have ever made great duck blind companion.

Another giant in the field of psychology was of course Sigmund Freud. He wasn't a duck hunter, but did study another favorite topic in great and titillating detail. Much has already been written about Les Maxwell, he of several legendary pursuits. Remember brother Bobby doing a census of Les's wives, and then adding the comment "Plus a whole lot of chippying around."?

Too bad Sigmund never made it to Pete Dahl. Bobby's older brother would have been a fantastic Case Study.

Freud was big on symbolism, I vaguely and perhaps incorrectly recall. I am sure he would have been fascinated by one of our neighbor's favorite pastimes. Les didn't want to waste his time on sparse flights of early season birds. On the other hand, Randy and I, both weekend warriors, weren't too selective about whether we were shooting skinny local ducks that had nested on the Delta, or the big full-plumed Northern birds that migrated through late in the season.

Almost daily, Les would stand shirtless on the porch of his cabin in Carhart pants, untangle binoculars from suspenders across his hairy chest, and scan the horizon for large bands of migrating birds. Between an oil space heater running full bore, shelves tilting with spirits, and high powered B.S. around the clock, the thermostat at Maxwell's place was always running hot. Sometimes he probably stepped out just to cool off.

Like any good scientist, Les liked to reinforce his visual observations with physical data. When we returned from the morning shoot and strung our birds outside the cabin, he would wander over and carefully feel their breasts. Every now and then he would get this glazed look in his eye. Which meant either the duck was a plump Northerner, or he was dreaming of some thing else, likely Wife #3, who was a stunning blonde Nordic beauty. Freud would have loved it.

Darwin, most famous for his evolutionary theories, was also central to the development of comparative psychology, whose main question is the relative intelligence of different species. Duck hunting lends itself to countless opportunities in this field, particularly in comparing human intelligence to that of waterfowl. We often come out lacking.

A simple illustration. Duck hunters will sit in a blind for hours, no birds moving, drinking hot coffee to stay warm. Finally, after two gallons of the stuff, it's time to either raise the pond level or fill up your boots. This urge, unlike wisdom, accelerates with age. Being polite, you step out of the blind, frantically undo several layers of clothing, and drop your waders. Ah, relief. Nine times out of ten, standing there with something other than shotgun in hand, is exactly when fifty widgeon land in your decoys.

If you pee, they will come. Pete Dahl Duck Hunting Axiom #1. I once wrote a letter to Cabelas suggesting they make a plastic life-size model of a duck hunter that could be filled up with water and project a stream into the pond for hours. The ultimate Motion Decoy. No batteries or moving parts. Didn't receive a response.

For years this repeated behavior was attributed to the devious mentality of wily ducks, personally waiting for just the right moment to drop in for a visit. The psychological term for this is anthropomorphism.

Of course, it's likely the ripples on the pond are what attracted the birds. Just as when one leaves the blind to rearrange the decoys, or cut fresh brush for camouflage, or to warm up by briskly walking, here they come. Probably attracted by motion. One day I told my partner that ducks couldn't count, so if we would take turns standing outside the blind doing jumping-jacks, the other could blaze away. Worked out really well. We headed back to the duck shack with no birds and a big thirst. Not the first time IQ was discussed late into the night.

Part II: Evolution 101

One of the most fascinating instructors at the University of Alaska (Fairbanks) during my undergraduate studies back in the early 60s was Ivar Skarland. Had the good fortune to take Anthropology 101 from one of the institute's most legendary teachers in my freshman year.

Ivar was the real deal. In fact, so real, you couldn't understand half of what he said, with that thick Scandinavian accent. Born in Norway, came to the U.S. in 1921. Spent many years with Eskimos much further north. Truly had been there and done that. Ph.D. from Harvard. Lived in a little log cabin right on campus.

Fascinating person. Short, stocky, his broad brow had vestiges of the Early Man that he loved to describe. One thing became quickly clear: if you didn't believe in the Theory of Evolution, you were in the wrong class.

I seem to recall that it took our early ancestors considerable time to gradually evolve from one stage to the next. Time periods for change were astonishingly long. Homo sapiens have been around for two million years. Duck hunters probably for most of that stretch, and still can't outsmart a teal.

Looking at bones and photos certainly verifies our development and evolution. Yet nothing proves the theory of evolution more clearly than ducks and decoys. Evidence abounds, and arrives on regular basis in the mail.

Cabelas and Mack's Prairie Wings catalogs should be required reading for any course on evolution. Ducks have to be one of the most rapidly changing species on the planet, and the Principle of Natural Selection imposed on them by hunters would make Darwin proud.

When I first started duck hunting in the 50s, we carried half a dozen rubber Deeks in the game pouch of our shell vests. Remember them? Roll em up, a marble(!) in a little protrusion on their stretchy chest on which to tie a short anchor line, which was usually attached to a half inch galvanized nut. With a nut of larger size packing them around.

Small. Lightweight. Inflatable. A hard metal ring in an opening in their bottom; drop them from a foot above the pond, they filled with air, and merrily bobbed away. Some hunters just stood on the bank and gave 'em a toss. Nothing fancy about the layout.

The birds loved em. Deeks only came in mallard decor back then. But widgeon, pintail, teal, spoonbill, gadwall, canvasback, and scaup came to join the party. Only drawback was the metal ring in the bottom that not only kept the air in place, but also served as a weight to keep them upright. Exposed to salty water, it quickly rusted. At the end of every season, the rings had to be removed and oiled. Otherwise the rubber around them would become attached, and quickly deteriorate. Meticulous hunters even powdered their Deek interiors with Baby Talcum before storing them for the winter.

Gotta take care of those babies.

Before Deeks, duck hunters used decoys carved out of wood or cork. While things of beauty, both were bulky and hard to carry. Waxed fiberboard decoys by Johnson's, mainly for geese, soon came along. Johnson's also made folding fiberboard duck decoys. I found one tucked in the rafters of our old boathouse on Odiak Slough.

Even then, English Majors looking for work had applied lessons from Creative Writing to describe the latest innovation. Directions printed on the bottom of the decoys, which expanded into triangular shape and hence could float on ponds or sit on grass, included: "The construction of these decoys allows them to be constantly moved about by the slightest breeze which is a most important factor in decoying ducks." Right. Can imagine where they would move if a stiff wind came up?

Plus this gem: "Too much cannot be said for these decoys when used in large numbers over shallow water or stubble. The old-time market hunters seldom used less than a hundred decoys but he carried them in a wagon. A hundred of these decoys can be easily carried by inserting a dozen heads into each loop of a duck strap and will take up about as much space as eight dead ducks."

Finally, "If your dealer does not carry these decoys insist that he get them or they will be sent postpaid from factory upon receipt of price. PRICE 55 CENTS EACH." Wonder what the postage was back then.

By the late 60s and early 70s, molded plastic decoys hit the market. These decoys looked so realistic that hunters would shoot their own spreads early in the morning. They were bulky but far more effective and durable. Styles and models skyrocketed. Catalog sales, and then online marketing, made them available to hunters everywhere.

Soon there was a model for every known species, in multiple sizes and shapes. The magnitude of decoy spreads exploded. If six rubber Deeks worked, imagine what sixty plastic decoys would do?

So it has come to this. The 2013 Mack's Prairie Wing's 189 page Waterfowl catalog has 34 pages devoted to decoys alone; Cabelas 216 page Waterfowl Edition tops that with 54 pages of fake ducks. The latter's thousand page "Limited Edition" hard bound catalog stays at home, too heavy to haul down to the cabin given the restricted weight capacity of my river boat. Did you know that a case of Alaska Amber weighs more than 20 pounds?

Of course, both outfits have even more options available on-line. No internet service at the duck shack, thank goodness. However cells phones do work, and two numbers I have memorized are 1-800-237-4444 and 1-877-MACKSPW. Plus my VISA card digits.

The diversity of imitation ducks available makes it impossible to sleep prior to the morning shoot. Countless choices for every species in every size imaginable. Pro-Grade. Over-size. Lifesize. Standard. Classic. Elite. Floating. Field. Sleeper. Rester. No-head feeders. Butt-up feeders. Real Image. Northern Flight Plus. Premier. Storm Front. Tanglefree. Battleship Super-Magnum. 3-D Silhouette. Grand Prairie Harvester. Full Body. Dakota.

And my favorites, as well as Freud's: Hard Core Magnum Goose Butts and Edge Quivering Duck Butts. Oh my.

But wait! There's more. That was just the first half of the decoy section.

In the last ten years, through Twitter and Tweet, plus Survival of the Fittest, ducks and geese have figured out that decoys which do not shake, rattle, and roll are just not worthy of their company. The pace of modern Natural Selection is now measured in gigabytes.

Enter the World of Motion Decoys. These babies have the moves of topless duck dancers and drive drakes into a frenzy. Some are powered by wind, others by batteries. The Boys at Eyak spend half their time recharging 9 volt Mojo batteries, while filling their own cells with Who-Hit-Johnny.

Juice of an electric sort is needed to power splash ducks such as Mallard Master Feedn' Frenzy, Quiver Duck, Mighty Duck Board, Flocked Drake Swimmer, Rapid Flyer Lucky Duck, or Splashing Flasher II and Pulsator II. Mojo's series including Floater, Flyway Feeder, Mallard Machine, and Thrasher; and Wonderduck's line includes Cyclone, Twister, Paddle Wheel, and Tornado.

All are designed to stir up the water and attract ducks with motion on flat calm days. The paddle wheel is a dual purpose model similar to amphibious assault vehicles of WWII. Not only does it have bright orange paddles that splash merrily away, it also has spinning wings.

Which leads to airborne-appearing Mojo's and such. These are lifesize plastic decoys mounted on poles above pond or ground with wings that relentlessly rotate. One wing side is white, the other black with a horizontal white and blue band to simulate the speculum of mallards. Also now available in teal, wood duck, and gadwall models.

Mojo Mallards, Regular and Super, were among the first to hit the market, and have proven so effective they are banned in some states. It is amazing how far away one can see the white of their flashing wings and not even know a big spread of decoys is floating around them. One of the early Mojo's even had LED lights on the leading edge of the wings. Hmmm.

These decoys come in the three digit price range. So Mojo came out with a simple and much less expensive item called the Wing Thang. It is a single white and black-sided simulated plastic wing pointing straight up vertically that operates on four AA batteries, which is much easier to operate and maintain. May have been inspired by some intrepid hunter who inadvertently blasted his Super Mojo while trying to pick out a mallard landing near it, and noticed that the remaining wing, which kept spinning in an now upward fashion, still attracted birds.

As every duck hunter knows, if one motion decoy works well, why not add more? Like Vortex Rotating Spinning Wing System, which features four ducks spinning in a 10 foot circle off a tall pole. Silloscks offers a similar Tornado Rotary Decoy Machine. If a duck flies into either, why, you won't even have to pluck it. Both require a 12 volt battery. Try carrying one of those to your blind.

The number and design of battery powered decoys is becoming so complex a Black Box device called the Decoy Boss is now available. A control panel worthy of a F22 fighter allows the operator to manage four remote-controlled decoy at once. Imagine the grief you will get for turning on Mojo Teal when it's a pintail coming in.

Perhaps in response to the ban on battery-motorized decoys in some areas, or because of the constant issues with keeping them charged and operating, wind operated decoys have come into vogue.

The Mojo Wind Duck is an illustration. Its wings spin and create white flashing motion that attracts the birds, if the wind is blowing. Winduk and Air Lucky operate in similar fashion. Of course, spinoff concepts also go flying. They include Ultra Reel Wings and 360 degree Motion Airwings, plus Jackite goose kites, that are actually attached to a string like in days of yore. Just don't shoot the string.

Then there are windsock decoys, fastened to a small rod in the ground, that rotate and flash in the wind. Sillosocks Full Body Wind Socks come in mallard, Canada and snow goose, plus Sandhill crane. Just a light breeze makes them very realistic. The Boys at Eyak have a spread of crane models in an open meadow adjacent to the deck of their cabin, which makes for a leisurely evening shoot.

Another recent innovation is the Bobblehead decoy. A round metal ring supports this decoy, which sits atop a flexible metal rod fastened to the ring. Even the slightest wind causes a bobbing motion from these lifelike decoys.

Last year local duck hunter Tom Justice mentioned Deeks could still be found by going on-line. I ordered two dozen as a sort of collector's item. They are now available in both mallard and pintail design, so naturally I needed twelve of each. A couple weeks later I decided to give mine an experimental trial run. A trip down Memory Lane, as well as a Test of Darwin's Theory.

My partners were blazing away over plastic decoys enlivened with motion splash ducks and Wing Thangs. Half mile away, over my spread of never-before-used Deeks, I watched ducks roar by out of range, and swear I could hear laughter intermingled with their quacks. Somewhere Ivar was also chuckling.

According to National Geographic, wild ducks have a life span of 5 to 10 years. More if they fly over my blind. Using 7.5 years as an average, it is amazing how in just nine generations spanning the 50s to the present how much smarter ducks have become. Or how much dumber we have grown.

Ah, for the good old days. Jim Webber told me a story about he and Larry Kritchen taking a couple newspapers to Walhalla and crumpling them up for snow goose decoys. This was in the early 50s, when Alaska was still a Territory, newspapers cost ten cents, and the boatload of geese they brought home kept many locals quite happy.

Darwin developed many of his theories while circumnavigating the globe as a scientist aboard HMS Beagle from 1831 to 1836. If I ever decide to get another hunting dog, his name will be Darwin, and you can guess the species.

Part III: Shooting 101

Obviously, one of the justifications for having a duck cabin is hunting. How could we make it through the winter without all those ducks in the freezer? Harvesting said birds requires shoots and shooting.

A. Shoots
Pete Dahl shoots are carefully categorized: Morning Shoot, Noon Shoot, Evening Shoot, Moon Shoot, Tide Shoot, and Northern Shoot. A brief description of each.

MORNING SHOOT: This is the biggie. Rise to the rattle of multiple alarm clocks 90 minutes before shooting hours, which begin 30 minutes before sunrise. Pitch black out the window. Coffee, rolls, pile in the riverboat, run up the slough with barely enough light to see, pray a moose isn't standing in the narrow channel. Tromp over to the blinds, crank up all the motion decoys. Waterfowl are notorious early risers. Whistle of wings in the early dawn; light gradually streaking the skies to the east; the favorite time of day for all duck hunters. Every morning different, even after 54 years of Pete Dahl daybreaks. Weather fair or fowl; hunting hot or slow; fall colors of grass and brush changing from green to gold to brown; snow line on mountains marching downward and birds marching south; seasons. In all those years, I can count one one hand the number of morning shoots I have missed. Every Delta dawn proves there is much more to duck hunting than shooting ducks.

NOON SHOOT: This usually takes place in the bunks. Return from Morning Shoot, have a big breakfast, including famous Pete Dahl Snappers, and everyone is shot. P.D. Snappers are a top secret form of Bloody Mary's. The name evolves from a canned tomato juice drink no longer available called Snap-E-Tom. Came in little 6 oz cans, and was basically spiced tomato juice. Perfect for Bloody Mary's. When the Del Monte product was no longer available in Cordova, many experiments were conducted to duplicate its secret ingredients. The famous result:

Pete Dahl Snapper
1. Fill a large glass mug with ice.
2. Pour in an overflowing jigger of vodka
3. Add 1/2 jigger of lemon juice
4. Add several dashes of Lea & Perrins
5. Fill space left with tomato juice, to within 1 inch of top
6. Add celery stick, spiced bean, and lemon slice
7. Top with pepper and celery salt
8. Optional: add Tabasco sauce, and more L & P, to taste

This has become a Cabin Tradition. Daughters Heidi and Gretchen drank Virgin Snappies beginning at age two. When their college days began, they were promoted to the real deal. Granddaughter Ellie is on the same cabin regime. As a result, she now requires three spiced beans as part of her Cold Lunch at Kindergarten. Her mother Gretchen, who teaches at the same school, would be a bit embarrassed if Ellie pulled out her little thermos and poured a Snappie right there in the lunch room.

One year, hunting partner John Davis had students do a demonstration activity in his 5th grade class at Mt. Eccles Elementary. Gretchen brought in all the ingredients except one, and earned an "A" for whipping out Pete Dahl Snappers in front of the class.

In her later years, it was she who coined the phrase "Three Snapper Dawn," which is immediately followed by a long mid-day siesta by all patrons.

TIDE SHOOT: before the earthquake uplift, this was another biggie. Especially when combined with bad weather. Duck and geese prefer to hang out on the Flats beyond the Delta's cutbank, feeding and resting on the open muddy terrain. Incoming water and wind would force them into the ponds. This no longer occurs below Pete Dahl, except on extremely high tides. However, due to less uplift on the western end of the Delta, tides are still the key to hunting success at Eyak. Often, the Eyak Boys sleep in, and make a leisurely cruise down to nearby blinds beyond the river mouth for the Tide Shoot. They also monitor the weather closely. The worse, the better, for hunting.

EVENING SHOOT: When we were Weekend Warriors, this was a must. Not so anymore. Birds do tend to fly a bit before settling in for the night. We observe this from the front deck, while sitting in lawn chairs listening to ball games on the XM Satellite radio. With shots of a different sort in hand.

NORTHERN SHOOT: The Les Maxwell Special. When big strings of birds start zipping by below the cabin, it is time to head to the blinds, regardless of time of day. Often thousands can migrate through in the course of a day, and then it is all over. Breaks in weather can be a key factor. Birds have built in barometers, and tend to move just before a big storm, or immediately after.

MOON SHOOT: Ah, the Days of Our Youth. And Statutes of Limitation. On occasion, in the pre-earthquake days, when it was flat calm and a full moon was out, it was possible to hunt over nearby ponds, very late in the evening. Birds silhouetted against the moon, flames out of shot gun barrels, and then silence, listening for the plop of ducks landing in the pond.

Finally, one shoot that was not formally listed, but dominates duck hunting, the B.S. Shoot. No shooting hours or time restrictions on that one.

B. Shooting

Entire books have been written on the fine art of wing shooting. These days there are countless training videos seconds away on Google and You Tube. The pros in these demo's never miss. Yet, like everything else, it ain't as easy as it looks.

I personally subscribe to the Golden BB Theory. A three inch #4 shotgun shell contains as many as 200 pellets. Therefore a three shot volley fills the air with 600 bb's. Good grief. A duck is bound to fly into one of them. Dad's Mantra "Shoot, the air is full of widgeons," resonates in my mind from his early tutorials back in the 50s. Of course, after all the baldpates flew away, he muttered Corollaries such as "Pick out a bird" and "Don't flock shoot." Sound advice, which neither of us

The ducks get a day off, as neighbors Roger Trani, John Goodridge, and Tom Trani enjoy an Noon Shoot, Pete Dahl Style, in the early 1980s.

followed. Back then shot gun shells were a lot cheaper. These days, almost every BB is golden, in value, at least.

I have discovered I do my best shooting when I don't think about it. Hell, the Great Yogi knew that: "You can't think and hit at the same time." I went through basic training at Ft. Lewis, Washington back in 1968 during the height of the Vietnam War. The Army actually sent us through a week long course called "Quick Kill," in which we learned to react and shoot, rather than aiming. The idea was to think of your M-16 as an extension of your arm. We used BB guns in the

Mike McHone demonstrates the proper way to enjoy Snapper # 3 at Pete Dahl, September 1988.

program. You were paired up with a partner who stood four feet away and tossed a 3 inch metal disk up in the air. You raised the BB gun from port arms and reacted. Believe it or not, within a week many of us were knocking quarters and then dimes out of the air on a consistent basis.

So you would think with a full pattern of airborne BB's, ducks would just fall out of the sky. Right.

C. Shotguns

My sequence of duck hunting shotguns is: a. bolt action .410; b. single shot 16 gauge; c. Winchester Model 12 pump 16 gauge; d. Browning Semi-Auto 12 gauge; e. Beretta 303 semi-auto 12 gauge.

I used the .410 for two years, ages 11 and 12. The number of ducks taken never totaled my age.

The single shot 16 gauge taught me how to flinch. Wow. That baby would knock you over. Nothing but your shoulder to absorb all the recoil. It was extremely safe and reliable, and often frustrating. One and done, although I learned to hold an extra shell in my forward hand while shooting that first volley, so I could quickly reload.

After two years, Dad decided I was ready for the same gun he used his entire life, the classic Model 12, in 16 gauge. His dated all the way back to Seward and ptarmigan hunting, and was his father's shotgun.

More than two million of this popular pump action Winchester were produced, included modified versions that were used in WWI, WWII, the Korean War, and the early part of the Vietnam War. Model 12 really is a shortened nomenclature for Model 1912, the year this amazing firearm first came on the market. It was the first truly successful internal hammer pump action shotgun ever produced, and set the standard for 51 years until production was discontinued in 1964. Dad and I both sent our Model 12's back to the factory to be rebuilt. Finally, they just plain wore out. Both now sit side by side in my gun cabinet, countless memories stored there with them.

In 1980, Sue's father John Ekemo sold his popular local grocery store, K & E Foodland. Not one for for idle time, he moved across Cordova's Main Street and went to work in Flinn's Clothing and Sporting Goods store. At least he could take a weekend off for duck hunting now and then, so I was able to take him down to our cabin. Not surprisingly, he proved to be an excellent wing shot. And a keen observer of the issues his hunting partner was having with a beloved but aging Model 12 that often would not feed shells properly, and have a penchant for misfiring when flocks of ducks were attacking.

Lo and behold, under the Christmas tree that winter, was a new shotgun. A Belgian-made Browning A-5 12 gauge, right off the shelf from Flinn's. Beautiful recoil-operated semi-automatic shotgun, the bird gun of choice for deadeyes such as Les Maxwell. Wow. Not only did I pick the right wife, I got a helluva father-in-law in the process.

It was the first 12 gauge, and semi-auto, I had every shot. And the birds loved it. I couldn't hit a widgeon if it was standing on the end of the barrel. Incredible. John Goodridge, high school shop teacher who also was the Rifle Club Advisor and purchased the duck cabin two doors down from us, cut down the stock to fit. I'm only 5 ft 5 inches, and it was way too long. Well, I was now a couple inches closer to the birds, but that didn't help.

Flinching didn't factor in. The gun action absorbed most of the recoil. But some of its unique design features proved to be the root source of my shooting woes. The A-5 has a distinctive high rear end, earning it the nickname "Humpback." The top of the action goes straight back with the level of the barrel, before dropping sharply to the butt stock. Plus the barrel itself slides back to eject the spent shell; it's called a long recoil. Well, I wasn't hitting any long shots, or short ones, for that matter.

Finally, one evening at our cabin, over Peachtree Schnapps for me and Yukon Jack for neighbor John, we decided to analyze the issue. Took the cleaned and unloaded A-5 off the gun rack, and Rifle Coach John told me to close my eyes and throw the gun up to my shoulder as if a flock of ducks were coming in. My eyes were already at half-mast, so that didn't take too much effort. He then told me to open my eyes and describe what I saw.

Which was a vertical black wall of metal, namely the "Humpback." After 25 years of shooting a nicely curved Model 12, instinctively getting "down on the barrel," I was now attempting to adjust, unsuccessfully, to a foreign-shaped "rise." Ah ha. Knowing the issue, I spent many hours and days in the blind, thinking about what I must do to adapt. And of course, as I mentioned earlier, once you start thinking, you start missing. At least that is my M.O.

I tried the Browning for another season. And finally gave up. Goodridge had a gun dealer's license, and offered to find me a new shotgun in exchange for the Browning, which he let his twin sons use. We looked at different options, all shotguns with a profile similar to the old Model 12. And picked a Beretta 303 12 gauge semi-auto.

Which, thirty year later, is the gun I still shoot. Amazing. The smoothest, most reliable, easy to maintain, shotgun I know. Unlike the newer models, its stock and forend are wood. Recently, son-in-law Tom, who owns Whiskey Ridge Trading Company and of course has a gun license, was able to find a replacement for the forend, which was beginning to deteriorate after countless days in rain and cold.

And when I miss an easy shot, or for that matter any shot, I never never never blame my shotgun. In fact, I chant an apology to Phil Beretta, whose name is engraved on the receiver. And then tell myself, after 54 years, "Don't flock shoot.

Pick out a bird. Get your head down on the stock. Don't get too excited. Relax. Swing with the bird."

Dad, I hear you.

Finally, a shotgun tale about my hunting companion Randy Bruce. He used 12 gauge from the get-go, and his early guns of choice included the Winchester Model 12 and 1200 pumps, and then Browning A-5 and A-500 models.

For one Pete Dahl hunt in the early 60s, he borrowed Uncle Kenny Van Brocklin's A-5 Browning. Couldn't hit a thing. Sound familiar? Sitting on a shelf in our cabin is the solution. A two inch thick slice of the stock. The Saturday evening shoot that weekend involved several BXB's and a handsaw. I'm sure his shooting was much better on The Sabbath Morn.

Randy now hunts at Eyak with a Benelli, the Lamborghini of Shotguns. Their ad boasts that Benelli gives shooters and hunters an edge. At their price, I'm surprised they don't toss in one of their famous motorcycles too. Can visualize Randy and Julius like Steve McQueen in *The Great Escape*, roaring off and jumping brush lines and gutters enroute to their intertidal blinds.

The jump from Browning to Benelli involved another shotgun that starts with "B." The Eyak Deadeyes hunt offshore in relatively open terrain, with modest blinds in sweet gale brush. They take their camo seriously, and hunt with face masks in place. Which makes sense. From our cozy blinds at Pete Dahl, with roofs, backs, and sides buried in piles of brush, the one thing I can see 500 yards across the pond is Tom's visage peering out. However, our blinds are situated with the morning sun at their backs, so we sit in the shade with grass and brush hanging down from the top, and flaring off exposed white faces is not a significant issue.

Evidently, one morning at Eyak, Julius mentioned to Randy that from his blind he could see light reflecting off the barrel of his partner's old Browning, and needed to have it re-blued. The A-500 had been through the paces, and Randy decided to graduate to a newer camouflaged synthetic stock and forend shotgun, solving mechanical and reflection problems at the same time.

Anyone who has fired the same shotgun for many years knows how difficult it is to change. You and your faithful gun have been through countless hunts, partners in times good and bad. "Do you take this shotgun to be your lawfully wedded hunting partner, through wind and rain…"

Randy had heard me sing the praises of Beretta, and finally decided that would be his choice. Contrary to all manufacturers' claims, no two models of shotguns are equally reliable. Randy had constant problems with his new Beretta, despite meticulous maintenance after every hunt. The gun would misfire, not eject spent shells properly, nor feed the next round correctly. The camo job was great; in fact, if he had thrown it in the brush in disgust, I am sure he would never have found it.

Instead he mailed it back to Beretta for repairs. Twice. Shipping guns is complicated these days, so the shotgun had to be sent by a known gun dealer. In this case, Tom Carpenter. Who loves to "pull people's chain."

The first repair job came back with reminders about careful maintenance, and explained the problem likely had something to do with water accumulating in the stock, where a part of the gas-operated bolt recoils after every shot. The issue had been addressed.

After another frustrating season with the same problems, the box containing the Beretta was again addressed. With another missive describing the same issues. At least the shipping box was working well. Randy was not in town when the repaired shotgun arrived back at Whiskey Ridge. Tom opened the box to check it out, and called me immediately.

"You will not believe what the letter from this gunsmith at Beretta says. You have gotta come down and check this out."

I went roaring down to Tom's oversized green and camo-colored quonset-style shop.

The letter has undoubtedly been torn to shreds by Randy, who discovered the gun continued to misbehave. You can tell a Swede, but you can't tell him much.

In essence, the enclosure indicated the problem continued to be the accumulation of water in the stock, and directed that all efforts should be made to prevent it from entering the barrel of the gun and seeping downward into the action. It suggested keeping the barrel horizontal, and if that wasn't possible, to put a balloon over the barrel to keep the water out. Honest to Pintail. This is a shotgun for hunting WATER fowl, that fly in the air, right? And all duck hunters know the worse the weather, the better the hunting.

"Oh boy," said Tom, who loved to needle Randy about football, duck hunting, or anything else available. "I can't wait to see Randy's reaction when he picks up the gun."

To Tom's dismay, when Randy stopped by, he didn't open the box, nor call later to comment on the letter.

Tom and I agreed this was completely unacceptable. So we came up with the idea of a folllowup "letter" from "Beretta Corporation." I went on-line and order 500 camo balloons that would fit over the barrel. When they arrived, I typed up a "letter" from "Beretta" indicating they had forgotten to enclose the recommended balloons, free of charge. Packed the info and balloons in a small box, with Beretta's return address attached, and took it to Tom's.

He called Randy. "Hey, Randy, there's another box here from Beretta. I don't know what it is, come down and pick it up sometime."

Evidently, it's the shooter, not the shotgun, that makes the difference.
Randy Bruce, with his sons John and David, September 1977.

Wish I had been hidden in the back room, which is where Tom and the Boys play poker late at night, when Randy showed up.

Tom tossed the small box on the counter. Randy looked at the parcel. Tom, with straight face: "Maybe it's something to do with your shotgun." Randy opened it up.

Tom later admitted he was happy there were no other customers in the store at that time. It took considerable time to air out the blue smoke.

And not too long for Randy to figure out he had been had.

Soon after that he bought a Benelli. Which is the gun he uses to this day.

Part IV: Recreation 101

As much as they would like to, duck hunters simply cannot hunt 24 hours a day. First of all, there's this thing called Shooting Hours. Which all law abiding Delta hunters obey. Just ask Leer and Dad. Secondly, there's the issue of endurance. As Pete Dahl hunters became older and wiser, the Noon Shoot became longer and more popular, morphing into the Afternoon Shoot. Which increased the demand for entertainment.

A: Radio

Perhaps no single item has been a greater source of cabin entertainment than the radio. It began with the classic battery-powered Zenith TransOceanic and a simple piece of wire running the length of the roof for an antenna.

5–7 September 1959—Labor Day Weekend

A grand weekend away from town and with ariel installed enjoyed marvelous radio… —Anita

A year later, along with replacing pilings and a tilting outhouse, fixing the radio was a top priority, as part of Mom's entry noted:

24 June 1960

Rather bumpy trip, rain and blow. Boys fixed the ariel… —Anita

Music, news, weather, sports. From local Cordova station KLAM, or filtered through static from KFQD, KBYR, and KHAR in Anchorage. Stations featuring Oldies but Goodies always a favorite. Shortwave late in the day and evening when atmospherics were right, marveling at skies full of stars including the Alaska's flag Big Dipper right off our porch, while listening to broadcasts from all over the world.

Eventually we switched to a car radio powered by 12 volt battery for better reception; and in recent times, to XM Satellite Radio. The latter has an incredible variety of selections, and comes in crystal clear. But guess what the most popular channels are?

Music from the 50s and 60s, plus baseball and football.

Countless entries appear in the cabin logs about the World Series, the Washington Huskies, and of course, my Oregon State Beavers and Los Angles Dodgers. Starting in the first cabin year.

3–4 October 1959

Listened to World Series game from L.A… —Anita

Speaking of L.A., I am often asked why I root for the Dodgers. Ironically, because of radio. My love for the Boys in Blue started back in 1955, when they still played in Brooklyn. Back then all the games were day games, and the World Series pitted the Dodgers against the Yankees. At that time, because of its longitudinal width, Alaska alone had four times zones. So Dad and I would get up early in the morning, huddle over the shortwave radio, and with the pop, snapple and crack of Rice Krispies adding to the hiss of static, listen to Gil, Pee Wee, Campy, Duke, Jackie, and Crew battle the Bronx Bombers. Sal the Barber Maglie, a mean-spirited relief pitcher who liked to give hitters a close shave, was one of our favorites. What a name. A young sportscaster named Vin Scully was marvelous. He still is. Plus it was the American Way to root for the Underdog. Go Dodgers!

Ah technology. A few years ago, Tom arrived at the cabin on Saturday. From Illinois, and raised a Catholic, he is a huge Notre Dame fan. Still hasn't recovered from the 41-9 drubbing Oregon State gave the Irish in the 2001 Fiesta Bowl. Anyhow, he came racing up the steps, and asked if I was listening to the Notre Dame - USC game. I replied that it wasn't on the radio. He marched to the XM Radio and turned the dial to Channel 211, and here were the Fighting Irish, loud and clear. What channel is that, asked I naively? Dick, it's CBN. What the hell is CBN? Why, the Catholic Broadcast Network, of course. After choking on my Alaska Amber, I said something other than Hail Mary to that one. He admonished me, with a reminder that Touchdown Jesus overlooks their stadium.

B: Betting

An entire book could be written on wagers made at Pete Dahl. For example.

1. Beavers

No, not the ones that clog up gutters, or wear Oregon State Orange and Black; Dehavilland Canada DHC-2 Beavers, the workhorse of Alaska bush operations. Designed shortly after WWII ended, these amazing planes are famous for load capacity as well as short take-off and landing capabilities. Originally powered by war-surplus 450 hp Pratt and Whitney engines, they sound like tanks and fly just about as fast, while packing six passengers or payloads of a ton or more. So it is no surprise that Cordova Air Service flies one, on wheels or floats.

One early 70s weekend, when hunting and associated activities were in full swing at Pete Dahl, Cordova Air's red and white Beaver circled and then splashed down gracefully in front of the cabins. It was a big tide, so the pilot taxied right up to the bank in front of Maxwell's. Six guests, a mixed bag of hunters and their wives, packing sundry gear, stumbled out of the cabin, managed to tiptoe along the plane's pontoons, and then pile board without falling in.

Randy Bruce, Frank Sherby, and I were watching this operation from the deck of our cabin. The Noon Shoot was in full swing, and it was a dandy. Frank was a certified Air Frame Mechanic, and did considerable work on small planes at his hanger near the town's small airport. As the Beaver turned and then idled past our cabin, floats almost submerged, we speculated on how long it would take the plane to get off the water when it turned around down stream and then raced past us before going airborne. Frank obviously had the best idea, and gave us his opinion. Which was met with immediate skepticism.

Ah ha. A bet was born. We jumped off the deck, and each of us raced to the point on the bank where we thought the pontoons would leave the water. The pilot, aware of his considerable load and lack of significant headwind, taxied all the way around the slough bend below the cabins before turning to take off. We had ample time to choose our spots, Lucky Lagers in hand, spaced 50 yards apart. With the roar of the engine, we all began jumping and cheering, waving our arms in upwards gestures to encourage flight. The Beaver emerged from around the bend, engine roaring, floats angled upward, spray flying behind, struggling to get on step. Finally it began planing, and we could the pilot in the cockpit leaning forward as if to help the aircraft go faster. And we could also see wide-eyed commuters looking at us out round windows along the fuselage, panic in their faces, as they tried to understand what we were communicating.

The floats lifted off the water halfway between our cabin and Maxwell's, and the Beaver, still growling on full throttle, cleared the slough bank above Les's place by ten feet. Luckily there was no tall brush lines back then.

I cannot honestly remember who won the bet. We were too busy laughing at the reaction of the passengers.

2. Shooting the Score

Anyone who has placed friendly wagers on sporting events knows that most of the fun is in the inspired verbal give and take that accompanies the ups and downs of the game. The size of the bet is typically harmless in economic terms, but before the contest is over, one might think the wager is wife or home. Invariably, considerably more moola is spent on the liquid and solid refreshments consumed during the event than is won or lost on the wager. Super Bowl Sunday has to be worth at least a 100 point jump in the Dow Jones based in an upsurge of particular stocks, regardless of what happens in Vegas.

Keeping track of the score of a baseball or football game is essential to the raucous pursuit of its inevitable conclusion. Which led to some strange occurrences at Pete Dahl. Les had to be scratching his head when he would hear shotgun blasts from our cabin deck, walk outside, and see sunny cloudless skies with nary a duck in sight.

It was someone shooting the score. That is, every inning, stepping out on the porch, and for example, firing a shotgun three times, pausing, reloading, and then blasting twice. At nothing.

Yipee, or oh no, would the hunters at Walhalla think. The Dodgers are ahead, 3 to 2. Obviously, shells were a lot cheaper back then. And equally evident, this system did not work for football.

But it was especially popular during the World Series. However several issues arose. What if the score was 2 - 0? The cabin score keeper fires twice. Then what? So who's ahead? All of us were adept at shooting zeros when attack by flocks of ducks, put how to shoot a numerical zero? Plus keeping track of which team's score came first was imperative. And surprisingly difficult to remember, after the previous night's Evening Shoot. Three shots, followed by two. Is that Cards 3, Bosox 2, or vice versa?

And finally, what if a darn flock of ducks landed on the cabin outhouse? The system was shot to hell.

3. A Canvasback Shave

Perhaps the most uncommon duck taken on the Copper River Delta is the canvasback. While these large diving ducks are plentiful in many Lower 48 states, they are rarely seen in this area.

Most Delta hunters shun diving ducks in general, and when a unusual canvasback comes roaring by, it is usually mistaken for scaup, which are common. Canvasbacks travel at 70 mph, and there isn't a lot of time for identification. Much of their coloration, as well as their wing beat, is similar to that of bluebills, another name for scaup. Often it's the unusual high profile of the canvasback's bill that serves as a give-away, and by that time, with afterburners kicked in, it is out of range.

Canvasbacks are one of the finest eating birds around. If you could, just ask Otto Koppen, the famous USFWS Enforcement Officer who patrolled the Delta for decades more than 50 years ago. One fall I bagged a canvasback, and knowing Otto's fine appreciation of duck, took it into town for the Annual Elks Duck Feed. Otto was a Cordova BPOE Lodge Icon, and well into his years by that time. More than one hundred Elks and their families packed the Lodge for the popular event, prepared by Cordova's best waterfowl cooks, including Bobby Maxwell, Gary Raymond, Jim Webber, Pete Fridgen, Randy Bruce, and Frank Siemion. Usually, by the time the ducks were ready, they were also well roasted, but certainly not crisp around the edges.

Otto had been critiquing their performance for years. Out of all the ducks they prepared that day, only one was a canvasback. Mallards, pintails, widgeon, spoonbills, and even teal for the tots, were the main fare.

The Top Chefs didn't expect Cordova's most famous Elk to wait in line to dish up in the traditional buffet style, and instead brought Otto his duck at a table reserved just for him. They nervously waited to see if their masterpiece passed muster. The venerable Koppen took a bite, chewed thoughtfully, set down his napkin, and said: "Not bad for a canvasback."

So given their rarity and succulence, it should come as no surprise that Les Maxwell often pitted himself against Old Redeye, the nickname given the drake canvasback for its unusual bright ruby-hued iris. In 1972, little did this particular species know that Les vowed, once duck season began, not to shave until he had bagged one. It took a bit longer than he anticipated.

9 October 1972

On opening day of season made biggest mistake I've ever made in my life!!! Said I wouldn't shave until I killed my first Canvasback of the season. Today I bagged one and let Shellhorn shave me, which was the second biggest mistake of the

season. No skin left and few scattered whiskers!!!!
—Les Maxwell

Major operation gave Les a shave, had to give him major sedative but operation a success. —Don

The event was so significant it inspired more Delta Verse.

Ordeal at Pete Dahl

Happened by Pete Dahl to see what's going on. Everyone was there.
—Les, Shirley, Anita, and Don

October 1972. "On the opening day of the season made the biggest mistake I've ever made in my life ..." With support from wife Shirley, Les Maxwell braces himself for a Canvasback Shave from Pete Dahl barber Don Shellhorn, October 1972.

Stopped at Les's cabin to deliver the oil. Don hollered over, the beans are starting to boil. Les felt bad that he had made a pact. To shave when he shot a canvasback. Don said Don't worry got a razor over here. Les advanced but was adorned with fear. Don said come on Les, you fearless knave. And covered his face with electric shave. Off came his whiskers skin blood and all. I knew I should have never stopped. To see what was going on at Pete Dahl.
—Jack McCullough

After reading the preceding page, my story has been told, but must say something about the beautiful dinner prepared by Anita. Outstanding "Ham Hocks and Beans." Enjoyed my part in the "torture"of Les. Gosh after three weeks at the cabin, he sure looks handsome. —Shirley Maxwell

Not much more to add, a lot of BS sure was flying around before, during and after the shaving of Les...We are all even on the betting on the baseball playoffs, come on your Pirates and Oakies!... Les says he's going to take Don out in the airboat tomorrow and give him a thrill equal to the shaving torture.—Anita

C: Toasting

It didn't take much to inspire a Toast at Pete Dahl. Anything out of the ordinary was met with "I'll drink to that." For example, just getting the oil or water barrel hooked up was cause for jubilation.

Yet perhaps the most famous toast occurred not at Pete Dahl, but at the

"It didn't take much to inspire a Toast at Pete Dahl." The local Mayor proposes a B&B as Paul Cole and Randy Bruce finish a successful oil transfer, September 1977.

Powder House. Pierre DeVille's rustic waterhole was located a mile outside downtown Cordova, and gained its sobriquet from its origins as a storage shed for powder and dynamite during the construction of the railroad. Pierre passed away many years ago. A bust of him created by local artist Joan Bugbee Jackson stand's on the back bar, and current owners Gary and Libbie Graham offer sweatshirts with the logo "I got blasted at the Powder House" for sale. Hmm.

When Pierre ran the operation, nothing as fancy as sweatshirts were on sale. A crusty sourdough Alaskan who at one time was a sparring partner for heavyweight boxing champions, Pierre often tended bar in old-fashioned longhandle underwear, and there was no blender on the back counter. Beside the bar, there were a few tables, and much of the remaining space was filled with stacks of beer. Restocking the coolers didn't require much time or footwork.

Every now and then a folding stairway in the ceiling to upstair living quarters would lower, and down would come Pierre's wife Kit, an attractive lady who always dressed well and behaved in similar manner. She ran an upscale lady's apparel store in Cordova called Kits Boutique. An unlikely, and entertaining, couple.

It didn't take much to get on Pierre's wrong side, and once that happened, your toasting took place at any of the multiple other available downtown dram shops lining Main Street. However, given its location and inherent character, the Powder House was a natural stopping point for duck hunters returning on Sunday afternoon from a weekend at their cabins. A place to warm up after a cold boat ride, recap the hunt, exchange intelligence with other ducksters, plan the next weekend's adventures, and further agitate already unhappy wives waiting a mile away.

Which Randy and I were doing one October Sunday afternoon. The tide had been early, so our post op was not hurried. We had actually had quite a weekend, and laying out in the trailered boat were numerous ducks as well as six Dusky geese. Pierre had set us up with a BXB, the latter a generous shot glass of Blackberry Brandy. We wanted to give our wives a sweet kiss upon arrival home.

Somehow it occurred to us that the six geese, which came from an unusually successful dual barrage that brought down the entire flight, may have been a single family. A twinge of remorse convinced us they deserved a farewell toast.

So we went out to the parking lot, picked up the strings of geese, brought them back in, propped them individually on chairs around the table, and ordered Blackberries for all. Business was slow, and to our surprise, Pierre went along with it. We carefully propped each goose with its beak in the brandy, and enjoyed a Hail and Farewell.

Pierre also enjoyed one of his most successful Sunday afternoon's ever, as patrons who meandered in applauded our tribute and joined in salute.

Our greeting at home were not quite as triumphant.

D. Weather

Much has already been written about weather. Every day on the Delta is a lesson in meteorology. Patterns become evident to even the most ignorant. For example, if the bunks on the back wall of the cabin shake, it's blowing at least 40 southeast.

The ways of the wind are truly entertaining. At one time we had a Dwyer Wind gauge mounted atop the cabin roof. Plastic tubing connected it to a small display on the inside wall just above the main cabin table. The wind speed was indicated by a clear tube filled with red fluid that climbed up a curve marked with numbers as the force increased. We would ooh and aah at the magnitude of gusts, and fortify ourselves for impending adventure on the way to the blinds or upriver to the landing. Occasionally, wagers were even made on the height the red fluid might reach. Imagine that.

Graves wrote that "there is nothing rational about the response we give to storms. A man is a fool to welcome bluster and wet and cold, and yet he often does, and even indoors he is seldom indifferent to their coming."

A man is also a fool to become a weather forecaster Even today, weather prognosticators are often bamboozled, despite huge advances in technology such as satellite imagery. Forecasts on the Delta are correct about 50% of the time, in our experience at Pete Dahl. Why we even listen is somewhat of a mystery. It is much simpler to just look out the window and observe what it is.

However, despite our eventual cavalier attitude about what Mother Nature was going to do with Her Atmospheric Forces, one particular weather event that occurred only once in our 54 years at Pete Dahl deserves mention.

The Twister
Cordova Times

17 September 1970

Several People Saw "Twister" on the Flats

Something new has come to this area, so hence the rest of the country can read about us and our tornado - it's a waterspout, if that's what is at its base. Last Sunday p.m. at Pete Dahl Slough - about 15 miles east of town, the weather phenomenon was viewed by several people. The nearest ones were at Don Shellhorn's cabin, where Don and Dick Shellhorn, Harry and Dean Curran and Randy Bruce all were near enough to hear as well as see it. There was thunder and lightning with heavy rain and hail. Some distance away were three local people in a canoe on the slough. They had a good view of the show which lasted only a few minutes. They were Mr. and Mrs. Wally Watts and a Forest Service man. Mr. Watts is the Forest Ranger for this part of the Chugach National Forest. Other people, including this reporter, have noted cloud formations this summer that are common to conditions where tornados and water spouts are frequently viewed.

The unusual weather event actually occurred on Labor Day, 7 September. All of us except for Dad were up hunting near Walhalla. He had opted to putter around the cabin and then take an afternoon stroll down the slough.

7 September 1970

*Witnessed one of Nature's phenomans which I never had seen before. Heard a
sound like an airboat - then a minature tornado came across the river picking up
water etc then started to hail (very interesting!) —Don*

What Dad failed to mention was his actual course of action, which was to run
like hell for cover behind the nearest log. When we returned from our hunt, Dad
had calmed himself with multiple B & B's, but couldn't wait to tell the story.

Dean Curran, who was closest to the cabin on the opposite side of the slough,
described it as much more than a water spout. "It was picking up sticks, dry alder
leaves, and grass, and tossing them more than 200 feet up in the air, while making
this loud roar."

"I also remember it chased up ducks everywhere. The sky was full of birds, and
I was so excited I kept dropping shells. Then came the thunder, lightning, and
hail. I couldn't keep my gun loaded, there were birds everywhere."

Forty four years later, in hindsight, he admitted Duck Fever had gotten the
best of him.

"I don't suppose sticking a metal gun barrel up in the air in the middle of lightning was probably the smartest thing to do, but I had never seen so many ducks
in the air at once."

Dean also recalled we all agreed, before returning to the cabin, that "we would
not admit to Don we saw it." A way to tease Dad, which was a Curran Specialty.
When we arrived back, the Mayor of Pete Dahl was standing on the doorsteps,
eager to recount his adventure. Taking Harry's cue, we all acted perplexed. The
Scotsman asked Dad: "Now tell me again, Don, what did you actually see? A
twister? Really? We better have a B & B."

Dad would repeat the story, becoming more excited each time, as each recital
earned another toast, followed by the same repeated question. The evening shoot
of 7 September 1970 ended at a record earlier time for the Oldtimer.

Not long after that we gave Dad the first Dwyer Wind Gauge, which was quickly
dubbed The Tornado Detector.

Chapter 19

Cycles

CYCLE: 1. A round of years or a recurring period of time in which certain events or phenomena repeat themselves. WEBSTER 2. The duck cabin outhouse moves in cyclic fashion. It is relocated roughly every ten years, based on rate of deposition.

"The wheels of the bus go round and round, round and round, The wheels of the bus go round and round, all day long."

CHILDREN'S SONG

Time marches on. The Delta has changed, and so have we.

As sloughs continue to silt in, it has become more and more challenging to navigate the upper portion of Pete Dahl. In the summer, with runoff from the Copper, it now takes at least an 11 foot tide to make it through that shallow stretch in a jet-powered riverboat. During the fall, with water flow from above dropping, that number increases to 12 feet.

And of course, it is impossible to run that area in the dark. The narrow channel through broad reaches of sand and mud takes extreme turns that are invisible without light.

There are two high and two low tides daily, and the sun barely sets during midsummer, so at least during June and July, there are two chances per day. Not so during the fall, when daylight vanishes at an accelerating rate.

On average, there will be 15 days in both September and October in which there is both enough tide and light to make it to the cabin. If the weather isn't blowing like hell.

The Family Labor Day Weekend hunt is a tradition that dates back to 1959. Last year, due to bad weather, I was unable to make it upriver to pick up Sue, Gretchen, and Ellie. Then tides and weather intervened on following opportunities. It was one of the rare years that we did not have a Labor Day celebration at Pete Dahl.

The Tradition continues. At age 9 months, Heidi, with help from her father Dick Shellhorn, makes her first entry in the Pete Dahl Cabin Log, July 1974.

Factor in the declining quality of hunting due to the change in habitat, and the cabins are now rarely occupied. A list of yearly cabin guests and visitors verifies the trend.

In 1959, our first year at Pete Dahl, four of our family, and 34 guests or visitors, shared the cabin. Contrast that to 2013, in which the total was 8 family members and 3 guests. The biggest year in cabin history was in 1975: 8 family members and 44 guests or visitors.

And let's face it. Not only has the river presented increasing challenges, we've all mellowed out. With age comes some wisdom, maybe just because we can't keep up the pace. During hunting season, it really is early to bed and early to rise. I finally understand what Dad meant when he counseled "Moderation in all things."

The greatest joys at Pete Dahl have come not from shooting ducks, but from sharing special times together.

1 July 1974

Down to cabin with Randy, Jackie, and boys for a quick picnic on the tide. Beautiful day - Heidi on her first trip to the cabin. She is 9 months old. —Dick

My first trip down in two years -missed last summer cuz of Heidi (too pregnant for boat ride) - had a great boat ride. —Sue

"I like Pete Dahl" —Heidi (written entry with assist from her mom)

20 August 1974

Heidi's asleep on a mattress on the floor, the sun's setting, and the geese are honking. Her first overnight stay at the cabin - she is 11 months old today. —Dick

On 24 August 1975 Donita and Paul, plus Sharon, Heidi, and I made a quick trip to the cabin in two boats with a birthday cake for Dad. He and Mom had been working away on the addition.

24 August 1975

Heidi's first trip this year. Sue at home with #2 overdue, and still baked a cake for the Oldtimer.. —Dick

"Happy Birthday Grampa" —Heidi (written with assist from her Dad)

A great day to have the kids come down, was really surprised and sure appreciated it. Thanks Sue for the birthday cake. Sorry you couldn't come, but next year or before, we hope you will be here with both the grandchildren. —Don

29 August 1975

Happy Day! Just heard on KLAM radio Dick and Sue Shellhorn had a baby girl last night - 8 lb 3oz. Yippee. Congratulations and Welcome, Gretchen. Needless to say, Grama and Grampa are so proud. —Anita

26 June 1976

Sue, Heidi, Gretchen and I made our first family trip to the cabin this year. Gretchen is ten months old. Had a bouncy ride down in the west wind. Heidi loved it, Gretchen slept. Mom and Dad came down yesterday afternoon, so we all spent the night, and enjoyed a nice fire in the fireplace... Heidi at the age where she really enjoys it, Gretchen a bit young yet. —Dick

"I saw a goose nest with 5 eggs." —Heidi (written with assist from her Mom)

On 16 August 1977 Sharon, Brian, Heidi, Gretchen, and I made a quick supply trip to the cabin. The following day Grampa Don, Heidi, and I returned with another load. Plus some valuable cargo going back to town.

17 August 1977

Had to pick up the blanket and teddy bear that Heidi left yesterday. —Dick

20 August 1977

Was laying a rug when Dick, Sue, Heidi, and Gretchen arrived. Dick cooked steak plus all the trimmings - plus ice cream. Great dinner and real nice evening. —Don

Well for the first time 6 Shellhorns sat down to dinner at the cabin at Pete Dahl. Quite an event and very nice. Heidi and Gretchen said Grace as we all held hands around the table. —Anita

3 October 1977

Don told me of Gretchen's remark about JoAnn Tilgner's dog Toka. She told me "Heidi stepped in dog poop," but she also said "Toka has a high pooper" and she is only 2 years old. Laughed all day on that one. —Anita

29 July 1978

Heidi got some feathers and waded in the mud. I got feathers too. Then we got to clean off in a big tub. —Gretchen

3 September 1979

I saw a hawk and owl when hunting with Daddy and Gretchen. —Love, Heidi

I won the Queen of Hearts game at the duck cabin. I like the duck cabin. I ate two tacos. —Gretchen

August 1977.
"Well, for the first time 6 Shellhorns sat down to dinner at the cabin ... quite an event and very nice." Daughters Gretchen and Heidi, ages 2 and 4, make their own entries in the Cabin Log before heading back upriver, August 1977.

31 August 1980

I'm in second grade. I went for a walk to the point. —Heidi

I started kindergarten this year. I turned 5 on Thursday. I picked flowers for everyone. —Gretchen

28 September 1980

I helped Dad steer the boat. I am seven. My birthday was the 20th. I won Blackjack. —Heidi

I won the Queen of Hearts game at the duck cabin. I like the duck cabin. I ate two tacos. —Gretchen

Dick and the girls took a ten minute walk Sat. afternoon and when Gretchen got back she said: "Bad news Mom, we didn't catch a duck!" —Sue

14 June 1981

I petted a baby goose. I beat Mom at Fish. —Gretchen

I held two baby geese. A moose crossed the river in back of us. I went to the duck blinds. We saw a beaver. —Heidi

It was a fun relaxing day - sunbathed Saturday afternoon - ate steaks - lost at Old Maid - what more could a person want? —Sue

7 September 1981

We went duck hunting. We saw a flock. We did not get any. We had fun. —Heidi

We went to the blind. I had fun steering the boat. —Gretchen

4 October 1981

When we went back we wore our pajamas to keep warm. —Love, Gretchen

14 July 1982

We went rowing around in the pond. While I was writing four geese were walking along the bank. We had popcorn. I had fun. —Love, Heidi

Me and Hide looked at the comics. I hated the outhouse. Playing on the bunk bed was my favorite thing. —Love, Gretchen

6 September 1982

I made a puppet. It is funny, it can stick it's tongue out. We got stuck in the grass in the boat. —Gretchen

I made cartoons and drew pictures. We took the Lower Cutoff. Grampa's motor caught on fire. We had fun. —Heidi

3 October 1982

Ardy (Hanson) and I had fun. We were shooting at an American Golden Eye with my bb gun. Got some nagoonberries for grandma so she could plant them. —Love, Heidi

3 June 1983

We saw lots of eagles on the way down. We sang songs from Day Camp in the boat. I played with my teddy bear. (brought lots of clothes) also brought cards and jacks. The real bear didn't visit anyone else (Ha Ha). —Heidi

A bear came to the cabin. We saw his tracks in the garden. We saw some swans and lots of geese. P.S. The outhouse still smells good. —Gretchen

Perhaps that's because it's just been relocated. —Sue

8 July 1983

We had a rain festival and a war with seeds. It was fun playing in the rain.
—Gretchen

Yesterday we saw a BIG brown bear. And Dick almost shot it. I was scared.
—Jessica *(Pingatore, a young friend of Gretchen)*

5 September 1983

On my birthday I got two Barbies and one Ken. School started on Monday.
—Gretchen

11 September 1983

I forgot my night gown so I had to wear Grandma's. The Goodridges were here too. We had fun. —Gretchen

I made a blind with Wade and Cade. Had fun. Love you. —Heidi

23 June 1984

We got here at midnight! A few minutes later we lit off fireworks. Some of them didn't work too good. Gramdma (Ekemo) got to come. It hasn't changed a bit since the last time I was here. Love, —Gretchen

Finally made it to the cabin with Dick, Sue, Heidi, and Gretchen. Beautiful trip, beautiful cabin - flags in full bloom. Enjoyed every minute of it. Love to you all
—May *(Sue's Mom)*

I had a lot of fun. I screamed at birds (Arctic terns) and they dove at me. I found 4 eggs in a swallow nest under Tilgner's cabin and 5 eggs in a nest above our window. There was a next one I couldn't reach though. Love, —Heidi

23 June 1985

We were going to have boiled dinner but DAD forgot the carrots and cabbage. I am going to get glasses. Oh boy! There pretty. —Gretchen

P.S. We are the first people to be here this year!

Heidi did a census of all the swallow nests, and summarized her data in an elaborate table. There were eight nests, with eggs varying in number from 6 to 0. She commented of her lengthy entry: Boy, I took up a lot of space. —Heidi

18 August 1985

Heidi's sick with the flu. But Pam could come. Well, the cabin's fine, and the outhouse still stinks. My birthday is in a week. —Gretchen

A mink was in the outhouse. It was big. —Pam (Van den Broek)

30 June 1986

Another first for the cabin - the kids - Heidi, Linda (Van den Broek), Gretchen, and Amy (Thorne) went swimming in the slough - swam all the way back from the point in fact! —Sue

26 June 1987

I went outside to explore and all of a sudden mom started screaming. I ran in and there was a live swallow trying to get out the kitchen window. I caught it and let it go outside. Didn't see one live baby bird; kind of worried about that. Rained the whole time we were here, but we're used to that by now. Gretchen is at Girl Scout Camp. —Love, Heidi

Another day in paradise - wind, rain! Dick was saved from being skunked by one peg - now who's the lousy crib player! Got a make-up and hair-do by Heidi. —Sue

12 July 1987

We came down yesterday and surprized the Ermold's. Dad taught us how to play poker. Lost all my chips! —Gretchen

Had a great time playing poker. Had $3.10 at one time!!! I saw a family of mink. They were really cute but one of them had a duckling in its mouth. They also killed an Arctic Tern. The baby birds at Goodridges cabin could be able to fly soon. —Heidi

7 September 1987

Trip down OK. Very wet! Mom lost her glove in the water and dad ran into a sandbar. —Gretchen

... I'm sorry I didn't write very much, but I have to do enough of that in English! —Heidi

15 July 88

Guess what happened to us? We almost didn't make it down here. The ride in Larry's car was great! But the ride in Larry's boat was unforgettable. Smooth sailing up until Petedahl, where we hit a sandbar! We screamed for an hour, in the rain, with the bugs. We had no shotgun, no firecrackers, no matches, and no food! We all thought we were going to spend the night there. We called out things like "Dad," "Dick," "We want boiled dinner," "Help," "We're stuck on a sandbar," We're stuck," "Yo." An hour later, someone on the roof saw us. It was Marni! (youngest Goodridge). Larry piggy-backed us to a sandbar, where John Goodridge rescued us in his airboat. Whew! Now we're back and hungry for boiled dinner. Yum. —Drippiing Wet, Gretchen
(Note: Sue and Heidi were at Rainbow Grand Assembly in Fairbanks)
It's been mentioned often, so here is the recipe.

Pete Dahl Boiled Dinner
1. Fill eight quart pot with 3 quarts of water, bring to boil
2. Add six potatoes and six carrots, peeled and chunked
3. Bring back to boil
4. Add pack of regular hot dogs, and pack of coarse hotdogs, plus juice
5. Add 2 polish sausage, cut in chunks; plus 1 hot/spicy sausage of choice, also chunked
6. Add 1 onion, chunked, and 6 stalks celery, chunked
7. Once this reaches boil, add 1 head cabbage, cut into 8 wedges. Make it two heads if lots of company.
8. Pepper, garlic powder, and other seasoning to taste
9. Cook until cabbage on top is done. Try not to boil so much that the spuds fall apart.

Serve with vinegar, catchup, mustard, butter, salt and pepper, and ice cold beer. The leftovers are served for brunch the next day with Pete Dahl Snappers and french toast.

The years zipped by. Heidi and Gretchen graduated from high school and college, both now teach, Gretchen at the elementary school here in Cordova, Heidi at a middle school down in Austin, Texas. Both have married, and now we are the proud grandparents enjoying the cabins with another generation.

5 June 2008

Down solo on 15 ft tide thru upper. My usual cabin opening partner didn't make it - because she is expecting our first grandchild!!!! Way to go Tom and Gretch. Due in late August, everything going well. Glad Gretchen passed on trip. It's cold! Fresh snow on peaks, birds just starting to nest, bullrushes in back pond still brown, flat, dead. Crazy. No Copper River salmon yet either. —Dick

20 June 2008

So this may be my one and only trip to the cabin this year! As Dad mentioned in his first entry on the year - I'm pregnant! 31 weeks, due on August 25 (our anniverary, and Grandpa Don's birthdate). So I'm thinking I won't make it down for Labor Day Weekend. Had a great couple days despite the fact that I had to pass on the traditional Snappy (had a virgin one), etc. We played games and I got some scrapbooking Done. And, as always, had some good laughs. —Gretchen

*Yay! Great trip to the cabin. Ate (a lot), read (a lot), slept (a lot), and drank... a lot. Mom's taking another **picture** as I write. She beat us at rummy - probably due to her lucky sweater. She is **still** taking pictures. Dad is tearing down Lohse's cabin all by himself. (Formerly the original Swartzbacker cabin, it was falling apart due to lack of use over the years)... Thanks for a great trip!* —Heidi

Always fun when we are all here! Next year we'll add Ellie to the group - can't wait for her first trip!! I might have won at Rummy today but i got beat (badly) yesterday at Chixfoot, Rummy, & Scrabble! Everything perfect except for the mosquitoes - I think I got bit every time I left the cabin. We're up early in the A.M. (3!) to head up river on the tide, then breakfast at the CoHo - sourdoughs. Shower for Gretchen & baby Ellie Monday - Mom get's here Wednesday, Heidi leaves Friday. As always, relaxing down here. —Sue

Ellie Dahl Carpenter was born on 22 August 2008 to Tom and Gretchen. Guess the source of her middle name.

30 July 2009

Tom & Gretch planning to bring Ellie Dahl to Pete Dahl on August 22 for her first birthday. —Dick

Unfortunately, tides and weather conspired to make that impossible. And also messed up the Labor Day Weekend. It wasn't until the following year that Ellie first visited her namesake slough. Heidi and her husband-to-be Scott were up from Austin to witness the event.

14 July 2010

First trip down in 2 years! I missed this place! It was a great time - Ellie's first trip down, she is almost 2 years old. Fun to watch her take it all in. She loved the chips, cookies, ducks, and fire in the fireplace. Having Scott here was fun too. We had some great laughs. See you soon cabin. —Gretchen

It was so great to get down here again! Also really wonderful to get Scott down here. I had so much fun that I'm a bit worn out actually... Snappies, cards, napping, reading stories by the fire - yay! So glad we were here for Ellie's first trip. **Thanks Mom and Dad.** *—Heidi*

30 August 2010

Came down for one night as our "Labor Day Weekend." Tom, Ellie, Gma & Gpa. Fun trip. Sunny boat ride down. Ellie sat on my lap, facing the wind in Tom's boat & loved it. Ellie pooped in the outhouse! Yay! Great relaxing time before getting back into teaching school (newly renovated) tomorrow. Ellie had a blast playing w/ the DU model duckies from the window sill, splashing in the rain - water bucket & helping Gpa build the fire in the fireplace. Wonderful trip. —Gretch

Another fun trip with Ellie - another first -Tom found a frog for Ellie to play with - she also "fished" with Grampa from the punt in the pond - plus all the usual - As always it was a great time. —Sue

11 September 2011

Came down for an overnighter w/Ellie, Mom and Dad - since we didn't make it over Labor Day Weekend due to weather. Great fall weather now - beautiful colors, sunny, and cool wind. Ellie was quite entertaining. The most hilarious was when she was doing "moves" on the table - you'll have to see the pictures. Her and grandpa had a wonderful time together exploring, making a fire, & fishing with cattails from the little boat in the back pond. And her and grandma had fun coloring and playing princesses at the table. It was a great weekend & I'm so glad Ellie loves this place as much as I do. She just asked, "Why do we have to leave?" I agree Ellie. —Love, Gretchen

It was a great last minute decision to come down - we kept trying to out guess the weather! After a little downpour on the drive to the landing, it has been beautiful… As always - Fun - with Ellie providing the entertainment this trip - new dance moves… She helped clean up, telling Grandpa he did a "good job."… Right now the entertainment continues with more dance moves, without any clothes on of course, a stall tactic because she wants to spend another night down here. —Sue

In July 2012 Tom's sister-in-law Julie and her daughter Kate came from Chicago to visit Cordova. A trip to the cabin was of course part of the tour.

21 July 2012

Great trip! Got Julie and Kate down here finally! Ellie had some firsts - sleeping on the bottom bunk, using the outhouse and picking flowers by herself. Such a big girl. Fun trip. See you soon. —Gretchen

I liked eating snappies best because they had beans in them. I liked sleeping on the bunk. —Ellie

Thank you Dick and Sue for a fantastic first trip to the duck cabin. I am overwhelmed by the beauty of this place… I loved watching the girls pick flowers in the sun, watching the mountains change, and playing in the mud at the point. But most of all the food was gourmet, the Snappies refreshing, and the company fantastic! —Love, Jules Carpenter

My favorite thing was going on the rowboat. It was so much fun! —Love, Kate

Tides and weather again conspired against us in early September.

2 September 2012

This erratic weather and non-stop revised forecasts is driving me crazy. Blowing 40 plus at 2 pm, flat calm by 4:30 pm. Was going to pick up Sue, Gretch, and Ellie, but had to call and cancel, as tide is now ebbing. Words cannot express how disappointed I am to not have them down for our traditional big weekend. —Dick

14 September 2012

Hunting has been dismal. Eyak Boys (Randy & J.R.) report the same; didn't even hunt for 4 days; plus 1 or 2 birds last 3 days. Of course, all of that is irrelevant. Sue and I leave on 19th September to Austin, Tx to be there for the birth of our first grandson, already named "Little Harry" by Ellie. —Dick

Huckleberry Cole Moorhead arrived a bit early, and our plane out of Cordova was a couple days late. Due to weather. Sound familiar? Scott and his mother Rosalon met us at Austin airport with a little bundle of joy, as Heidi was still recovering.

Ten months later, the Little Longhorn was cruising down the river. To Pete Dahl.

9 July 2014

Hooray! Huck's first time to the cabin! So much fun! We've all been dreaming of this for a long time. Cards, snappies, magic routines, mud dances, beer & tacos, shrimp (from Marv Van den Broek's pots in Simpson Bay), all the usual - and - wonderful stuff. Thank you! Back again soon we hope! —Heidi

Came down with Ellie, Heidi, Huck, Scott, Mom and Dad. Tom showed up today in the airboat. Great food and drink. Highlight was watching Ellie take a "mudbath" in the slough. She had a blast jumping, rolling, running, and laying in the gooey mud. Tom came just in time to "bathe" her in the back pond. Yay Daddy! —Love, Gretchen

What an awesome trip with everyone here. Ellie playing naked in the mud! Huck's first trip - a real trooper now. Tom showing up in airboat! Me losing at rummy to everyone - how did that happen? —Sue

24 hours, excellent weather and good food and plenty to drink. Great 2nd visit, look forward to more. Huck a champ. —Scott

Came down w/airboat for afternoon. Nice day, new prop seems to work well. Headed home with gang from Texas getting their first airboat ride. —Tom

What a crew, and trip. Great weather; Heidi, Scott, & I hiked Crater Lake yesterday; they both went swimming despite snow on the banks. Scott and I used both lawn mowers to cut all the grass. He's hired! Huck and Ellie were awesome! —Dick

Chapter 20

Ashes

ASHES: 1. The powdery residue that remains after burning.
WEBSTER'S
2. "Ashes to ashes, dust to dust," a phrase from the Anglican
burial service. WIKIPEDIA

"My life has been a tapestry of rich and colored hue..."

CAROLE KING, "TAPESTRY"

July 5, 2011

The sun had risen in glorious fashion over the Queen's Chair, and was sparkling off slight ripples from a light north wind on Eyak Lake.

In the words of John Masefield, "The sky was of blue unspeakable."

Sharon and I stood holding an innocuous box, as bright American flags planted by the U.S. Coast Guard fluttered over the graves of Cordova's veterans.

It was Mom and Dad, together again, at last.

After spending most of her life in Cordova, Mom had ebbed away at Providence Hospital in Anchorage with my sister and I spending days and nights sharing her room. I was holding Dad's hand when he closed his eyes for the last time in the local hospital sixteen years prior.

And now here we were, as per their wishes, about to scatter their combined ashes over Bobby's grave. A simple concrete site, filled with blossoming red Sitka roses, marked by a bronze plaque depicting Mount Eyak, with inscription "Bobby Shellhorn, 1941–1955."

Cordova Times

18 May 1955

As a result of an accident sustained on the annual school picnic, young Bobby Shellhorn died at approximately 4:30 Wednesday afternoon. It has been a hard blow to the community, because Bobby was one of those youngsters who was known and well liked by everyone.

The sixth, seventh, and eight grades went out to Alaganik for their picnic. As they pulled in to the side of the road to stop, a group of youngsters broke through the railing at the side of the truck and fell. Several sustained minor bumps and bruises, but Bobby went under a wheel. This was about 11 o'clock.

Rushing back to Mile 13, they called Doctor Coffin who arrived on the scene as soon as possible. Bobby was brought in to the Cordova Community Hospital on a stretcher at approximately 1:00 p.m. Despite the best in medical attention he died at 4:30.

Fourteen year old Bobby was born in Cordova and spent most of his life here, attending the Cordova Public Schools. He is survived by his mother and father, Mr. and Mrs. Don Shellhorn; two sisters, Donita and Sharon; a brother Dicky, and his grandmother, Mrs. Meda Shellhorn.

Funeral services will be held at 2 p.m. Saturday at the Community Baptist Church with the Rev Howard May officiating. Interment will follow in the New Cemetery.

The family has requested that those who might wish to Donate flowers make a contribution to the Hospital Fund instead.

Lives changed forever. By an accident only five hundred yards from the launching point of our first, and only, duck hunt together. Oh Brother, Where Art Thou?

Three small Alaska flags Sharon and I had placed at the end of the grave waved gently and brightly. Eight stars of gold on a field of blue. Dad, Mom, and Bobby, our three pieces of gold, gone.

To this day it hurts so much to think of that day, and what was endured in those hours from 11 a.m. to 4:30 p.m.

"At odd moments life will take an abrupt bite out of the heart."

JIM HARRISON, *The Road Home*

My brother Bobby on Little League Basketball All-Star team, January 1955. Top row, L to R: Wayne Gilmore, Pete Anderson, Henry Blake, David Glasen. Bottom row, L to R: Jack McCullough, Jake Tysling, Bobby Shellhorn.

Bobby and I shared a small upstairs bedroom, and like many young brothers, had gotten into a minor scrap that morning. We headed our ways on a warm sunny day still a bit angry at each other. I went to a grade school end-of-the-year party in the basement gym of the old Baptist Church. Mom had packed a tuna sandwich and chips in my black lunch pail. Bad news travels fast in small towns. I first learned of the accident in the midst of eating lunch; and to this day, a tuna sandwich triggers memories. A few years later, after playing pickup softball on the old City Field, one of the boys who was on the truck that day took it upon himself to describe the accident in detail. I wanted to run, but my legs wouldn't move. Each of us has listened to words we never want to hear. Why is it the things you don't want to remember you never forget?

"Pieces of the past stay on as pieces of us."

Ivan Doig, *Heart Earth*

Sharon and I stood quietly. Birds chirped in the background, our eyes blurred in memories.

It was time to say a few words.

Mom and Dad, as per your wishes, Sharon and I are here to place your ashes over Bobby's grave. Some of his ashes - your life would not be complete without the rest being scattered at Pete Dahl.

Bobby was born in 1942, and died way too early in 1955.

The loss of a child, any child, is a tragedy. It leaves a hole in the heart forever, an empty space that can never be filled.

Only having your own children and grandchildren, and loving them every day, can make one truly grasp how devastating their loss would be. The sudden tragic loss of your first son Bobby had to be the worst event in your lives.

Seeing photos of you in the years close after his death shows this toll, and the stress it caused in your lives and health. Yet you both bounced back, channeling your energy into the rest of your family and building a beautiful new home for us all.

And truly, the luck of the draw, in 1958, changed your, and our lives, forever - when Dad was picked for a cabin site in a U.S. Forest Service lottery, at a place called Pete Dahl.

Little did we know then how that good fortune would impact our family and our future. The building of a cabin on a remote slough on the Copper River Delta re-energized us all and became a binding focal point of joy and adventure in our lives.

Last week, while running down the river with a load of supplies for the cabin, in the same route we pioneered 53 years ago, now just steering on instinct because of darkness, it occurred to me how life is like a river - you never know what's around the next bend, but you steer on, trusting that the tides - and the Gods - will get you there.

You taught us that trust. And we trust, as we scatter these ashes, that you are finally back with your long lost son.

Next it was Cruising Down the River. Time to scatter the rest of Mom and Dad's ashes at Pete Dahl. Due to the tide, we headed down early in the evening. Nice weather, and all of us - Sue, our daughters Gretchen and Heidi, our almost three year old granddaughter Ellie, Sharon and her daughter Holly - piled into Tom's new 17 river boat for a pleasant ride through so familiar waters.

Both our parents lived long lives, Dad to 83, Mom to 90, so the slough-side Tribute we had planned wasn't to be nearly as solemn as the graveside Memorial of earlier that day. We had been brainstorming this Celebration of Life for quite some time, wanting to honor our favorite moments at the cabin.

Dad was always a huge fan of the Alaska flag. His family arrived in Seward in 1915 when he was three years old. He went through school there, graduating from Seward High before moving to Cordova in the mid-30s. He came to know and admire the designer of Alaska's flag, Benny Benson, through their competition as track and cross country runners in Seward.

Benson was a 13 year old 7th grader at the Jesse Lee Home in Seward when a contest was held to create a flag for the Territory of Alaska. His father had put him in the Jesse Lee Home in Unalaska at the age of 3 when his mother died, and the Mission School moved to Seward in 1925. More than 700 designs from throughout Alaska were submitted, all on 8.5 by 11 inch paper. Benson's winning design was a simple but elegant eight stars of gold on a field of blue, the Big Dipper and the Northern Light. The blue symbolized Alaska sky and the forget-me-knot, a common Alaska flower. The North Star represented Alaska's northernmost location; the Dipper stood for the Great Bear

"The luck of the draw changed our lives forever." Captain Shellhorn cruising down the river on a Sunday afternoon, July 1977.

of both early European and Native American mythology, symbolizing strength.

The story goes Benson learned about his winning design while in class at school. His teacher's husband brought in a telegram, she looked at it and her mouth dropped open. Benson recalled she was speechless, and "I darned near fell out of my seat when I found out." Benson passed away in 1972.

Dad had two flag poles attached to the top of the carport at our home in Cordova, one for the U.S. flag, the other for the Alaska flag. At the Pete Dahl duck cabin, he erected one tall pole for both flags. After retiring, Mom and Dad spent many autumns there. We could all remember coming around the bend below the cabin to smell the alder smoke from the fireplace chimney, and seeing flags snapping in the breeze. And of course there was Dad's handcrafted, beautifully-painted plaster Alaska flag sculpture mounted over the mantle of the cabin fireplace.

So as part of the farewell tribute we had a multitude of Alaska flags: a big 3X5 one to fly on the cabin flag pole, smaller ones to wave as we spread the ashes. We also had music to play.

September 1978. "Dad came to know and admire the designer of Alaska's flag, Benny Benson, through their competition as track and cross country runners in Seward." U.S. and Alaska flags flying at Pete Dahl, September 1978.

Alaska's State Song

Eight stars of gold on a field of blue,
Alaska's flag may it mean to you,

The blue of the sea, the evening sky, the
mountain lakes and the flow'rs nearby;

The gold of the early sourdough's
dreams, The precious gold of the hills
and streams; The brilliant stars in the
northern sky, The Bear -the Dipper
- and, shining high,

The great North Star with its steady
light, Over land and sea a beacon
bright,

Alaska's flag - to Alaskans dear, the
simple flag of a last frontier.

And of course, there had to be Lucky Lager, Dad's iconic beer. Rare was a picture of a Dad at the cabin, without one of those stubby bottles in his hand or by his side, and a smile on his face.

This is where it became interesting, and I'm sure the Oldtimer would have chuckled at the length we went trying to find this vanishing brand for his farewell. The Hunt for Lucky Lager was on.

It started by checking liquor stores in Cordova. No luck. Next it was the bigger outlets in Anchorage, such as Brown Jug Liquor. They scratched their heads and said "What? Never heard of it."

Finally Internet and Google, to discover the Lucky Lager brand was sold to a Canadian firm and was no longer brewed in the United States. It was reportedly popular in western Canada, especially British Columbia. So I asked a fisherman who was running his seine boat up from a remodel job in Washington if he could stop at Campbell River, call a cab, have them run a case down, and bring it up on his way north through the Inside Passage.

Not a problem. Except the boat ended up being finished six weeks behind schedule, an alarmingly consistent trend in boat building. Seine season had already started by the time it was finished. Captain and crew came roaring north, non-stop, for good reason. Dang.

Desperate times breed desperate measures. Searching on his computer, friend, outhouse mover, and frequent cabin guest John Davis came up with the image of a genuine Lucky Lager label . We printed off 24 copies, and on the next trip to Anchorage I bought a case of unfamiliar beer in stubby brown bottles, used clear packing tape to affix the red and white Lucky labels over the original brand, and wa la, we had our Lucky.

But wait. It get's better.

A week before the Ceremony, a small box with an unfamiliar return address arrived in the mail. Opened it, and there inside was a single can of genuine Lucky Lager beer. Mailed from Idaho by Mike McHone's brother-in-law, who resides close to the Canadian border. McHone, who lived in Cordova as High School Principal and Superintendent for several years before retiring back to his Spud State roots, had made several eventful trips to the Pete Dahl cabin. Word of our Beer Quest had spread all the way to his ranch in Idaho. Turns out his in-law liked the hoppy-tasting ale, and drove into Canada to buy a case every now and then. One 12 ouncer followed the Big Dipper's directions North.

Finally, fireworks. For years, the start of the duck season on September 1 has been marked with an evening fireworks show. Skyrockets, Roman candles, the whole bit. Partly to commemorate that wild evening in our first year at the cabin in 1959, when Dad, Leer, and I were busted for shooting after hours, and the ensuing shotgun display late that night.

Just this side of the Eyak River bridge a fireworks stand pops up a few weeks before the 4th of July every year. I proceeded to spend half my Permanent Fund Dividend check on several honking big skyrockets. For good reason. Child of the Sputnik Era, I had always dreamt of being a rocket scientist, and these were not going to be run-of-the-mill missiles. They were going to carry a Very Special Payload, namely Mom and Dad's ashes, zipping skyward across the Pete Dahl sky. Crashing on the launchpad or quickly self-destructing, as many of our country's early Vanguard and Jupiter rockets did, would not be acceptable.

Several rainy days were spent down in the Odiak Slough Rocket Research Center, also known as my warehouse, experimenting with packets of dry sand attached to the rockets in various amounts and positions; followed by test launches at the Eight Mile Missile Range, also known as The Golf Course. From the bolted doors of the top secret workshop emerged evolving versions V1, V2, V3, and V4, in honor of my German ancestry, although I was not related to

Werner Van Braun. In hindsight, they should have been PD 1 through 4, in honor of Pete Dahl.

By the time we arrived at the cabin, unloaded all the gear, and had the traditional taco dinner, everyone was well exhausted. In early July it barely becomes dark at night, so we decided it didn't really matter if we waited until the next day for all the action. Plus we wanted the big sand bar in front of the cabin to be fully exposed by low tide for scattering the ashes. We built a blaze in the fireplace, drank jelly glasses of Peachtree Schnapps, told stories, and called it a night.

The next day was as nice as they come at Pete Dahl. Delta dawn, a 3 a.m. sun rising far to the northeast behind blue-green mountains surrounding the upper reaches of the Copper River. Wild iris and shooting stars fluttering in a sea of waving green grass; waxy emerald leaves on the cottonwood trees rustling in the light breeze. Swallows chirping, ducks quacking, geese honking, and gentle stirrings in the bunks. Is there anything more wonderful than a little three year old snoozing away in a cozy sleeping bag at a cabin you built 53 years ago, surrounded by family, memories, and traditions she will learn and inherit?

The troops gradually arose. Sweet rolls, coffee, or hot chocolate with marshmallows. Walks outside, games inside. Soon it's time for taco omelette and famous Pete Dahl Snappers. And then, of course, a nap. Life on the Oldtimer's "slow bell."

Murky slough water slowly ebbed outward, the sand bar gradually emerged and grew in size. Finally, low tide, time for The Celebration.

We all headed outside to the cabin deck, each waving a small Alaska flag mounted on a short black stick. Together we unfurled the big Alaska flag, and hoisted Dad's beloved Blue and Gold up the flag pole attached to the cabin addition. It snapped in the breeze.

Now the hard part. A few words, and tears, before scattering their ashes.

A Farewell Tribute

Truly, parents are the greatest influence on our lives. The special legacy of place and time Mom and Dad have given us, in this place called Pete Dahl, makes us double blessed.

It is here we have all enjoyed the times of our lives. This is where we return, to reunite, to relax, to recharge, to be family together. When was the last time we did not head back upriver happier, re-energized, closer to each other; and with a fond farewell wave to the cabin as boat pulled away in the slough.

The cabin logs are not only a testimony to our great adventures here, but also to our good fortune. And most of all to that truest value of all, family and friends.

"Truly, parents are the greatest influence on our lives." Mom & Dad take a stroll down to the point below the cabin, gathering wild iris, also knows as "flags," and driftwood, September 1973.

And so, Mom and Dad, as we scatter your ashes and say farewell, we say thank you. With a promise to continue the traditions that have been such a wonderful part of our lives.

And, as the Oldtimer would say, let's have a Beer and a Blast!

Which we did. With ice cold Lucky Lager-labeled beer, and Dad's good old V.O. Even my wife Sue, who favors nothing stronger than wine coolers on rare occasions, imbibed. And gasped. Wow. That broke the spell.

Next, with waders on, I headed down over the bank with Mom and Dad's ashes, plodding across a sticky mud patch to get to the top of the fully exposed sand bar. A face plant right about then would have been perfect. Seriously.

From there, a wave at the gang 60 feet away standing in front of the cabin. With the Alaska's Song playing on a tape deck, Mom and Dad's ashes were scattered across Earth and Water. They were finally together where they wanted to be.

Back on the bank in front of the cabin, it was time to send them off with a Blast. Of a different sort.

All the rocket models performed well, lifting ashes several hundred feet up before exploding and scattering The Founders skyward.

It was grand. Almost. Little Ellie, frightened by the noise, retreated to the cabin to watch out the window with ears covered, trying to figure out just what was going on. Life can be perplexing, for young and old alike.

Soon, the tide began to flood. It was time to pack up and head back to town.

10 October 1972

To The After Hours Club
Shellhorn Boid Branch Cabin
A heavenly place to get away
Forget the pressures of each day
Relax and do just as we please
Just plain living a life of ease
All who come enjoy with pleasure
And leave with moments to treasure
The Boys all hoist some B and B's
I'm not referring to Birds and Bees.
So what the heck it's all in fun
And always some "fixing" to be done
September 1st is always the big day
Thrilling to anticipate and wish to stay
But each of us must return
To our jobs so that we can earn
The always necessary daily bread
But longing to stay here instead
So good-bye Cabin till next spring
When the ice is gone and birds will sing
Then comes out the "Misty" Number 3
And on the way back we will be.
Adios —Anita

6 July 2011

Smooth sailing to the cabin in honor of Dad & Mom. A wonderful tribute to their memory and the times we shared together as a family. Allah be with you Mom & Dad as you waltz together in the big sky over-looking Pete Dahl.
—Your loving daughter Sharon

"The tide began to flood. It was time to head back to town." Back row, L to R: Heidi Shellhorn, Gretchen Carpenter, Sharon Ermold, Holly Glasen. Front row: Grampa Dick Shellhorn and Ellie Dahl Carpenter, July 2011.

Came down with Mom, Dad, Heidi, Ellie, Shar, and Holly to have a tribute to Grandma Anita and Grandpa Don. it was a great 2 days. The weather was beautiful yesterday and this morning. After breakfast we had our ceremony to honor the two of them. Ellie had a blast. She loves it here and doesn't want to go home. Heidi recorded her top 5 cabin favorites - which are listed after this entry. It was so wonderful to have everyone down here and laugh/cry together remembering Grandma & Grandpa. A trip I will never forget…We love you Grandma and Grandpa & miss you! Thanks for leaving us with such a special place! We are a blessed family! —Love, Gretchen & Ellie

Ellie's Top 5 (6)

1. I did like to go to sleep.
2. I did like sitting.
3. A fort. That was my favorite.
4. I liked eating beans. (pickled green beans for Snappers)
5. I love building a fire.
6. I love making fireworks. (I call B.S. on that last one)

Heidi

Heidi's Top 5:

1. Honoring Grandpa Don & Grandma Anita in a way they would have loved! Thank you Dad & Sharon for setting it all up… flags, flag song, B&B, Lucky Lager, log entries and tributes, ashes on fireworks, and laughing as we remember them both.
2. Ellie's ballet moves and singing.
3. Snappy Toms with the whole crew around the table, Ellie with her own mini-Snappy
4. Cards with everyone
5. Just being here in such an amazing place with my wonderful family

Thank you and love you guys! —Heidi

Wow!… it had been awhile since I was down here and I realized how much I miss it. It brought back lots of memories. It has been a bitter sweet trip with the memorial for GG and all. I hope to come back this summer with my kids! See ya later cabin… —Love Holly

It was a great time with everyone here - haven't been down with Sharon & Holly in awhile, and Heidi is here from Texas. Ellie was entertaining as usual. Mostly it was just a reminder of how important this cabin has been to all of us - a wonderful legacy left by Don & Anita. You will both be missed - but remembered with love and wonderful memories. God Bless You Both - we will look for you in the stars! —Sue

10 October 1984

Departure day for us, always a sad time, kinda get butterflies. However we shall return next year the Lord willing. Bye now —Anita

Me too. —Don

And they had. As Nord would say, Indeed.

We all piled in the riverboat, looking at the cabin from mid-slough. The incoming water and a gentle westerly had pushed us upriver slightly as we were bidding our farewell. Involved in Dad's traditional ceremony of bowing to Allah, our place at Pete Dahl, no one noticed we had drifted atop the sandbar in front of the cabin, now barely covered in grey tidal water.

"I muttered Uh-Oh. Ellie Dahl had already learned to recognize certain phrases as verbal precursors to impending disaster ... What that mean, Grampa?"
6 July 2011.

As I tried to start the jet engine, it ground in the muddy sand.

And Mom and Dad's ashes.

I muttered Uh - Oh. If a little child and ladies hadn't been on board, it might have been something else.

Our perceptive little granddaughter Ellie Dahl had already learned to recognize certain phrases as verbal precursors to impending disaster. Buried in layers of clothing, raingear, knit hat, and life jacket, a voice piped up: "What that mean, Grampa?"

Somewhere Dad smiled.

Time and Tide Wait for No Man.

Ring around the rosy
A pocket full of posies,
Ashes, ashes,
We all fall down.

CHILDREN'S NURSERY RHYME, AUTHOR UNKNOWN

Appendix

I: Pete Dahl Cabin Company, By Year

Family, plus Guests and Visitors (Guests overnighted, visitors dropped by. They are grouped together.) All names are listed in Cabin Logs. Unfortunately there were many others who did not sign.

1959

Family

Shellhorn, Don, Anita, Dick, & Sharon

Guests & Visitors

Banta, Bud

Bernard, Smokey & Dennis

Borer, Dick, Pat,& Mark

Curran, Harry

DeLeo, John

Downing, Dick

Ekemo, Bill & Wanell

Flinn, Pat

Kelsey, John

Leer, Dr. Harrison

Lovseth, Pete

Martin, Dr. & Mrs. Asa

Maxwell, Les & Virginia

Mulcahy, Bob

Noonan, Mike

Nordman, Harold & Julia

Paulson, Pogey

Pettingill, Fred & Kent

Renfro, Mr.& Mrs., & son Mike

Smith, Merle

Swalling, Al, Minnie, Mike, & Chris

Swartzbacker, Andy & Trudy

Traub, Dan

Van Brocklin, Ken

1960

Family

Shellhorn, Don, Anita, Dick, Sharon, & Donita

Guests & Visitors

Behymer, Jerry

Corliss, Jessie

Daniels, Bob

DeLeo, Ann

Fitzpatrick, Paddy

Flinn, Pat

Hansen, Harold (H.Z.)

Hasbrouck, Louie

Lee, Sig

Leer, Dr. Harrison

Mitchell, Herb

Mulcahy, Bob

Mulcahy, Paul

Nicolet, Debbie

Nordman, Harold,Julia, & Ann

Otey, Bill

Paulson, Bob

Pernula, Harold

Renner, Dick

Savoy, Dave

Swartzbacker, Allen

Swartzbacker, Andy Jr.

Traub, Dan

Van Brocklin, Ken, Bobby, & Pam

Wilson, Linda

1961

Family

Anderson, Al & Evelyn

Shellhorn, Don, Anita, Dick, & Sharon

Guests & Visitors

Behymer, Jerry

Borer, Dick & Pat

Bruce, Randy

Cook, Don

Curran, Dean

DeLeo, John & Ann

Durkee, John

Ekemo, John Jr.

Knaack, Bill

Knight, Art

Maxwell, Les & Virginia

Nordman, Harold

Pernula, Harold

Simpler, Bob

Stanton, Barton

Traub, Dan

Van Brocklin, Don & Hattie

Van Brocklin, Pam

1962

Family

Shellhorn, Don, Anita, Dick, & Sharon

Guests & Visitors

Behymer, Jerry

Borer, Dick & Mark

Cudahy, Dan

Curran, Harry & Dean

Ekemo, Johnny & Sue

Flinn, Pat

Hansen, Herb

Knight, Art

Van Brocklin, Don & Hattie

Van Brocklin, Pam

Wright, Chuck & Peggie

1963

Family

Shellhorn, Don & Dick

Shellhorn, Willard, Carl, & Bill

Guests & Visitors

Baxter, Rae

Cartwright, Virgil

Ekemo, Bill & Billy

Ekemo, Johnny

Everly, Don

Jardinski, Al

Kissane, Paddy

Knight, Art & George

Korn, Bob

Leirer, Steve

Lydick, Jack

Nordman, Harold

Wilcox, Fr. Glen

Wilson, John & Jim

1964

Family

Shellhorn, Don & Dick

Guests & Visitors

Balog, Chuck

Blair, Harry

Chase, W. B.

Curran, Dean

Dooley, Tom

Ekemo, Johnny

Ekemo, Ron

Everly, Don

Hayes, Len

Hunter, Bob

Kaiser, Nick

Linton, Jack

Lowe, Alex

Nelson, Beaver

Nordman, Harold

Porter, Chuck

Renk, Al

Roth, J.

Rowland, Frank

Simpler, Bob (Iggy)

Stewart, Al

Stookey, Bill

Taylor, Bill

Taylor, Gary

Thurston, Donald

Watsjold, David

Van Brocklin, Don

1965

Family

Shellhorn, Don

Guests & Visitors

Borer, Dick

Nordman, Harold & Dennis

1966

Family

Estes, Bill

Shellhorn, Don, Anita, Dick, & Sharon

Guests & Visitors

Borer, Dick

Cassidy, Mike

Curran, Harry & Dean

Ekemo, Johnny & Sue

Finrow, Dave

French, John L.

Hammersmith, Mike

Henrichs, Hollis

Johnson, Ken & Paul

Larson, Bob

Lowe, Alex

Morgan, Pat & Janis

Nordman, Harold & Dennis

Porter, Chuck

Pritchard, Jack

Renk, Al & Buddy

Steen, Karl

Steen, Kaye

Taylor, Mike

Ujioka, Steve

Wilcox, Fr. Glen

Zahradincek, Bill

1967

Family

Shellhorn, Dick & Sue (Ekemo)

Shellhorn, Don, Anita, & Sharon

Guest & Visitors

Ballard, Jess

Bruce, Randy & Jackie

Davis, Arlen

Jardinski, Al

Maxwell, Les

Nicolet, Harry

Nordman, Harold & Dennis

Pernula, Harold

Putansu, Doug

Steen, Karl & Ruth

Steen, Kaye

Stevens, Don

Stewart, Al

Urie, Martin

Van Brocklin, Mike & Pat

Wickett, Susie

Zahradincek, Bill

1968

Family

Shellhorn, Dick & Sue

Shellhorn, Don & Sharon

Guests & Visitors

Behymer, Jerry

Brown, Roger

Bruce, Randy

Criner, Glen

Curran, Dean

Davis, Arlen

DeLeo, John

DeVille, Marty

Hammersmith, Mike & Patty

Henrichs, Bob "Moose"

Iverson, Mary Jo

Maxwell, Les

McCullough, Bill

Mulcahy, Bob

Mulcahy, Paul

Nicolet, Harry

Nordman, Harold, Julia, & Dennis

Ochs, Pete

Pettingill, Fred

Siemion, Ted

Taylor, Gary

Webber, Jim

Wheeler, John

Wickett, Linda

Williams, Walt

Van Brocklin, Don & Pat

Van Brocklin, Ken & Pam

Zahradincek, Bill

1969

Family

Shellhorn, Don & Sharon

Guests & Visitors

Bruce, Randy

Criner, Glen

Curran, Dean

Gillam, Don

Graham, Joe

Hammersmith, Mike

Jatzeck, Tom

Lovseth, Pete

Martin, Skip

Nordman, Harold & Dennis

Sherby, Donna & Frank

Wheeler, John

1970

Family

Shellhorn, Dick & Sue

Shellhorn, Don, Anita, & Sharon

Guests & Visitors

Bruce, Randy

Butler, Don

Chisum, Mark

Curran, Harry & Dean

French, John L.

Jardinski, Al

Kissane, Paddy

Kolenut, Ed

Maxwell, Les & Shirley

Nestor, Charlie

Nordman, Dennis

Taylor, Chuck & Exie

Wheeler, John

1971

Family

Cole, Paul, Donita (Shellhorn), Butch, & Bobby

Ekemo, Candice & Janice

Shellhorn, Dick & Sue

Shellhorn, Don, Anita, & Sharon

Guests & Visitors

Bruce, Randy, Jackie, David, & John

Butler, Don

Curran, Harry & Dean

Davis, Dick

Ekemo, Bill Jr.

Foode, Jim

Franzel, Dick

Fridgen, Pete

Jones, Byron

Kazazean, Mark

Lovseth, Pete

Lyons, Jean

Maxwell, Les

Nordman, Dennis

Parker, Tom

Reynolds, Julius

Taylor, Chuck, Exie, & Terry

Thorne, Fred

Tracy, Wes

Van Brocklin, Barb

Van Brocklin, Don

1972

Family

Cole, Paul, Donita, Butch, & Bobby

Ekemo, Candice & Johnny

Shellhorn, Dick & Sue

Shellhorn, Don, Anita, & Sharon

Guests & Visitors

Bruce, Randy, Jackie, David, & John

Downing, Al

Fridgen, Pete

Hammersmith, Mike & Patty

Maxwell, Les & Shirley

McCullough, Jack

Mix, Pam

Nichols, Jim

Rabinowitz, Leon

Robinson, Kathy

Sherby, Frank

Sherby, Lee

Simonson, Diane

Smith, Kenny

Smith, Sheila

Taylor, Chuck

Tilgner, Dr. Art & Barbara

Wunncke, Bill & Paul

1973

Family

Cole, Paul, Donita, Butch, & Bobby

Ekemo, Johnny

Shellhorn, Dick

Shellhorn, Don, Anita, & Sharon

Guests and Visitors

Banta, Bud

Bolon, Bruce, Karen, Kelly, & Gary

Bruce, Randy

Carter, Dave

Chisum, Mark

Curran, Dean

Ermold, Dr. Larry

Fridgen, Pete

Marshall, Ralph

Maxwell, Les & Shirley

Nestor, Charlie

Nichols, Jim

Sherby, Frank, Donna, & Joe

Tilgner, Dr. Art, & Theron

1974

Family

Cole, Paul, Donita, Butch, & Bobby

Ermold, Dr. Larry & Sharon (Shellhorn)

Shellhorn, Dick, Sue, & Heidi

Shellhorn, Don & Anita

Guests & Visitors

Bromley, Bob

Bruce, Randy, Jackie, David, & John

Curran, Dean

Hanson, Merle

Hill, Robbie

Keitel, Jack

Maxwell, Les

McCracken, Connie

Mickelson, Pete

O'Brien, Dan, Margie, & Dan Jr.

Robbins, Art

Taylor, Chuck

Wheeler, David

Wheeler, John

1975

Family

Cole, Paul & Donita

Ekemo, Johnny

Ermold, Dr. Larry & Sharon

Shellhorn, Dick, Sue, & Heidi

Shellhorn, Don & Anita

Visitors & Guests

Booth, Wilbur

Bruce, Randy

Butler, Don

Chandler, Dr. "Crash"

Chisum, Mark & Dovey

Crooks, Dr.

Curran, Dean

Curran, Dr. & Mary

Davis, Chuck

Fridgen, Pete & Pete Jr.

Glasen, Dan & Dan Jr.

Glasen, Don

Issacs, Dr. Paul

Hanson, Merle

Hill, Robbie

Justice, Tom

King, Mark

Maxwell, Mike & Robby

Maxwell, Les, Shirley, & Matt

McCracken, Charlie

Novak, Scott

O'Brien, Dan & Margie

Sellen, John

Sherby, Frank

Simpler, Charlie

Stenger, Dr. Herman

Stevenson, Jack Jr.

Taylor, Chuck

Thibodeau, Emery

Tilgner, Dr. Art, Theron, & Les Tilgner

Wheeler, John

Weiss, Tony & Sheila

1976

Family

Cole, Paul & Donita

Ekemo, Johnny

Ermold, Dr. Larry & Sharon

Shellhorn, Dick, Sue, Heidi, & Gretchen

Shellhorn, Don & Anita

Guests & Visitors

Bacon, Bill

Behymer, Jerry

Bruce, Randy

Butler, Don & LaDonna

Butler, Larry

Christmain, Deb

Curran, Dean

Dolan, Rob

Dunn, Mrs.

Farnes, Jerry & Richard

Fridgen, Pete

Honkola, Bob

Jensen, Herb

Marlou, S.J.

Maxwell, Les & Shirley

McGuire, Dr. Dave & Cheri

Nottingham, Dennis

Oleszeank, Rich

Pingatore, Lenny & Siga

Pirtle, Ralph

Seldon, Dr. John, & sons

Sherby, Frank & Donna, plus Frank's Dad

Stanton, Bart & Bert

Taylor, Chuck & Exie

Tilgner, Dr. Art & JoAnn

Weinrick, Gary & Ruth

Williams, Len

1977

Family

Cole, Donita, Butch, & Bobby

Ermold, Dr. Larry, Sharon, & Brian

Shellhorn, Dick, Sue, Heidi, & Gretchen

Shellhorn, Don & Anita

Guests & Visitors

Bendzak, Jerry

Bruce, Randy, David, & John

Butler, Don

Chisum, Mark & Dovey

Curran, Dean

DeLeo, John & Bill

Fridgen, Pete & Peter Jr.

Giles, Dr. Ray

Glasen, Danny & Donny, & sons

Hanson, Merle

Keitel, Jack

Maxwell, Les & Matt

McCracken, Charlie

Pirtle, Ralph

Sherby, Frank & Donna

Steen, Karl & Karl Jr.

Taylor, Chuck & Terry

Tilgner, Dr. Art, JoAnn, Eric, & Theron

Weiss, Tony & Sheila

Wheeler, John

1978

Family

Ermold, Dr. Larry, Sharon, & Brian

Shellhorn, Dick, Sue, Heidi, & Gretchen

Shellhorn, Don & Anita

Guest & Visitors

Behymer, Roger

Bridgeman, Art

Bruce, Randy

Butler, Don

Chisum, Mark

Curran, Dean

Evans, Mary Jo

Fridgen, Pete

Giles, Dr. Ray

Hanson, Merle

Issacs, Dr.

Noe, Mike

Osborn, Dr. Oliver

Pingatore, Lenny

Pirtle, Ralph

Segerman, Ray

Seldon, Dr., & two sons

Tilgner, Dr. Art

Trapp, Denny

1979

Family

Ekemo, John Sr. & Johnny

Ermold, Dr. Larry, Sharon, & Brian

Jacobs, Roy & Virginia

Shellhorn, Dick, Sue, Heidi, & Gretchen

Shellhorn, Don & Anita

Guests & Visitors

Bruce, Randy

Butler, Don

Chisum, Mark

Curran, Dean

Fridgen, Pete

Hanson, Merle

Hilliker, Ben

Justice, Tom

Lange, John

Maxwell, Les & Shirley

Maxwell, Rob

Nelson, Swede

Pingatore, Lenny

Rizer, Bruce

Seldon, Dr. John & kids

Taylor, Chuck

Tilgner, Dr. Art

Van Brocklin, Dorothy

1980

Family

Ermold, Dr. Larry, Sharon, Brian, Wendy, & Holly

Shellhorn, Dick, Sue, Heidi, & Gretchen

Shellhorn, Don & Anita

Guests & Visitors

Bruce, Randy, Jackie, David, & John

Butler, Don

Chisum, Mark

Fiansean, Art

Goodridge, John

Hanson, Merle & Ardy

Herder, Dale

Hood, Adam

Osborn, Dr. Oliver

1981

Family

Cole, Butch

Ermold, Dr. Larry, Sharon, Brian, Wendy, & Holly

Shellhorn, Dick, Sue, Heidi, & Gretchen

Shellhorn, Don & Anita

Guests & Visitors

Anderson, Teenie

Bruce, Randy, David, & John

Hanson, Merle & Ardy

Kramer, Dean Jr.

Schultz, Dr. John

Steen, Karl Jr.

Tilgner, Dr. Art

1982

Family

Ermold, Dr. Larry, Sharon, Brian, Wendy, & Holly

Shellhorn, Dick, Sue, Heidi, & Gretchen

Shellhorn, Don & Anita

Guests & Visitors

Goodridge, John, Cade, & Wade

Hanson, Merle & Ardy

Pingatore, Lenny

Schultz, Dr. John

Van den Broek, Linda

1983

Family

Ermold, Dr. Larry, Sharon, Brian, Wendy, & Holly

Shellhorn, Dick, Sue, Heidi, & Gretchen

Shellhorn, Don & Anita

Guests and Visitors

Arvidson, Gus & Judy

Curran, Dean

Goodridge, John,

Glenda, Cade, Wade, & Marni

Lillebridge, Dr. Clint

Mickelson, Pete, Belle, & Mike

Narrance, Don

Noe, Mike Jr.

Pingatore, Jessica

Rose, Melissa

Trani, Roger & Dee

Van den Broek, Linda

1984

Family

Ekemo, May

Ermold, Dr. Larry, Sharon, Brian, Wendy, & Holly

Shellhorn, Dick, Sue, Heidi, & Gretchen

Shellhorn, Don & Anita

Guests & Visitors

Arvidson, Gus & Judy

Goodridge, John, Glenda, Cade, Wade, Marni, & John's Mother

Hinfor, Steve

Jorday, Glenn

Lenz, Bob

Mickelson, Pete

Narrance, Don

Schultz, Dr. John

Trani, Roger & Dee

Wamser, Bill

1985

Family

Ermold, Dr. Larry, Sharon, & Holly

Manwiller, Mr. & Mrs. Ralph, & Allen

Shellhorn, Dick, Sue, Heidi, & Gretchen

Shellhorn, Don & Anita

Guests & Visitors

Brudnell, Dr. Ross

Cowell, Fuller, Chris, & Alexis

Goodridge, John, Glenda, Cade, Wade, & Marni

McHone, Mike

Schultz, Dr. John

Tilgner, Dr. Art

Van den Broek, Pam

1986

Family

Ermold, Dr. Larry, Sharon, & Holly

Shellhorn, Dick, Sue, Heidi, & Gretchen

Shellhorn, Don & Anita

Guests & Visitors

Burgard, Amy

Beaudin, Lyle & Gwen

Lenz, Bob & Deb

McHone, Mike

Thorne, Amy

Van den Broek, Marvin & Linda

1987

Family

Ermold, Dr. Larry, Sharon, & Holly

Shellhorn, Dick, Sue, Heidi, & Gretchen

Shellhorn, Don & Anita

Guests & Visitors

Beaudin, Jay

Brudnell, Dr. Ross

Cave, Al

Davis, John

Giles, Dr. Ray

Gilmore, Oma

Goodridge, John, Cade, & Wade

Lenz, Bob

McHone, Mike

Schultz, Dr. John

Trani, Roger

Weinrick, Gary

Van den Broek, Marvin

1988

Family

Ermold, Dr. Larry, Sharon, Wendy, & Holly

Shellhorn, Dick, Sue, Heidi, & Gretchen

Shellhorn, Don & Anita

Guests & Visitors

Brudnell, Dr. Ross

DiMattie, Francis

Goodridge, John Glenda, Cade, Wade, & Marni

Lenz, Bob & Dennis

McHone, Mike

Schultz, Dr. John

Thibodeau, Emery

Van den Broek, Marvin, Linda, & Pam

Webber, Jamie

1989

Family

Ermold, Dr. Larry, Sharon, Wendy, & Holly

Shellhorn, Dick, Sue, Heidi, & Gretchen

Shellhorn, Don & Anita

Guests & Visitors

Arvidson, Gus

Cave, Barb

Davis, Mary

Goodridge, John, Glenda, Cade, Wade, & Marni

Johnson, Mayland

Lenz, Bob & Dennis

McCarty, Hannah

Narrance, Don

Trani, Roger

Van den Broek, Marvin

Webber, Jamie

1990

Family

Ermold, Dr. Larry, Sharon, & Holly

Shellhorn, Dick, Sue, Heidi, & Gretchen

Shellhorn, Don & Anita[1]

Guests & Visitors

Blair, Mike

McHone, Mike

Popelka, Thorne

Van den Broek, Marvin

Webber, Jamie

1991

Family

Ermold, Dr. Larry, Sharon, Wendy, & Holly

Shellhorn, Dick, Sue, Heidi, & Gretchen

Shellhorn, Don

Guests & Visitors

Alazabal, Ana

Blair, Mike

Cave, Barb

Davis, Mary

Goodridge, John, Cade, & Wade

Lohse, Becky

McHone, Mike

Van den Broek, Linda

Webber, Jamie

1992

Family

Ermold, Dr. Larry, Sharon, & Holly

Shellhorn, Dick, Sue, Heidi, & Gretchen

Shellhorn, Don[2]

Guests & Visitors

Goodridge, John

Lauderdale, Gary

Lenz, Bob, Dennis, & David

Rock, Jesse

Trani, Tom

Van Brocklin, Ken

Van den Broek, Marvin

Webber, Jamie

---

1 Mom's last trip to cabin, 31 August – 2 September 1960

2 Dad's last trip to cabin, 29 Aug 1992

1993

Family

Ermold, Dr. Larry, Sharon, & Holly

Shellhorn, Dick, Sue, Heidi, & Gretchen

Guests & Visitors

Carpenter, Tom

Davis, John

Goodridge, John, Glenda, Cade, Wade, & Marni

Morace, Jeremy

Van den Broek, Marvin

Webber, Jamie

Williston, Jim

1994

Family

Ermold, Dr. Larry, Sharon, Wendy, & Holly

Shellhorn, Dick, Sue, Heidi, & Gretchen

Guests & Visitors

Carpenter, Tom

Cave, Barb

Dahle, Tore

Dunlap, Chris

Gaspar, Dr. Matt

McHone, Mike

Milillo, Dr. Phil

Tilgner, Dr. Art

Van den Broek, Marvin

1995

Family

Ekemo, May

Ermold, Dr. Larry, Sharon, & Holly

Shellhorn, Dick, Sue, Heidi, & Gretchen

Guests & Visitors

Carpenter, Tom

Gaspar, Dr. Matt

Goodridge, John, Glenda, Cade, Wade, & Marni

Hottinger, Cecily

Narrance, Don

Rose, Melissa

Tilgner, Dr. Art

Wilcox, Shanny

1996

Family

Ermold, Dr. Larry, Sharon, & Holly

Shellhorn, Dick, Sue, Heidi, & Gretchen

Guests & Visitors

Carpenter, Sue Ellen & Tim

Carpenter, Tom

Gaspar, Dr. Matt

Groff, Dick

1997

Family

Ermold, Dr. Larry, Sharon, Wendy, & Holly

Shellhorn, Dick, Sue, Heidi, & Gretchen

Guests & Visitors

Bednarz, Paul

Carpenter, Tom

Cave, Al & Jason

Clayton, Kevin

Davis, John

Lauderdale, Gary

Masolini, Nick

Schultz, Neil

1998

Family

Belcher, Donita

Blakeslee, Ted & Janice

Brooks, John

Ermold, Dr. Larry, Sharon, & Holly

Robbins, Candice

Shellhorn, Dick, Sue, Heidi, & Gretchen

Guests & Visitors

Carpenter, Tom

Davis, John

Groff, Dick

Lipson, Ross

1999

Family

Belcher, Donita

Cole, Brandon

Ermold, Dr. Larry, Sharon, Wendy, & Holly

Shellhorn, Dick, Sue, Heidi, & Gretchen

Guests & Visitors

Carpenter, Tom

2000

Family

Ermold, Dr. Larry, Sharon, Wendy, & Holly

Shellhorn, Dick, Sue, Heidi, & Gretchen

Guests & Visitors

Carpenter, Tom

Groff, Dick

Lake, Bryce, USGS

2001

Family

Belcher, Donita

Carpenter, Tom & Gretchen (Shellhorn)*

*(Married on Dad's birth date, 25 August)

Carpenter, Sue Ellen, Dave, & Tim

Shellhorn, Dick, Sue, & Heidi

Guests & Visitors

Allen, Les

Cave, Al

Corrington, Dave

Davis, John

Groff, Dick

Hanson, Ardy

McDonald, Bob & Cathy

Threlkeld, Mike

Vollmer, Frank & Sharon

Wheeler, Leonard

Zollner, Tim

2002

Family

Belcher, Donita

Carpenter, Tom & Gretchen

Ekemo, Janice

Ermold, Sharon

Shellhorn, Dick, Sue, & Heidi

Guests & Visitors

Davis, John

Groff, Dick

Lauderdale, Gary

Popelka, Thorne

Veal, Chip

2003

Family

Carpenter, Tom & Gretchen

Shellhorn, Dick, Sue, & Heidi

Guests & Visitors

Arvidson, Mike

Bruce, Randy

Groff, Dick

Janson, Buddy

King, Kyle

2004

Family

Brooks, John & Candice (Ekemo)

Carpenter, Tom & Gretchen

Ekemo, Janice

Ekemo, Johnny

Shellhorn, Dick & Sue

Guests & Visitors

Bruce, Randy

Cave, Al

Davis, John

Muma, Gordon

Steen, Karl Jr.

2005

Family

Carpenter, Tom & Gretchen

Morris, Doug

Shellhorn, Dick, Sue, & Heidi

Guests & Visitors

Bue, John

Cave, Al

Collins, Mike

Davis, John

Groff, Dick

Hanson, Ardy

Lauderdale, Gary

Wayne, Jimmy

Wheeler, Leonard

2006

Family

Belcher, Donita

Carpenter, Tim

Carpenter, Tom & Gretchen

Cole, Butch

Ermold, Sharon

Glasen, Holly (Ermold), Mikee, Kayley

Shellhorn, Dick, Sue, & Heidi

Guests & Visitors

Burcham, Milo

Davis, John

Fode, Jason

Groff, Dick

Johnson, Roger

Moore, Bud

Truex, Mike

2007

Family

Carpenter, Tom & Gretchen

Shellhorn, Dick & Sue

Guests & Visitors

Arvidson, Gus & Mike

Cave, Al

Davis, John

Koch, John

Moore, Bud

Morrisett, Rob, Alaska State Trooper

Shipman, Fred

2008

Family

Carpenter, Tom & Gretchen

Shellhorn, Dick, Sue, & Heidi

Guests & Visitors

Arvidson, Gus & Mike

Davis, John

Goodridge, John & Glenda

Groff, Dick

Lee, Andy & Marni (Goodridge)

Moore, Bud

2009

Family

Carpenter, Tom

Cole, Butch

Ermold, Sharon

Glasen, Kayley

Shellhorn, Dick

Guests & Visitors

Arvidson, Gus, Mike, & Inga

Balero, Joe

Cave, Al & Jason

Corrington, Dave

Davis, John & Jim

Grady, Zeb

Groff, Dick

Kleinding, Jackie

2010

Family

Carpenter, Tom,
Gretchen, & Ellie
Dahl

Shellhorn, Dick,
Sue, & Heidi

Guests & Visitors

Arvidson, Gus,
Mike, & Inga

Davis, John

Mallory, Chris

Moorhead, Scott

2011

Family

Carpenter, Tom,
Gretchen, & Ellie

Ermold, Sharon

Glasen, Holly

Shellhorn, Dick,
Sue, & Heidi

Guests & Visitors

Arvidson, Mike &
Inga

Moore, Bud

2012

Family

Carpenter, Julie &
Kate

Carpenter, Tom,
Gretchen, & Ellie

Shellhorn, Dick &
Sue

Guests & Visitors

Arvidson, Mike &
Inga

Davis, John

2013

Family

Carpenter, Tom,
Gretchen, & Ellie

Moorhead, Scott,
Heidi (Shellhorn),
& Huckleberry

Shellhorn, Dick &
Sue

Guests & Visitors

Leirer, Steve &
Linda

Moore, Bud

II: References

Alaska Department of Fisheries, "History of Salmon Canneries in Central Alaska, 1882-1950," Alaska Department of Fisheries Annual Report for 1951.

Allen, Lt. Henry T., *Report of An Expedition to The Copper, Tanana, and Koyukuk Rivers in 1885*, Alaska Northwest Publishing, 1985.

Ambrose, Steven E., *Undaunted Courage*, Simon & Schuster, 1997.

Alstad, Ken, *Savy Sayin's: True Wisdom from The Real West*, Whippersnap Press, 2004.

Berra, Yogi, *The Yogi Book*, Workman Publishing, 1998.

Boots, Michelle, "Fire Destroy Historic Copper Center Lodge," *Anchorage Daily News*, 20 May 2012 .

Bromley & Rothe, Conservation Assessment for the Canada Goose, USDA, General Technical Report, PNW-GTR-591, December 2003.

Building The Mile 13 Airport and Cordova Military Base 1941-1944, Cordova Historical Society, Cordova City Museum, Cordova, Alaska.

Caswell, Christopher, *The Greatest Sailing Stories Every Told*, Lyons Press, 2004.

Copper Nugget 1962, Published by Annual Staff of Cordova High School, Cordova, Alaska, 1962.

Cordova Times Archives, Microfiche File, Cordova Library, Cordova, Alaska.

Cordova Historical Society, *Building the Mile 13 Airport and Cordova Military Base 1941-1944*, Cordova Museum, Cordova, Alaska.

Curran, Harry, Taped Interview, 25 September 2011, Cordova, Alaska.

Doig, Ivan, *English Creek*, Penguin Books, 1984.

Doig, Ivan, *Heart Earth*, Harcourt Inc., 1993.

Ducks Unlimited: Dusky Canada Goose Nesting Enhancement, 2012 Report.

Fondell, Dusky Canada Geese: What Have We Learned Since the Last CRD Science Symposium, 13th Copper River Delta Science Symposium, Cordova, Alaska 2011.

Fondell, Grand, Miller, & Anthony: Predators of Dusky Canada Goose Goslings and The Effect of Transmitters on Gosling Survival, Journal of Field Ornithology 4, 399-407, 2008.

Giles, Donna Estes, *The Funny River Hunt*, Between The Lines Publications, 2000.

Graves, John, *Goodbye to a River*, First Vintage Departures Edition, 2002.

Gutherie, A.B, *The Big Sky*, First Mariner Books, 2002.

Hanable, William S., *Alaska's Copper River, The 18th and 19th Centuries*, Alaska Historical Commission Studies in History No. 21, 1982.

Harrison, Jim, *The Road Home*, Washington Square Press, 1998.

Hayden, Sterling, "The Fisherman's Cup Races: Last Act," from *Wanderer*, 1977, W.W. Norton & Co.

Hirsch, Kett, & Trefil, *The Dictionary of Cultural History*, Houghton Mifflin, 1993.

Lamott, Anne, *Bird by Bird: Some Instructions on Writing and Life*, Anchor Books, 1994.

Leavy, Jane, *Sandy Koufax, A Lefty's Legacy*, Perennial Publishing, 2003.

Lethcoe, Jim and Nancy, *History of Prince William Sound, Revised 2nd Edition*, Prince William Sound Books, 2001.

Logan, Dan, USFS, retired Cordova District Ranger, Taped Interview, Cordova, Alaska, 29 October 2011.

Maggiulli & Dugger, Factors Associated with Dusky Canada Goose Nesting and Nest Success on Artificial Islands of the Western Copper River Delta, Dept. of Fisheries and Wildlife, Oregon State University, 2011.

McCutcheon, Marc, Roget's Super Thesaurus, 4th Edition, Writer's Digest Books, 2010.

Meyer, Philipp, *The Son*, Harper Collins Publishers, 2013.

Nielsen, Nicki J., *From Fish and Copper, Cordova's Heritage and Buildings,* Alaska Historical Commission Studies in History No. 124, Cordova Historical Society, 1984.

Payne, Jim, "Local Fishing Methods and Gear Progressed," *Cordova Times*, 30 April 1981.

Pels, Jacquelin Ruth Benson, *Unga Island Girl*, Hardscratch Press, 1995.

Proulx, E. Annie, *The Shipping News*, Simon & Schuster,

Sherman, Cathy R., *Images of America: Cordova*, Arcadia Publishing, 2012.

Snaith, William, "About Figaro," from *On the Wind's Way*, Penguin Putnam Inc., 1973.

Swalling, A.C., *The Cordova That I Knew*, Word Masters Publishing, 1997.

Tower, Elizabeth, *Big Mike Heney, Irish Prince of the Iron Trails*, Publication Consultants, 2003.

Webster's College Dictionary, Random House, 1991.

Wikipedia, The Free Encyclopedia, www.wikipedia.org.

Young, G.O., *Alaskan Yukon Trophies Won and Lost*, Wolfe Publishing Company, 2011.

III: A History of the Names of Sloughs of the Copper River Delta

By Dick Shellhorn

Submitted in Partial Fulfillment of the Course Requirements of The History of Prince William Sound

April 1983 (With revisions and additions in 2011)

Introduction

Traversing the Copper River Delta from Whitshed to Martin River, one encounters a veritable litany of historical names for the myriad sloughs and geographic features one sees. Having spent a lifetime hunting and fishing in this area, I have often wondered about the historical background of the names of these features. This paper is a brief summary of research to date on the history of nameplaces of the Copper River Delta.

Sources of Information

Primary sources of information were as follows:

Dictionary of Alaska Place Names, U.S. Dept. of Interior Geological Survey Professional Paper 567, Cordova Library. This is a fascinating publication documenting history of an incredibly detailed number of Alaskan places.

Taped conversation with Norman Swanson, a true oldtimer who first became involved with the Copper River Delta fisheries in the late 1910s. This tape was made in April 1983.

Phone conversations with Pete Lovseth, a pioneer Cordovan who spent his youth hunting and fishing the Flats and lived here until recently moving to Homer, Alaska.

Excerpts of interview with Art Tiedeman, Sr., from *Out of Our Times,* a paper produced by the Career Education Class at Cordova High School.

Article by Jim Payne, titled "Local Fishing Methods and Gear Progressed," April 30 1981 *Cordova Times.*

6. *An Expedition to The Copper, Tanana, and Koyukuk Rivers in 1885*, Lt. Henry T. Allen, Northern History Library, Alaska Northwest Publishing Company, 1985

General Categorization of Names

Names for sloughs and other key features seemed to naturally fall into four broad categories.

NATIVE NAMES: Names which include Eyak, Chugach, and Ahtna roots. Examples are Kokinhenik, Eyak, Alaganik, Softuk, Katella, Kanak, and possible Okalee.

GEOGRAPHIC FEATURE NAMES: Names for many sloughs or islands are clearly geographic in origin. Examples include Mountain Slough, Center Slough, Glacier, Castle Island, Grass Island, Cottonwood Point, Little River, and Mirror Slough.

ACTIVITY BASED NAMES: Several islands and waterways were named for activity in that particular area, such as hunting, fishing or navigation. Examples include King Salmon, Egg Island, Steamboat, Government, and Walhalla.

INDIVIDUAL BASED NAMES: Many sloughs were named after local commercial fishermen who traditionally fished these particular areas from very early on. Examples include Joe Reeve, Johnson, Tiedeman, Whiskey Pete, Gus Stevens, Storey, Gus Wilson, and Cudahy.

Brief History of Fishery

Since so many of the place names on the Flats are closely related to the salmon gill net fisheries, a brief review of the early fishing activity is important.

Incidentally, the term "Flats" refers to the area between the mainland edge of the Delta, primarily a cutbank drop-off which stands four to eight feet tall, and the inside edge of a band of sandy barrier islands that prevent the Pacific Ocean surf from pounding against that muskeg face. In most places the Flats are three to four miles wide, and at low tide a muddy maize of exposed sand bars and shallow meandering grey gutters and sloughs. Many a craft, including Lt. Henry Allen's canoes in 1885, has been stranded there at low tide in lousy weather.

Allen, in his Narrative of the Copper River section of his report *An Expedition to The Copper, Tanana, and Koyukuk Rivers in 1885*, discovered the Eyak natives had coined the phrase "flats." It took his party three tries to cross this terrain from Whitshed to the mouth of Alaganik Slough, a major tributary of the Copper. He states: "They spoke much of the mud flats, which we afterwards became acquainted with through sad experience."

Later he described their first attempt to cross them: "To reach the principal channel of Copper River, which we were to ascend in order to obtain water to float our boats, necessitated a start from Point Whitshed at 3 in the morning, about the time of flood tide. The wind was dead ahead, from the southeast, producing a heavy surf, and darkness was supreme. Our boats were constantly shipping water, yet for several hours we struggled against all difficulties, keeping close to the rugged and rocky shore, without a beach. The more the tide fell the oftener we grounded on the mud. We had hoped to reach the channel of Copper River before this state of affairs could arrive. Finally, as a means of economy, we tried to make headway by going out from the shore, but the tide was receding too fast and left us on the mud about eight hundred yards from shore."

"Welcome to the Club" would have been his greeting from countless future fishermen and hunters.

The following quotes from Payne delineate the early fishing efforts that started in Eyak Lake itself, and gradually shifted downstream to the slough mouths and then the Flats.

"Salmon fishing was common in Cordova long before settlement by outsiders and commercialization of the product. To the Eyak Indians who lived around the present day Cordova area, salmon was the most important source of food and the "staff of life" according to historians. The Eyaks had no exclusive fishing locations owned by individuals because there were so many salmon in the Copper River that they could catch a whole year's supply early in the season. They usually fished in pairs using dipnets, stone corrals and scaffolds from which they speared fish. Chugach Eskimos in Prince William Sound placed subsistence emphasis on sea mammals, but also fished for salmon with weirs, harpoons, gaffs and fish traps."

"The first commercial salmon canneries began operating in 1889 in what was to become the Cordova region. The Central Alaska Company and the Peninsula Trading and Fishing Company built canneries on Little Kayak Island (Wingham Island) that year. Also building canneries in Odiak Slough in 1889 were Pacific Packing Company and Pacific Steam Whaling Company. Eventually, Pacific Packing Company joined the Alaska Packers Association. In 1895, the Pacific Steam Whaling Company moved up the coast about four miles to Orca. The areas fished for the canneries encompassed an ever-increasing circumference after the first year. The first pack in 1889 was obtained almost exclusively from Lake Eyak and the Eyak River. The following year, fishing started in the Copper River Delta and a few locations in Prince William Sound."

This would be when individual early pioneer fisherman such as Pete Dahl had their names attached to their particular traditional fishing spots.

"Up to 1912, much of the yearly pack continued to come from Lake Eyak. The major capturing technique used there was stake nets. One historian notes that "these nets form an almost impossible barrier, and the wonder is that any fish ever get through to the spawning grounds." Small steamers transported fish caught in

Lake Eyak to a tramway at the western end of the lake. From there, the fish were transported by tram the short distance (thought the current Old Town area) to the canneries at Odiak Slough. This same route was used by lighters and smaller vessels, including small steamers, to transport fish from the Copper River Delta to the Odiak canneries. The steamers operating on the Delta had a draft of only 24 inches and often went aground. Fishing in the Eyak River was so intense, that it was noted in 1900, regarding the transport boats, "In most cases the nets are laid so that it is barely possible to get through them with a boat, and occasionally, in order to get up the river, the boats have to pass entirely over the nets." In the earliest years on the Delta, fishermen lived in bunkhouses along the sloughs, where fish were consolidated for pick-up by steamers. Columbia River double enders with two men and 450 fathoms of linen web composed a typical fishing crew at the turn of the century." (Reprinted by permission of the *Cordova Times*)

Payne then goes on to describe how in the 1930s double enders with power came into use, launching the advent of the drift net fishery as we know it today, mentioning that a few fishermen still continued to use cabin sites at the mouth of Eyak River as the base for their operations.

Swanson provided a more detailed description of fisheries along the sloughs in the early 1900s. He indicated many of the sloughs were named after the first fishermen to stake them out for pole (set net) fishing. This traditional form of fishing may have come from early operations in Eyak Lake. Rights to sloughs and gutters came on a first come, first serve basis, with camps being set up on points early in the spring, sometimes while the sloughs were still frozen. Methods to claim sites included being dropped off by sternwheeler to row in; using one's own sailboat (Tiedeman did this), or skiing across land from the railroad (Whiskey Pete's method).

Originally small tent frames were constructed; these later developed into cabins, some as elaborate as the bunkhouses Payne mentions. To harvest fish, poles were set up along the cutbanks of the sloughs, with up to 400 fathoms of net set on the poles. Fish were harvested 7 days a week throughout the season, using a row boat to pick the fish and then transport them to tenders who came by to gather the fish and take them to the canneries, as well as drop off supplies to the fishermen. This type of fishing continued until 1923. No one fished in the breakers and open ocean outside the bars (barrier islands) prior to that time, until Utness started experimenting with power boats and drifting those areas. Prior to that small boats didn't have the power to combat the tides and rough weather.

Tiedeman mentioned first going out on the Flats on stern wheelers during this era. The stern wheelers would go across the Flats and up to the mouths of the sloughs to take in supplies and remove fish. He stated: "Those canneries had a house on every point of every slough, with three or four fishermen and a couple boats, and oars and sails for power."

Hence it is clear that many of the place names of the Copper River Delta relate to this particular early style of fishery.

Detailed History of Slough and Name Places

Listed below is the historical data gathered to date on particular sloughs and places. The names are listed approximately from west to east, and maps of the area showing the locations of each are attached in an Appendix.

1. MOUNTAIN SLOUGH: local name reported in 1897 by Moser, Commander of U.S. Bureau of Fisheries steamer Albatross that did extensive research in the summers of 1897, 1898, 1900, and 1901. (Moser visited most of the Alaska canneries and important salmon streams, and his name is associated with the names attached to many of these places. He was later promoted to Admiral in the U.S. Navy.) The name is geographic in origin, based on the slough's proximity to the east side of the Heney Range.

2. CENTER SLOUGH: name derives from its location midway between Mountain Slough and Eyak River. It was fished in the pole/set net era by N.P. Nelson, who later became a partner in the Crystal Falls Cannery, located near a large waterfall a mile up Mountain Slough. Listed in 1951 USGS Survey. (Note: USGS stands for United States Geological Survey).

3. EYAK RIVER: Native name derives from the village and lake above it. The word *eyak* (igya'aq) refers to the "throat" of a river. (Sherman: Images of American: Cordova). According to the Dictonary of Alaska Name Places, a former Eskimo village reported in 1869 as "Yhacks" by Maj. Gen. Halleck, U.S.A. Listed by Petraff in the 1880 Census as "Ihiak; population was 94 in 1890, 222 in 1900. In 1899, Moser reported it as a cannery called Odiak, pop. 273. (Note: this was probably at the western end of Eyak Lake, not to be confused with the lake outflow to the east or the mouth of the Eyak River.) Swanson mentioned that most of the cabins at the mouth of Eyak River used to be on the opposite (west) side of the slough, since the water was deeper there, due to the natural course of the river. In 1919 a Parks rigging scow cabin (two stories) was set up on the opposite bank, and others followed. Incidentally, this rigging scow cabin is still standing, and is the only two story cabin on the Delta.

3a. EGG ISLAND: a 2.5 mile long barrier island six miles southeast of Pt. Whished and directly below the mouth of the Eyak River; a primary nesting areas for Glaucous-winged sea gulls, and the world's largest colony of this species. Site of egg gathering by local natives; local name reported by G.D. Martin, USGS, in 1905. Note: The Dictionary of Alaska Name Places lists 18 Egg Island or Islands.

4. JOE REEVE SLOUGH: a small slough between Eyak and Government, named after the set netter who utilized it from 1919 to 1922. Swanson stated that Reeves was an old man at that time, single, and with no sons. Lovseth recalled Reeve living in a cabin by Eyak Lake in the winter, and traveling Eyak River by rowboat and later a skiff powered by a 5.7 Alto outboard. This fishing site was later acquired by Bob Korn, who expanded it into a popular duck hunting cab fondly known as the Korn Hole. The cabin is still in use; upon Korn's death, Merle Hanson and Chuck Taylor took over its maintenance and hunted out of it, until its recent sale by Terry Kissane, to outside interests. Lovseth mentioned that Black Nels also fished a small tributary near Joe Reeve Slough, using a skiff with a tarp over it, and "5000 dogs." This is probably the unidentified character shown in Nancy Bird's slide collection on early Cordova scenes that shows a man in a tarp covered skiff with a pack of dogs.

5. GOVERNMENT SLOUGH: named after a large highly visible geodetic tripod located there that served as a triangulation point in surveying the Flats. USGS also used Government Rock to the west of the mouth of Mountain Slough for this purpose. Swanson remembered the name was somehow connected with mapping; Lovseth remembered actually seeing the tripod, which "stood for years."

6. JOHNSON SLOUGH: Swanson indicated a fisherman named Oscar Oman had this site in the pole fishing era, and the slough was named from earlier days. Neither Lovseth or Swanson felt the name was related to any of the many local Johnson families. Despite its evident early naming, the Dictionary of Alaska Place names states simply "local name, 1954, USGS."

7, 8. BIG GLACIER AND LITTLE GLACIER: geographic names, both are branches of waters from Sheridan Glacier, so named as Glacier Slough in 1900 by USGS "because it heads at a glacier." Local fisherman made the distinction between the two branches at the edge of the Flats based on the width of the sloughs, according to Swanson.

9. TIEDEMAN SLOUGH: named after August Tiedeman, who originally reached this site by sailboat, living in Sheep Bay in Prince William Sound during the offseason and sailing around to set up his camp after the spring break up.

10. ALAGANIK SLOUGH: an Eskimo name derived from the upstream village of Alaganik; reported as Algonek River in 1899 by Moser. The word "alaganik" (*alarneq*) means "switchback in the river." (Sherman: Images of America: Cordova). The Dictionary of Alaska Name Places mentioned Alaganik Village as "former Eskimo and Ahtena Indian village visited in 1848 by Serebrenikov, who reported it as "Alagnak." Its population (including Eyaks) was 117 in 1880; 48 in 1890.

11. WHISKEY PETE SLOUGH: named for Pete Olsen, father of local Cordovans George and Gilbert Olsen. Swanson indicated Olsen's rights to this slough were respected, and that he reached this site early in the year by overland travel while things were still frozen up. Swanson described Whiskey Pete as a small, tough, hard fishing individual infamous for his prodigal drinking ability.

12. STEAMBOAT: not actually a slough cutting through the grass banks and marshes of the Delta, but rather a channel from Copper Sands, a long sand island outside the mouth of Eyak, to Pete Dahl Slough, inside the barrier bars and breakers. So named because sternwheelers drawing three feet of water went through here, it was a big and deep channel that has altered and silted in over the years. Lovseth recalled riding the sternwheeler Bancroft through here as a boy; and mentioned that the remains of the Bancroft are to be found at Fleming Spit.

13. PETE DAHL SLOUGH: a local name reported by Moser in 1898. Swanson said Dahl fished the area from that time until 1904, while Northwestern Cannery operated, but left or died prior to Swanson's arrival. A tributary near the mouth of Pete Dahl Slough is the site of four duck cabins originally built in the mid and late 1950s. The owners, by cabin, were: Dick Borer; a group including Andy Swartzbacker, Bill Ekemo, and Pete Lovseth; a group of six headed by Les Maxwell; and my father, Don Shellhorn.

14. WALHALLA SLOUGH: actually name was "Valhalla," according to Lovseth. Several Norwegian fishermen set net here, and regarded it as Fish Heaven. Swanson also mentioned a set net cabin site on a small gutter between Pete Dahl and Walhalla sloughs; I have often duck hunted that particular area but all trace of such a cabin is gone.

15. GUS STEVENS SLOUGH: named after an old time fisherman who lived in Cordova up until the 1950s, residing "on the hill" near Larry and Kathleen Kritchen's home. Fished this slough for as long as Lovseth could remember. Local name was listed by USGS, 1951.

16. KING SALMON SLOUGH: Swanson described this slough as formerly one of the major branches of the Copper, a very deep tributary that produced large numbers of king salmon for many years.

17. CASTLE ISLAND AND CASTLE ISLAND SLOUGH: named by H.P. Ritter, USC&GS, 1898. His description of the significant land feature was: "The Knoll is about 30 feet high and covered with Alder bushes. There are five large Cottonwood trees on this knoll, and from a distance they resemble the towers of a castle." Note: Ritter was in charge of a survey party on the USC&GS steamer Taku, which from 1898 to 1903 surveyed the Copper River Delta and eastern Prince William Sound.

18. STOREY ISLAND AND STOREY SLOUGH: local name listed in 1898 by Ritter. Storey Island in Prince William Sound was reported by Schrader, USC&GS in 1898, as "the island is named for Walter Storey of San Francisco." Swanson stated this slough on the Flats was named after the same individual, who was involved in both fishing the Copper River and fox farming on Prince William Sound.

19. GRASS ISLAND: not a slough, but a prominent barrier island with a geographical name given by Ritter during his survey work in 1898. Swanson described the gradual shifting of this island and others westward due to prevailing surf and wind action, citing the relocation of Egg Island Light three times this century as evidence of this phenomena.

20. KOKINHENIC ISLAND: an Indian name reported in 1897 by Moser as Coquenhea, and listed by Ritter in 1898 as Kokinhenik. Swanson described a cannery that was located on this prominent sandy island on the edge of the main Copper River for a few years. It had been moved to that location from Kanak Island, and ended up being the cannery that the Copper River and Northwest Railway bought out on Odiak Slough in the early 1900s as the staging area for building the railroad to the copper mines at Kennecott. A deep channel to this island, called Kokinhenic Slough, allowed steamboats drawing as much as 12 feet of water to reach the cannery; however fresh water for processing fish was a problem. A catch basin was built to trap rain water; additional water was shipped in and transferred to a large storage tank; but lack of water was one cause for the eventual second move, this time to Odiak slough adjacent to Cordova. (Note: by the early 2000s, this island has almost completely vanished, due to wind erosion and changing river flow of the main Copper River.)

21. COTTONWOOD POINT: a prominent point on the western edge of the main Copper River named by Abercrombie in 1898 for the large stands of high visible cottonwood trees.

22. DAGO SLOUGH: named after the many Greek and Slavonian fishermen who "homesteaded" there, according to Lovseth.

23, 24, 25. RUSSIAN RIVER, LITTLE RIVER, SHIT RIVER: small sloughs on the far eastern side of the flats, named in order for a. ethnic use, b. size, and c. amount of snags and "crap" one seemed to get in his net while fishing there, said Lovseth. The names are more recent, and post-date the set/pole net era.

26, 27. CUDAHY, GUS WILSON SLOUGHS: named after fishermen who traditionally used these areas, according to Lovseth.

28. MARTIN RIVER: named after the Glacier from which it emerges by Abercrombie in 1899. Martin River used to follow the base of a mountain range nearby until a rock slide in the 1920-1930 time period choked it off, forcing it to flow directly into the Copper, said Lovseth.

29. MIRROR SLOUGH: local name reported in 1904 by Martin, USGS. Swanson said the well protected waters were always glassy like a mirror and a safe place to anchor in even the worst storm.

30. SOFTUK: an Eskimo name listed by Marten and Pratt, 1903

History of Some Adjacent Non-Delta Places of Interest
The above list completes data to date on places names on the Copper River Delta. While doing research, I also found some intriguing information regarding some non-Delta locations that are added below.

31. BERING RIVER: river flowing from Bering Glacier and Bering Lake, named in 1880 by USGS in honor of Vitus Bering, a Dane in service of Russia's Peter the Great, and credited with Alaska's discovery. First landfall was made by Bering near here in 1741. The Spanish explorer Arteaga named the same river Rio de Lagartos

(River of Lizards) in 1779, although he never reached the river itself, so "the name had to have had some other source than any knowledge he had of lagartos in it," according to the Dictionary of Alaska Name Places. It is possible Arteaga may have confused sea lions, seals, or otter with lizards, or perhaps at that time the Spanish language did not have a word for such "creatures." It is clear that the Spanish did not communicate with the English and Russians about maps and places already discovered and named. They merrily went about giving Spanish names to features that had been named years before by British or Russian explorers, or Native groups. As another example, the Spanish came up with their own name for the Copper River; Arteaga called it "Rio do los Perdidos," meaning the "River of the Lost, in 1779.

32. WINGHAM ISLAND: named in June 1794 by Peter Puget, a member of Vancouver's Expedition. Called Mitchell's Island by Capt. J. Mares in 1788; Eskimo name was Shiganik Island, according to Tebenkov in 1852. Also called Isla Dudose by Malaspina in 1791, since "he thought it might be connected to Kayak Island and hence a peninsula, according to the Dictionary of Alaska Name Places.

33. KAYAK ISLAND: called Kayak by Russian Sarichev in 1826 because of the fancied resemblance of its outline to the Eskimo skin canoe. This island was Russian Vitus Bering's first landfall, and the basis for that country's claim to Alaska. He named it St. Elias in 1741. Naturalist Georg W. Stellar, surgeon aboard Bering's ship St. Peter, went ashore here briefly to examine flora and fauna as well as to attempt contact with natives and find fresh water. Among his discoveries was a colorful blue jay now known as Stellar's Jay. "Captain Cook visited it on May 12, 1778 and buried a bottle with a paper and two small pieces of silver given to him by Dr. Kaye, the chaplain to King George III of England, for this Purpose," according to the Dictionary of Alaska Name Places. Because of this Cook named it Kaye's Island. The Spanish, as per course, had their own name for it, by Arteaga in 1779, calling it Isle de Carmen, for the Saint to whom the day of its sighting was dedicated, July 16, 1799.

Conclusion

Place names reveal a fascinating menagerie of information. They are like pieces in a historical puzzle. The names of features of the Copper River Delta gives insight into native culture, exploration, geography, development of fisheries, and characters of local folklore. To find the roots of a place, look to the names.

Supplemental Information

The location of our duck cabin on Pete Dahl Slough generated special interest, and I continued researching this name for years after the 1983 paper. In November of 2007 I learned from Cordovan Toni Hosick that Pete Dahl was her husband Hughie Hosick's grandfather on his mother's side, and that Pete Dahl's wife was of Tlingit origin.

From the Valdez Museum, a year later, I obtained a photo copy of page 19 of the Twelfth Census of the United States, Census of Alaska, dated July 21,1900, of the Copper River District, Alaganick, Alaska, by Special Agent Albin Johnson.

It listed the following information about Dahl: Date of Location in Alaska, April 1890, Post Office Address at Home: San Francisco, Cal.; Relationship of each person to the Head of the family: Head; Color: White; Sex: Male; Age at Last Birthdate: 45; Birth date, Month and Year: February 1855; Conjugal Condition: S; Birth Place of this Person: Sweden; Birthplace of Father: Sweden; Birthplace of Mother: Sweden; Year of Immigration to the United States: 1875; Number of Years in United States: 25; Naturalization: 14 (years); Profession, Trade, or Occupation of each Person ten years of age and over: Occupation at Home: Seaman; Occupation in Alaska: Prospector; Months employed: None; Education: Attended School, Months: X; Can Read: yes, Can write, yes; Ownership of Farms and Homes: Farm: no, home yes.

Census takers certainly asked some interesting questions back then.
Immediately under Pete Dahl's line of data on the 1900 Census was listed Dahl, Elizabeth, his four year old daughter that was born in February 1896 at Alaganik. The birth place of her mother was Kayak Island, likely verifying her Tlingit roots. However the mother was not listed in the Census.

And in an amazing example of how historical data shows up at unexpected times, while shoveling snow on the steps of my house in November of 2011, the City garbage truck pulled up. Cordova is a small town, so I was shooting the breeze with the garbage crew while helping them toss my trash in their truck.

Chancy Harmon, a local artist moonlighting in the sanitation trades, was admiring the craftsmanship of my garbage can holding bin which I built after tiring of chasing my plastic cans down Odiak Slough every time the wind blew. After stating I had the nicest garbage holder in town, he mentioned hearing that our duck cabin in Pete Dahl was also quite well maintained. And then dropped a bombshell: a friend of his, local carpenter Frank Jones, traps in the winter at Katella, Alaska, and had discovered a graveyard in some tall timber the previous year. Amongst the 30 or more graves was a wooden marker for none other than Pete Dahl. I called Jones that same day, and he shared as much information as he could recall. He had walked within 80 yards of the graveyard several times while working his trap line, and never noticed it. One day he got off track a little bit and noticed a small white fence typically used around Russian Orthodox graves. Several hours of exploration led to many graves, all with individual's names and information, in remarkably good condition.

Many were made of cement, or granite that was still polished, as well as painted wood markers with still legible data. Pete Dahl's marker was painted wood, listed his birth date as what Jones thought was 1885, but was actually 1855, according to the census. Birthplace was Sweden; and he died in Katella in either 1918 or 1915, with the 8's and 5's hard to read. Jones also mentioned that most of the graves in the area had the 1915 to 1918 span as time of death; and that most individuals didn't live past 40 in that era.

"If you lived to 50 you were an oldtimer in Katella, based on that cemetery," said Jones, who camped in a wall tent, flying down from Cordova for three weeks of solo trapping, mainly for marten. He visited the grave sites several times. "It's an amazing place, and I treated it with the utmost respect."

/

Index